ROAD BELONG CARGO

W9-BCG-377

FOR

THE TANGALOOMA

UNIVERSITY OF CONNECTICUT — GROTON, CONN.

JAN 6   1977

# ROAD BELONG CARGO

*A study of the Cargo Movement
in the Southern Madang District
New Guinea*

*by*

PETER LAWRENCE

MANCHESTER UNIVERSITY PRESS

© 1964 PETER LAWRENCE
Published by the University of Manchester at
THE UNIVERSITY PRESS
316–324 Oxford Road, Manchester M13 9NR

ISBN 0 7190 0457 8

*First published* 1964
*Reprinted with new preface and*
*postscript,* 1971

Distributed in the U.S.A. by
HUMANITIES PRESS, INC.
303 Park Avenue South, New York, N.Y. 10010

Printed in Great Britain by Butler & Tanner Ltd, Frome and London

# FOREWORD

In New Guinea nature divided the land with almost insurmountable barriers. There were the broken ranges, the deep forests, the malarial swamps, the swift torrents, and the sea that separated the great island from the many small. As if following the design of nature the people of the land were divided also—divided by hatred and mistrust that expressed themselves in the practice and fear of sorcery, and in internecine war that could split even tribes into palisaded communities. The languages numbered hundreds; the dialects tens of hundreds.

How could such a people possess a common philosophy?

\*       \*       \*

To a tremendous degree the basic philosophy of the New Guineans remains a mystery to the non-native and it is true to say that until recent years no general serious thought was ever given that such a philosophy, embracing principles common to all, ever existed among them. There is a mass of documentary evidence about their ways of life and traditional beliefs. Most of it has been recorded by way of factual reporting and with comparatively little attempt on the part of the writers to show how the age-old thinking influences present behaviour. For many years I have thought that an understanding of the cargo cult might reveal the foundations upon which a common philosophy may lie. We might learn if we could get deeper.

My friend, Peter Lawrence, has dug deep indeed. His assiduous digging has taken him far beneath the surface; his trained skill and acceptance by the people have done the rest. The result is this book.

It tells of the religious beliefs of the people of the southern Madang District prior to the coming of the first European, the courageous Baron Miklouho-Maclay, in 1871. Then there are the changes when the people are confronted with harsh, foreign domination. Physical rebellion is ruthlessly crushed. The white man's God and knowledge, with strict demarcation between sacred and secular, are incomprehensible. Again the aid of the old gods is sought but the magic is of no avail and new ways have to be found.

The story is brought to the present day and still the eternal question is asked, 'Where is the road that leads to cargo?' Although unanswered, there is no loss of faith in the world of gods and spirits; it is a matter of discovering the right method of approach—a matter of trial and error until at last the gods and spirits will listen and so bring the black man equality with the white.

All through, the strong thread of cargo is ever present.

*     *     *

The cult of cargo, occurring as it does in widely separated parts of Papua and New Guinea—among people who have no physical communication with each other—and in varying manifestations, has an underlying basic principle: that the intruding white man has prevented the material betterment of the native people. Western goods and knowledge originate in the world of gods and spirits (this despite the existence of the white man's factories and schools) and the European withholds them from the people of New Guinea by keeping for himself the religious secrets by which they are obtained. The ever-arising prophets of the cult constantly seek to find new ways in order to succeed where the old leaders have failed. Their aim is to release the gods and spirits held in bondage by the white man so that they will send goods to the people.

Dr Lawrence's book is aptly named for it follows the devious road with all its false trails, hardships, and pitfalls that the prophets of Madang have travelled—and, be it remarked, are still travelling, for there is hardly a month that passes without, somewhere in the vastness of New Guinea, another prophet arising among its two million souls to preach the cult of cargo.

As District Officer, I was the Senior Government official at Madang when I met Peter Lawrence there in 1949. I had then served over twenty years in New Guinea and had known many of the men who had tried to lead their people to better things by way of the cargo doctrine. Some of them, like Batari of Talasea, New Britain, claimed that they were reincarnated spirits in human form. (Batari claimed a like transformation in myself so that I was a spirit in rather bulky human shape.) Most of them had lost their power when the promised cargo failed to arrive.

I have long known Yali of the Rai Coast and I hope I have kept his friendship. Dr Lawrence records the sad history of the man: Yali's simple and rather naive plans, based on what he had observed in Australia, to lead the people to betterment; his initial support by the Government; and the gradual and subtle infiltration of the old beliefs into his teachings. Poor Yali! Reluctantly he allowed himself to become a messiah. The power of cargo was too much for him and at the height of his career he was tempted and fell.

Yali's subsequent sentence of over six years' imprisonment was, in my opinion, harsh—but what was worse, his prosecutors took no pains to understand how the innate beliefs of the people had played their part. Perhaps if this book had been written at the time a better understanding would have been possible.

*        *        *

Any honest documentation brings forth controversy. I must mention two points about which I have some reserve and a third which I should like to elaborate.

The author has given my views on the first two points in footnotes in context so that I can deal with them only briefly here. Firstly, there is reference to the forceful methods used by native mission helpers to make the villagers accept Christianity. From long years spent in New Guinea I can vouch for the native people's skill in playing white man against white man. It is indeed an essential art among the directly ruled and one necessary for survival. Officials are played against missions—and sometimes both against planters! Again, even the primitive native is aware of at least one item of Government policy: he is free to follow whatever religion he chooses—be it pagan or Christian. Therefore, any coercion by the native mission helpers would certainly have been reported to the District Office; that it was not inclines me to believe that such instances as are mentioned were isolated. One has no guard against the over-zealous individual.

Secondly, Yali tells of the seduction and rape of native women prisoners by their European and indigenous gaolers. It would be presumptuous to deny that such crimes *ever* occurred. However, it would be unjust to regard Yali's statement as a general accusation against a Service that deservedly bears a high reputation. The record may have been besmirched—but not ruined—by the acts of a few.

The third point concerns Dr Lawrence's account of the promises that were given native troops during the war and the first flush of victory in 1945. Looking back it will be found that most of these were made during farewell speeches when the men were paraded prior to demobilization. That the promises were impossibly lavish, incautious and made without any official approval made no difference to the men's belief that they would be kept.

But in all fairness, other factors should be borne in mind here. At least official policy resulted in generous War Damage payments (and ultimately pensions). Perhaps Madang did better than most Districts for as District Officer I was quick to take advantage of an Administration rehabilitation scheme when £A17,000 worth of tools was issued to the villages. I need not dwell on the tremendous advances that have taken place in social, medical, political, and educational services since 1945— and especially since 1950. They go towards honouring the 'unofficial' promises but, satisfactory though this may be in putting the European mind at rest, it does little to cure the bitter disappointment of the earlier years when irresponsible promises were naturally unredeemed.

*          *          *

Years ago I described the cult of cargo as the belief of a people without hope. The ways of the white man gave no immediate light and so in their darkness the New Guinea people looked back to their own. It is a belief now so widely held that it might well be regarded as a fundamental part of their life; if it is to be replaced, then it must be approached with basic sympathy.

Cargo cult cannot be overcome by the penalties of the white man's law; the gaoling of its followers makes martyrs and gives weight to the belief that the Europeans are worried lest the natives have discovered the cargo secret. Yet overcome it must be for, while a sympathetic appreciation is required in its handling, this does not mean that the cult should be condoned. Bluntly, cargo cult is one of the great barriers that impede the advancement of the people. It must go if progress is to be achieved. But the changing of men's minds is a slow process; a step forward in the changing is the recognition and admission on our part that intricate belief systems such as cargo cult exist. You cannot fight with your head in the sand.

Unthinking and mischievous critics of the Australian Administration of Papua and New Guinea frequently carp at the apparent slow progress that is being made to develop the native people. 'Why don't you go faster?' is the usual complaint and the difficulties in the way of progress are either brushed aside or deliberately ignored. Never have the critics considered that the very thinking of the people may be the main obstacle in the path of their development. That this is a fact is shown in the several 'dissentient' groups that have continued to resist the Administration's efforts to bring them into Local Government Councils. The so-called 'Submarine Men' of Kokopo—a cult that had its genesis in the cargo cult belief—is an example of how a group, sophisticated and economically well off, preferred magical and religious ritual to the white man's ways in their endeavour to find betterment. Once more the Administration has been confronted with the age-old beliefs of the people it is trying to develop.

What *Road Belong Cargo* achieves, then, is to shed light on the New Guineans' basic philosophy by showing the complexity, elaborateness, and logic of cargo thinking. It reveals the connecting links of cargo doctrine; it proves that cargo doctrine is no mere series of isolated superstitions joined only by coincidence, but a highly integrated and organized belief system so widely held that it is entitled to be regarded as a philosophy in its own right. Beyond all else, it shows how cargo cult maintains its grasp on the minds of the people. Once we understand and accept this we will be on the way to tackling the problem and the value of the book is that it gives us this understanding. As I have said—you cannot fight with your head in the sand.

*          *          *

For this reason I am glad that Peter Lawrence has written this revealing exposition of the cargo religion. It cannot but help those who seek understanding with the people of New Guinea—and understanding is the foundation of friendship. In the near future I hope, too, it will be read by the New Guinea people ... *Road Belong Cargo* would do much to teach them how the white man thinks.

J. K. McCarthy

*Port Moresby*
  *Territory of Papua and New Guinea*
*October, 1963*

# CONTENTS

# MAPS

# TABLES

# DIAGRAM

# PLATES

# PREFACE TO FIRST EDITION

As the field work on which this book is based lasted for about three years between 1949 and 1958 and documentary research was prolonged until 1961, I have inevitably incurred debts to many people. I regret that I can repay them only with the briefest acknowledgement. I carried out the bulk of my field work as a Research Scholar, Research Assistant, and Research Fellow of the Australian National University, Canberra, A.C.T. I am grateful to the University for providing the necessary funds, and also to the Department of Territories, Canberra, A.C.T., for enabling me to visit the field again for a short time in January 1958 and to consult valuable documentary material.

At a more personal level, my thanks go, first, to my teachers and colleagues at several academic institutions for their stimulus, encouragement, discipline, and patience. I started anthropology at Cambridge under Professor J. H. Hutton and did my early post-graduate work under his successor, Professor Meyer Fortes. Dr Reo Fortune, my supervisor, awakened in me a special interest in the belief content of Melanesian religions. Professor Raymond Firth of the London School of Economics enabled me to go to the Madang District of New Guinea, and both he and Professor Max Gluckman (then at Oxford) taught me, among other things, the elements of field research. Before and during my first period in New Guinea, Dr Ian Hogbin of the University of Sydney was specially helpful with information about the post-war scene and advice when he visited me in the field. At the Australian National University, I had the very great privilege of working under the late Professor S. F. Nadel.

I am particularly indebted to the staff of the Australian School of Pacific Administration, Mosman, N.S.W., where I spent three and a half most profitable years (1957–60). Mr C. D. Rowley, the Principal, with characteristic generosity allowed me to make use of his then unpublished research. Mr Ian Grosart gave me crucial insights into my historical material. Mr John Reynolds went to very great pains to locate map positions of obscure native villages mentioned in the text. Mr (now Professor) J. P. McAuley spent many hours patiently reviewing and helping me elaborate many of the concepts I have used.

Other scholars assisted me in similar ways. Dr C. A. Valentine helped me find vital documents in the A.N.G.A.U. War Diary. Dr C. A. Schmitz provided me with German texts not readily available

in Australia. Professor Meyer Fortes (Cambridge University), Mr
C. D. Rowley (Australian School of Pacific Administration), Dr M.
Harris (University of Western Australia), and Professor K. F. Walker
(University of Western Australia) read and criticized the second draft
of the manuscript, and Dr A. L. Epstein and Professor Max Gluckman
(both of the University of Manchester) the third draft. Mr G. A.
Bartlett (University of Western Australia) commented on the manu-
script as an ex-serviceman, and Mrs T. Robertson (University of
Western Australia) as a non-specialist reader. Professor Gluckman also
very kindly sponsored the work for publication. Dr P. M. Kaberry
(University College, London) was always encouraging, especially
when I began my research, and Mr E. W. P. Chinnery (formerly
Government Anthropologist of the Mandated Territory of New
Guinea) gave me sound practical advice and letters of introduction
when I first went to the field.

Second, my thanks go to many people in New Guinea, the United
Kingdom, and Australia (Administration officers, missionaries, and
private individuals), without whose consistent advice, co-operation,
and hospitality my field work would have been very difficult to
complete.

In the Administration, I am specially indebted to Mr and Mrs J. K.
McCarthy of Port Moresby. Mr McCarthy, now Head of the Department of Native Affairs, was District Officer of Madang when I began
my field work and it is only fitting that I should have asked him to
write the Foreword to this book. I received many kindnesses also
from Mr A. A. Roberts, Mr McCarthy's predecessor at the Department of Native Affairs, who enabled me to read relevant official documents; Mr and Mrs C. D. Bates; Mr L. Williams; Mr and Mrs T. G.
Aitcheson; Mr A. Gow; Mr M. Pitt; Mr T. Ellis; Mr and Mrs R.
Galloway; Mr and Mrs D. Parrish; Mr J. Page; Mr and Mrs Royce
Webb; Mr and Mrs Keith Dyer; Mr and Mrs J. Norton; Mr and Mrs
P. Fienberg; Mr M. Neal; Mr and Mrs Roy Vickery; Mr and Mrs T.
Cunnington; and Mr Reg Bentinck, Mr Lex Lennoy, and their house-
mates of 1950.

I have to thank members of two missions: Fr John Wald of the
Roman Catholic Mission (S.V.D.) and many members of the American
Lutheran Mission—especially Rev. J. Kuder, Mrs A. Welsch, Rev.
and Mrs G. O. Reitz, Rev. and Mrs A. Maahs, Rev. and Mrs H. Wuest,
Rev. and Mrs E. F. Hannemann, Dr and Mrs T. Braun, Mr D. Daech-
sel, Mr D. Kohn, and Mr A. Fenske.

The private individuals who helped me are too numerous to list in full. I can mention only a few particularly. My parents tolerated the irregular comings and goings of a field anthropologist. My wife shared them with me during my two last major field trips and contributed incalculable wisdom. Mr Paul Maclay of Sydney enabled me to consult private documents of the Miklouho-Maclay family. There were many European friends in New Guinea: Mr and Mrs C. Reason of Cape Rigney Plantation; Mrs M. Pitt, Mr and Mrs R. Mitchell, Mr and Mrs Roy Macgregor, Mr and Mrs J. Gilmour, and Mr Franz Moeder—all of Madang; and Mr Frank Luff and Mr and Mrs Claude Rouse of the northern Madang District. I have endeavoured to acknowledge the frequent and extraordinary generosity of Mr and Mrs Eric Snook of Madang by inscribing this book to their cabin-cruiser, on whose quarterdeck I obtained one of my most important pieces of information.

I do not forget the patience and generosity of my many native informants—especially Apuniba, Kasumala, Labaia, Yalokai, Pioba, Imoguli, and Watutu among the Garia; Kinaingge, Kupangat, Toringa, Gegang, Sui, Nainggi, Kuria, and Yali among the Ngaing; and Bär of Yabob, Gulu of Amele, and Pastor Liwa of the Lutheran Mission near Madang.

I began writing this book while I was Senior Lecturer in Anthropology at the Australian School of Pacific Administration and completed it when I was Senior Lecturer in Anthropology at the University of Western Australia. I am greatly indebted to Mr M. Taylor of Perth for drawing the maps from those prepared by my wife in the field, and to the late Mrs W. Radvansky of Perth, who typed the manuscript with the greatest devotion and skill.

In the writing of Pidgin English and native vernacular words I have used the following orthography: all consonants are pronounced as in English; 'a' is pronounced approximately as in 'father', 'e' as in 'day', 'i' short as in 'it' or lengthened as in 'he'; 'ng' is soft as in 'sing', and 'ngg' hard as in 'dangle'; 'ä' is pronounced as the half-open unrounded front vowel (IPA $\varepsilon\cdot$)—that is, approximately as the first vowel sound in 'air'.

PETER LAWRENCE

*Sydney, N.S.W.*
*October, 1963*

# PREFACE TO SECOND EDITION

IN 1965 I returned to the southern Madang District after seven years' absence, revisiting Madang, the Rai Coast, and the Bagasin Area. I am grateful to the District Commissioner, Mr D. Clifton-Bassett, members of the District Office, Rev. and Mrs G. O. Reitz of Madang, and Mr and Mrs P. Moloney of Saidor for help and hospitality.

In this Preface, I amplify, modify, and corroborate several statements in the original edition and in my Postscript on pp. 274-5 I discuss events in the area since 1958.

Mr Moloney told me of an alternative rumour after 1945, that Yali was God-Kilibob returned from Australia to give people cargo. Native informants stated that it was neither widespread nor long-lived, and that it played no part in the Fifth Cargo Belief. But it may have had some bearing on Yali's accredited power over sorcerers (p. 152). I state wrongly, on p. 153, that girls sent to Yali were expected to produce exceptional children after sleeping with him. In fact, it was assumed that Yali would give them his power so that they would produce such children after marrying other men. On p. 191, I state wrongly that the word *parambik* ('myth'), used by Yali to describe indigenous artefacts in the Queensland Museum, connoted 'New Guinea culture'. In this context, *parambik* means 'statues of the gods', which the Ngaing, like coastal people (p. 24), used to carve before the war. When Yali said, *'Parambiknining iretigang'*, he was stating directly, 'Statues of our gods are [in the Museum]'. Gurek easily misrepresented this statement as, *'Our gods* are [in the Museum]'. I have since visited the Museum and found its exhibits as Yali described them: an old-fashioned aeroplane, skeletons of giant prehistoric creatures, and cases of Melanesian artefacts including statues of deities. But the mummy is from Torres Strait, not the Kukukukus. Yali interpreted what he saw in terms of his own culture and experience. I am now fully satisfied that many coastal Sengam opposed the Fifth Cargo Belief because they assumed that reversion to paganism would prevent God or Jesus-Manup from sending goods (see p. 199). Finally, the lover and the N'dau assassin (p. 215, n.1) were definitely trade partners.

*Brisbane, October,* 1966

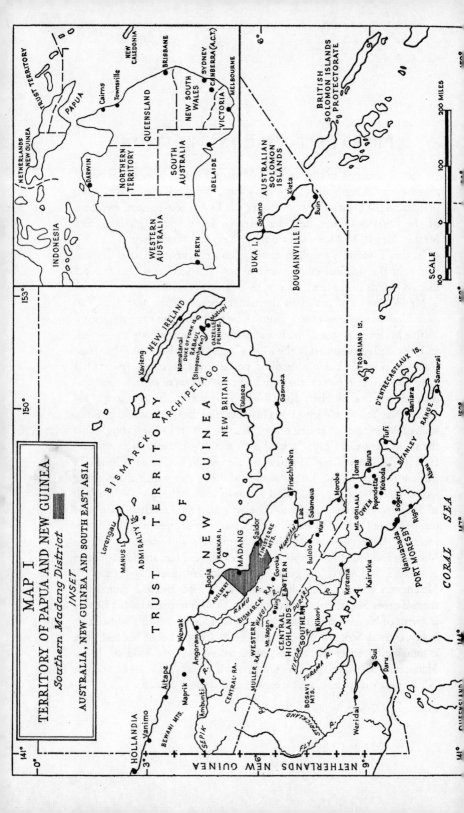

MAP I
TERRITORY OF PAPUA AND NEW GUINEA
*Southern Madang District*
INSET
AUSTRALIA, NEW GUINEA AND SOUTH EAST ASIA

# INTRODUCTION

THE New Guinea cargo cult has attracted a great deal of public attention since the last war. It is based on the natives' belief that European
goods (cargo)—ships, aircraft, trade articles, and military equipment
—are not man-made but have to be obtained from a non-human or
divine source. It expresses its followers' dissatisfaction with their status
in colonial society, which is to be improved imminently or eventually
by the acquisition of new wealth. It has, therefore, a disruptive influence and is regarded by the Dutch and Australian Administrations as
one of their most serious problems. In Australian New Guinea, it is a
penal offence, involving terms of imprisonment of up to six months.
It has had its counterparts in many areas of the world: the millenarian
cults of medieval Europe; the Chinese Taiping Rebellion; the Mahdiya
in the Sudan; the American Indian Ghost Dance; various cults in
Africa, South-East Asia, and Polynesia; and flying saucer cults in
modern industrialized America.

There is now a considerable literature on cargo cults.[1] Until recently
it consisted of many short papers describing individual outbreaks and
several longer general accounts, the most important by Worsley.[2]
Other scholars—Bodrogi, Inglis, Stanner, and Mair[3]—have published
papers on problems of interpretation. All these works provide
stimulating hypotheses but are handicapped by their authors'
lack of first-hand knowledge of actual cults. The information on
which they are based is often very thin. The time is ripe for detailed
accounts of cargo cults by scholars who have studied them in the
field.

A beginning has been made by Guiart and Burridge[4] with monographs on single cult complexes in the New Hebrides and around

[1] My select bibliography contains only works mentioned in the text. Excellent general
bibliographies are given by Leeson, *Bibliography of Cargo Cults and other Nativistic Movements in the South Pacific*, and Worsley, *The Trumpet Shall Sound*. See in my bibliography, also, works by Berndt, Salisbury, Read (1958), and Reay (pp. 194–202). Freeman,
'The Joe Gimlet or Siovili Cult' in *Anthropology in the South Seas* describes cult phenomena in nineteenth-century Polynesia.

[2] Worsley, op. cit.

[3] See Bodrogi, 'Colonization and Religious Movements in Melanesia'; Inglis, 'Cargo
Cults: The Problem of Explanation'; Stanner, 'On the Interpretation of Cargo Cults'; and
Mair, 'Independent Religious Movements in Three Continents'. See also Wallace,
'Revitalization Movements', for a theoretical interpretation of American Indian material.

[4] Guiart, *Un Siècle et demi de Contacts Culturels à Tama, Nouvelles-Hébrides*; Burridge,
*Mambu*.

Bogia (north-eastern New Guinea). Schwartz', Mead's, and Maher's[1] descriptions of primarily secular movements in Manus and the Purari Delta provide valuable comparative material. The present book has the same limited aims: it is a specialized case study, based largely on my own field research, although supplemented with documentary material, and dealing with cargo cult in one socio-cultural field, the southern Madang District of New Guinea. Before outlining the way in which I present the material, I describe how I came to study it.

In 1949, I went to Madang to carry out my first piece of anthropological research. I knew little about the District's administrative problems. I had been told that there were outbreaks of cargo cult but that they were being combated by a new native leader, Yali of the Rai Coast, who had a large following among the people, his own organization, and strong administrative backing. But after my arrival, it became obvious that the situation was very confused. Not only was cargo cult widespread but also there was no agreement whether Yali was its arch apostle or staunch opponent. Missionaries unanimously regarded him as its secret director from Saidor to Bogia. Yet the opinion of the business community, which could have been expected to be uniformly hostile to any native leader, was divided.

At first, I was interested in the problem but the Administration, not wanting an untried worker in an area where he could add to its difficulties, understandably refused me permission to go to the Rai Coast, the apparent centre of disturbance. I was not greatly upset: I was too inexperienced to challenge the decision and my chief interest at the time was traditional socio-political structure. I willingly agreed to work in Garialand, some thirty miles west-south-west of Madang and, according to all accounts, free from cargo unrest and Yali's influence.

I soon learnt that it was impossible to go anywhere in the southern Madang District without encountering cargo cult in some way. For a while my research went according to plan. The people's old way of life was still very much intact in spite of twenty years of Administration and Lutheran influence, and they did not appear interested in cargo cult. Then the whole situation changed and I found myself the centre of some very suggestive rumours.

After two months in the field, I heard it said that my mother and sister were in Madang with a shipload of goods for me. I was then asked to inspect a site for an airstrip. I did so but pronounced it unsuitable because of the mountainous terrain. When I asked why

---

[1] Schwartz, 'The Paliau Movement in the Admiralty Islands, 1946–54'; Mead, *New Lives for Old*; Maher, *New Men of Papua*.

they wanted an airstrip, my informants said lamely that, as the Administration had made them plant rice as a cash crop, they wanted aircraft to transport their small harvest to Madang. After three months in the field, I visited Madang to buy new supplies. I asked for six natives to accompany me but instead got fifty volunteers, who would not be turned back. On arrival, they were obviously disappointed not to find my mother and sister with the cargo they intended carrying back to Garialand. I then heard that my mother and sister were expected by the next ship, and learnt that the rumour was current among non-Garia in the Madang Labour Compound. After returning to the field, I was directly asked to organize the clearing of an airstrip.

Thereafter I began a cautious inquiry. 'What', I asked, 'is the purpose of this airstrip?' 'To fly in your cargo and ours', came the embarrassed reply. It eventuated that the expected cargo consisted of tinned meat, bags of rice, steel tools, cotton cloth, tinned tobacco, and a machine for making electric light. It would come from God in Heaven. The people had waited for it for years but did not know the correct procedures for getting it. This was obviously going to change. They now had their own European, who must know the correct techniques and had demonstrated his goodwill. I would 'open the road of the cargo' for them by contacting God, who[1] would send their and my ancestors with goods to Sydney. My relatives living there would bring these goods to Madang by ship and I would distribute them to the people. An airstrip would eliminate the labour of carrying.

I now saw cargo cult as a fascinating intellectual challenge. Previously I had never considered that it had a serious logical basis. Yet in these early discussions, informants' explanations of the conceived source of our goods and the means of acquiring them expressed highly systematized ideas about man's place in a cosmic order far wider than the limited pattern of purely social relationships I had set out to study. I should have to understand the structure of the total cosmos as the people believed it to be and the forces they believed governed it. This would involve a thorough examination of their traditional religion and interpretation of Christianity. Moreover, as I went on, I realized that I could not confine my investigations to the Garia. Cargo cult embraced many peoples in the Madang District, and leadership and allegiance had nothing to do with language boundaries. I had to

[1] I avoid the use of capital letters for pronouns and relative pronouns referring to God and Jesus Christ. This is sanctioned by the Anglican Authorized Version of the Bible and equivalent Catholic translations. It also avoids ambiguity where God and Jesus Christ are equated with pagan deities.

study events elsewhere. But my immediate problem was that the cargo belief seemed extremely variable. Yali was revered everywhere (including Garialand) as the Movement's paramount leader, who originated all important ritual. Yet, while the Garia claimed that faith in God was 'the road of the cargo', the Madang and Rai Coast peoples had renounced Christianity, claiming that the secret lay in traditional religion. The Garia, too, before their quasi-Christian protestations to me, had adopted the pagan cargo belief for a short time. Clearly, one belief could replace the other after a period of failure, although both could be held in Yali's name.

I could not solve problems like these until I had carried out more research in other parts of the southern Madang District. I was able to spend, in all, three years in the whole area. I worked among the Garia between April 1949 and June 1950, and between October 1952 and February 1953; and on the Rai Coast—mainly among Yali's people, the Ngaing—between March–November 1953, and July–December 1956. In January 1958, I spent a further three weeks in the general area. During each field visit, I did some work around Madang. Many difficulties had to be overcome. As it was illegal to watch cargo ritual, I had to rely on descriptions of past events.[1] Early on, I made many mistakes because I failed to recognize the flexibility and elaboration of cargo myths, and had to correct them by repeated discussions on the same subject with as many informants as possible. I had also to learn to interrelate information from conversations in widely separated places and at distant points of time.

Gradually the material fell into place. By 1953, I could describe the main features of the quasi-Christian and pagan cargo beliefs, and show why the Garia, Ngaing, and Madang peoples could hold both without any sense of incongruity.[2] But the total pattern did not emerge until I began to follow up new lines of inquiry, which forced me to reconstruct the history of European contact in the southern Madang District from the arrival of the first white man in 1871. This enabled me to see the growth of the different cargo beliefs, their essential interconnexions, the post-war cargo disturbances, and Yali's relation to them in clearer perspective. This means that my research is far from complete. I could not cover the whole area as intensively as I should have wished. Many

[1] In any case, although they were still interested in news of it, the Garia had virtually withdrawn from the Cargo Movement by 1949–50. The rumours circulated about myself were transient. During my later research, the Movement had come to a close on the Rai Coast also.

[2] See my 'Cargo Cult and Religious Beliefs among the Garia' and 'The Madang District Cargo Cult'.

events must have escaped my notice and have had an influence I cannot at the moment assess. Also, the events I describe are not finite but only the prelude to the now rapidly developing situation discussed at the end of Chapter IX.

## Presentation and Analysis

Cargo phenomena in the southern Madang District constituted a single movement. We can distinguish the following facets: A cargo *belief* (myth) described how European goods were invented by a cargo deity and indicated how men could get them from him via their ancestors by following a cargo prophet or leader. Cargo *ritual* was any religious activity designed to produce goods in this way and assumed to have been taught the leader by the deity. But, as already indicated, cargo beliefs and rituals were never fixed: they could be revised or replaced after failure. Thus the history of the Cargo Movement represented a succession of different mythological explanations and ritual experiments. Each of these was a cargo *cult*—a complex of ritual activity associated with a particular cargo myth and more or less distinct from other complexes of the same general kind but associated with other myths.

The Movement must be understood in terms of both its sociopolitical and epistemological[1] aspects. My purpose is to lay equal stress on both. The first has been given close attention by recent scholars, but the treatment of the second has so far been inadequate.[2] I begin by asking three obvious questions, which immediately puzzle newcomers to a cargo cult situation and which, although interrelated, can be kept separate for analytical purposes:

1. Why did the people regard European wealth as so important that they spent decades of patently fruitless effort to discover its source? Why did they set such a high social value on it?
2. Why did they believe that this wealth could be obtained almost entirely by ritual activity? Why did they tend to ignore purely secular activity?
3. What is the general importance of the Cargo Movement? What sort of situation has it contributed to or created?

[1] The *Oxford English Dictionary* defines epistemology as 'the theory or science of the method or grounds of knowledge'. I am using the term to cover the general questions: From what sources do the people of the southern Madang District believe knowledge to be derived? And what kinds of knowledge do they hold to be available to themselves?
[2] To avoid sacrificing ethnographic detail, I forego a preliminary examination of the views of other scholars and refer to them only specifically in context. But, as this is an important issue which I do not wish to evade, I intend to discuss it in a separate publication.

I answer these questions of motivation, means, and effects by considering the Cargo Movement from three different angles. *Motivation* can be understood by examining the nature of European contact, the people's reactions to it, and the attitudes and values these reactions expressed. *Means* can be understood by analysing the processes by which the people believed all human destiny was governed, and their attempts to harness them. *Effects* are shown to be the changes for which the Cargo Movement was directly responsible, and those which it envisaged, in the traditional socio-political system in the past, and the influence it will have on native adjustment to increasing Western encroachment in the future.

These answers cannot be provided simply by describing the Cargo Movement on its own. They necessitate careful analysis of the total setting in which the Movement grew up—the interaction between the people's traditional socio-cultural background and the situation created by European occupation. Such an account cannot be restricted to a single plane of time but must be presented chronologically. In Chapter I, I reconstruct the natives' pre-contact cosmic order: their economic and socio-political structure, and their religion. I assess their social values and epistemological assumptions. This stresses the significance of material culture in their lives: the importance they attached to it and the intellectual meaning they ascribed to it.[1]

In Chapters II–VIII, I describe European contact in the southern Madang District between 1871–1950[2] from two strongly contrasted points of view. I deal with the period, first (in Chapter II), from that of a European, recounting the establishment of a colonial economy and socio-political system, and the introduction of Christianity;[3] and second (in Chapters III–VIII), from that of the people themselves, showing how they tried to control the new situation. The native version is, at the same time, a description of the origin and development of the Cargo Movement.

In Chapter IX, I analyse both accounts of contact history in the light of the three questions initially asked. It is shown from an exam-

[1] For reasons of space, I have had to reduce the account of the pre-contact cosmic order presented in Chapter I. I refer the reader to supplementary publications in context and hope to make good the deficiency in due course with full-length monographs on the Ngaing and Garia.

[2] I close the account in 1950 because this date saw the end of cargo activities as a single movement. Cargo cults since then have been relatively sporadic.

[3] For reasons of space, I am unable to present as full an account of contact history as I should have liked but must limit myself only to those facts directly relevant to the Cargo Movement. I plan to amplify Chapter II in a later publication, to which specialist readers are referred.

ination of the European account (Chapter II) that, in spite of commercial, administrative, and missionary pressures, colonial rule, while changing the outward form, never struck at the heart of native life. The indigenous value- and epistemological systems, especially as far as material wealth was concerned, were barely affected. As can be seen from the native account (Chapters III–VIII), they constituted, from the separate standpoints of motivation and means, the essential framework of the Cargo Movement, gave it its remorseless logic, and shed important light on its effects.

The crucial factor in motivation was a pattern of race relations, which left the people with the conviction that they could have satisfactory dealings with Europeans only if they acquired large quantities of cargo. This did not produce a stereotyped reaction. Native attitudes to whites passed through several alternating stages of friendship and hostility, and the types of goods desired, and the purposes for which they were to be used, varied accordingly. Yet these attitudes were always in keeping with the values current in traditional society.

The people's adoption of largely ritual means in their attempts to acquire cargo was consistent with their basic epistemological assumptions, which were always dominated by religion. These assumptions could be built up into a system of ideas, which made the new situation completely intelligible and offered hope of bringing it under control. This system was so versatile that, whenever a particular explanation was proved wrong, it could be replaced immediately with a substitute.

The political effects of the Cargo Movement are discussed for both the past and future. For the past, I show how the Movement eventually gave the natives of the southern Madang District a sense of unity they had never known before European contact and, especially in its last stage, developed into a form of 'embryonic nationalism' or 'protonationalism'.[1] I consider how far this was an expression of, and how effectively it exploited, the desire for unity. For the future, I suggest that the ultimate significance of the Movement will be the influence of its underlying values and intellectual assumptions on the Administration's new policy of native economic, political, and educational advancement, implemented during the last decade.

---

[1] See my 'Cargo Cult', op. cit., p. 20, and Worsley, op. cit., p. 255. Belshaw, 'The Significance of Modern Cults in Melanesian Development', Guiart, 'Forerunners of Melanesian Nationalism', and others have used similar terms to describe the political significance of cargo cults.

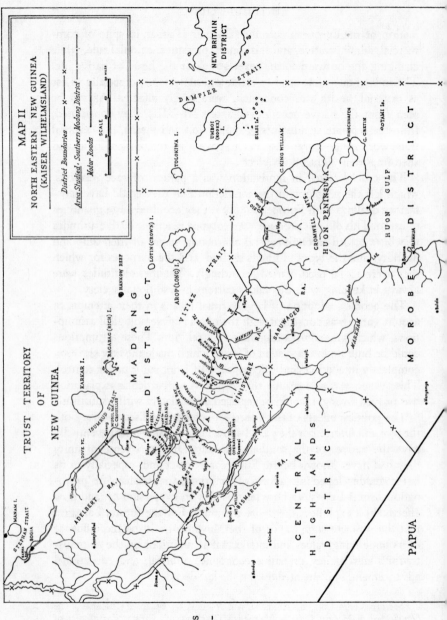

This map shows the District Boundaries as in 1950

MAP II

NORTH EASTERN NEW GUINEA
(KAISER WILHELMSLAND)

District Boundaries ———×———×———
Area Studied: Southern Madang District
Motor Roads ——————

SCALE

TRUST TERRITORY
OF
NEW GUINEA

MADANG DISTRICT

NEW BRITAIN DISTRICT

CENTRAL HIGHLANDS DISTRICT

MOROBE DISTRICT

PAPUA

HUON PENINSULA

HUON GULF

VITIAZ STRAIT

DAMPIER STRAIT

# CHAPTER I

# THE NATIVE COSMIC ORDER

## TRADITIONAL SOCIETY, RELIGION, VALUES, AND EPISTEMOLOGY

THE term southern Madang District does not denote a socially or politically unified territory. It represents merely the area in which I gathered coherent information about the Cargo Movement: some 3,000 square miles bordered by a line running south-west from Sarang (north of Madang) to the Ramu, then south-east along the river to Dumpu, from Dumpu to Saidor on the Rai Coast, and from Saidor back to Madang and Sarang. (See Maps I -II.) Its indigenous population is just over 24,000, comprising an as yet unknown number of small linguistic groups, each of which has probably anything from 150 to 3,000 members. Linguistic fragmentation correlates with a good deal of cultural idiosyncrasy but the people's basic outlook is essentially homogeneous.

Traditionally, the natives regarded[1] their cosmos as a finite and almost exclusively physical realm, in which man was the focal point of two systems of relationships: actual relationships between human beings (social structure); and putative relationships between human beings, deities, spirits of the dead, and totems (religion). In this chapter, I begin by describing the general features of the natural environment, economy, social structure, and religion. Then, to illustrate these generalizations and provide the ethnography relevant to later chapters, I summarize the social structures, religions, and trading systems of peoples studied in the area. Finally, I abstract the values and epistemological assumptions which underlay the traditional cosmic order and, as stressed, were carried over to the Cargo Movement. The keynotes of social and religious life were materialism and anthropocentrism, and knowledge was ascribed to divine revelation rather than the human intellect.

## The Natural Environment

The area is very rugged—a series of mountain ranges, covered with

---

[1] To suit my presentation and analysis, I have written this reconstruction (except in the case of the natural environment) in the past tense, although it cannot be fully accurate because the field work on which it is based was carried out comparatively late in the contact period after there had been inevitable cultural losses. But these losses are probably not crucial to the argument and can be disregarded.

dense bush, and sandwiched between the narrow coastal plain and
the Ramu Valley. To the south and east are the Finisterres, which
rise over 11,000 feet above sea level within fifteen miles of the Rai
Coast littoral and fall away equally abruptly to the Ramu. To the west,
the coastal plain runs inland from Madang further than on the Rai
Coast until it reaches the Hansemann Mountains and the low hills
overlooking the Gogol. In the hinterland of Madang are the mountains
of the Bagasin Area (1,500–3,000 feet above the sea), which spread
out into the Ramu Valley. To the north again lies the Adelbert
Range.

In the past, this terrain hindered swift communication and the for-
mation of large socio-political groups. Yet there was never complete
cultural stagnation. Travel, however slow, was always possible, so
that the two trading systems to be described counterbalanced the
tendency to community isolation and fostered an overall cultural uniformity by enabling the periodic diffusion of ideas.

### Economy and Social Structure

Setting aside local idiosyncrasies, the general social pattern was typical
of coastal New Guinea. It is best understood in terms of the economy,
of which the obvious features were these: The people lived in small
villages or hamlets, were primarily agriculturalists, and secondarily
herders and hunters. They domesticated pigs, dogs, fowls, and cassowaries. They hunted and trapped wild pig and other game in the bush,
and caught fish in the sea and rivers. Their technology was simple.
They built houses from bush materials. They had no knowledge of
weaving or metallurgy, but made artefacts from clay, stone, wood,
bark, bone, and shell.

At a deeper level of analysis, the economic system had three charac-
teristics sharply distinguishing it from that of Western society. First,
it had very little specialization. Every individual was expected to perform or contribute to all the tasks necessary for survival: growing food, building houses, and making tools, weapons, and clothes.
Specialization occurred only in the manufacture of major artefacts
(canoes, slit-gongs, and sacred instruments) and in ritual, which were
the prerogatives of male experts.

Second, the primary emphasis was on subsistence with no concept
of profit. The economy was designed to produce only enough wealth
(mainly food) to keep people alive. There was no idea of creating
a surplus which could be ploughed back to create greater wealth in
the future. Vegetable food was consumed almost immediately, for

daily needs or at feasts. Even storable goods (pigs, shell and bone ornaments, and trade articles) were exchanged not on the basis of gain but of strict equivalence, each item having its fixed value.

Third, lacking the concepts of profit, saving, and reinvestment, the economy had no strong internalized forces of change and tended to be stationary. Without the search for new resources, and hence the incentive to produce new goods or improve old productive techniques, it never expanded or contracted to any appreciable extent, maintaining an annually repetitive rhythm. That some changes did occur there can be no doubt, but they were imperceptible and hardly disruptive.

These economic factors determined the salient features of native societies. Because specialization was little stressed, there were no occupational groups. Social structure was based on ties of descent, kinship, marriage (monogamy and polygyny), locality, and trade. It was undifferentiated and egalitarian. In contrast to the relatively flexible structure of Western pyramidal society with its separate systems for economic, political and legal, and religious activities, the same structure performed multiple functions in all these fields. There was little stratification by occupation, wealth, or birth. Although the size of a society's descent or local groups tended to fluctuate, none claimed any great degree of precedence over the others.[1] Apart from a few island groups, all had equivalent access to basic resources in proportion to their numbers, which never in fact became excessive because of infant mortality, abortion, and infanticide.

As indicated, there was no political unity within, or single authority over, the whole area or even any one of its component societies. Wars between even fairly close neighbours within the same society were common. They were fought rarely to improve a group's economic position but for revenge, when disputes arose over love magic, adultery, sorcery, and homicide. Leadership was democratic and limited in scope. Leaders were not hereditary or elected officials: their positions depended on success in war and economic activities, and mastery of ritual. Their authority was restricted primarily to their own local groups, although the most eminent might attract followers from elsewhere. It was really effective only for organizing vital annually recurrent undertakings involving the whole community. It was insignificant in the policy-making and judicial fields: leaders rarely initiated entirely new schemes of action or gave binding decisions in disputes.

[1] Hannemann, *Village Life and Social Change in Madang Society*, p. 15, refers to the ranking of Yam patriclans but this was probably not very marked.

## Religion

It is difficult to give a precise definition of traditional religion because no native society had any single word for it as a separate cultural component. The best approach is to examine the implications of the initial statements: that the cosmos was an almost exclusively physical realm; and that religion represented a system of putative relationships between human beings, deities, spirits of the dead,[1] and totems existing within it.

We must dismiss at once the concept of the supernatural: a realm of existence not only apart from but also on a higher plane than the physical world. The religions of all peoples studied in the area fully corroborate Bidney's argument that it is often impossible 'to distinguish' among non-literate peoples 'between the sphere of the natural and that of the supernatural, since gods and spirits are just as much a part of the order of nature as birds and animals'.[2] Gods, spirits, and totems were regarded as a real, if not always visible, part of the ordinary physical environment. In nearly every case, gods and spirits were thought to live on the earth, either in the bush or in sanctuaries (clumps of trees, rocks, or river pools) near human settlements. They were described as more powerful than men but always as corporeal, taking human, animal, or insect form at will. They could handle material objects and had human emotions.

We must consider also the nature of these putative relationships. There was no clear separation between religion and magic on the basis of Tylor's and Frazer's dichotomy: that religion is man's belief in spiritual beings, whom he tries to propitiate and to whom he thereby concedes freedom of action; while magic is his belief that he can control occult forces by ritual. Although there were elements in native belief and ritual corresponding exactly with both these categories, they were only marginal. In the vast majority of ritual activities, it was fully accepted that, provided he first satisfied certain stipulated conditions, man actually *guaranteed* the co-operation of gods and spirits. Failure was attributed not to their caprice but to the incompetence of the ritual operator.[3]

Thus I use the one term religion to mean man's beliefs about deities, spirits, and totems, whom he regarded as superhuman or extra-human beings living with him in his own physical environment, and—to a

---

[1] I distinguish clearly between deities and spirits of the dead. Deities were believed to have existed more or less always, except in special cases. I use the word spirit throughout to refer *only* to a departed ancestor, who was *never* equated with a deity.

[2] Bidney, 'Meta-anthropology', p. 333.

[3] See Firth, *Elements of Social Organisation*, p. 223, who discusses this point.

more limited extent—about impersonal occult forces. The function of religion was to explain, through myths, how the deities and, in one recorded case, totems (but never the spirits of the dead) originally brought the cosmic order into being, and to give man the assurance that, through ritual, he was master of it. By ritual, I mean normally practices which had to be buttressed by initiatory taboos and by which man assumed that he maintained correct relationships with gods and spirits, so that they would automatically employ themselves to his advantage.[1] Otherwise, there were two specialized forms of ritual. I call occasional examples of human attempts to control impersonal occult forces sympathetic magic, and reserve the term sorcery for ritual used to kill or harm human beings.

## Case Studies

There is reliable information about only few peoples of the area. But, being distributed from one end of it to the other and representing sub-coast, seaboard, off-shore islands, and hinterland, they were probably typical samples. Structurally, they exhibited a degree of local variation and fell into three categories: double unilineal (Ngaing); patrilineal (Sengam, Som, and Yam); and cognatic (Garia). Their religions were more stereotyped. Trading systems are dealt with separately to show how they linked the different societies described.

## The Ngaing[2]

The Ngaing of the Rai Coast (today somewhat over 800) occupied the sub-coast mainly between the Nankina and Mot Rivers. They lived along the tops of the ridges which ran down from the Finisterres towards the sea. Their neighbours were the Sengam, Gira, Som, Neko, M'na, and N'dau.[3] (See Map III.) Their staple crop was taro and their most important artefact the wooden slit-gong, used partly in the Male Cult (ceremonies honouring the spirits of the dead) but also for sending messages over long distances. Every adult male had his personal call-sign.

[1] Cf. Horton, 'A Definition of Religion, and Its Uses', p. 211: '. . . Religion can be looked upon as an extension of the field of people's social relationships beyond the confines of purely human society.' See also my 'Cargo Cult', op. cit., pp. 10–11, where the same point is implicit.

[2] The following account is based entirely on my own field work. See also my forthcoming 'The Religious System of the Ngaing', in a symposium on *Some Religions of Seabord Melanesia and the New Guinea Highlands*, ed. P. Lawrence and M. J. Meggitt, for supplementary material.

[3] The Gira, Neko, M'na, and N'dau are not described because of lack of field data.

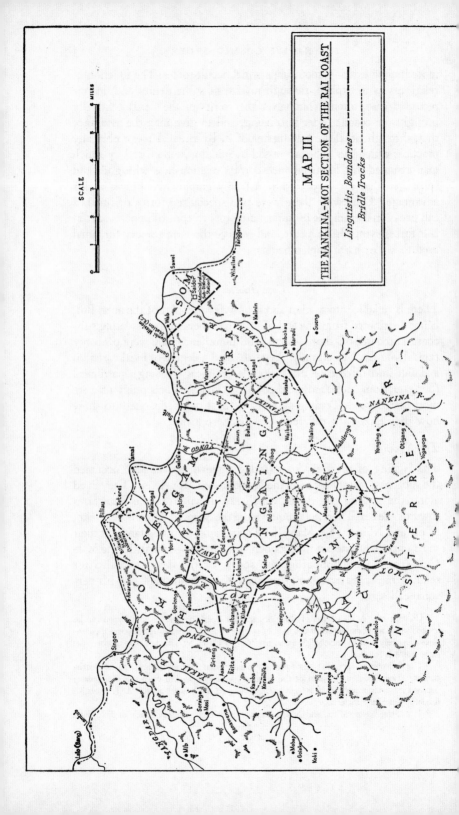

SCALE

MAP III

THE NANKINA–MOT SECTION OF THE RAI COAST

Linguistic Boundaries ━━━
Bridle Tracks ┄┄┄┄┄

*Social Structure:* Ngaing territory comprised about twenty named bush areas. The inhabitants of each can be called a bush group and were a political unit. They avoided bloodshed among themselves, combined for offence and defence, and had a common war god. Bush groups were allied by trade relationships and linked, at the personal level, by intermarriage.

The bush group was divided into a number of small, named, exogamous patriclans, each consisting of several patrilineages of between three and five generations deep. The patriclan was the basic unit of local organization, forming either a settlement on its own or part of a settlement. It had its own land and ritual property for the Male Cult. It had its own ornaments with which it could decorate its settlement cult house (around which the dwelling houses were grouped); its own slit-gong, gourd trumpets, and sacred melodies, from the gong beats of which its members took their personal call-signs; and its own sacred or spirit pool. It normally had its own leaders although, if it were small or its older men ineffectual, it would have to place itself under the aegis of another patriclan in its settlement or bush area.

Cutting across the patrilineal structure was a number of named, exogamous, totemic matriclans, whose component matrilineages were again from three to five generations deep. Every individual belonged to a matriclan as well as to the other groups mentioned. But, apart from common totemic allegiance, the members of a matriclan had no corporate identity. They were always dispersed because women, the sole transmitters of membership, lived with their husbands after marriage. Besides exogamy, the most important matriclan rule was that members should never harm their totem or one another even if they belonged to enemy bush groups. Thus the dispersal of the matriclan extended the range of a man's effective social relationships.

A man had to marry a cross cousin—the daughter of a true or classificatory mother's brother or father's sister. Outside marriage, he could indulge in casual liaisons with all his other female cross cousins without incurring enmity provided he compensated their husbands with gifts of clay pots and food. Liaisons with other female relatives were condemned as incest and adultery. A boy was initiated by his mother's brothers and, when they died, repaid their services by laying out their corpses and disposing of their bones. Rites of passage were solemnized by the ceremonies of the Male Cult and by formal exchanges of pigs, food, and valuables (dogs' teeth and Siasi beads[1]) between the patriclans involved: between patriclans contracting a

Siasi beads are small shells pierced with holes so that they can be strung on thread.

c

marriage; between those of a boy and his mother's brothers after initiation; and between those of a man and his mother's brothers after a funeral.

*Religion:* The Ngaing believed that their world was brought into being by their deities (*tut*) and totems (*sapud* or *supud*), and that they controlled it by performing ritual to their deities and spirits of the dead (*kabu* or *asapeng*). Although treated with respect, totems were of no ritual importance. Boys learnt religious secrets during and after initiation.

The cosmic order came into existence in two stages: the emergence of the natural environment followed by that of human beings and their culture. For the first stage, the natural environment—land, rivers, wild animals, birds and plants (including totems), and even war gods—was 'put' by the remote creator god Parambik.[1] For the second stage, there were elaborate myths. One set told how people appeared when totemic birds, animals, and plants gave birth to or turned into the human ancestresses of matriclans. Another set told how, at the same time as the appearance of human beings, deities created the important parts of the culture. War gods invented bows and arrows, and other gods bullroarers, slit-gongs, hand drums, and wooden bowls. The goddess Meanderi gave taro and other important plants to mankind. The god Yabuling invented the pig exchange and Male Cult by creating pigs and the gourd trumpets used to honour the spirits of the dead. In the inland region (Aiyawang, Sindama, and Sibog), myths told how local deities made dogs' teeth and Siasi beads.[2]

The sanctuaries of the deities were in various parts of the Rai Coast. Their distribution did not correlate closely with group membership. Although war gods belonged to specific bush groups, and some myths and deities to a limited number of bush groups, rights to others were common to all Ngaing and even extended across linguistic borders. Yabuling belonged to all peoples of the Nankina-Mot section of the Rai Coast.[3] Meanderi originated at Asang, west of Ngaing territory. But there was always a recognized area for each myth and deity, and any attempt by outsiders to acquire them without formal purchase was regarded as theft.

[1] Parambik was the only Ngaing deity without a fixed sanctuary. He was regarded as all-pervasive. His name was the word for myth.

[2] Ngaing near the coast (as in Amun, Sor, and Paramus), being closer to the true source of supply, did not have similar myths.

[3] The Sengam may once have had a separate myth. See Hannemann, *Papuan Dances and Dancing*, pp. 6–8 and 9–10. But today they claim that they always had the Yabuling myth.

The deities were believed also to have taught men to exploit the environment. During the period of creation, each deity appeared to men in a dream or lived with them and instructed them how to produce his or her special part of the culture. This included both secular and ritual techniques. Ritual techniques (*pananak* or *mana*) involved the symbolic repetition of actions performed by the deity at the time of creation and the knowledge of an esoteric formula or spell, the secret name (*wawing buingna*) of the deity or artefact invented. The distribution of rights to ritual correlated with that of its associated myth. Each patriclan had ritual for warfare, slit-gongs, bullroarers and hunting, agriculture, and pig husbandry and the Male Cult. Inland groups had special ritual to ensure that their deities sent dogs' teeth and Siasi beads via the ancestors. Every group had sorcery and love magic.

It was assumed that, as long as ritual was correctly performed, the relevant deity had no option but to grant immediate success in any serious undertaking. Before a raid, the leader took leaves from his war god's sanctuary, breathed the deity's name over them, and fed them to his warriors, who also shouted the god's name as they attacked. The bullroarer was used before hunting not associated with feasts honouring the dead. The leader breathed a spell over the bullroarer and whirled it in the bush, out of sight of women and children, so that the deity would provide plenty of game. When the dead were to be honoured, the bullroarer was carried as a hunting talisman but never whirled. For agriculture, a garden leader breathed Meanderi's secret name over shoots of her crops before planting them around a special shrine, near which he had set up an *atatagat* branch to symbolize the staff she used to carry. Sorcery and love potions were based on sympathetic magic. A sorcerer, for instance, stole something that had been part of, or in contact with, his victim and either burnt it or heated it over a fire to cause death or illness.

The ancestors were regarded not as creators but as the protectors of their surviving relatives. They lived either in their war gods' sanctuaries or with the guardian deities of their sacred pools. The bones of the dead were deposited in either place after preliminary exposure of corpses in old slit-gongs. Spirits helped the living in the following ways: by warding off illness; by protecting crops from wild pig; by accompanying raiding and hunting parties; and by visiting their relatives in dreams with messages about the future and, in the inland, gifts of valuables.

The ancestors' goodwill was ensured by according them ritual honour. At a funeral, personal possessions were placed with a corpse for the spirit's use and mourning was designed to emphasize its relatives' sense of loss. Members of raiding and hunting parties, in addition to the ritual already described, offered food to the spirits and carried relics of dead kinsmen—locks of hair and finger bones tied to bullroarers, and jaw-bones or skulls. In garden ritual, the ancestors were invoked to protect the crops, and food offerings were often put out for them and the goddess Meanderi.

Special honour was paid the spirits in the Male Cult: the Harvest Festival and Kabu Ceremony. The Cult imposed strong taboos, prohibiting women and uninitiated boys from witnessing its secrets, whirling of the bullroarer, and those participating from making war. The Harvest Festival took place early in the year when the new crops were ready for eating, and the Kabu Ceremony during the dry season (April–November). They involved formal exchanges: in the Harvest Festival specifically to honour the spirits for having watched over the crops; and in the Kabu, to solemnize marriage, initiation, and death.

Both functions began in the same way. When the exchange principals, helped by their patriclansmen, had assembled enough pigs, game, valuables, and vegetable food, they went at dusk to their patriclan sacred pools to wash and decorate their trumpets. They invoked Yabuling and the guardian deities of the pools to send the spirits back with them, and the spirits to follow. They then returned home, leading the spirts by playing melodies.

In the later stages of the Harvest Festival, the spirits were escorted to the cult house, where their personal call-signs were beaten out on the slit-gongs in welcome. They were offered cooked food, and silence was maintained while they were supposed to eat. Next day exchanges were held between the various patriclans involved. The ancestors were entertained with music for a few days, after which they were escorted back to their pools.

The later stages of the Kabu were of longer duration. The spirits were welcomed to the settlement by a dance (*ola*), in which both men and women participated, and which lasted till dawn. Then exchanges were held. From now on, music was played on trumpets and slit-gongs in the cult house every night from sunset to sunrise. Women and children, although debarred from the cult house, could dance outside. At this time no food was offered the spirits but pig fat was rubbed on gongs and trumpets to please them. Ritual was performed for the growth of pigs by giving them food over which a trumpet, bespelled with Yabuling's secret name, had been played. The Kabu ended with a final dance outside the cult house and the formal departure of the spirits to the sacred pools. The whole ceremony could last as long as three months, additional exchanges between different principals being held during the period.

A boy's first religious experience was initiation, which could take place during the ordinary Kabu Ceremony. Novices were segregated for about a month, during which their mothers' brothers taught them to play the sacred instruments, recited the Yabuling myth, and gave them a symbolic beating.[1] Then, dressed in fine ornaments, they paraded before the women, and formally exchanged pigs and valuables with their mothers' brothers.

Initiation had two aims: First, the novices were supposed to gain strength from their ancestors and grow into healthy adults. Second, they began their true education. They were introduced not only to the secrets of the Male Cult but also to their own patriclan myths and ritual. While segregated, they had to observe strict taboos on washing, drinking water, and eating food cooked in water and all types of meat. They ate only roasted taro and sugar cane. These taboos, believed to have been ordained by the gods, were said to make teaching effective and protect the novices. Those who ignored the taboos would never use the spells correctly and would become ill should they attempt to use them. Those who showed the greatest ability in learning, and the greatest prowess in using, ritual eventually became leaders.

### The Sengam, Som, and Yam[2]

The Sengam and Som of the Rai Coast, and the Yam of Madang spoke interrelated languages, and had similar cultural and social systems. The Sengam (now about 600) and the Som (now about 150) inhabited the Rai Coast plain. (See Map III.) The Yam (about 700 in the late 1930's) lived on four islands outside Madang Harbour: Graged, Biliā, Siar, and Panutibun. (See Map IV.) These peoples cultivated the yam as their staple crop and had extensive coconut groves. They were keen fishermen and—especially the Madang peoples—good sailors. The Yam and their neighbours built large seagoing single-outrigger canoes.

---

[1] In Amun only, penile supra-incision, performed by the mother's brother, was included in initiation. Other Ngaing bush groups did not have this custom, which belonged properly to the peoples of the seaboard.

[2] The material on the Sengam and Som was collected by myself but is supplemented by Schmitz, 'Zur Ethnologie der Rai-Küste in Neuginea', pp. 27–56. For the Yam, I rely mainly on Hannemann, *Village Life and Social Change*, op. cit. Other material is acknowledged in context.

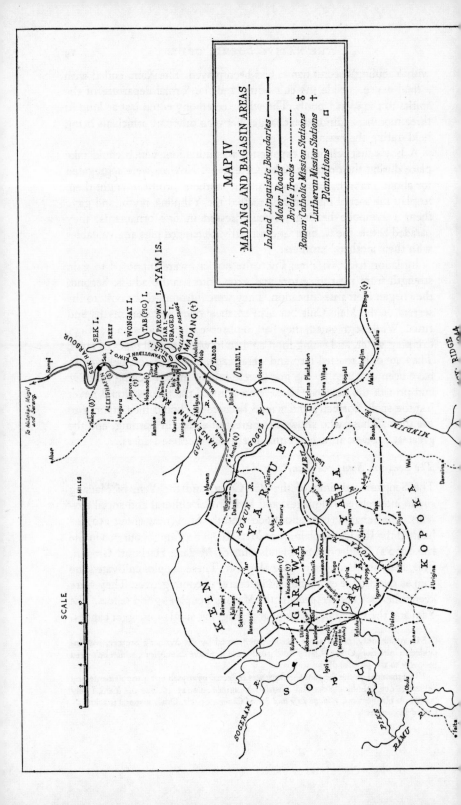

MAP IV

MADANG AND BAGASIN AREAS

Inland Linguistic Boundaries ⎯⎯⎯
Motor Roads ⎯⎯
Bridle Tracks ⎯ ⎯ ⎯
Roman Catholic Mission Stations ✝
Lutheran Mission Stations ✝
Plantations ☐

SCALE

MILES

To Alexishafen, Nagill and Sarang.

*Social Structure:* These societies had exactly the same social groups as the Ngaing, except for the totemic matriclan. Sengam territory comprised about nine bush areas, and Som territory two. As noted, Yam territory consisted of four islands. The inhabitants of bush areas and islands were again political units, possessing their own war gods, allied by trade, and linked by intermarriage. The bush or island group was divided into named, exogamous patriclans, subdivided again into unnamed patrilineages of from three to five generations deep. A settlement contained several patriclans, each with its own land, fishing reef, leaders, and the same kind of ritual property as among the Ngaing (carved ornaments, slit-gong, gourd trumpets, and sacred pool). In addition, each patriclan had its own totemic animal, bird, or plant, which it regarded as an emblem but not as an ancestor.

Marriage, initiatory and mortuary duties, and the exchanges solemnizing them followed the same pattern as among the Ngaing.[1] The sole difference was that marriage was enjoined, and extramarital licence permitted, only between classificatory but not true cross cousins.

*Religion:* The Sengam, Som, Yam, and other seaboard peoples shared a complex of origin myths, which the sub-coastal and hinterland peoples did not possess, and which played a major role in the Cargo Movement. Ritual and initiation were similar to those of the Ngaing.

All these peoples believed in a creator god (*tubud* or *tibud*), called Anut by the Sengam, Som, Yam, and Yabobs,[2] and Dodo by the Seks.[3] The Sengam, Som, and Seks attributed to him the existence of the whole natural environment. The Yabobs believed that the earth had always existed, but that Anut emerged from a cave and 'put' the other natural phenomena. Thereafter the creator brought into being two deity (*tubud* or *tibud*) brothers, Kilibob and Manup. Their birthplace was generally accepted as Karkar Island, although the Seks and Milguks (inland from Yabob) separately claimed the honour for their own areas. The Yabobs believed that Anut first made a man and woman, who were their parents, while the Seks said that Dodo created and himself impregnated a woman, thus becoming their father. A separate version from Milguk is given in Chapter IV. But these differences were

[1] Hannemann gives no specific information about marriage rules and ceremonial exchanges among the Yam. But the fact that sisters' children had to perform burial duties for their maternal uncles suggests that the overall system was similar. See Hannemann, *Tibud*, pp. 85–6.

[2] Where the name of a linguistic group is unknown, I pluralize the village name.

[3] Anut and Dodo were conceived as the same person, although each society viewed him in a slightly different way. Among the Sengam and Som, Anut was the esoteric name of Barnun and Balaulau respectively, again the words for myth in their languages. For convenience, I use the names Anut and Dodo only, for they now have general currency.

generally ignored, the two brothers being always spoken of as the sons of Anut or Dodo.[1]

For the rest of the myth there were two main versions, each with local variants: the first from the Yam, Yabob, Milguk, Rempi, Sarang, Erima, Bogati, and Bongu peoples; and the second from the Sek, Bilbil, Sengam, and Som peoples.

The first version, paraphrased here from Yam texts and Yabob variants,[2] begins with a quarrel between Kilibob and Manup. Kilibob invented canoe-building and wood-carving. One day Manup's wife stole one of Kilibob's arrows and forced him to tattoo its incised design on her pudenda. Manup was furious and tried to murder Kilibob. Eventually the two brothers left Karkar. Manup made a canoe and sailed north. But Kilibob made a very large canoe and then created men, pigs, dogs, fowls, food plants, and artefacts, all of which he put on board. He sailed to Madang, where he carved out Dallman Passage and the Yam Islands by shooting arrows at the mainland. He then sailed down the Rai Coast, again leaving new islands and reefs in his wake. At each coastal village, he put a man ashore, giving him the power of speech, food plants, a bow and arrows, a stone axe and adze, rain, and ritual formulae. East of Saidor, he crossed over to Siasi, where he settled and was visited by Manup, with whom he was reconciled.

The Yabobs had two main variants. Whereas Kilibob invented useful arts, Manup was responsible for love magic, sorcery, and warfare. It was Manup who tattooed Kilibob's wife rather than the reverse. Also, the reconciliation between the brothers had not yet occurred but was prophesied for the future. They would return to Madang, heralded by portents: Kilibob by the discovery of a Siasi wooden plate at sea to the south, and Manup by the arrival of a canoe from the north. There would be an eclipse of the sun, and a volcanic eruption and fall of ash that would destroy the gardens and lead to war and cannibalism. The crisis would end only when the brothers settled their dispute.

In the second version,[3] the same events were recounted but the

---

[1] In my 'Cargo Cult', op. cit., p. 17, n. 1, I have said that Kilibob originally came from the Nobanob area. This was an ethnographic error caused by inexperience at the time.

[2] The Yam texts paraphrased here are from Hannemann, *Tibud*, op. cit., pp. 11–29. The Yabob variants were collected variously by Aufinger and myself. See Aufinger, 'Die Mythe vom Brüderpaar *Kilibob* and *Manup* auf den Yabob-Inseln Neuguineas', pp. 313–15.

[3] I heard accounts of the second version of the myth from Sek, Sengam, and Som informants. But the most complete accounts from the Sengam were recorded by Schmitz, 'Zum Problem des Balum-Kultes in Nordost-Neuguinea', pp. 265–7, and 'Zur Ethnologie der Rai-Küste in Neuguinea', op. cit., pp. 46–9. The Bilbil account was recorded by Dempwolff in 1906. See Dempwolff, 'Sagen und Märchen aus Bilibili', pp. 63–102. That

roles of the brothers tended to be reversed. There were variants on the origin of the quarrel: the Seks, Sengam, and Som (like the Yabobs) claimed that Manup tattooed Kilibob's wife, although the Bilbils followed the Yam account in this respect. But all four groups held that Kilibob sailed north, while Manup journeyed via Madang and the Rai Coast to Siasi, putting men ashore, and giving them language and culture. The Bilbils said that Manup established them and the Yabobs as master potters, and the Seks that he gave them a dance he had invented, the Letub.

The coastal peoples integrated this myth with their other beliefs in different ways. For the first version, the Yam claimed that Kilibob gave them all their culture and ritual formulae. The Yabobs said that after Kilibob established the war and reef gods (tibud), and the people and their culture, he empowered certain men and women to preside over various food plants and artefacts. These persons were not tibud and had no collective term. But as their secret names were used in ritual, they can be called demigods and included in the broad category of deities.[1]

For the second version, the Sengam and Som[2] claimed that after Anut 'put' the natural environment, and the war and reef gods (tubud), Manup arrived and started the two linguistic groups. At Biliau, he put Aisan ashore to found the legendary village of Ran-Tanggom, and at Teterei another man, Madi, whose descendants founded the other Sengam bush groups. At Wab, Yosei was put ashore, and one of his descendants went to Sawoi. Later both peoples formed patriclans and adopted totems. But they attributed much of their culture to indigenous deities rather than to Manup. War gods invented bows and arrows; humans with special powers invented food plants and other artefacts. Thus the Sengam were given yams by a woman from east of Saidor, who brought them to Ran-Tanggom, where she married Aisan. Again, these human originators were not tubud but can be called demigods (deities) for the same reason as above.

Ritual formulae incorporated secret names of deities and sympathetic

---

the Bilbil people should have had the second rather than the first version is puzzling. The geographical proximity of Bilbil to Yabob and Bogati suggests that its people should have had the first. I myself did no work in Bilbil and for the moment we must accept Dempwolff's account as it stands.

[1] My Yabob informant stated: 'They are not tibud but our little gods (Pidgin English, liklik god bilong mipela).' That the beings I call demigods should be classified as deities is supported by the fact that they as well as tibud are translated today by the same Pidgin English word, masalai.

[2] I have no comparable information from Sek and Bilbil.

magic, the latter being more powerful if derived from Kilibob or
Manup. Elaborate ritual was performed for trading expeditions, on
which reef gods were believed to accompany and protect sailors. The
wives of Kilibob and Manup were invoked for calm seas.[1] Anut's
name, as well as those of specifically relevant deities, was used for war
and gardening. Beliefs about the ancestors corresponded with those
of the Ngaing.[2] Spirits helped the living in war, trade, fishing, and
agriculture, and were honoured in the Male Cult, for which dancers
wore carved face masks.[3] Around Madang, some dances were followed
by a great deal of sexual licence, stimulated by love magic. One very
important feature of coastal religions was the *telum*—statues carved to
represent and honour both deities and spirits of the dead.[4] The mother's
brother's initiatory duties were the same as among the Ngaing but
included also the operation of penile supra-incision. Boys now learnt
myths and ritual, for which they had to observe strict taboos.

## The Garia[5]

The Garia (now about 2,500) inhabited about thirty-five square miles
of the Bagasin Area overlooking the Ramu and Naru valleys. Their
neighbours were the Kein, Yarue, Girawa, Sopu, Kopoka, and Yapa.
(See Map IV.) They lived in small hamlets consisting of dwellings
grouped around a cult house. Their staple crop was taro.

*Social Structure:* In Garia society, unilineal descent did not provide
the framework of local organization, and of clear-cut property-owning
and political groups. The structure must be seen from the standpoint
of the individual and the network of interpersonal relationships sur-
rounding him. A man divided the inhabitants of his locality into those
who belonged to his security circle—those with whom he had safe
relationships—and those who did not. His security circle included all

[1] See Hannemann, *Village Life and Social Change*, op. cit., p. 23, and 'Le Culte de
Cargo en Nouvelle-Guinée', p. 944; Aufinger, 'Wetterzauber auf den Yabob-Inseln in
Neuguinea', p. 288; and Schmitz, *Historische Probleme in Nordost-Neuguinea (Huon-
Halbinsel)*, pp. 323–4.

[2] Sengam and Som ancestors were said to live near the patriclan sacred pools. Those of
the Yam were said to live at Sel, east of Saidor. This did not, apparently, impede their
communication with the living. The people of Amele had a similar belief. Their ancestors
were thought to live at Erima.

[3] Bodrogi, 'Some Notes on the Ethnography of New Guinea', p. 133.

[4] See Schmitz, 'Zwei *Telum* Figuren aus der Astrolabe-Bai in Nordost-Neuguinea',
pp. 56–65, and the illustration by Miklouho-Maclay in Bodrogi, 'Some Notes', op. cit.,
p. 183.

[5] The following account is based entirely on my own field work. For supplementary
material see my *Land Tenure among the Garia* and my forthcoming 'The Political
System of the Garia', in *Political Systems in Papua and New Guinea*, ed. K. E. Read.

bilateral kin up to the fourth ascending generation together with other people with whom he had normally no blood ties but specific contractual relationships: trade partners; persons with whom he exchanged pigs; and affines, to whom he gave or from whom he received periodical instalments of bride price. Outside marriage there was no form of permitted sexual licence whatever.

The kindred was divided into named patrilineages of up to five generations deep. But persons descended from a patrilineage's female members had close association with it, using its name (as well as those of their own patrilineages) for several generations until their ties with it were forgotten. Put another way, a man's kindred consisted of a number of linked cognatic groups, each with an agnatic core. Affinal and cognatic ties, and trade and exchange partnerships, linked hamlet to hamlet. Because marriage across the linguistic borders was frequent, the system was extended well outside Garialand.

The members of a man's security circle could be scattered anywhere in his locality because of the land tenure system. Apart from inheritance from their fathers, people could purchase rights to land and agricultural ritual from their mothers' brothers and transmit them to their patrilineal heirs. Thus their garden plots were often in many different quarters. To use them all they had regularly to move from one settlement to another. The members of a patrilineage were rarely localized, and hamlets consisted of irregular clusters of people, some of whom were interrelated and others not. The patrilineage could maintain no exclusive rights over esoteric formulae, which it shared with cognates, or ritual property for the Male Cult. Gourd trumpets and bamboo pipes were owned privately, slit-gongs by the current inhabitants of a hamlet, and dances and melodies by those of a whole locality. A leader's authority was always ill-defined: he could not represent a specific group but only the often transient inhabitants of his own and possibly neighbouring hamlets. Dispersal of land holdings and consequent migration enabled his followers to divide their allegiance between him and his rivals, or withdraw it immediately if his prowess was eclipsed.

*Religion:* The Garia believed that the natural environment, human beings, and their culture were created by deities (*oite'u*). They had no totemic ancestors or emblems. First, certain deities 'put' the ground. Second, Obomwe, a snake god, gave birth to human beings. Third, the deities who 'put' the ground grouped people into hamlets, gave them their basic customs, and became their war gods. Finally, other deities invented food plants, pigs and pig exchanges, the Male Cult, sorcery, and artefacts. A few deities were common to all Garia. War and pottery gods were associated with particular hamlets. Otherwise, Garialand was divided into four zones, whose members had inviolable rights to their own deities for agriculture and domesticated animals. Ritual techniques (*osa*) involved breathing the deities' secret names (*wenum minikoro*), said to have been revealed in dreams during the period of creation. The most feared type of sorcery was *ämale*, attributed to a god who enabled men to turn invisible and project missiles into their victims' bodies.[1]

There were two kinds of spirits of the dead: *kopa*, spirits of those who died naturally; and *kaua*, of those who had been killed. *Kopa* inhabited a land of the dead with Obomwe, where existence was a replica of human life. *Kaua* roamed the bush. Spirits helped their descendants in important enterprises, and brought them messages and gifts of valuables in dreams. They were honoured by mourning ceremonies, food offerings, various dances (including some traded in from the coast), and the Male Cult (Nalisägege). Personal property was placed with corpses, which were exposed in trees, partly for the spirits' use and partly to buy off an evil deity waiting to devour them *en route* to the land of the dead.

The initiatory period was longer and more exacting than on the coast. It lasted from puberty to marriage, and involved training in mythology and ritual (including sorcery). Taboos, again sanctioned by the deities, were very severe. Apart from those on food and water during the ceremony, youths had always to avoid most kinds of meat and all contact with women until marriage.

### Trade

The two trading systems in the area linked the peoples as follows: the Ngaing, Sengam, Som, and Yam belonged to one system which operated along the coast; and the peoples of the Bagasin Area belonged to another which operated in the interior.

### The Madang-Rai Coast Trading System

Although there was little intermarriage between the different linguistic groups of the Rai Coast seaboard and sub-coast, they co-operated in activities such as burning off grassland for communal game drives and celebrating the annual arrival of the palolo worm. Most important

---

[1] The Garia and other Bagasin Area peoples are still greatly respected in the southern Madang District as sorcerers. For a fuller account see my 'Sorcery among the Garia', pp. 340–3.

were the trade ties between Madang and the Saidor area, which formed part of a system embracing the mainland east coast, Huon Peninsula, and Siasi Islands.[1] As well as trading dogs' teeth and Siasi beads, the Madang peoples—especially the Yabobs and Bilbils—provided the Rai Coast with cooking pots, for they had large clay deposits which the Saidor area lacked, although there were some deposits to the west at Mindiri.[2] In return, they received wooden bowls and bark cloth made by the Ngaing. The Sengam, Gira, and Som were middlemen.

Trade relationships reached at least from the foothills of the Finisterres to the Hansemann Mountains. On the Rai Coast, bush groups inhabiting the same ridge running down towards the sea, together with the bush group at its tip on the coastal plain, formed a trade league. In each bush group, every patriclan had its opposite number in the next bush group, and between the patriclans individuals were paired off in private partnerships. The coastal bush groups had similar patriclan and personal links with the Madang island groups, which had partners on the mainland as far inland as Kurog, Kauris, and Nobanob. Trade relationships imposed strong loyalties at both group and personal levels: they precluded all hostility, and enjoined mutual protection and hospitality.

Trade was both informal and formal. Informal trade went on continually. On the Rai Coast, Ngaing brought bowls and bark cloth to the coast, and returned with fish, salt, dry coconuts, pots, and valuables. At Madang, mainland groups exchanged wooden plates for pots and valuables from the islands. For formal trade, the Madang groups assembled canoes, which they loaded with pots and valuables. They made for the Rai Coast, putting in at all villages from Singor to somewhere east of Wab. When the fleet was known to be at sea, Sengam, Gira, and Som prepared to receive it. They got any additional bowls or bark cloth they needed from their Ngaing partners. When the canoes reached each port, hosts and guests danced in each others' honour and exchanged wares.[3] The visitors were entertained with feasts. In these formal exchanges, Rai Coast seaboard and Madang island groups took the lead. They tended to patronize the inland peoples, who were not expected to participate, although they were always free to do so.

[1] See Neuhauss, *Deutsch Neu-Guinea*, Vol. I, pp. 366–9, and, for a modern reconstruction of the system, Bodrogi, *Art in North-East New Guinea*, pp. 31–3.

[2] Some pots were sent to the Saidor area from Mindiri, probably through a subsidiary trade system, about which unfortunately I did not make detailed inquiries.

[3] I saw the last of these exchanges at Yamai on the Rai Coast in 1953. See also Hannemann, *Papuan Dances*, op. cit., p. 4.

## The Bagasin Area Trading System

In the Bagasin Area, the Garia and Girawa, who had the best clay deposits, made pots. The Sopu made wooden plates, and bows and arrows. The Yapa and Kopoka provided stone axes[1] and tobacco. All these articles were traded. Near at home a man dealt with affines and cognates, but further afield he had special partners. Shell ornaments and dances came in from Madang and, more particularly, up the Naru Valley from Bogati, which the Bagasin Area peoples always regarded as their true beach port.[2] This kept them, however tenuously, in touch with the coast.

### Values and Epistemological Assumptions

The essential materialism and anthropocentrism of the people's outlook, and the religious basis of their intellectual system, were implicit in their conception of the cosmic order. Man's primary concern was his own welfare, which he strove to guarantee by careful regulation of the two systems of relationships in which he saw himself as involved within the physical world.

The existence of at least three different forms of society implied, of course, variation in social attitudes. Yet this was important only in minor details. There was always broad homogeneity. Nobody in any of the societies outlined clearly understood its total structure. Rather, individuals conducted their affairs from a purely egocentric standpoint: in terms of constellations of person to person relationships, some denoting membership in a descent or local group, and others affinal, cognatic, exchange, or trade ties. These relationships were verbalized mainly by means of kinship terminologies which, allowing for language differences, were very consistent through the whole area.

The content of these social relationships can be described as the exchange of equivalent goods and services. A purely nominal relationship had little value. What counted was that each party to a relationship should be forced to 'think on' (Ngaing, *inahok ra-*; Garia, *nanunanu pulowobu*—literally, 'to get a man's thinking') the other by the fulfilment of specific obligations—as in kinship and exchange commitments—which demanded an automatic and equal return at the risk of losing personal reputation and mutual advantage. Material wealth,

[1] I never determined whether stone axes actually originated in the Ramu Valley or were traded in from further inland.

[2] The tradition is still maintained. Today there is a Garia-Girawa colony engaged in copra production near Bogati. Also, as will be seen, soon after the Second World War a Girawa native started a cargo cult in the area.

apart from its primary utility, had a secondary and perhaps greater value as the symbol of social relationships. Its existence enabled co-operation between, and its abundance conferred prestige on, both individuals and groups. Where there was no exchange of goods and services, there could be no sense of relationship, mutual obligation, and value, but only suspicion, hostility, and the risk of warfare.

This stress on the value of individual and group equivalence had its correlates in the economic system. Absence of specialization demanded that everybody should have approximately equal rights to basic re-sources, which alone could make the principle of equivalence a reality. Absence of a profit motive gave the economy its stationary tendency, and this in turn fixed relationships between persons and groups in a virtually stereotyped pattern. Even allowing for imperceptible changes, the socio-economic structure was a practically static order. Despite the prominence of materialism, there was nothing akin to the Protestant Ethic to sanction attempts at individual economic advancement at the expense of the group.

Anthropocentrism and materialism were undisguised in religion. The world existed for man and he was master of it. The deities had made and given him his culture as a concomitant of living. The ances-tors, although not creators, helped him enjoy it. He was dependent on these superhuman beings only in so far as he had to fulfil his obligations to them by performing ritual, respecting their sanctuaries, and observ-ing taboos. If he ignored these stipulations, they would be angry and harm him. But as long as he complied, they would at once submit to his direction by giving him their aid. Spiritual values such as purity and sin were non-existent. There was no idea of rewards in the next world in return for good works in the present or of separate destinations for 'good' and 'bad'. The affairs of the dead automatically ordered them-selves. Even the initiatory taboos had no abstract ethical meaning. They were 'good' only because, having been ordained by the deities, they were necessary for success in ritual activities.

Thus man regarded religion as 'above all a technology',[1] which he used to maintain his central and paramount position in the cosmic order. What he could take for granted—the general physical environ-ment and form of the social structure—he tended to neglect. But whatever caused him anxiety, or involved risk or failure—essential resources and artefacts, and relationships necessary for producing and distributing wealth—all these he strongly emphasized. It was staple crops, valuables in short supply, trade, and key institutions such as

[1] McAuley, 'My New Guinea', p. 18.

the Male Cult and pig exchange that were explained by the most elaborate myths and buttressed by the most intensive ritual. Men would go to any approved lengths to acquire the most efficient secret formulae. Garia who had rights to taro goddesses of different zones through their fathers and mothers' brothers would experiment to see which yielded the better crop and concentrate on her thereafter. There was no notion of punctilious devotion to a jealous god. Yet, although myths and ritual could spread, there was no conscious idea of proselytism. Rights to deities had to be established by genealogy or purchase. Otherwise, they were invariably withheld from outsiders who, it was believed, would exploit them to their own advantage and so impoverish the original owners.[1]

Religion did far more than reflect man's social values. It governed his whole intellectual life. We may define two categories of knowledge: secular or empirical knowledge, which the people actually possessed; and sacred knowledge, which had no empirical foundation but which they believed had been revealed by their deities.[2]

That the people had a sound body of secular knowledge is attested by their skill in agriculture, use of slit-gongs for communication, and seamanship. Using our own concepts, we can regard these as the people's own achievements in the field of human intellectual endeavour. Yet the natives themselves did not interpret and evaluate their secular knowledge in this way. Except in minor matters, they dismissed the principle of human intellectual discovery. They accepted myths as the sole and unquestionable source of all important truth. All the valued parts of their culture were stated to have been invented by the deities, who taught men both secular and ritual procedures for exploiting them. The deities lived with men or appeared in dreams, showing them how to plant crops and make artefacts. They taught men to breathe esoteric formulae and observe taboos. Even when a man composed a new melody or dance, he had to authenticate it by claiming that it came from a deity rather than out of his own head. The same assumptions applied when men used secular and ritual techniques without having learnt the substantiating myths, as happened with dances traded into the Bagasin Area from the coast. Ignorance of a myth did not matter as long as it could be accepted that a myth of some sort existed and was known in the place of origin. It was enough to be sure that the relevant deity had revealed his secrets in a recognized way.

---

[1] See my 'Cargo Cult', op. cit., p. 9, for a discussion of this point.
[2] The problem is more fully discussed in my 'The Background to Educational Development in Papua and New Guinea', pp. 52–60.

Furthermore, not only were the deities assumed to be the sole authentic sources of both types of knowledge but also, of the two, it was sacred knowledge that was emphasized as paramount. Secular techniques were described as 'knowing' but only at a very elementary level. The hard core of knowledge was mastery of esoteric formulae, as was stressed in education and leadership. A small boy's upbringing was very informal. He was generally left to do as he pleased, but he continually imitated his elders' activities—dancing, hunting, and even garden work. In this way, by adolescence, with little formal instruction, he had picked up much of the secular knowledge of his society. Yet this was not rated as high intellectual achievement. 'True knowledge' was gained only during and after initiation, when a boy was introduced not to secular skills but to mythology, ritual, and taboos. Again, leadership depended on personal pre-eminence in important activities, but secular skill alone was inadequate. What counted was mastery of ritual by which men could ensure success. The leaders were men who 'really knew' and who could direct the activities of others—those who did not 'really know'[1]—to the best advantage. It was popular conviction of this ability that enabled the particularly successful leader, who had an outstanding personality and had never been defeated by unforeseen circumstances, to lure followers away from his less fortunate rivals.

To regard this as proof of a high degree of mysticism in native thinking would be a misinterpretation in European terms. The people's thinking was, in fact, extremely pragmatic, as can be seen by reconsidering how they conceived their cosmos both spatially and through time.

Spatially, as was stressed, the cosmos was conceived as a unified physical realm with virtually no supernatural attributes: in which human beings interacted not only with each other but also with deities, spirits, and totems. The content of the putative relationships between human and superhuman beings was understood and expressed in the same way as in the case of those between men themselves. The fulfilment of social obligations created a network of face-to-face ties between men by ensuring that they continually 'thought on' and co-operated with each other. Similarly, the observance of taboos and performance of ritual were attempts to establish the same sort of personal ties between human and superhuman beings. They were meant to place deities and ancestors in a position where they had automatically to

---

[1] In this context, the 'purely elementary' empirical knowledge referred to earlier was entirely discounted, of course.

D

'think' and confer material benefits on men.[1] But the imagined activities of deities and spirits in helping mankind had no mystical quality. They were believed to take place on the same plane of existence and to be, therefore, just as real as those of human beings combining for any joint task.[2] Thus, although the people regarded important work as a compound of secular and ritual techniques,[3] they assumed that both were equally pragmatic. Both were derived from the same source and both involved collaboration between beings in the same environment.

Viewed through time, the cosmic order was essentially changeless. There was no historical tradition. Adapting Evans-Pritchard's terms,[4] we may define two kinds of time: oecological and cosmic time. Oecological time, the annual succession of the seasons, was reckoned by rudimentary calendars, but it had no chronological meaning. Time depth could be measured only in relation to the recognized age of the cosmos. Cosmic time may be regarded as genealogical time (Evans-Pritchard's structural time) or the period of remembered events, plus the age of antiquity, when the natural environment, man, and his culture were believed to have come into being.

Yet even cosmic time had little chronological meaning. It did not represent an immense and ever-increasing span of years. The depth of empirically recordable genealogies was not only very shallow (five generations at most) but also kept more or less constant. With each new generation distant forbears were forgotten. Thus the age of antiquity was only just beyond the horizon of the period of remembered events, and the division between the two extremely blurred. The age of antiquity itself was virtually timeless. There was no concept of a detailed sequence of creation. Although the natural environment was assumed to have been brought into existence at the very beginning, thereafter food plants, artefacts, domesticated animals, ceremonies, and, in the case of the Ngaing, human beings emerged at random.[5] Not only the whole mythology but even individual myths reflected the

---

[1] The essential quality of a leader was expressed in the same way as was that of the person successful in social relationships: he could *tutyerak inahok ra-* (Ngaing) or *oite'u po nanunanu puluwobu* (Garia)—literally 'get the deity's thinking'. The same phrase was used in relation to the ancestors.

[2] Cf. Berndt, 'Reaction to Conquest in the Eastern Highlands of New Guinea', pp. 262-3, who says of the Eastern Highlands peoples that they do not merely believe but *know* that the spirits exist, just as they know that people in the next village exist, although they cannot at the moment see them.

[3] See also my 'Cargo Cult', op. cit., p. 15.

[4] Evans-Pritchard, *The Nuer*, p. 94.

[5] Evans-Pritchard, op. cit., p. 108, discusses the same problem among the Nuer.

absence of the idea of time depth. There was no suggestion of a gradual advance from a rudimentary to a more elaborate way of life. Each part of the culture was described in myth as if it had at the time of its invention exactly the same form as during living memory. Also each myth depicted the culture of antiquity as recognizably up to date and complete except for that part of it the relevant deity had to introduce and explain. In short, the tendency to stasis in the actual socio-economic order was repeated in, and validated by, the intellectual system. Events of antiquity were events of the present and would be events of the future as well. Hence relationships between men, deities, and spirits within the cosmos were finally established: all had their unalterable roles to play towards each other.

By the same token, the body of knowledge was conceived to be as finite as the cosmic order within which it was contained. It came into the world ready made and ready to use, and could be augmented not by human intellectual experiment but only by further revelation by new or old deities. It was hardly surprising that epistemological assumptions fossilized in this way. The religion was intellectually satisfying because it operated within a framework which normally demonstrated its validity. Because of the relative monotony of social and economic life, there was hardly any event which could not be explained by or attributed to it. The whole visible world—annually ripening crops, fertility of pigs, success in hunting—far from allowing it an aura of mysticism, proclaimed that it was solidly based on verified and empirical fact. There was no need—in fact, no room—for an independent human intellect.

It was these values and epistemological assumptions that provided the threads of consistency in the otherwise variegated socio-cultural pattern of the southern Madang District: the assumption that a true relationship existed only when men demonstrated goodwill by reciprocal co-operation and distribution of wealth; and the unswerving conviction that material wealth originated from and was maintained by deities who, with the ancestors, could be manipulated by ritual to man's advantage. One of the main results of European occupation was that these threads of consistency were accentuated so that local idiosyncrasies became irrelevant. This made possible the uniform native reaction to, and interpretation of, the new situation, to which we now turn.

# CHAPTER II

# THE COLONIAL ORDER

## 1871–1950

THE Cargo Movement in the southern Madang District between 1871 and 1950 represented native reactions to two distinct phases of European contact. First, there was initial contact, ending with the German Occupation in 1884; and second, intensive contact—the sixty-five years of German, Australian, and Japanese rule. In this chapter, I begin by outlining the main events of these two phases of contact through the eyes of a Westerner relying on documentary sources. I then consider their significance for race relations, showing how the first phase correlated with friendship between coastal natives and occasional European visitors, and the second with racial segregation and antagonism, sometimes tempered by cordiality between the people and limited or transient sections of the white community. This gives the historical background to the cargo beliefs and activities described in Chapters III–VIII, where I retrace the whole period as it was interpreted by the natives themselves.

### Initial Contact, 1643–1884

Although north-eastern New Guinea was unoccupied by any colonial power for sixty years after Dutch acquisition of the western mainland in 1824, it had been known to European explorers for two centuries. In 1643, Tasman sighted Umboi and Bagabag Islands. In 1700, Dampier sailed past and named Cape King William on the Huon Peninsula, Rooke Island (Umboi), Long Island (Arop), Crown Island (Lotin), and Rich Island (Bagabag). In 1792–3, d'Entrecasteaux travelled through the Huon Gulf. In 1827, Dumont d'Urville entered Astrolabe Bay, naming it after his ship. None of these visits had any immediate results. No trading posts were established, and even the blackbirders, who had been recruiting labour in the eastern Melanesian islands since 1860, never operated in the area. At this stage, the only Europeans who could have had any prolonged contact with the southern Madang District were the Marist Catholic missionaries, who had a station on Umboi Island between 1847 and 1855. It is also

possible that Indonesians and Malays visited the north-eastern mainland as far south as Finschhafen from early times.[1]

Real contact began in 1871, when the Russian Baron Nikolai
Miklouho-Maclay arrived at Bongu on the Rai Coast. He paid three
visits: September 1871 to December 1872; June 1876 to November
1877; and for about ten days in 1883. His interest in New Guinea was
scientific. He recorded the people's language and culture. He explored
the foothills of the Finisterres, and the coast between Rempi and
Teliata. He called the coast on which he lived by his own name[2]
and the place where he landed Constantine Harbour after his patron.[3]

After Maclay's second visit, Europeans began to show commercial
and political interest in north-eastern New Guinea. In 1878, Australian
gold prospectors in the *Dove* put in at Bongu but left almost immediately. In 1881, Romilly (British Deputy High Commissioner of
the Western Pacific) paid an official visit to the Rai Coast. He was followed in the same year by Finsch, who was investigating the area's
economic potential on behalf of von Hansemann's German trading
consortium. Finally, in November 1884, when Britain occupied
Papua, a German party under Finsch (now representing von Hansemann's new consortium, the New Guinea Company[4]) took possession
of the north-eastern mainland and Bismarck Archipelago. The German
flag was hoisted at Matupi (New Britain) on 3 November; in the Duke
of York Islands on the 4th; at Madang on the 12th; and at Finschhafen
on the 27th.

*Intensive Contact: Administrations and Missions, 1885–1950*

Between 1885 and 1950, the two main agents of contact in the southern
Madang District were the Colonial Administrations and the missions.
There were seven Administrations: two German, four Australian, and
one Japanese. There were three missions: Lutheran, Roman Catholic,
and, after 1945, Seventh Day Adventist.[5]

[1] For a summary of early exploration see Schmitz, *Historische Probleme*, op. cit., pp.
11–12. For a fuller account see Reed, *The Making of Modern New Guinea*, esp. pp. 72–125.
[2] The Rai Coast is still sometimes called the Maclay Coast but there is probably no
connexion between the two names.
[3] The Grand Duke Constantine, President of the Imperial Russian Geographical Society.
[4] Neu Guinea Kompagnie. For fuller accounts of events leading up to the German
Occupation see Jacobs, 'Bismarck and the Annexation of New Guinea', pp. 14–26, and
'The Colonial Office and New Guinea, 1874–84', pp. 106–18. See also Mackenzie, *The
Australians at Rabaul*, esp. pp. 21–2.
[5] Inselmann, *Letub, The Cult of the Secret of Wealth*, p. 125, indicates that a Seventh
Day Adventist missionary was making first contacts with Madang natives before 1942,
but the Mission does not seem to have been established there until after 1945. It is not
listed for the Madang District in *The New Guinea Handbook* (Reprint 1943).

*The Seven Administrations: Trends of Policy*

The outlooks of the seven Administrations were never consistent. They varied from severity to liberalism. The various policies they represented must be summarized before their impact on the southern Madang District is described.

*The German New Guinea Company's Administration under Charter from the Imperial Government (1885-99):* Company rule was based on Bismarck's principle: a colony was to be exploited for primary resources to feed home industries. This would be done most efficiently by encouraging large-scale European development, because of the backwardness of the natives, and leaving administration to a chartered company, which would pay the costs from its profits, guaranteed by a trading monopoly. The New Guinea Company established a viable economy but its native policy was incompetent and oppressive. Between 1891 and 1899, its administrative authority was modified and then entirely resumed by the Imperial Government.

*The Imperial German Administration (1899-1914)* introduced two main improvements: First, it made some separation between commerce and government. The Company and other firms were left to exploit the colony: taxes on their profits, helped by an Imperial subsidy, paid for administration. Although these firms were still influential, Imperial officers could devote themselves more disinterestedly to native affairs. Second, the Imperial Regime ushered in the policy sponsored by the Colonial Society and endorsed by the Colonial Office after 1906.[1] The principle of economic exploitation was upheld but, because many of the commodities needed by German industry were being produced by the natives themselves, it was realized that efficiency demanded native as well as European development. Schemes were implemented to ensure native progress, especially in the economic and educational fields.

*The Australian Military Administration (1914-21)* scrapped the German native development programme and allowed European commerce once more to dominate policy. The Imperial officers were repatriated but, as Australia wanted to monopolize the colony's copra trade, German planters were enabled to carry on and everything was done to foster their interests at the natives' expense. Also, the Australian officers had to administer the colony, as captured territory, according to German law, for which they were unqualified. They were forced to rely on the advice of the planters, who thus became extremely influential.

[1] For a scholarly account of the policy see Rudin, *Germans in the Cameroons*, pp. 120-77.

*The Australian Administration under Mandate of the League of Nations (1921–42)* confirmed the supremacy of commercial interests. As the Australian Government did not subsidize the colony, revenue was derived largely from taxes on copra and gold produced, after the expropriation of the Germans, almost entirely by Australian settlers, who could thus dictate their own terms to the Administration. The Imperial German native development policy, in spite of many promises, was never seriously revived.

*The A.N.G.A.U.*[1] *and Japanese Military Administrations (1942–6)* based their rule on military considerations.

*The Australian Administration under the Trusteeship Agreement of the United Nations Organization (after 1946)* introduced a liberal programme of native economic, political, and educational development because of native resentment of pre-war conditions and world criticism of colonial powers.

## The Two German Administrations in the Southern Madang District (1885–1914)

*Administrative Organization:* The Company placed the colony under the authority of its Director, and divided it into the Western District (the mainland or Kaiser Wilhelmsland) and the Eastern District (the Bismarck Archipelago, Buka, and Bougainville). Each District had its subordinate officials and native police. After 1891, the Company Director was replaced by an Imperial Governor and Imperial Judges were appointed to the two Districts. Finschhafen was the first capital but was abandoned in 1892, owing to malaria, for Stephansort (Bogati). Stephansort proved unsuitable for shipping and, in 1897, the capital was moved to Madang (Friedrich Wilhelmshafen), where there was a fine harbour. After 1899, the Imperial Administration transferred the capital to New Britain, first to Herbertshöhe and later to Rabaul. Kaiser Wilhelmsland remained a separate District with its own District Officer, and District and Magistrate's Courts at Madang. Its European population was 97 in 1901, reached its peak of 290 in 1912, and fell to 283 in 1913. It consisted largely of settlers scattered in coastal plantations. The Administration never had more than eight officers at Madang. To strengthen its organization, it allowed private settlers to act as assessors (*Beisitzer*) in the law courts[2] and, together with lay members of the missions, punish their native employees for minor offences. This included the right to flog.

---

[1] The Australian New Guinea Administrative Unit.
[2] Rowley, *The Australians in German New Guinea, 1914–21*, pp. 233–4.

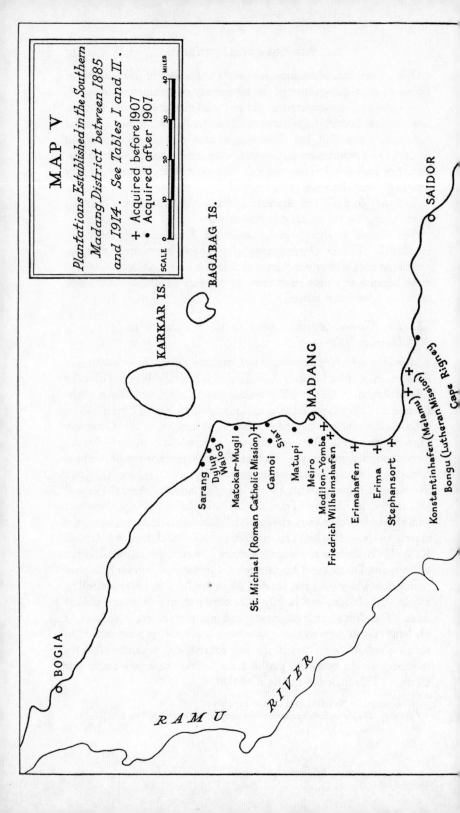

MAP V

*Plantations Established in the Southern Madang District between 1885 and 1914. See Tables I and II.*

+ Acquired before 1907
• Acquired after 1907

SCALE

0    10    20    30    40 MILES

BOGIA

RAMU RIVER

KARKAR IS.

BAGABAG IS.

MADANG

Sarang
Dylup
Walog
Matokar-Mugil
St. Michael (Roman Catholic Mission)
Gamoi
Siar
Matupi
Meiro
Modilon-Yomba
Friedrich Wilhelmshafen
Erimahafen
Erima
Stephansort
Konstantinhafen (Melamu)
Bongu (Lutheran Mission)
Cape Rignau

SAIDOR

## TABLE I

Plantations established near Astrolabe Bay and Alexishafen, 1902–7

| Plantation | Cleared Area (ha.) | | |
| --- | --- | --- | --- |
| | 1902–3 | 1904–5 | 1906–7 |
| Friedrich Wilhelmshafen | 137·5 | 150 } | 1094·9 |
| Modilon-Yomba | 401·7 | 554 } | |
| Stephansort | 619·7 | 800 | 1329·59 |
| Erimahafen | 39·4 | 109 | — |
| Konstantinhafen (Melamu) [Constantine Harbour] | 154·2 | 303·9 | — |
| Erima | — | 363·5 | — |
| St Michael (Alexishafen) | — | — | 30 |
| Total Area Cleared | 1352·5 | 2280·4 | 2454·49* |

* *Note:* There are no figures listed for Erimahafen, Konstantinhafen, and Erima in the 1906–7 Report. But if the figures for these three plantations for 1905 are added to the total given above for 1906, the full area cleared in that year would have been at least 3,230·89 ha. By 1910, St Michael had an additional 20 ha. under rice cultivation. This would be included in the total area of c. 3,900 ha. cleared by 1914.

## TABLE II

Dates of acquisition and first clearing of other plantations, and their area in 1926

| Plantation | Purchased from Natives | Initial Clearing | 1926 Area (ha.) | | |
| --- | --- | --- | --- | --- | --- |
| | | | Cleared | Uncleared | Total |
| Bongu (Lutheran Mission) | By 1907 | ? | ? | ? | ? |
| Sarang | 1910–11 | Before 1914 | 256 | 291 | 547 |
| Matupi | 1912 | Before 1914 | 121 | 179 | 300 |
| Meiro | 1912 | Before 1914 | 194 | — | 194 |
| Walog | 1914 | 1913–14 | 321 | 70 | 391 |
| Dylup | 1914 | 1912 | 522 | 126 | 648 |
| Siar | 1912 | Before 1914 | 547 | — | 547 |
| Gamoi | 1912 | Before 1914 | 109 | — | 109 |
| Cape Rigney | 1914* | 1916 | 210 | 26 | 236 |
| Matokar-Mugil | 1914* | After 1914 | 74 | 519 | 593 |

* Purchase approved but not concluded by August 1914.

*Land Policy:* The Company's immediate aim was to establish plantations on a grand scale. It made no attempt to extend political control as a prerequisite for orderly economic development. It alienated huge tracts of land from natives whom it left in their traditional state and with whom it had only tenuous relations. In theory, alienation was governed by strict regulations in the Imperial Charter: the Company had to survey and register all land acquired; and all such land had to be ownerless or bought subject to a contract protecting native interests. These responsibilities were assumed and endorsed by the Imperial Administration after 1899.

In practice, however, both these regulations were ignored. Surveys and registration were so unsystematic that it is difficult to state exactly how much land was acquired. According to figures compiled by the Australian Custodian of Expropriated Property,[1] about 33,000 hectares (ha.) were officially alienated along the coast between Sarang and Saidor[2] by 1914. But probably little more than 3,900 ha. had been actually taken up by that date. This would include 3,230 ha. planted on seven properties by 1906, and allow for later extensions on them, clearing on the Lutheran Mission property at Bongu, for which there is no information, initial clearing on seven plantations started after 1910, and areas marked for clearing on two others in 1914. Yet even this conservative estimate meant rapid European economic expansion along the Sarang–Saidor coast by the end of German rule. The extent of the Company's plantations around Astrolabe Bay and the Catholic Mission's property at Alexishafen (acquired in 1904) for the years 1902–3, 1904–5, and 1906–7 is shown in Table I.[3] For the other plantations, comparable figures are unobtainable. Only dates of acquisition and first clearing, and areas in 1926, can be given. These are set out in Table II.[4] (See also Map V.)

German officials failed to safeguard native interests. The Company's Administration, which acquired most of the holdings, especially around Astrolabe Bay, was primarily to blame. After 1899, the Imperial Administratio tried to improve the situation but, in the face

[1] See Custodian of Expropriated Property, *Catalogue of New Guinea Properties, Second Group* (1926), *Catalogue of New Guinea Properties, Third Group* (1927), and *List of New Guinea Properties Sold by the Custodian of Expropriated Property as at 1st January 1928* (1928). My discussion of German and Australian land dealings is not definitive. Supporting information has been omitted. This will be rectified in a later publication. I am most indebted for help and advice to Messrs C. Greig and I. Cartledge (Department of Territories, Canberra, A.C.T.), Mr J. Gibney (Government Archives, Canberra, A.C.T.), and Mr C. P. McCubbery (Commissioner of Titles, Port Moresby).

[2] No land was ever alienated on the sub-coast or in the interior of the southern Madang District.

[3] Figures from *Annual Reports* (1902–3; 1904–5; 1906–7).

[4] Figures from Custodian of Expropriated Property, *Catalogue . . . , Second Group*, op. cit., and *Catalogue . . . , Third Group*, op. cit.

of commercial pressures, often had to compromise with illegalities. This was the case at Madang.

Land was acquired at Madang in 1887–8, when Kubary[1] (Superintendent of the Company's Outstation at Bongu) paid M202.50 to the Bilbil islanders and M54.40 to the Yabob islanders for 5,500 ha. comprising the site of Madang and its hinterland. Neither purchase was valid. The Bilbils and Yabobs had no absolute rights on the mainland, and the true owners were never consulted. Kubary did not even go ashore to survey the area. Although the land was not registered until 1896, Company agents began clearing it in 1892. The native owners protested through the Lutheran Mission but the Company insisted on the authenticity of its claims. Although the bulk of the land was untouched, nearly 540 ha. were under cultivation on Friedrich Wilhelmshafen and Modilon-Yomba plantations by 1903, and over 1,000 ha. by 1914. After 1900, District Officer Berghausen of the Imperial Administration, realizing the illegality of the situation, negotiated with the Company on the natives' behalf. Eventually, in 1904, he had to accept the Company's titular ownership of the 5,500 ha., subject to the excision of native reserves. But the scheme never came into operation. The survey of the proposed reserves did not begin until 1911 and was still in progress in 1914, when it was abandoned. The issue was settled only in 1932.

This affair, which had repercussions for many years, challenges the legality of the Company's land purchases elsewhere in the southern Madang District. Kubary probably did not examine native rights in the Bogati-Gorima region, where he bought vast estates also in 1887, any less cursorily than at Madang. The Imperial Administration's suspicions were clear from Governor Hahl's reluctance for Berghausen to take the Madang natives' case to court lest a judgement in their favour led to litigation all along the coast. This would hinder the colony's economic progress.

*Exploration:* Plantations created two needs. The first, for labour,[2] was not met by the small coastal population, which was unwilling to be recruited, or by the importation of South-east Asian coolies,[3] which

---

[1] For details see Phillips, J., *Judgement: Delivered at Madang, on Wednesday the 25th day of May, 1932.*

[2] The demand for labour can be gauged from the numbers of natives employed on Friedrich Wilhelmshafen, Modilon-Yomba, Stephansort, Erimahafen, and Konstantinhafen plantations: 468 in 1900–1; 815 in 1903–4; 1,027 in 1904–5.

[3] It was believed that Asians would be easier to handle and more familiar with tropical crops. By 1900, 122 Chinese and 184 Javanese were employed at Madang, and 13 Chinese and 54 Javanese in the Bogati area. In the same year another 190 Chinese were imported to Madang and, in 1901, another 270. No more Asians were imported after 1909.

was never profitable. The second was for additional cash crops (especially rubber and guttapercha, urgently needed by German industry) to supplement copra exports. The solution of both problems was seen in the exploration of the interior. There were two important expeditions: the first (October–December 1890) followed the Gogol from its mouth to the Naru and explored the inland plain; and the second, begun in 1896 and taking the same route, reached the Ramu. Later, using a small steamer, the Imperial Administration plotted the Ramu from its mouth almost to its source. Exploration led to the discovery of considerable native populations that could be tapped for labour, important botanical specimens, and alluvial gold.[1]

*Political Control:* By 1900, it was clear that economic expansion depended on full political control: to protect settlers and induce natives to enter European employment or help development in other ways. The Company did nothing in this field. It had no clear programme for native administration and its officials did no more than establish its rule near the plantations. The task was left to the Imperial Administration. Staff shortage and the rugged terrain restricted operations largely to the coast. By 1906, the controlled area reached from Cape Rigney to Cape Croiselles; by 1910, from Hansa Bay to Helmholtz Point; and by 1912, from the Sepik to the Papuan border. Full control went inland about eight or ten miles, and partial control or influence a little further.

The Imperial Regime's initial aim was pacification: to stamp out cannibalism and warfare with police expeditions and collective punishment. In the southern Madang District, there was little immediate resistance. The Rai Coast natives were probably the most unruly but they appear to have been brought to heel by 1910. The second aim was constructive administration. Madang was developed as the District's capital. In 1901, it had fourteen European inhabitants; in 1902, nineteen; and in 1903 (the last year in which figures are given in the *Annual Reports*), twenty-six. The last figure was probably about doubled by 1914 and was augmented by a slightly larger Chinese population engaged in small trade. Erima, Madang, and Alexishafen were linked by vehicular roads, and Madang and Nobanob, where the Lutheran Mission opened a station in 1906, by a mule track. All villages had to keep open bridle paths for official patrols.

Public works in Madang and road-building increased the demand for labour. The Administration met it by strengthening its hold on the pacified area. After 1904, each village or hamlet cluster was placed

[1] For details see **von Beck**, *Das überseeische Deutschland.*

under a native headman or *luluai* (one of the more co-operative older men), who had to maintain order, guard the village census book, report epidemics, and settle minor disputes. He was assisted by a *tultul*, who acted, where necessary, as his interpreter and had, therefore, to be fluent in Pidgin English, the *lingua franca*. After 1907, adult males, other than indentured labourers, those who had already worked ten months of the current year for Europeans, and those who had given fourteen days' free labour to the Administration, had to pay an annual head tax of M5.00. The Administration used local officials to impress natives for labour, and the tax, of which headmen kept 10 per cent, forced them into European employment. The system was established in the whole pacified area of the southern Madang District by 1914 but, unlike pacification, met with opposition. In 1904 at Madang, where the people had lost the most land and had to provide the most labour, there was a revolt which was put down with an iron hand. In 1912, there was further unrest, which led to the exile of the local population and the confiscation of their land by the Administration.

*Native Development:* Administrative control not only forced natives to submit to exploitation but was also the prerequisite for the policy adopted after 1906. This policy involved the reform of labour laws, and native economic and educational development. Labour laws were amended in 1907 to lay down better working conditions, although part-payment of wages (reckoned at less than M5.00 a month) in trade goods assessed at more than their true value still allowed abuses.[1] Revised laws were drawn up again in 1914, to be implemented a year later. After 1906, labourers were given quinine and native *Heiltultuls* trained to practise elementary medicine in the villages.

In the economic field, the Administration goaded natives into primary production as a means of earning money other than by labour, and regarded the head tax as a legitimate pressure for this purpose.[2] As native copra for a long time exceeded that produced by Europeans, it was planned to establish and extend native-owned plantations.[3]

In education, as well as encouraging the missions, the Administration

---

[1] For German labour regulations see Mair, *Australia in New Guinea*, pp. 135–7, and Rowley, *The Australians in German New Guinea, 1914–21*, op. cit., pp. 106–16.

[2] Rowley, op. cit., p. 173.

[3] See *Annual Reports* (1909–10 and 1912–13). In 1902–3, of the 2,800 tons of copra exported from the whole colony, 2,200 tons were native grown. In 1909–10, total exports were 8,750 tons, of which the bulk was still native grown. Rudin, *Germans in the Cameroons*, op. cit., p. 260, states that, in 1912, most of the palm products exported from the Cameroons were native grown.

opened a native school at Namanula near Simpsonhafen (New Britain) in 1907, and planned four others—one of them at Madang—by 1917. The school's aims were to replace Pidgin English with German, spread German ideals and culture, and enable pupils to take over the junior administrative posts held by Asians. The curriculum included reading, writing, German folksongs, local geography, printing work, simple mechanics, carpentry, locksmithing, and bookbinding. In 1907, it had 27 pupils; in 1909, 60; in 1911, 71; and in 1912, 92.[1]

The development programme was only in its infancy in the southern Madang District by 1914. The reform of labour laws benefited the people but *Heiltultuls* were not appointed in the area until after 1921. Economic development made little progress. After 1906, natives near Madang were trained to produce rubber and guttapercha, which had been discovered in the hinterland. They sold several thousand kilograms through the District Office.[2] They played little part in the copra industry until 1910, when they planted 32,000 new coconut palms. The Namanula school made only a slight impact on them. In 1911, there were only sixteen pupils enrolled from Kaiser Wilhelmsland and, in 1912, twenty-three.

## The Australian Military Administration in the Southern Madang District (1914–21)

German rule ended in 1914. The A.N. and M.E.F.[3] occupied Rabaul on 13 September and on the 21st received the surrender of the colony. Madang was occupied three days later. After the departure of the Imperial officers, the existing administrative framework was retained. Australian officers replaced German District Officers and Australian N.C.O.s German Policemasters.

The Madang Garrison was well staffed: 1 District Officer (Garrison Commander); 1 N.C.O. Policemaster; 21 N.C.O.s and other ranks; and between 75 and 80 native police. Yet its administrative record was negligible. It allowed roads to fall into disrepair and, apart from

---

[1] For fuller accounts see *Annual Reports* (1907–8; 1911–12; 1912–13) and Rowley, op. cit., pp. 252–3. It should be noted here that the Germans did not introduce Pidgin English to New Guinea. It probably originated with the labour traffic to Queensland, Samoa, and Fiji before the German Occupation. See Reed, *The Making of Modern New Guinea*, op. cit., pp. 271–2.

[2] See *Annual Reports* (1902–3; 1909–10; 1911–12). Rudin, *Germans in the Cameroons*, op. cit., pp. 255–65, describes German efforts in the Cameroons to encourage native palm, cacao, and rubber production.

[3] The Australian Naval and Military Expeditionary Force. The most important and up-to-date work on this period is Rowley, op. cit., on which I rely for this section.

punitive expeditions to Bogia, the Rai Coast, and Karkar, and an exploratory patrol to the Hansemann Mountains in 1915,[1] it did nothing to re-establish or enlarge the German boundaries of control. Its only positive achievement in native affairs occurred towards the end of 1914, when it gave the Madang exiles permission to return home.

The Military Administration's chief concern was the production of copra. The initial clearings on Sarang, Matupi, Meiro, Dylup, Siar, and Gamoi were extended, and a start made at Cape Rigney and Matokar-Mugil. The Lutheran and Catholic Missions also expanded cultivation. There was little interest in the natives beyond trying to ensure that they satisfied the demand for labour, which the wartime copra boom made acute. In 1915, new labour laws, based on those drawn up by the Germans in 1914, were promulgated, prohibiting private employers from flogging, recruitment by force or fraud, and signing on boys under twelve. In 1919, all flogging was abolished. In the limited area under the District Office's surveillance, these rules may have been obeyed, but recruiters who entered places not yet brought under control—such as the Bagasin Area and, probably, the inland Rai Coast—appear to have broken them consistently. According to Garia informants, coercion, kidnapping, and shooting were common. The Administration took no notice as long as no complaints were made and sufficient recruits provided.[2] In the same way, the people were ordered to sell their copra to traders but not in a way to promote the well-organized native industry the Germans had wanted.[3] Needless to say, the Namanula school, which closed down in September 1914, was never re-opened. Nothing was done about the four others originally planned.

## The Australian Mandate Administration in the Southern Madang District (1921–42)

*District Organization:* The colony, now the Mandated Territory with its capital still at Rabaul, was administered by Australia separately from Papua, which had come under her control after Federation. The Madang District's boundaries now included the coast from the Ramu to Gal (east of Saidor) and part of the Central Highlands.[4] Its administrative framework lasted, with few changes, until 1950. Civil order was

[1] See Rowley, op. cit., p. 40 and pp. 199–200, and Mackenzie, *The Australians at Rabaul*, op. cit., pp. 311–12.

[2] See Lyng, *Island Films*, pp. 183–6, for a graphic account. Lyng was District Officer at Madang for a time during the Military Occupation.

[3] Rowley, op. cit., p. 187.

[4] The Highlands remained in the Madang District until the last war.

in the hands of the Department of District Services and Native Affairs (henceforth called the Department of Native Affairs), with a District Officer, Assistant District Officers, and Patrol Officers. Its staff never rose above six. At the disposal of the District Office yet administratively separate from it, was a detachment of native police. The District Court sat in Madang, and Courts for Native Affairs, presided over by officers of the Department, sat in Madang and on the sub-stations. Courts for Native Affairs tried minor cases, the most important being adultery. Native plaintiffs and defendants were given legal representation, and due consideration was paid to native custom. The other Departments were those of Agriculture and Public Health.

Native administration followed the German pattern, although harsh punitive measures were forbidden. The aim was to open up the country by peaceful patrols. By 1937, the whole southern Madang District— including the Bagasin Area and inland Rai Coast, and excepting only the higher ranges of the Finisterres—was under full administration. In 1932, a patrol post was set up at Saidor. It became a sub-station in 1936. Also, after 1932, the District Office sent patrols to the Central Highlands.

The inland peoples offered as little resistance as the coastal natives had done to the Germans. There was only one ugly incident. On the Rai Coast in 1936, Patrol Officer Nurton sent six police to the inland Ngaing area. At Saing, they stole some gourd trumpets and played them in front of local women whom they had appropriated. The Ngaing were infuriated by the double insult and killed one of the constables. Nurton led a patrol to Aiyawang and put the culprits on road work. One day, when most of his police were away supervising the labour line, he allowed apparently friendly M'na and N'dau to enter camp. They suddenly fell on him until his few remaining police drove them off. The police out on the road, hearing the noise of the disturbance, came back and restored order. They shot a number of the attackers. Nurton was replaced, and his successor finally established full control on the Rai Coast.[1]

To consolidate its authority, the Administration suppressed warfare and made adultery, its main cause, a penal offence. For reasons of hygiene, it banned old methods of exposing corpses and instituted village cemeteries, but otherwise left religious and marital custom alone.

[1] For details of the Nurton incident I rely on Ngaing informants, Reed, op. cit., p. 170, and *Annual Report* (1936–7). All accounts tally. For details of patrol work generally see *Annual Reports* (1921–2 to 1939–40), and of the administrative structure of the District see *The New Guinea Handbook*, op. cit.

(a) Cargo: natives work ship, Madang (1950)

(b) Patrol Officer interviews Garia Village Headmen (1952)

PLATE 3

It regrouped settlements under *luluais* and *tultuls,* who had the same duties as before but lost the authority to keep 10 per cent of head tax and settle minor disputes. It introduced two new types of native officials: the village medical *tultul* (German *Heiltultul*); and the Paramount *Luluai,* who had general authority over other headmen in his area and, unlike them, received a salary ($£3^1$ a year). It fixed head tax at 10s. a year for all adult males except village headmen, indentured labourers, and mission helpers and students. It had Rest Houses (Pidgin English, *haus kiap*[2]) built for officers visiting the villages to line the people for census-taking or tax-collection. Although forced labour was abolished, it saw that bridle paths were kept open between the villages.

Political control gave the people some protection against unscrupulous recruiters. Headmen could report malpractices to the District Office and, by checking village books, Patrol Officers could see that no more than $33\frac{1}{3}$ per cent of adult males were drawn off from a village at any one time and that its food supplies were thereby maintained. But the imposition of head tax throughout the whole area forced ever-increasing numbers of natives into European employment which, with the collapse of the Administration's promises for native development, was the only means they had of earning the necessary cash. The plantations and, after 1926, goldfields at Wau and Bulolo still made heavy demands for labour, which were not greatly affected by the depression of the 1930's. As wages were pegged at between 5s. and 10s. a month and keep, labour costs were hardly prohibitive.

*Expropriated Properties:* Apart from supplying them with labour, the Administration's main concern was to take over German properties (other than those owned by the missions) so as to get full control of internal security and revenue. By 1928, all such properties in the southern Madang District had been expropriated and sold to Australians. The area involved was about 33,000 ha., of which about 6,800 ha. had by now been taken up for plantations and about 4,800 ha. were actually under cultivation. The Administration confirmed freehold titles but, to protect native interests, prevented further alienation between Sarang and Saidor. It also tried to redress past wrongs. In 1932, when it realized that Kubary's acquisitions at Madang in 1887–8 were invalid, it took legal action. The court ordered the New Guinea Company's successors to restore the virgin land in question—about 4,400

[1] All monetary values are given in Australian currency except, of course, in the case of German marks.
[2] *Kiap* is the Pidgin English word originally for any Native Affairs officer down to the rank of Assistant District Officer but now, in fact, for any Administration officer.

E

ha. of the original 5,500 ha.—to the native owners and to pay them £99 compensation so as to acquire legal title to the two plantations (now called Modilon-Yomba and Wagol) on the residue.[1] The decision showed official rectitude, but the new Administration could champion native rights no more strongly than the Imperial Regime. Unproductive virgin land could be given back to natives but, in the interests of the colony's economy, valuable plantations had somehow to be kept in European hands. The Madang natives were forced to give up about 1,000 ha. for ever.

*The Failure of Native Development:* The Administration's record in native development, as has often been remarked, was hardly impressive. The labour regulations of 1915 and abolition of flogging in 1919 had improved working conditions, but otherwise little was achieved. In the economic field, it was difficult to expand native copra production owing to the depression, opposition from the planters, and the lack of trained staff. Only small trading continued,[2] although in the Madang District one native-owned plantation was started on Karkar. After the loss of the guaranteed market in Germany, the Madang natives' rubber and guttapercha enterprises were useless, for the people could not compete with growers in Malaya and elsewhere.

In education, the official aim was to teach English and train natives for the lower grades of the Public Service. But between 1923 and 1937, annual expenditure for the whole Territory fell from £18,000 to £5,000. By 1939–40, there were only six Administration schools with a total of 491 pupils: four in New Britain; one in New Ireland; and one at Chimbu (Central Highlands).[3] Few Madang District natives were enrolled: one went to New Britain in 1927; three in 1928; and six in 1929 (after which no figures are given in the *Annual Reports*). In 1941, a seventh school was opened near Madang with 150 pupils but was closed down a year later because of the Japanese invasion. The failure of native education meant, of course, the retention of Pidgin English as the *lingua franca*.

*The A.N.G.A.U. and Japanese Military Administrations in the Southern Madang District (1942–6)*

After 1939, the Administration made every effort to preserve calm among the natives by hiding news of the European war from them.

---

[1] Details from Phillips J., *Judgement: Delivered at Madang*, op. cit.

[2] Reed, *The Making of Modern New Guinea* op. cit., p. 256, states that in 1935–6 native income from copra for the whole Mandated Territory was £13,000.

[3] See Reed, op. cit., p. 188, for details of expenditure and *Annual Report* (1939–40) for list of schools and pupils.

Apart from training the New Guinea Volunteer Rifles (N.G.V.R.), all local preparations were kept secret, especially the Coast Watching Service, a group of officers and settlers willing to stay in their areas in the event of attack and report enemy movements.[1] With the Japanese invasion in 1942, the colonial structure in the southern Madang District collapsed. By the end of January, Rabaul was in enemy hands, and on the 21st Madang was bombed from the air. Many of the police rioted and deserted. Civil Administration was at once replaced by a small force of N.G.V.R. and A.N.G.A.U.[2] All Europeans other than missionaries and coastwatchers were evacuated.

The Japanese by-passed Madang during 1942. They took only Lae as a staging base for their Papuan operations but, when these and their venture in the Solomons failed, they occupied the whole north-eastern mainland. They landed at Madang on 18 December 1942. The N.G.V.R. and A.N.G.A.U. force retreated to the Central Highlands. Enemy light forces occupied the Rai Coast seaboard and Bagasin Area in 1943. The Japanese either confirmed existing headmen or installed others willing to collaborate, replacing Australian insignia with their own. The headmen's main duty was to provide workers for the occupying troops. The Japanese also created a Native Police Force, recruits coming from Madang, and the Gogol and Bagasin areas. Its duties were to maintain contact with inland villages and provide scouts for army patrols. The European missionaries on the Rai Coast and at Nobanob managed to escape through the inland. Those near Madang carried on for a time but were eventually rounded up, publicly humiliated, and deported. The Chinese community was treated in the same way. The only Europeans left were the coastwatchers on the Rai Coast.

In 1943, the tide of war turned. The Allies recaptured Lae, Salamaua, and Finschhafen by early October. In January 1944, American troops won a beachhead at Saidor, where they were joined on 22 April by Australians who had fought their way from Finschhafen. Meanwhile Australian troops from Lae captured Kaiapit and Dumpu in September and October 1943. At Dumpu, they were joined by other Australians from the Highlands. The combined force split into two groups. One went to Yapa and the other, after the hard-fought Shaggy Ridge campaign of February 1944, to Bogati and Bongu, where it was reinforced by Australians brought by sea from Saidor. This new group recaptured

---

[1] For a graphic account of this service and the war in New Guinea see Feldt, *The Coast Watchers.*

[2] The Australian New Guinea Administrative Unit was formed early in 1942 to take over from the Civil Administration in areas not in enemy hands.

Madang and Alexishafen on 24 and 25 April. Japanese troops were pushed towards Hansa Bay and, with the reoccupation of Hollandia and Aitape, hemmed in at Wewak.[1] In all these operations, natives serving with Allied forces played a distinguished part: as ships' crews, carriers, policemen, and members of three special units, the New Guinea Infantry Battalion (N.G.I.B.), the Papuan Infantry Battalion (P.I.B.), and the Allied Intelligence Bureau (A.I.B.).

After the close of military operations in the southern Madang District, A.N.G.A.U. was once again in control. Headmen were either reinstated or replaced and collaborators arrested. Patrols went through the area to recruit as many labourers as possible to help the troops fighting to the north.

## The Trusteeship Administration in the Southern Madang District (after 1946)

The new Civil Administration took office from A.N.G.A.U. on 1 January 1946. It had literally to rebuild the whole District. Material reconstruction and routine administration were its least worries. The planters returned and got their properties into production again. Madang, which like all coastal towns had been completely destroyed, was gradually rebuilt. In many places, the native population was scattered and, especially along the coast, the villages were deserted. Native Affairs staff, although still very small, regained contact with the people.

The greatest problem was the implementation of the Labor Government's new progressive policy, which paralleled but exceeded that of the Imperial German Regime after 1906. Papua and the Trust (old Mandated) Territory were placed under a joint Administration with the capital at Port Moresby. War Damage Compensation was paid to those natives whose property had been destroyed or lost. Head tax was abolished.[2] Labour laws were again revised: the basic wage was increased to 15s. a month and keep. Most important were the far-reaching economic, political, and educational reforms. Native Rural Progress and Co-operative Societies were to promote local industries and cash crops—copra, rice, coffee, and cocoa. There was to be native representation on the Legislative Council to be constituted in Port Moresby.[3] Village (or, after 1954, Native Local Government) Councils were to be formed on a regional basis, each village returning a councillor. They

---

[1] For further details see Australian War Memorial, *Jungle Warfare*.

[2] Head tax was reintroduced in 1958 for natives not taxed by Local Government Councils.

[3] The Legislative Council was inaugurated in 1951, its first meeting being held on 26 November of that year.

were to levy taxes (about £2 from every adult a year) to finance such schemes as building Medical Aid Posts. There were plans for primary and secondary schools, at which teaching was to be in English, and for advanced training of Native Medical Assistants. To ensure the success of the policy, the Government guaranteed an annual subsidy to the combined Territory.[1]

These reforms were long overdue in the southern Madang District. During the war, many natives had been blatantly disloyal and now, although outwardly friendly, were no longer automatically obedient. There was a succession of labour troubles, which began the first day the Civil Administration took office. Natives recruited during 1944–5 had been promised that their contracts would end when A.N.G.A.U. was disbanded. But the new District Officer, not wanting to leave the town without essential services, would not release them. The labourers in Madang, led by a Kopoka native, rioted. The ringleaders were gaoled.

Yet during the first five years of peace, the Administration made little progress with its new economic, political, and educational schemes. Specialist staff had to be recruited and trained. Although there were a few ventures with copra and vegetables at Bogati and Madang, it was not until 1950 that the first important native economic undertaking was started: the Amele Rural Progress Society for the production of rice. Co-operatives were not introduced until 1952. The first Native Local Government Council (Ambenob[2]) was not proclaimed until 1956. An Administration secondary school was opened at Madang soon after the war but there were no schools at Saidor or other centres until 1955. A few Native Medical Assistants were trained at Lae.

*The Missions in the Southern Madang District (1885–1950)*

Of the three missions in the southern Madang District, the Seventh Day Adventist, which went to Madang only after 1945, can be ignored in the present chapter. By 1950, apart from gaining a few converts, it had very little impact. The two most important missions were the Lutheran and Roman Catholic, which were virtually entirely responsible for

---

[1] Annual subsidies paid by the Commonwealth Government since 1945 have been: 1945–6—£252,740; 1946–7—£2,018,673; 1947–8—£1,866,942; 1948–9—£3,196,668; 1949–50—£4,184,454; 1950–1—£4,354,563; 1951–2—£5,284,309; 1952–3—£4,657,022; 1953–4—£5,421,983; 1954–5—£7,128,289; 1955–6—£8,431,899; 1956–7—£9,446,590; 1957–8—£10,796,491; 1958–9—£11,498,910; 1959–60—£12,808,282; 1960–1—£14,796,648; 1961–2—£17,300,000. (Information kindly supplied by the Hon. Minister for Territories, Mr Paul Hasluck.)

[2] The Ambenob Council covers the Madang, Amele, and Nobanob area.

bringing the people under Christian influence. The Lutherans, who began as the Lutheran Rheinische Mission, went to Bongu in 1887. The Roman Catholic Mission (S.V.D.) went to Aitape in 1896, Bogia in 1901, and Alexishafen in 1904. It is necessary, however, to include in the account the early history of a separate Lutheran Mission—the Neuendettelsau Mission, which went to Finschhafen in 1886—because of the general influence of its policy in the area as a whole.

Until 1942, the Lutheran and Catholic Missions had tremendous prestige in the southern Madang District. They were subsidized to teach German by the Imperial Administration. During the Australian Military Occupation and Mandate, because the Administrations had no serious educational programmes of their own, they had an almost complete monopoly of native intellectual development. Their organizations rivalled—even overshadowed—those of the Administrations.

*The Lutheran Mission:* Of the two Lutheran Missions, the Neuendettelsau had the greater initial success. By 1914, it had spread its influence through the Finschhafen interior, Huon Gulf area, and Markham Valley. It claimed 3,637[1] zealous, if not baptized, adherents. This success was due partly to the absence of bad race relations in the mission's area and partly to the boldness of its approach. Relatively little land was alienated at Finschhafen[2] and, after the capital was moved to Stephansort in 1892, there were few Europeans to make demands for labour. Moreover, after 1899, the Rev. C. Keyszer revolutionized the mission's evangelical system.[3] He realized that the policy of singling out individuals for conversion was useless, for individual converts could not resist the pressures of their own communities and relapsed into paganism as soon as they left the mission station. The wisest approach would be to move out into the villages and remould whole native societies as Christian congregations. The most energetic converts should become leaders, serving as congregational elders and evangelists or teachers in other pagan villages. This system of group approach soon proved its worth: it enabled the natives to adopt Christianity on their own terms and increased the mission's effective field staff.

The Rheinische Mission, by 1914, had very little success. Working

[1] Unless otherwise acknowledged, figures of adherents are taken from German and Australian *Annual Reports*.

[2] According to the German *Annual Reports*, by 1905, only 300 ha. were under plantation cultivation at Finschhafen. The plantation involved was subsequently acquired by the Neuendettelsau Mission.

[3] For fuller accounts see Keyszer, 'Mission Work among Primitive Peoples in New Guinea', pp. 426–35, and *Eine Papuagemeinde*. See also my 'Lutheran Mission Influence on Madang Societies', pp. 73–89.

in the area of closest European settlement, it was embarrassed by bad race relations and, because of shortage and illness of staff, could not as yet adopt the policy of group approach. Apart from getting a foothold on Karkar, it did not at this stage operate outside the crescent formed by Bongu, Madang, and Nobanob (where it was established after 1906). Even in this area its influence was slight: it met with apathy, even antagonism, from the people. Its first converts—fourteen adults and six children—were not made until 1904, and few of them remained faithful. By 1900, it had four schools with a total of 136 pupils: at Bongu, Bogati, Siar, and Graged. By 1910, it had eight schools with 367 pupils, 109 baptized converts, and 35 candidates for baptism. By 1911, it had nine schools with 365 pupils but its baptized converts had dropped to 83. In 1912, it had eleven schools with 486 pupils and its baptized converts had risen again to 103. But the exile of the Madang natives in the same year deprived it of many of its adherents.

During the First World War, the Rheinische Mission's fortunes improved. Like the other missions, it overcame its financial difficulties, caused by the freezing of funds from Germany, partly by accepting aid from religious bodies in Allied countries and partly by exporting copra. It expanded cultivation on its plantations at Bongu and Madang to 260 ha.[1] Moreover, its evangelistic work began to prosper. After 1912, it turned its attention to the Rai Coast, where many of the Madang exiles were living. Although the mission had taken over much of the land confiscated from the exiles by the Administration, the experiment turned out well. When the exiles were allowed home in 1914, they adopted Christianity *en masse* and became the first Lutheran congregation in the southern Madang District. By 1916, the mission had twenty-four schools with 3,702 scholars.[2] In 1918–19, it opened Amele Station and, as its staff increased, began to employ Keyszer's system of group approach.

In the interwar years, to assuage Australian resentment at the continued presence of ex-enemy nationals in the Mandated Territory, the Rheinische Mission ceased to be controlled from Germany. In 1921, it was placed under an Australian Director and its staff supplemented by Americans, Australians, and Samoans.[3] In 1932, it was finally taken over by the American Lutheran Church.[4] But these changes did not interrupt its successes. By 1940, its influence had spread throughout

[1] Lyng, *Our New Possession*, pp. 228–9.
[2] Lyng, op. cit., pp. 219–20.
[3] The Samoans belonged to the Congregational Church. They were withdrawn in the 1930's.
[4] From now on I refer to it simply as the Lutheran Mission.

most of the District south of Alexishafen, except for a pocket on the Rai Coast taken over by the Catholics, and its adherents numbered about 12,000.[1] Although only some of these adherents were baptized, most had received instruction in basic Christian doctrine.

Expansion proceeded by regular stages. In 1922, Bagaşin Station was founded. From there mission parties went through the whole inland region as far as Dumpu. The Garia were evangelized during the late 1920's and early 1930's, and were beginning to be baptized in 1937. There were workers in Kopoka villages after 1931. In 1922–3, a Samoan went to Biliau on the Rai Coast with a party of Yam evangelists, who were eager to take Christianity to their trade friends. He was replaced in 1929 by a European. By 1942, the mission had won over the Sengam, Som, and coastal Gira. It gained a foothold in Sibog (Ngaing) until about 1930, when it gave way to Neuendettelsau evangelists from Ulap. These men worked among the inland Ngaing, M'na, and N'dau. Only the sub-coastal Gira and Ngaing refused to be converted.

By 1942, the Lutherans had built up in the southern Madang District an organization, the main features of which persisted until 1950. Their ultimate objective was to found an independent Native Lutheran Church in New Guinea. In Madang, the mission had a high or central school, technical school, general store, and printing press. Its hospital was at Amele. Its area was divided into congregations based on Madang, Karkar, Amele, Bongu, Nobanob, Biliau (Rai Coast), and Bagasin.[2] Each congregation, which consisted of several thousand people (often of different linguistic groups), had its station and secondary school under a European missionary, helped by senior native evangelists and teachers. In the larger villages, junior evangelists and teachers ran churches and schools. If possible, neither evangelists nor teachers were employed in their natal congregations. Their educational qualifications varied: evangelists often attended only village primary school, although some went higher; teachers had to go to the high school in Madang.

The ideal was that every boy and girl should pass through village primary school, and that abler boys should go on to secondary and then

[1] The official figures of the mission's adherents in the *Annual Reports* are as follows: 1932–3—11,888; 1933–4—13,777; 1934–5—14,296; 1935–6—14,269; 1936–7—15,393; 1937–8—14,946; 1938–9—14,796; 1939–40—18,098. These figures include, after 1933, adherents in the Central Highlands. Thus it is safest to assess the total for the southern Madang District at a little over the 1932–3 figure. Of the other c. 12,000 natives in the area, many were adherents of the Catholic Mission and others inhabited the more inaccessible interior.

[2] The Bagasin Congregation began as an offshoot of the Amele Congregation and was becoming fully autonomous only just before the Japanese invasion. It became a separate congregation in 1949.

high or technical school. The subjects taught were: in primary and secondary school, reading, writing, arithmetic, Bible stories, catechism, singing, and hygiene; in high school, Basic English, geography, world and Church history, and elementary science; and at technical school, carpentry and mechanical work. Except at high school, where English was used, the missionaries taught in vernacular languages.[1] They avoided Pidgin English, although nearly all Lutheran natives spoke it as a *lingua franca*.

There were other important congregational duties apart from church work and teaching. Money had to be collected to pay native staff. Every congregation had to be self-supporting and was given little financial help by the mission. As a result, it could afford to pay its native helpers only token salaries—about £1 a year. Also, each congregation was expected to provide evangelists to help convert pagans in outlying regions. Although the European missionary was ultimately responsible, these duties were largely taken over by a Council of Native Elders, who discussed problems at regular meetings and at the annual Mission Conference held on one of the stations. This gave the Elders considerable control over congregational policy. Furthermore, evangelists and teachers often worked in villages where their European missionaries could rarely visit them. They were, therefore, largely accountable for the Christian doctrine and Western secular knowledge held by members of their congregations.

For this organization to be effective, Christianity had entirely to replace paganism. But to minimize social disruption, the mission proceeded very circumspectly. It tried to preserve rather than change native secular economic and cultural life where it did not clash with its own ideals. The only purely secular customs it attacked were polygyny and extramarital sexual licence. It tried to introduce even its religious reforms slowly. Native helpers were explicitly instructed to win over pagans by patient discussion and Christian example. Baptism had to be withheld for several years until the people had been carefully prepared and honestly desired it. But when that stage was reached, the conditions were stringent: monogamy, and the renunciation of all pagan belief and ritual, which the men had to symbolize by declaring their knowledge and displaying secret paraphernalia to women and children. Native helpers made even greater demands on baptized converts. At the

---

[1] Not every vernacular was used. In many places, a language from another area was introduced as a school language. Graged (Yam) was used in Madang and on the Rai Coast; Amele in the Bagasin Area until 1950, when it was replaced by Graged; and Kâte (a Finschhafen vernacular) in the inland Rai Coast area.

Nobanob Conference in 1923,[1] the Elders banned all dancing in Lutheran congregations, even as a secular amusement.

With the Japanese invasion, all mission work was suspended until 1945, when the stations were gradually reoccupied and rebuilt, and the congregations reformed. There were only a few local changes in the pre-war organization, such as the removal of Bagasin Station to Konogur in 1949. The main changes occurred after 1950, when the mission began to work strenuously for an independent Native Church.[2] Natives were now chosen to be trained as pastors to replace European missionaries in the congregations.

*The Roman Catholic Mission (S.V.D.):* The history of the Catholic Mission was relatively untrammelled. Alexishafen, acquired in 1904, became its main station in 1909. In that year, it had a boarding school with 121 pupils and founded Mugil Station. It surmounted the financial difficulties of the war years by selling copra from its huge estates.[3] In 1917, it opened Halopa Station and thereafter created a sphere of influence in the hinterland of Alexishafen bordering that of the Lutherans in the Muguru area and running north to Bogia. In 1932, it opened a station on Karkar and, in 1933, another at Gumbi on the Rai Coast. From Gumbi it started work among the sub-coastal peoples, including the Ngaing and Gira, who had earlier resisted the Lutherans. The mission was forced to close down during the Japanese Occupation. The priests returned after May 1945 and had reopened their stations by 1950.

The Mission's organization was fully established also by 1942. The Bishop's seat was Alexishafen, where there were a high school, store, boat-building works, and other installations. The Catholic area was divided into congregations, each with a station and secondary school under a European priest. In the larger villages, there were native catechists (paid £3 a year by the mission), who ran both churches and schools. The priests used only Pidgin English for teaching, although many of them spoke vernacular languages. The priest had sole responsibility for his congregation, for there was no Native Elders' Council. But, like their Lutheran counterparts, catechists in outlying villages were rarely visited by the priests and so were largely answerable for

[1] Hannemann, *Village Life*, op. cit., p. 40, and *Papuan Dances*, op. cit., p. 24.

[2] This was established in 1956.

[3] According to Lyng, *Our New Possession*, op. cit., pp. 228–9, by 1916, the mission was cultivating 2,100 ha. on the whole mainland. This included properties at Bogia and in the Sepik District. It is impossible to quote figures of Catholic converts in the southern Madang District at any time up to 1950. All figures given in the *Annual Reports* are for the whole mainland.

Christian doctrine and Western secular knowledge in their congregations.

The Catholics, like the Lutherans, attempted to preserve native secular economic and cultural life, again with the sole exceptions of polygyny and extramarital sexual licence. Their religious reforms were relatively lenient. Priests not only instructed catechists to deal carefully with pagans but also were tolerant of their converts' shortcomings, although their prerequisites for baptism were, in theory, as strict as those of the Lutherans. In fact, however, they denounced only sexual offences and sorcery, disregarding other beliefs as long as they were not entirely repugnant. They took notice only of those deities whom the people themselves regarded as dangerous and whom they purported to neutralize with holy water.

### Race Relations in the Southern Madang District, 1871–1950

The natives' reactions to Europeans were governed by two considerations: the personal behaviour of white men they knew; and an unsatisfied demand for Western goods, on which they became increasingly dependent. These two themes are best discussed chronologically from the standpoint of, first, lay Europeans and, second, missionaries.

During initial contact, the coastal natives had no unpleasant experiences with the few white men they met. Maclay treated them very well; the gold prospectors in the *Dove* did not stay long enough to do them harm; and Romilly and Finsch won their friendship. Most of these visitors ensured their goodwill by giving them presents—the first steel tools and cotton cloth they probably ever handled in any quantity.[1]

Intensive contact brought very bad race relations. Under Company rule settlers regarded natives purely as economic assets, to be exploited with a minimum of outlay and flogged into obedience. Because of the absence of administrative control, the Astrolabe Bay natives' first experiences of Europeans were often forcible dispossession of their land and incessant demands for labour. In return, they received little of the new wealth, in which they were by now extremely interested.

The Imperial Regime initiated a struggle between official and settler attitudes. The new Administration tried to give the people a stake in their own country. Although often forced to compromise over important issues, such as the Company's land at Madang, it did what it could to protect their interests. For instance, in 1911–12, it dismissed as largely groundless complaints by planters (whose properties were at

[1] Although there is evidence, quoted in Chapter III, that they had at least indirect knowledge of these things before 1871.

last coming into full production) about the very poor quality of native copra. The implication was that native growers were to compete with Europeans on a fair basis. There is evidence that the settlers so resented Governor Hahl's pro-native policy that they at least tried to force his recall shortly before the First World War.[1]

Nevertheless, Imperial rule was too short to eradicate the bad effects of settler attitudes and raise the native standard of living to an appreciable extent. Staff shortage forced the Administration to allow employers to discipline labourers and, in any case, natives could see little difference between the behaviour of settlers and officers. Although individual officers were trusted and even liked by some natives, the majority were so authoritarian that the bulk of the population failed to see the goodwill behind the stern exterior—as in the case of Berghausen, who supported the Madang natives against the Company. The people at large regarded the officers' actions only as harsh and meaningless coercion, and they reacted to all Europeans with equal hostility, as was implicit in the disturbances of 1904 and 1912. In view of the severe measures taken on these occasions, it is inconceivable that they should have thought otherwise. Again, by 1914 the development programme was too little advanced to satisfy the growing demand for European goods. Wages still had negligible purchasing power. Native industries were only beginning. Education had fitted few natives for well-paid positions.

When they were granted permission to return home in 1914, the Madang exiles thought that they would get fairer treatment. But settler attitudes again became supreme. German civilians, in spite of enemy occupation, now had a key position. Their prosperity and help were vital for the Administration. As informal advisers and court assessors, without restraint from the Imperial officers, they could slant decisions in their own favour. They soon indoctrinated Australian officers with their own racial attitudes.[2] They were forbidden to flog, but 'coon-bashing' could not be prevented. In these circumstances, no plan for giving natives greater access to Western goods had any chance of success.

[1] See *Annual Report* (1911–12) and Lyng, op. cit., p. 235, for these incidents. Lyng knew many German planters when he served with the A.N. and M.E.F. between 1914 and 1921. His statements have the ring of truth. It is significant, in this context, that Hahl was on leave in 1914.

[2] See Rowley, *The Australians in German New Guinea, 1914–21*, op. cit., p. 10 and pp. 233–4. Lyng's opinions, op. cit., pp. 158–69, about native character and intelligence are so stereotyped that he could have learnt them only from his planter friends. In *Island Films*, op. cit., p. 162, he indicates that the German planters, despite their patriotic convictions, preferred Australian officials as individuals to their own. The Australians were obviously more amenable.

During the Mandate, German settlers were deported but their attitudes were perpetuated without question by their Australian successors. The result was at best the paternalism described by Feldt. There were notable examples of devotion between Europeans and natives.[1] But, at its worst, the situation has been described more forthrightly by Reed and Hogbin.[2] Unassailable because of their economic position, many settlers were arrogant and brutal, as was apparent in 1929, when native police and labourers in Rabaul struck for higher wages. The strikers offered no violence and the Administration took a reasonable view. Yet the settlers were able to demand gaol sentences justifiable only in an emergency and, when they beat up those of their employees who had escaped imprisonment, the District Office did not interfere.[3] Again in 1929, settler opinion prevented seven natives from going to Australia for medical training. The few natives who did visit Australia—generally in the crews of small ships—stayed for very short periods and saw nothing but the bare externals of European life. The position of the Administration, without moral or financial support from Australia, was always embarrassing. Many officers, men of the highest integrity, did what they could. Others found it more convenient to comply with settler attitudes.

The southern Madang District was typical of the general pattern. The natives were kept firmly in their place. Their personal associations with Europeans were limited to annual meetings with officers on patrol, who had no time to get to know them or listen seriously to their problems, and to several years under indenture, which were invariably humiliating. They were given only menial tasks—such as house work and cutting copra—for which they received £3 a year and keep. Their employers had no interest in them as individuals and would often shout or hit them if they appeared incompetent or disobedient. Their low economic status, in contrast to the apparent affluence of Europeans, was bitterly frustrating. After 1920, in coastal and sub-coastal villages, with the loss of old skills, Western goods were no longer a luxury but a necessity. The people depended very largely on steel tools, cotton cloth, and other trade articles. Yet they still had nothing but the meagre basic wage with which to buy goods. The Europeans' failure to understand their economic problems was well illustrated by the payment of

[1] See Feldt, *The Coast Watchers*, op. cit., pp. 12–15. The better side of race relations was evident during the early stages of the Pacific War: some natives showed the greatest personal loyalty to their European employers at the time of the Japanese invasion.

[2] Reed, *The Making of Modern New Guinea*, op. cit., pp. 243–52, and Hogbin, *Transformation Scene*, pp. 276–89.

[3] For a very clear account see McCarthy, 'The Rabaul Strike', pp. 55–65.

£99 for Modilon-Yomba and Wagol plantations—land that was still the primary source of livelihood.

It was small wonder, therefore, that in 1942–3 natives in parts of the southern Madang District welcomed the Japanese as liberators and regarded its reoccupation by the Allies in 1944 as a mixed blessing. On the one hand, Allied troops treated them as human beings, sharing food, cigarettes and other luxuries, and paying handsomely for curios. Native soldiers attached to Allied units had been accepted more or less as equals, and those now employed by the Services in other capacities enjoyed similarly good relations. On the other hand, the behaviour of A.N.G.A.U. personnel was at times so inhuman that the Japanese, in places that escaped their brutalities while they were in retreat, were thought of with nostalgia.[1]

After 1946, race relations promised to improve. The Administration, now backed by a strong Government subsidy, was freed from dependence on commerce. But, as has been shown, the situation in the southern Madang District did not change appreciably by 1950. The development programme had to gather momentum and the commercial community fought hard to regain its old position. As late as 1953, there were attempts to downgrade native copra sold through the Native Co-operative Societies so as to stifle competition with the planters. The Administration officers' racial outlook was still uneven and it took time to wean them from the settlers' influence. The natives saw little difference in their position. After the departure of the friendly troops the old masters, as intolerant as ever, had returned. War Damage Compensation[2] and the wage increase did little to help the people economically. Coastal natives had lost most of their property and had to re-equip themselves. Also, the inland peoples were by now equally dependent on Western goods. With the higher prices in the stores, it was as much as they could do to bring their living standard up to the pre-war level.

Native relations with missionaries were not always ideal but generally better than with lay Europeans. Under German rule missionaries, although paternalistic, were never inhuman. They made only limited demands for labour and treated their workers relatively well.[3] Yet although in 1892 the Madang natives trusted the Lutherans sufficiently to complain through them to the Company about the theft of their

---

[1] For A.N.G.A.U. behaviour see Hogbin, op. cit., pp. 276–82, and Read, 'Effects of the Pacific War in the Markham Valley, New Guinea', pp. 95–116.

[2] I have no figures for War Damage claims for the whole southern Madang District. Except in some coastal villages, they probably rarely exceeded a few pounds a head. Larger sums were shared between relatives.

[3] Although, as noted, lay members of the missions could flog native employees.

land, in 1904 they marked them down for destruction together with other whites. It was not until the exile of 1912 that the Madang natives began to treat the missionaries as allies. With the subsequent spread of Christianity throughout the whole southern Madang District, natives and missionaries had very cordial relations. But missionaries' behaviour was never entirely satisfactory. They had comfortable houses, full storehouses, and lucrative plantations (in the Lutherans' case, on land confiscated from the exiles in 1912). Yet they were no more liberal with wages and trade goods than were other Europeans.

These, then, were the main themes in race relations. On the social side, there was friendship between the coastal natives and Maclay, Romilly, and Finsch between 1871 and 1884. Then there were six and a half decades during which the people came to regard most Europeans other than missionaries (for a time) and Allied servicemen of the Second World War with bitterness. On the economic side, Western goods gradually replaced so much of the old material culture that, whatever the natives might feel about Europeans, they were forced into a symbiotic relationship with them, from which there was no escape. In the following chapters, these two themes are elaborated as they were interpreted by the natives themselves.

TABLE III

The five Cargo Beliefs

| Cargo Belief | Date | Religion | Principal Cults | Cargo Deity/Deities | Leader(s) | Area Involved |
|---|---|---|---|---|---|---|
| 1st | c. 1871–c. 1900 | Pagan | — | Maclay and Germans conceived as pagan deities | ? | Sarang–Saidor Coast |
| 2nd | c. 1900–c. 1914 | Pagan | — | 1st Version Kilibob (Yam, Yabob, and Bogati area peoples) 2nd Version Dodo (Anut) and Manup (Sek and Bilbil peoples) | ? | Sek–Bongu Coast |
| 3rd | c. 1914–1933 | Christian | — | God and Jesus Christ | Renegade Mission Helpers | Most of southern Madang District |
| 4th | c. 1933–1945 | Syncretic Christian–Pagan | 1. Letub 2. Tagarab's Cult 3. Bagasin Rebellion | God-Dodo and Jesus-Manup God-Kilibob God-Kilibob | Kaut of Kauris and other local leaders Tagarab and associates Kaum and associates | Coast and Inland, north of Madang; and Bilbil, south of Madang Inland, south-west of Madang Northern Bagasin and Gogol areas |
| 5th | 1948–1950 | Pagan | — | All pagan deities | Yali and Gurek (Rai Coast) | Principally Sarang–Saidor Coast. Hinterland affected only slightly and briefly |

# CHAPTER III

# FROM PAGANISM TO CHRISTIANITY

## THE FIRST THREE CARGO BELIEFS, 1871–1933[1]

THE southern Madang District natives' interpretation of contact history took the form of five separate cargo beliefs, which are summarized in Table III. These beliefs were all based on traditional values and intellectual assumptions. They were periodically changed: each was revised or replaced in the light of new experiences. Thus they arose, and are presented here, in a distinct chronological order. Even so, the transition from one belief to another was not always automatic and uniform throughout the whole area. Although the major cargo beliefs cut across and bridged different language groups, geographical distance slowed up the spread of ideas and some of the nuclear doctrines were contained within limited regions by cultural barriers. More than one cargo belief could be current at the same time even within a single locality.

### The First Cargo Belief, c. 1871–c. 1900

The First Cargo Belief can be traced from 1871 until about 1900. Its origins, which appear to be earlier than 1871, are obscure. It was no more than a series of relatively unsophisticated statements about the identity of the earliest foreign visitors to the eastern mainland and its waters: Miklouho-Maclay, probably those who left no records, and the first German settlers. They were all identified mainly as pagan deities but also, to some extent, as spirits of the dead.

Maclay[2] arrived at Bongu, accompanied by a Swedish sailor and Polynesian servant, in the Russian corvette *Vitiaz* in September 1871. His immediate objective was to establish friendly relations with the natives, but it proved a formidable task. While his house was being built by the ship's company, several natives told him through sign language that he would be killed. Thus a circle of mines was laid around his house for his protection. When the *Vitiaz* departed firing a twenty-one gun salute, the people fled in terror but later returned and, without

---

[1] The dates given for the first three cargo beliefs are necessarily only approximate.

[2] Unless specific acknowledgement is made, this summary of Maclay's experiences is based on Greenop, *Who Travels Alone*, and Fischer, *Unter Südsee-Insulanern*. See also Worsley, 'N. N. Mikloukho-Maclay, Pioneer of Pacific Anthropology', pp. 307–14. (There are several different spellings of Maclay's full name in Roman script. In the text I have adopted that used by Greenop and Thomassen, which he himself is said to have preferred.)

warning, began to shower Maclay with arrows, aiming not to hit but miss him narrowly. Despite his two companions' terror, he ignored this unfriendly behaviour, and eventually the shooting stopped.

The next few months were a terrible ordeal. The Polynesian died. The Swede was a perpetual nuisance. In January 1872, Maclay himself was desperately ill with malaria. To cap it all, most of the natives would have nothing to do with him. But after a while the position began to improve. With great patience and by making suitable gifts, Maclay slowly won friends. Especially during his second and third visits, it became clear that the people not only respected him but also venerated him as someone more than a mere human being. There seem to have been several reasons for this.

For a start, Maclay was something quite outside the natives' experience. He was fair of skin and wore clothes. The huge ship in which he arrived, the things in his house (scientific equipment, firearms, and even the primus stove), and the presents he could give caused wonder and admiration. The people credited him and his companions with extraordinary powers. When the Polynesian died, Maclay buried him secretly at sea. When the natives asked where he had gone, Maclay pointed vaguely at the horizon and it was assumed that the man had flown away.[1] But what impressed the people most was Maclay's quiet courage and unfailing courtesy. He went everywhere unarmed, meeting every demonstration of hostility with complete nonchalance. Once, he was told that two men of a certain village were plotting his death. He called their bluff by visiting the place, and inviting them to kill him quickly because he was tired and at their mercy. He then lay down and slept. The challenge was not accepted. Maclay was also asked at a gathering of important men if he would or could ever die. Taking a spear, he invited one of them to try to kill him with it. Again, the challenge was refused.[2]

Maclay consistently told the people that he was a man from Russia but they did not understand him. Everywhere he went he was a focus of speculation. It was generally agreed that a being with such possessions, whose companions could disappear across the sea without visible means of transport, and who was so careless with his own life, was obviously superhuman. Some natives, having seen him walking at night with a ship's blue lantern, thought he was a man from the moon. Near both Bongu and Madang, men used to ask him about life on the moon,

[1] Fischer, op. cit., pp. 108–13.
[2] For details of the two incidents see Greenop, op. cit., pp. 145–7, and Fischer, op. cit., pp. 343–8 and 357–60.

apparently assuming that it was Russia.[1] Other natives thought that he was the spirit of a departed ancestor. But the large majority seem to have decided that he was one of their deities (*tibud*).[2]

In addition, this last view may well have drawn on even earlier speculation. There is evidence that at the time of Maclay's arrival the natives of Astrolabe Bay already knew about Europeans and their material culture, and had associated them with their creator god. In 1877, Maclay recorded that a Bongu native had 'heard about a distant (*dal' ilone*) land of Anut, where the people have iron axes and knives, big houses and wear clothes'. Again, the people of Sek showed him a '*Telum Anut*, which the sea brought up to one of the islands. This was a female figurehead of a European vessel.' Although these statements could be attributed to Maclay's first visit in 1871–2, it seems more likely that they represented ideas already current. These ideas could have been derived from Siasi traders' reports of the Marist Mission Station on Umboi Island two decades earlier, or from unrecorded contact with the explorers or other European mariners. That there was a shipwreck in the area seems almost certain.[3]

In view of this, it is hardly surprising that Maclay was in some way connected with Anut. During his first visit, he heard a conversation at Bongu, which he could not follow properly but in which he was obviously referred to as '*tamo Anut*', man of Anut. The Yam thought that the *Vitiaʒ*, which they could see far out from the shore, was Anut's ship.[4] Beyond this, although the evidence is far less certain, Maclay may have been identified as Kilibob or Manup. Yabob informants told me that their forbears believed that the first European ship they saw belonged to Kilibob, who was at last returning as their myth had prophesied. (The idea was supported by the belief that Kilibob was light-skinned like Europeans.) Madang natives told McAuley in 1958 that their forbears had thought that Maclay might be Kilibob but were not sure.[5]

[1] Thomassen, *Biographical Sketch of Nicholas de Miklouho-Maclay, Member of the Imperial Russian Geographical Society*, pp. 8–9, and Fischer, op. cit., pp. 190 and 214.

[2] Although coastal natives now know that he was only a human being, they still refer to him as Tibud Maclay.

[3] Both quotations in this paragraph are from Miklouho-Maclay, *Sobranie Sochenenii*, Vol. III, p. 149. I am indebted to Dr Peter Worsley for drawing my attention to the passage and to Dr A. C. Capell for this translation. The first quotation could, of course, refer to Indonesian or Malay traders. The use of the phrase *Telum Anut* (statue of Anut) in Sek is puzzling: Dodo is the local name of the creator god.

[4] See Fischer, op. cit., pp. 182–3, and Hannemann, *Village Life*, op. cit., p. 24.

[5] See also Aufinger, 'Die Mythe vom Brüderpaar *Kilibob* und *Manup* auf den Yabob-Inseln Neuguineas', op. cit., pp. 313–15, and McAuley, 'We are Men—What are You?', p. 74. The first ship could have been that of Tasman (1643), Dampier (1700), or d'Urville (1827) as well as the *Vitiaʒ* (1871), although it is unlikely.

Further conjecture would be useless. We can only recapitulate the general conclusion that Maclay was a local deity who had invented a new type of material culture and had now appeared to give it to the people. The first attempts to obtain the new goods were essentially pragmatic and can hardly be called a cargo cult. There is no suggestion that the natives performed ritual in Maclay's name. They endeavoured rather to have good face-to-face relations with him so that he would give them presents—steel axes and adzes, nails, mirrors, cloth, beads, paint, and seeds of new plants (pumpkin, melon, pawpaw, and pineapple). He had established his position at Bongu partly by gift-giving and his gifts were always returned. He received visitors from the Yam Islands, Yabob, Bilbil, Sek, Riwo, and even Karkar, who came to trade their wares for the goods they desired.[1]

The people saw Maclay as a source of not only wealth but also superhuman knowledge. They often turned to him for advice. By the time of his second visit, he was disturbed by the havoc caused by the labour trade and occasional European settlement in the eastern Melanesian islands. Recruiting by means of fraud and brutality, land theft, and indiscriminate shooting of natives had been commonplace. The mainland had so far been spared but Maclay realized that it would not be for long. When he left the Rai Coast in November 1877, he did what he could to protect the people by warning them about the Europeans who would follow him. They would be of two kinds: the 'good', to whom he would give a 'sign', who would announce themselves as his brothers, and whom they need not fear; and the 'bad', who would come to enslave them and rob them of their land, who would have no such 'sign', and from whom they should keep away. The coastal natives took the warning to heart: their next European visitors, the gold prospectors in the *Dove* in 1878, failed to announce themselves in a satisfactory way and were received so coldly that they left very quickly.[2]

Nevertheless, the warning was soon neutralized. Romilly and Finsch, who both visited the Bongu–Madang coast in 1881, won the people's confidence by claiming brotherhood with Maclay, who had met them in Sydney or in some other way told them how they should behave in the area.[3] That Finsch stifled suspicion on this occasion was very important: it ensured later German settlers a favourable reception. When, in 1884, he returned to Astrolabe Bay to occupy the area for Germany,

---

[1] Fischer, op. cit., pp. 110–11, and Hannemann, *Village Life*, op. cit., pp. 24–5.

[2] See Greenop, *Who Travels Alone*, op. cit., pp. 148–52, 205–9; and Faivre and Sokoloff, 'Mikloukho-Maklai (1846–1888): À l'Occasion du Centenaire de sa Naissance', pp. 98–9.

[3] Faivre and Sokoloff, op. cit., pp. 99–100; Fischer, op. cit., p. 430; and Romilly, *The Western Pacific and New Guinea*, p. 220.

the natives, unaware of what was going on, showed no alarm.[1] As he had already convinced them that he was a brother of Maclay, they regarded him and the other settlers as their deities, and hoped to get presents from them also by friendly behaviour.

The good impression created by Finsch was short-lived. The new Europeans were arrogant and mean. The worst shock came in the early 1890's when, as Maclay had predicted, the New Guinea Company began to take up the land Kubary had 'bought' in 1887–8. Although there is no record of what happened at Bongu and Bogati, it is possible to give a clear picture of events at Madang. In 1892, two Company agents landed at Kaisilan, the site of the Madang wharf. They gave the Biliā (Yam) natives, the owners of the immediate area, two steel axes, and some paint and matches. The natives, not as yet under administration and quite unused to dealing with Europeans, accepted the presents purely as rent for the small plot of land on which the newcomers built their house. But thereafter, to the people's horror, the agents began to cut bush through what is now Madang township and then towards the south. The Biliā natives lost most of their land and ever since have had to borrow or rent garden sites from affinal and cognatic relatives in other groups. The inhabitants of Nob, Yabob, and other villages also lost many of their holdings.[2]

The people had to explain this new situation. Their immediate reaction was that, whereas Maclay had been one of their own deities obviously well disposed towards them, the Germans were hostile deities from another area. Although few in number, they could enslave the natives because of superior material culture, especially firearms.[3]

It is uncertain how far these beliefs penetrated the whole southern Madang District by 1900. They were definitely current along the Sarang–Saidor coast, where Maclay and the Germans were known, and where news could travel along the trade routes.[4] Little can be said about the inland. Nevertheless, by 1900, the Naru, Gogol, and Ramu valleys had been explored. This must have caused speculation. The Garia preserve a tradition—which it is impossible to date—that the first

---

[1] Faivre and Sokoloff, op. cit., p. 100. Maclay bitterly opposed the German Protectorate but did nothing to prepare the natives against it, apart from giving them the general warning already discussed. He never returned to New Guinea after 1883. In 1886, he went home to Russia, where he died two years later.

[2] Details from Phillips J., *Judgement: Delivered at Madang*, op. cit. For details of clearing see Table I. Unlike the Biliās, the natives of Yabob and other islands off Madang had no absolute rights on the mainland but were allowed rights of access by other villages.

[3] Cf. Hannemann, *Village Life*, op. cit., p. 27.

[4] News could have reached the Ngaing and other sub-coastal groups also through trade channels.

Europeans they saw came up the Naru from Bogati. These visitors, who could have been either members of the 1890 and 1896 expeditions or recruiters between 1914 and 1921, were regarded as deities (*oite'u*) or spirits of the dead (*kaua* and *kopa*).[1] But even if the hinterland peoples held such a belief by 1900, they had so little contact with Europeans that they could have contributed little to the early development of the Cargo Movement, which should be regarded largely, if not purely, as a coastal phenomenon at this stage.

### The Second Cargo Belief, c. 1900–c. 1914

The Second Cargo Belief was current during the first one and a half decades of the present century. Like the First Cargo Belief, it explained the contact situation exclusively in terms of traditional religion, but it was more elaborate and introduced two new ideas. It expressed a changed view of the nature of Europeans, and its focus of interest was German military and political power, which had become absolute around Astrolabe Bay by 1905.

By about 1900, many natives realized that white men were not deities or spirits but human beings.[2] They had good reason. The death rate among early German settlers (both lay and missionary) was very high. Malaria had driven the Company out of Finschhafen in 1892. Near Madang in 1897, two native convicts, who had escaped with rifles and ammunition, shot Governor von Hagen when he led a patrol to recapture them.[3] In 1900, native police killed three Europeans and a Chinese in the Astrolabe Bay area.[4] This probably encouraged the people to resist. They did not have to be ruled for ever by a handful of Europeans, who were only mortal and therefore by no means invincible. Given the right opportunity and weapons, they could kill or drive them out. There was an upsurge of anti-white hostility, which culminated in the Madang Revolt of July 1904.

The groups involved[5] were the Yam, Yabobs, and Bilbils who, as noted, suffered most during the German Occupation. They were least able to escape forced labour and had lost the most land. They could see

---

[1] The tradition is perpetuated in linguistic usage. Garia call Pidgin English *oite'u kuna* (language of the deities), European articles red in colour *kaua po ulu* (goods from spirits of men killed by violence), and other European articles *kopa po ulu* (goods from spirits of men who died naturally).

[2] The initial belief that Europeans were gods probably co-existed for a time with the new belief, especially among the older people. Cf. Hannemann, *Village Life*, op. cit., p. 27.

[3] Von Beck, *Das überseeische Deutschland*, op. cit.

[4] Worsley, *The Trumpet Shall Sound*, op. cit., p. 46.

[5] The following account is based on Hannemann, *Village Life*, op. cit., pp. 26-8, *Annual Report* (1904-5, pp. 70 and 258), and my own information from the field.

no end to the settlers' greed. The Company claimed the whole of the Astrolabe plain and, as the plantation boundaries had not been properly surveyed and marked, the natives concluded that it would eventually clear the total area and leave them without any land at all.

Probably late in 1903, a full council of the conspirators was held on Bilbil Island, the Siars (Yam) taking the lead. It was decided that the island peoples should cross over to the mainland, rush the barracks and, before the native police could be alerted, seize their rifles. The attackers should then kill all the whites in Madang except for the few women and children attached to the Rheinische Mission.

The revolt was well organized. Although the Rheinische Mission at Bongu was warned about it as early as January 1904 and passed on the information to the Administration, little attention was paid. Moreover, although the Yabob and Bilbil people eventually defected, they kept the secret well hidden. Thus the Yam, led by the Grageds and Siars, were able to cross over in their canoes without detection. They might well have achieved their objective. The European population of Madang was so small (twenty-six in 1903) that, had the natives managed to seize the police rifles, the resistance it could have offered would have been limited. But at the last moment a Biliã native employed by the Medical Officer betrayed the plot. The police were alerted and swiftly restored order. Nine ringleaders were executed, and the remainder of those involved (including the people of Yabob and Bilbil because of their initial complicity) were forced to leave their island homes and settle on the mainland, where they could be watched more closely.

Although the basic ideas of the Second Cargo Belief were probably thought out some years earlier, it was against the background of these events that it seems to have taken its final form. Its essence was that Europeans were human beings to whom a special deity had given a superior material culture, particularly the rifles with which they had subjugated the natives. The answer was found in the Kilibob-Manup myth, which may have already been tentatively associated with the arrival of the first Europeans but was now revised so as to provide a more positive explanation.

The Second Cargo Belief[1] preserved the two forms of the traditional

[1] My source material for the two versions of the Second Cargo Belief is accounts given me by Yabob, Sek, Sengam, and Som informants between 1953 and 1958, and Dempwolff, 'Sagen und Märchen aus Bilibili', op. cit. The accounts differ in incidental detail, omitted here as irrelevant, but correspond on all important points. The most important account is that of Dempwolff, who recorded the second version in 1906, thus establishing a very early date for the Second Cargo Belief. A Sengam informant claimed to have heard a similar version as early as 1917.

myth described in Chapter I: the Yam-Yabob version, in which it was
the deity Kilibob who sailed from Karkar to Madang and the Rai Coast;
and that of the Sek, Bilbil, Sengam, and Som peoples, in which Manup
was the principal hero.

In the first version of the revised myth, when Kilibob and Manup
quarrelled and decided to leave their birthplace Karkar, Manup made
a small canoe while Kilibob secretly built either a large canoe of native
design or a ship with a steel hull.[1] The two brothers launched their
vessels. Kilibob's was immeasurably superior. Manup departed in shame
to the north, the area now identified with the mouth of the Sepik River.

Kilibob then provisioned his own vessel. He stocked it with native
men, artefacts, and food plants. According to some informants, he
next created European cargo and white men, took them on board,
and hid them below deck. When all was ready, he left Karkar for
Madang and the Rai Coast. At each of the major villages on his route
he anchored and put a man ashore, offering him the choice between
the two types of material culture he had created: between a rifle and
a bow and arrow; and between a dinghy and a native canoe. In each
case, the native rejected the rifle as a short and useless lump of wood,
and chose the bow and arrow because it was lighter and easier to
handle. He rejected the dinghy because it rocked in the choppy sea,
and accepted the canoe which, with its outrigger, rode steady and firm.

Eventually Kilibob left the Rai Coast for Siasi and then travelled
to another country where he put the white men ashore. He gave them
everything left in his vessel: the cargo, which the natives had forfeited
because of their own stupidity. He also taught them the ritual and
other techniques for obtaining new supplies. According to other informants, however, Kilibob did not create white men and place them
in his vessel. He found them already living in their own country and
gave them the cargo when he reached it.

The second version of the revised myth is again substantially the
same as the first apart from the substitution of Manup for Kilibob as
the main hero. Otherwise, there are a few variations. The Sek people
claim that Dodo (Anut), who had played a prominent part in the
creation of the traditional cosmos, himself invented the cargo and that
Manup learnt the art from him. In Dempwolff's account, the natives
are offered the choice between rifles and bows and arrows, but no
mention is made of dinghies and native canoes.

[1] Some informants between 1953 and 1958 described Kilibob's vessel as a European
ship, others as a large native canoe. Dempwolff, 'Sagen und Märchen aus Bilibili', op. cit.,
p. 77, hints that a European ship might have been conceived but is not absolutely clear.

The Second Cargo Belief had a necessarily limited distribution. There were two reasons why it did not spread beyond the Sek–Bongu coastal strip. First, this was the area in which contact was sufficiently intensive to cause the people to think continually about the nature of Europeans and to accentuate the desire for their goods, and German rule sufficiently oppressive to cause deep resentment. Natives elsewhere were as yet hardly affected by the situation. The Sengam, Gira, and Som of the Rai Coast may have heard of the belief but, as they were at most only just coming under political influence and had lost no land, appear to have shown no interest in it. Second, the Kilibob-Manup myth was the exclusive property of the coastal natives and hence the revised versions could not easily travel far inland. As far as is known, the peoples of the interior did not at this time modernize any of their myths in the same way.

For the natives of Astrolabe Bay, however, the new belief was extremely important, especially after the events of 1904. On the one hand, it explained not only the origin of cargo—how it had been created for man by a deity—but also their military defeat by the Administration. As they well realized, they could not resist the superior fire power of the Europeans.[1] The myth made it clear why the latter had rifles and they only bows and arrows. On the other hand, the new belief also held out hope for the future. In Yabob at least, there had always been the tradition that eventually Kilibob and Manup would return to usher in a period of peace and plenty after a general war. It appears that this idea was now taken up by the other natives, who associated it of course with the arrival of cargo. They waited for the homecoming of the two deities, either of whom would provide them with the goods he had taken away before, especially the new weapons which would enable them to fight not each other but the Europeans. Again, this cannot be described as a true cargo cult for there is no indication that the people performed special ritual to hasten the event. They merely hoped that what they regarded as a traditional prophecy would be fulfilled.

It is not surprising, therefore, that the eight years following the revolt were what Hannemann[2] has called the period of passive resistance. The Madang natives were sullen. They obeyed the Administration where necessary but obstructed it whenever they could. This was most obvious in road-building. As early as 1901, it was noted that the

---

[1] Hannemann, *Village Life*, op. cit., p. 28. Yabob and Sek informants stressed the same point to me fifty years after the event.

[2] Hannemann, ibid.

people moved their villages as far away as possible from roads or areas in which work was in progress so as to avoid forced labour. After 1904, the attitude seems to have hardened. For instance, in 1907, the year in which head tax was introduced as a means of coercing natives into employment, people from Rempi, Matokar, and the Madang mainland and islands were put to work on the roads. But repeatedly whole groups ran away into the bush and had to be rounded up by the police. This contrasted with the reaction of natives from further inland, who had not been affected by the recent disturbance and, in 1906, gave their labour without force having to be used.[1]

The period of passive resistance around Madang came to an end with the exile of the Yam and Yabob-Bilbil group in 1912. Tension had been steadily mounting. Plantation clearing around Astrolabe Bay had not ceased and, with the acquisition of Sarang plantation in 1910–11—and possibly with the initial negotiations for the others started along the coast north of Madang about 1914—the people had become more anxious than ever about their future. The matter came to a head after 1911, when the survey of the native reserves on the Gum-Gogol Plain, agreed to by the Administration and New Guinea Company in 1904, was begun. The natives seem to have regarded this as a new trick to drive them off their land completely.[2] They became increasingly surly. Although nothing has ever been substantiated, they probably discussed another conspiracy to murder the whites but later abandoned it for fear of Administration reprisals. Even so, their mood communicated itself to the District Officer,[3] who realized that the situation was once again dangerous. Alarmed by the unparalleled vehemence with which they were performing the ceremonies of the Male Cult, he posted extra sentries. When he received statements from several natives, including a Graged policeman with a grudge against his own villagers, that the plot which had already been given up was still live, he did not wait for conclusive proof. After a summary trial, at which a great deal of conflicting evidence was given, he deported the natives he thought to be implicated. He sent most of the Yam and Yabob-Bilbil people to the Sengam area of the Rai Coast, some of them to the north coast, and those he suspected of being the ringleaders to New Britain.

[1] *Annual Reports* (1901–2; 1906–7; 1907–8),

[2] Phillips J., *Judgement: Delivered at Madang*, op. cit. For further details of the unrest see Hannemann, *Village Life*, op. cit., p. 29.

[3] District Officer Berghausen, who had always been sympathetic towards the Madang natives, had been by this time transferred.

## The Third Cargo Belief, c. 1914–c. 1933

The exile of 1912–14 was, after the Annexation itself, perhaps the most important single event in the southern Madang District during the German Occupation. It profoundly affected the coastal natives' attitude towards Europeans in general and missionaries in particular, and led to the emergence of an entirely new cargo belief under the Australian Military and Mandate Regimes.

According to Hannemann,[1] who began to work among them about a decade later, the Madang natives seem to have spent much of their time on the Rai Coast reviewing their situation. They had achieved nothing by either active or passive resistance, having been openly defeated in 1904, and exiled and humiliated in 1912. Clearly, there was only one course open to them: to submit to the new order and try to achieve a *modus vivendi* with the Europeans.

What was more important, the exiles began to regard the missionaries in a more friendly light.[2] Hitherto, as mentioned in Chapter II, they had been indifferent, and even antagonistic, to Lutheran teaching. They had been quite convinced that they had nothing to learn from it: when they heard certain biblical names—Isaiah, Nahum, Aron, and Hur—for the first time, they claimed airily that they already had them in their repertoire of esoteric ritual formulae. Moreover, they could not conceive that outsiders would ever bring them the secrets of their own religion.[3] Thus they treated the missionaries with the general hostility they felt for all Europeans and planned to kill them (except for the women and children) in the rising of 1904.

The periodic visits of the Lutherans to the Rai Coast after 1912, however, were interpreted as demonstrations of goodwill. The people felt that they had some friends at court. Bilbil representatives tried to persuade the missionary at Bongu to intercede with the German Administration for their return home. Their petitions were finally successful after September 1914, when the necessary permission was readily granted by the Australian Military Officials.

The twenty years after 1914, therefore, were—again to borrow Hannemann's phrase—a period of accommodation. The Madang natives now made every effort to co-operate with both Administration

[1] Hannemann, *Village Life*, op. cit., pp. 29–30.

[2] This refers to the Lutheran Rheinische missionaries, who had taken over the area to which the exiles belonged. The work of the Roman Catholic Mission had not been interrupted by the disturbances described. But during the expansion of mission influence after 1914, native attitudes towards missionaries of both denominations were roughly similar.

[3] Hannemann, *Village Life*, op. cit., p. 29.

and missions. They visited the District Office to maintain friendly relations. They kept their villages and paths in good order without grumbling. They willingly paid taxes and provided labourers for the plantations. Furthermore, they appeared in groups outside the Lutheran missionary's house at Graged and asked to be prepared for baptism. As already noted, this led to the establishment of the first Lutheran congregation in the Madang area.[1]

The natives decided to become Christians partly from political motives. They saw in the Military Administration's permission for them to return home, and in the general benevolence of the Lutherans, the beginnings of the *rapprochement* they desired. It was obviously prudent to make the concessions the missionaries demanded.

There were, however, more significant reasons for conversion. Hannemann[2] implies that the people were consciously adopting a new culture. Just as their own culture represented a unity, explained and validated by their traditional religion, so they could not accept the new secular way of life imposed on them by the Administration without the new religion which, they supposed, would explain and validate it in the same way. The new culture had to be as fully integrated as the old. This can be understood in more practical terms. The natives wanted friendship with the Europeans. Yet, in their eyes, friendship would be impossible unless they themselves enjoyed a greater share of the trade goods on which by this time they were beginning to depend. Moreover, they assumed that Christianity by explaining and validating the new way of life, would automatically explain and grant control over its essential ingredient, the cargo. In other words, Christianity was attributed the same relationship to the new material culture as the pagan religion was thought to have to the old.

Christian teaching, therefore, was interpreted in such a way as to become the basis of the Third Cargo Belief. This was a distinct departure from the Second Cargo Belief, which was now overshadowed. Although the Kilibob-Manup cargo myth was not completely forgotten, it was remembered and perpetuated only by relatively few of the older coastal natives. The majority, led by some of the young men who had passed through the Lutheran and Catholic schools, paid virtually no attention to it and concentrated on working out a new version of Christianity.

Although some features of the pagan religion were fused with Christianity, syncretism was as yet given little prominence. The doctrine of the Third Cargo Belief was based initially on Bible Stories,

[1] Hannemann, *Village Life*, op. cit., p. 30.        [2] Hannemann, ibid.

which were preserved more or less in their original forms. The people selected those stories which they considered most pertinent and invested them with additional meaning. They construed them according to the values and intellectual assumptions of their own culture.

It will be remembered that the keynotes of the traditional religion were its materialism and anthropocentrism. It was not concerned with spiritual values—problems of moral good and evil—but was regarded as a 'technology', by means of which man could guarantee his own well-being. With the aid of ritual made effective by the observance of taboos (which had no ethical significance in themselves), he maintained proper relationships with gods and spirits, and so ensured that they conferred material benefits on him.

Christianity was recast in the same mould. The central theme was that God should look towards man and advance his worldly interests. Thus all the main teachings of the new religion—The Creation, The Fall of Man, The Great Flood, and even The Resurrection and Second Coming—were stripped of their spirituality and given a thoroughly pragmatic meaning. They became a new origin myth of the cargo, while Christian faith, worship, and morality were understood as the effective means of obtaining it: the *rot bilong kako* (Pidgin English), the road along which the cargo would come.

The following account of the Third Cargo Belief was given me by Garia (Lutheran) informants during 1949–50. Allowing for minor variations due to local cultural idiosyncrasies or other circumstances, it was typical of the versions current in other parts of the total area, which I heard from both Lutheran and Catholic natives in Madang and on the Rai Coast between 1952–3. The general uniformity of the belief was made possible by the overall homogeneity of the values and intellectual assumptions underlying the traditional religions. It appears to have been little affected at this stage by the differences between Protestant and Catholic doctrine,[1] although they were of some importance later on.

In the beginning, God—or Anut, as he was called by the missionaries when they spoke the vernacular languages of the Madang area[2]—created Heaven and earth. On the earth, he brought into being

[1] Even as late as 1956 most informants were quite unaware of the real differences between the teachings of the two missions. They could tell me only that the Lutherans taught in vernacular languages, whereas the Catholics used Pidgin English. Again, the Catholics were said to be more tolerant towards traditional religious ceremonies. Otherwise, it was assumed that the doctrines of the two missions were identical.

[2] With the spread of mission influence, God has become known as Anut throughout the whole southern Madang District. In Sek he is, of course, called Dodo.

all flora and fauna, and eventually made Adam and Eve. He gave
them control over everything on the earth and laid out Paradise (the
Garden of Eden) for them to live in. He completed their happiness by
creating and giving them cargo: tinned meat, steel tools, rice in bags,
tobacco in tins, and matches, but not cotton clothing. For a time
they were content but eventually offended God by having sexual intercourse. God in his anger threw them out of Paradise to wander in the
bush. He took the cargo away from them and decreed that they should
spend the rest of their days existing on the barest necessities. Later
Adam and Eve had two sons, Cain and Abel. Cain's murder of Abel
set the seal on his parents' 'wickedness', and the Fall of Man was
complete.

This situation continued until the time of Noah, who was a 'good'
man, obeyed God, and brought up his sons to do likewise. Other
human beings were still sunk in 'depravity' so that God decided to
destroy them in the Great Flood. Only Noah and his family were to
be saved. God showed Noah how to build the Ark—which was a
European steamer like those seen in Madang Harbour—and fitted him
out with a peaked cap, white shirt, shorts and stockings, and shoes.
Into the Ark Noah brought all his family—his wife, his sons, and their
wives—and a pair of all living animals. Then God sent rain. The waters
rose and covered the earth, and everyone else was drowned. When the
Flood subsided, Noah and his family went ashore. God instructed
them to repopulate the earth and gave them back the cargo as a pledge
of his renewed goodwill towards mankind.

Everything would have been satisfactory again had Noah's three
sons all obeyed God as he had done. Shem and Japheth continued to
respect God and Noah, and so continued to receive supplies of cargo.
In due course, they became the ancestors of the white races, which
profited by their good sense. But Ham was stupid: he witnessed his
father's nakedness. God was again very angry. He took the cargo away
from Ham and sent him to New Guinea, where he became the ancestor
of the natives, who were forced to make do with the inferior local
material culture.[1]

Like its forerunner the revised Kilibob-Manup myth, the natives'
interpretation of the Scriptures was no mere academic explanation of

---

[1] This belief was obviously derived directly from the teaching of European missionaries. It had a wide distribution. On the Rai Coast, Sengam informants told me that because of Ham's folly, natives could make only outrigger canoes as against steamships, and
build houses only out of bush materials as against the galvanized iron, sawn timber, and
nails used by Europeans. Hogbin, *Transformation Scene*, op. cit., pp. 242 and 284, refers
to a similar, if less widespread, belief at Busama near Lae.

the origin of cargo. It had its practical aspects. It was assumed that the friendliness of the missionaries was evidence that, whatever other Europeans might feel and do, they at least remembered and would honour their ties of brotherhood[1] with the natives as common descendants of Noah. They would reveal the ritual secrets which would ensure that God sent the natives supplies of cargo. God had said to the missionaries: 'Your brothers in New Guinea are lost in total darkness. They have no cargo because of Ham's folly. But now I am sorry for them and want to help them. You missionaries, therefore, must go to New Guinea and undo Ham's mistake. You must win over his descendants to my ways again. When they follow me again, I shall send them cargo in the same way as I send it to you white men now.'

The natives' expectation that cargo would arrive from God involved the reconstruction and enlargement of their cosmos so as to embrace the new ideas introduced by Christianity and what they had learnt from general contact with Europeans. The world in which they lived could no longer be conceived as a few square miles of jungle skirted by the sea. Its boundaries had to be extended so as to include the country of the Europeans and Heaven, both of which after 1914 began to be identified with Australia in general and Sydney, the main overseas port for New Guinea, in particular.

In the new cosmos, God was said to live in Heaven, which was believed by some to be on earth as part of Sydney itself and by others, who had listened more carefully to the missionaries, to be above Sydney in the clouds. In the latter case, however, it was thought that Heaven and Sydney were connected by a ladder. The spirits of the dead—the ancestors of both Europeans and natives—lived with God in Heaven. God was continually making cargo, although, according to some, he was helped by the ancestors, to whom he had taught the secret. According to others, however, the ancestors did not make cargo. They merely enjoyed the amenities of Heaven, for which the people yearned so vehemently on earth: European houses with tables, chairs, beds, and other furniture; meals of tinned meat, rice, and other European delicacies, which were served ready cooked by angels; and whisky, beer, and other alcoholic liquors freely provided for all.[2] There was no shortage of cargo in Heaven: there were stores everywhere, at which personal supplies could be replenished whenever they were

---

[1] As the joint descendants of a putative common patrilineal ancestor, the Europeans could be classified as 'brothers' in the native kinship terminologies of the whole area, so far as they are known, irrespective of differences of structural form.

[2] Until 1962, alcohol was forbidden to natives in Australian New Guinea and was consequently greatly desired.

running low.[1] In short, the natives' version of the Beatific Vision was an exact replica of the comfortable existence of Europeans they had seen in Madang and other centres. At this time, their chief interest was in civilian goods rather than military equipment.

In return for the luxuries of Heaven, the ancestors were expected to perform one special service. When God had prepared sufficient supplies of cargo, they had to carry them to the wharves in Sydney—either to that part of the city inhabited by human beings or down the ladder from Heaven—and load them in the ships which would take them to New Guinea. God, of course, would have them do this only as long as their descendants prayed to him and obeyed his commands —by observing the special taboos which he had instituted and which are discussed below.

So far only the Europeans had possessed this secret and thus only their ancestral spirits had been sent with cargo. But now the position was going to change. Provided that the missionaries' instructions were carried out in full, the natives' ancestors would be employed in the same way. Obedience to the missionaries would place the people in the correct relationship with God and give them what the Garia called *Anut po nanunanu*: the power to make God 'think on' them and send them cargo, just as the traditional leaders had had *oite'u po nanunanu* or the power to make the indigenous deities help them in important undertakings. It was believed by most that the cargo would arrive without any special portent, as it appeared to do for the Europeans. Ships would come to Madang with cases of goods specially addressed to the natives. But there were others who believed that the cargo would be ushered in only with the Last Trump, when there would be a volcanic eruption and Jesus Christ would return with the spirits of the dead laden with gifts for those of their descendants who had led Christian lives. These people believed that the Second Coming was imminent.

Nevertheless, although it dominated the Third Cargo Belief, Christian doctrine never entirely supplanted the pagan religion. One problem had to be solved: the relationship between God and Jesus Christ, on the one hand, and the local deities, on the other. The people had either to eliminate the local deities entirely or give them formal status in the new cosmic order. They adopted the second alternative. This

---

[1] Garia Christians place several shillings in the hand of a corpse to enable the spirit to make initial purchases in Heaven. In the past, as noted, property was placed with the corpse, partly for the spirit's use and partly to enable it to buy off the evil deity waiting to devour it.

appears to have been due, in part at least, to the missionaries' approach to traditional ritual.

Both Lutherans and Catholics, whether strict or permissive in their demands on their baptized converts, seem to have been unaware of the principles underlying local pagan ritual, and therefore failed to convince the people of its futility. They left them with the impression that they acknowledged the existence of the traditional deities. For a start, the Catholic practice of claiming to neutralize dangerous gods with holy water was tantamount to recognition of their power. Moreover, even when both Lutherans and Catholics denounced polygyny and sorcery, and the Lutherans other forms of ritual as well, they did not go beyond describing them as satanic, *samting bilong Satan* (Pidgin English). The natives interpreted this phrase in characteristically concrete terms. Virtually all their secular and sacred customs, especially their secret ritual formulae, were believed to have been given them by their gods and goddesses. Hence, if these customs came from Satan, it followed that the old deities were themselves 'satans'. They were identified with the Devil of official Christianity and, like the Devil, were assumed to have been brought into being by God himself, who had also enabled them to create the New Guinea material culture. This was neatly incorporated in the general doctrine of the Third Cargo Belief. It was said that when Ham came to New Guinea, God gave him and his descendants control over the 'satans' so that some sort of economic and social existence would be possible. Thus the pagan gods, far from passing into oblivion, were still accepted as real and powerful in their original spheres.

Although these syncretic elements were not at this stage given any great emphasis in formal expositions of the Third Cargo Belief,[1] in the long run they were of considerable importance. Superficially, the natives had been converted to Christian monotheism but, in reality, they were still thinking and acting in terms of polytheism. More precisely, within the new cosmos, apart from human beings and spirits of the dead, they now recognized two sets of deities: those belonging to the new religion and those belonging to the old.

These two sets of deities were classified as 'good' and 'bad' respectively. Yet this evaluation had nothing to do with ethical or spiritual values. It was based purely on materialistic considerations. Just as, in the past, one taro goddess might be discarded for another from whom a

---

[1] They were never included in the formal accounts of the Third Cargo Belief I was given at the beginning of my research. I discovered them later on only as the result of detailed discussions.

garden leader had had better results, so God and Jesus Christ were regarded as 'good' because they produced the cargo, whereas the local deities were 'bad' ('satans') because they were responsible for the inferior native material culture.

This in turn determined the way in which the natives understood the missionaries' instructions and translated them into practical action, which can be regarded as the first recognizable cargo cult in the southern Madang District: that is, the first organized ritual specially designed to actuate a deity to send Western goods. In the first place, it was believed that Christianity had to be accepted *in toto*. The people had to prepare themselves *en masse* for baptism: they had to go to church and prayer meetings; they had to sing innumerable hymns and listen to interminable sermons from evangelists or catechists; they had to receive catechetical instruction and send their children to mission schools. In the second place, it was thought that the above ritual would be effective only if the new taboos instituted by the missionaries were scrupulously observed. Satan had to be rooted out (Pidgin English, *rausim Satan*). In other words, all the customs of which the missionaries and God disapproved—polygyny, sorcery, the ceremonies honouring the spirits of the dead, initiation, dancing,[1] love magic, agricultural ceremonies—had to be eradicated. They 'blocked the road of the cargo' (Pidgin English, *pasim rot bilong kako*). Only when they had disappeared entirely would God feel obliged to honour his covenant with the people. A constant watch had to be maintained against Satan: the old gods and goddesses, who were always trying to lure the natives back to the 'bad' ways of the past. Garia Christians regarded this as implicit in the hymns they sang in church. Two passages read: 'Satan always cheats us. His ways are bad. We leave Satan's ways alone. We shall turn to God's ways'; and 'Satan always stalks us —O Jesus Christ support us'.[2] Informants explained these passages thus: 'The local deities always try to trick us into performing the old rituals again in their honour. But what they gave us was only rubbish

---

[1] It is very probable that the ban on dancing imposed by the Native Elders in 1923 was solely motivated by their fear that it would prevent God from sending goods. Their official reason was that, even as a purely secular amusement, it would stop the people from turning their hearts and minds to God as they should. It could never be divorced fully from its pagan religious background.

[2] The two passages quoted are from Wullenkord, *Duebuk*. The first is the third verse of Hymn 1 (p. 5), translated into Amele from the German (*Wie bist du mir so innig gut*) by Rev. A. Wullenkord. The second is the last line of Hymn 22 (p. 14), an original composition in Amele by Pastor Ud. As I do not read Amele, I present English translations from Garia translations. Even if the latter are inaccurate, they are significant as Garia popular interpretations of the originals.

—taro, yam, and all that stuff. If we yielded to temptation, God would not send us the real cargo—steel tools, tinned meat, and rice.'[1]

The Third Cargo Belief had spread throughout much of the southern Madang District by the early 1930's. It was current all along the coast between Bongu and Sek by 1920, and thereafter travelled inland as the country was opened up by Administration patrols and mission parties. It must have reached the hinterland of Alexishafen during the decade following the establishment of the Catholic station at Halopa in 1917. It was taken across the Gogol into the Bagasin and Ramu areas after 1922, and to the Rai Coast after 1922–3. On the Rai Coast, not only the Sengam, Gira, and Som but also many Ngaing, especially near the coast and in the Sibog region, were familiar with its doctrines by 1930, although most Ngaing paid little attention to them before 1933, when they formally accepted the Catholic Mission. The belief may well have penetrated the inland Nankina and Mot areas (inland Ngaing, M'na, and N'dau) during the 1930's with the general introduction of Christianity from Ulap. About 1932, a large gathering in the Sibog area was dispersed by Patrol Officer Nurton. According to local informants, these people were praying for and expecting the Second Coming of the Lord and the arrival of cargo.

It is, of course, impossible to state with any precision the proportion of the total native population which actively supported the Third Cargo Belief during the interwar years, but the figure was probably very high. Admittedly, there must have been some small and isolated groups in the distant hinterland which, although they knew about the belief, had been insufficiently activated to take much interest in it. Again, there was certainly a nucleus of completely sincere Christians among both mission helpers and laity. But such evidence as there is strongly suggests that these people were in a small minority. Hannemann, writing in 1948 after more than twenty years' mission work among the natives of Madang and the Rai Coast, suggests that 'more than fifty per cent, perhaps, of the population' subscribed to quasi-Christian cargo doctrines.[2] My own experience, however, in the Bagasin Area and Madang, and on the Rai Coast, leads me to suspect that even this estimate is too low. Virtually all my informants made it quite clear that they had always regarded the Third Cargo Belief as

[1] The attitude among Lutheran converts was probably always more extreme than that among Catholic converts because of the strictness of their missionaries. For comparable Lutheran attitudes in the Lae area, although no cargo doctrine appears to have been involved, see Hogbin, *Transformation Scene*, op. cit., pp. 232–75.

[2] Hannemann, 'Le Culte de Cargo en Nouvelle-Guinée', op. cit., p. 944. Cf. also Inselmann, *Letub, The Cult of the Secret of Wealth*, op. cit., p. 125.

official Christianity and assured me that it had had an extremely wide-spread following. Events after 1933 supported their view.

There were three reasons why the Third Cargo Belief should have been adopted so quickly throughout the southern Madang District. In the first place, as already noted, after 1920 Western goods had become necessities rather than luxuries in the coastal area. During the Mandate, with the opening up of the country and the decline of traditional local industries, the peoples of the hinterland began to depend on these goods in the same way. Yet, with low wages and few alternative means of earning money, the amount they could buy in the trade stores never satisfied their demand. Hence any doctrine that promised to solve this problem was bound to win ready acceptance.

In the second place, the old trade routes between Madang, the Rai Coast, and the Bagasin Area provided slow but reliable channels of communication. Information could be carried from village to village by labourers returning from indenture or by other natives visiting distant relatives or trade partners. It is significant that, after 1923, the Sengam, Gira, and Som were evangelized by their Yam trade friends. Because of the general cultural homogeneity of the area, the new ideas could easily be understood.

In the third place, there can be no doubt that quasi-Christian cargo doctrines were deliberately propagated by some Lutheran and Catholic mission helpers. Those native helpers who were sincere Christians scrupulously carried out their instructions to win the pagans over carefully and honestly. But so rapid was the expansion of the two missions during the interwar years—and, indeed, so keen the rivalry between them—that it was necessary to make use of men with very little basic education. Such men, working far away from the supervision of European missionaries and, because they were not employed within their natal congregations, in villages where they lacked the restraints imposed by kinship obligations, rapidly got out of hand. As they were so badly paid, they themselves looked to Christianity for a solution of their economic problems.[1] Moreover, because they were able to persuade the people that they possessed the key to the new wealth, they quickly came to dominate the Administration headmen, whose positions had no comparable sanction, and assumed *de facto* control of the villages in which they lived.

These irresponsible workers, who should never have been allowed in the field, soon won the missions many adherents but in the long run did irreparable damage. Convinced that the cargo would come only

[1] See also Hannemann, 'Le Culte de Cargo', op. cit., p. 945.

when everybody had embraced Christianity, they spared no efforts to hasten the event. They exhorted and abused the people, and threatened them with punishment from the Administration if they failed to send their children to school.[1] They caned pupils who were slow to learn. To symbolize the driving out of Satan, they felled the trees in the old deity sanctuaries without the owners' permission. They tore down pagan emblems and broke up initiation ceremonies. They tried to dissolve polygynous unions and arrange new marriages, often with scant regard for local laws of exogamy. As soon as they had settled in a new area, they tried to impose the ban on dancing, which even the Native Elders had meant to apply only to relatively sophisticated converts, without any discrimination. They either preached the cargo doctrines described or prophesied, as apparently at Sibog on the Rai Coast, the imminence of the Last Trump—an earthquake and fire, in which pagans would be consumed—followed by the return of Jesus and the ancestors with rewards of cargo for those who had joined their mission. They encouraged belief by painting glowing pictures of the European comforts enjoyed by the saved in Heaven in contrast to the misery of the damned in Hell. They reinforced the point by staging tableaux in which some natives wore Western clothes and other finery to illustrate the one, and other natives wore traditional clothing and ornaments, and were smeared with ashes, to illustrate the other.[2] In some areas —as on the inland Rai Coast—Lutheran evangelists tried to create new congregations, without permission from the European missionaries, long before the natives had sufficient knowledge of Christianity or the duties involved in holding congregational offices.[3]

[1] This was quite without foundation. All Australian Administrations since 1921 have always remained neutral in religious affairs.

[2] Professor R. M. and Dr C. H. Berndt have told me personally that they witnessed such tableaux in the Lutheran area near Kainantu during the early 1950's.

[3] As he states in his Foreword, Mr J. K. McCarthy has reservations about some of the material in this paragraph—especially that relating to the coercive practices of native mission helpers. While agreeing that there could have been isolated incidents of the type I describe, he believes that if they had been widespread they would have been reported to the District Office. Although I do not wish to imply that *all* native mission helpers were involved, I must differ from Mr McCarthy here. For a start, I doubt if southern Madang District natives (except those near Madang itself) at the time of which I write understood enough about the separation between missions and Administration to take such action. Furthermore, I took great pains to check my information. I had substantially identical accounts of the unorthodox behaviour I describe both in the Bagasin Area and on the Rai Coast. Regarding coercive practices, I directly observed one native mission helper browbeat villagers in the Bagasin Area. That this was common before the last war is supported not only by the many statements I was given by informants but also by the following passage which Yali incorporated in his 'Laws' drawn up in Port Moresby in 1947 (see Chapter VII): 'If a native mission helper behaves badly (*ino wok gut*, Pidgin English) in

After a certain point, however, personal responsibility for disseminating the Third Cargo Belief became relatively unimportant. When the doctrine was fully elaborated, it became, subject to local variations, part of the people's culture and had its own momentum. As such, it developed its own linguistic usages, expressed in both Pidgin English and the native vernaculars. Much of the phraseology was highly allusive or oblique (Pidgin English, *tok bokis*; Garia, *kuna ila'ila*). Two of the most obvious phrases have already been presented: 'to root out evil' was translated into Pidgin English as '*rausim Satan*', which was interpreted as 'to keep the local deities at bay'; and the Pidgin English '*opim/pasim rot bilong kako*' (literally, 'to open/close the road of the cargo') was understood as 'to reveal/hide the ritual secrets which would ensure the cargo's arrival'. In Pidgin English, God was known as the *as* (*bilong*) *kako* (the source of the cargo). Again, among the Garia, for example, ordinary Christian phrases assumed new meanings. 'God blessed Noah' (Genesis ix. 1) (Pidgin English: *God i bigpela long Noa*; Garia: *Anut Noale kokai älewoya*) came to mean 'God gave cargo to Noah' on the grounds that in Melanesian culture the concept of blessing could be given practical expression only by the presentation of wealth. The phrase 'the Mission wanted to help us' (Pidgin English: *misin i laik halivim/litimapim yumi*; Garia: *misin tianesigebule' eya*) came to mean 'the Mission wanted to give us cargo'. Such phrases as 'the period of ignorance' (Pidgin English: *taim bilong tudak*; Garia: *ägisigigem kolilona*) and 'the understanding of God is with us' (Pidgin English: *tingting bilong God istap*; Garia: *Anut po nanunanu pulina*[1]) were understood as 'the time before the cargo secret was revealed to us' and 'we now have the ear of God (and the means of getting cargo)' respectively.

This oblique language increased the complexity of the situation. It could be used in conversations with European missionaries without their being aware of its hidden implications and—although some of

---

his village, all the big men of the village such as the headmen must talk together and get rid of him. . . . A mission teacher must not beat the children in his charge. He is not the chief authority in the village: his job is just to educate men, women, and children.' Regarding the spreading of the Third Cargo Belief, some of my informants were practising mission helpers and others had given up the work after 1942. Several of these men admitted having heard quasi-Christian cargo doctrines or ideas that could have been construed as such while undergoing training, and having disseminated these doctrines and ideas before the war. I refer the reader also to later chapters in which I give examples of mission helpers involved in cargo cults after 1933. For an Eastern Highlands situation comparable to, if less extreme than, the one I describe, see Berndt, *Excess and Restraint*, pp. 381–2.

[1] Cf. also p. 78, where the meaning of the phrase is illustrated.

them suspected what was going on in the natives' minds—the extent to which their teachings had been misrepresented. As a result, they unconsciously allowed the people to assume that they confirmed the truth of the new doctrines. Either they or the sincere and disinterested native mission helpers had only to fail to correct an equivocal sentence, or innocently make a statement capable of two meanings, to substantiate the Third Cargo Belief in its entirety.[1] No stronger proof was necessary. In fact, during the 1920's, relations between natives and missionaries, although on the whole extremely amicable, were nevertheless based on complete mutual misunderstanding.

[1] As, for instance, 'But seek ye first the kingdom of God, and his righteousness; and all these things shall be added unto you' (Matthew vi. 33). Inselmann, *Letub*, op. cit., p. 124, makes exactly the same point. The following passage from the *Katekismo Katolik*, p. 17, par. 75, is also relevant: '*Long Heven i nogat trobel, i nogat pen. Em i fulap long ol gutpela samting. Heven i noken pinis. Em i ples bilong peim ol gutpela man. Oli kisim pe inap long ol gutwok bilong ol.*' This may be translated: 'Heaven is a place without trouble and pain. It is filled with every good thing. Heaven cannot end. It is a place where good men are rewarded. They are paid according to their good works.' (I have changed the Pidgin English spelling slightly to suit my own orthography.)

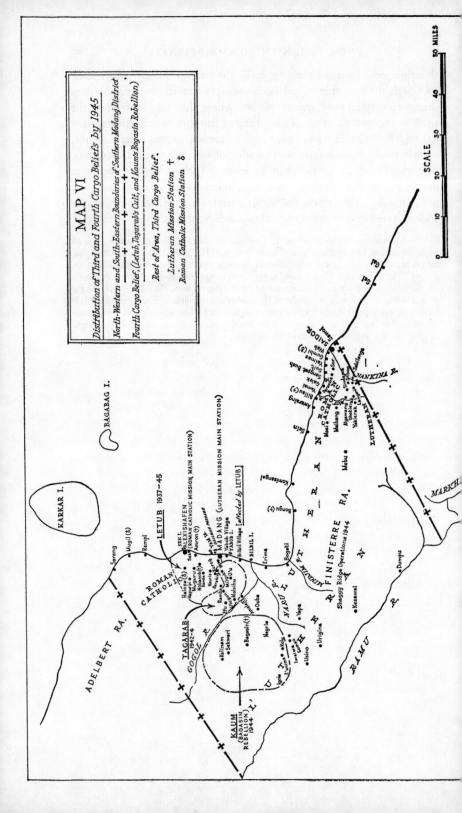

MAP VI

*Distribution of Third and Fourth Cargo Beliefs by 1945*

North-Western and South-Eastern Boundaries of Southern Madang District ...... +—+—+

Fourth Cargo Belief (Letub, Tagarab's Cult, and Kaum's Bagasin Rebellion) .......... •

Rest of Area, Third Cargo Belief.

Lutheran Mission Station ... +

Roman Catholic Mission Station ... ☩

CHAPTER IV

# THE FOURTH CARGO BELIEF

## 1933-45

THE Fourth Cargo Belief began to take shape some time after 1933.
It was preceded by a period of frustration, during which the teachings
of Christianity were called into question. Thereafter the natives near
Madang formulated new, syncretic doctrines and seceded from the
missions, although those in outlying areas still subscribed to the Third
Cargo Belief. The new doctrines were not finally renounced at Madang
until 1957, but in this chapter we are concerned with their development
only until the end of the Second World War.

### The Period of Frustration

By 1933, native Christians, especially in the coastal area, had become
restive. Their attempts to find an equitable *modus vivendi* with Europeans had failed. Near Madang, their grievances over the land 'sold'
over their heads some forty years earlier had not been fairly adjusted.
Although some groups had been 'given back' about 4,400 ha. of virgin
land, from which they had never been evicted, the seaboard natives
had irretrievably lost the thousand hectares actually taken up for plantations. In return they had received minimum compensation. Relations
with Australians generally were no better than they had been with the
Germans. The people realized that most Europeans still held them in
the greatest contempt. In fact, race relations were cumulatively a good
deal worse than they had been in the past. The spread of administrative
control, Christianity, and the Third Cargo Belief had already given
the natives a sense of common identity wider than they had ever
known.[1] This was now intensified: the arrogance of employers, poor
conditions of work, and the shortage of money with which to buy
Western goods were causing deep resentment against the Europeans.
The new attitude was fostered by perpetual discussions in the labour
compounds and by events such as the Rabaul Strike in 1929, in which
natives from the Madang District took part. As increasing numbers

---

[1] This was expressed in the Pidgin English phrase: '*Mipela Niugini*', 'We people of New
Guinea'. The concept embraced not only the peoples of the southern Madang District but
also those of all other parts of the Territory either visited or known to exist.

87

of labourers returned from the plantations and goldfields, it was taken to the hinterland.

To make matters worse, in spite of all the sacrifice and effort—the renunciation of the old religion, observance of the new taboos, careful attention to sermons and instruction for baptism, hymn-singing, and prayers—the cargo had not come. Once more the situation had to be explained. Two solutions were put forward.

The first solution was widespread throughout the whole of New Guinea at the time. It put the blame on the lay Europeans because of their generally unfriendly behaviour and absolved the missionaries, with whom the people were still on good terms. It was believed that both the missionaries and natives had fulfilled their parts of the bargain. Christianity had been substituted for paganism and God had answered the natives' prayers by sending their ancestors with supplies of cargo to the Sydney wharves. But God, natives, and missionaries were being cheated by the commercial Europeans, who had control of the ships. As soon as a ship put to sea, the crew would go through the holds with paintbrush and paintpot, striking out the names of the native consignees on some of the cases and replacing them with those of individual Europeans or European trading firms in Madang. Thus the cargo intended for the natives was being misappropriated.[1]

The second and probably later solution had far more serious implications. The natives began to question the *bona fides* of the missionaries —whose lack of generosity with trade goods was hardly in keeping with the material comforts they enjoyed[2]—and suspect that they were holding back information: some vital part of Christianity wherein the cargo secret lay. The conduct of individual missionaries was now most carefully scrutinized. It was believed that some of them were deliberately moved to new stations by their superiors, whenever they got to know the local people too intimately and were likely to reveal the truth to them.[3]

In some instances, these doubts were expressed apologetically and even covertly. About 1927, a much-trusted Lutheran evangelist in the Bagasin Area very cautiously confided his worries about the non-arrival of the cargo to his European missionary. When the missionary disillusioned him, he was bitterly ashamed and became, outwardly at least, more devoted to his work than before. In 1938, it was discovered

---

[1] Cheating gods and spirits is a common theme in the religions of non-literate peoples.

[2] The Lutherans also still held land confiscated from the exiles in 1912.

[3] The Bongu people said this of Rev. R. Hanselmann when he was removed from their congregation after 1933. Rev. G. O. Reitz (also of the Lutheran Mission) told me that he had the same experience in Karkar after the war.

that several Yam pupils had been sent to the Lutheran Mission Central School four years earlier to learn the cargo secret. At least one lad was taken away because this knowledge had not been given him[1]

In other instances, however, the complaints were more forthright. By 1929, Lutheran native helpers were openly criticizing their low salaries and personal standards of living. In 1933, natives from the Madang area sent the following message to Rev. R. Hanselmann, the missionary of the Bongu Lutheran Congregation, who had always expressed his Christianity in a practical way, and was extremely popular for his liberality with food and trade goods: 'Why do we not learn the secret of the cargo? You people hide the power of the Europeans from us. Our possessions are quite worthless; those of the white men are really worth while. We understand all the work of Europeans (*ologeta wok bilong wetman*) but they obstruct us (*tambu long mipela*). We want to progress but they keep us down as *kanakas*. True, the Mission has taught us Christianity but it does not help us black people in a practical way (*halivim long sikin bilong mipela*). The white men are hiding the cargo secret (*ting as kako*) from us. We are destined to be complete paupers, absolutely destitute.'[2]

The situation became critical during the mid-1930's, when specific accusations were made against the missionaries at two Lutheran conferences. The first was held at Mis (Sagalau) near Madang about 1934–5. For several years the missionaries had been worried about the general laxity and indifference in congregational life: unwillingness to attend church and send children to school. They wanted to know the reason. At the conference, they deliberately isolated themselves from the native delegates by stretching a vine from the altar to the west door of the church and sitting exclusively on one side of it instead of mixing with them, as was their usual practice. This provoked discussion, in which the mission helpers admitted that they believed the Europeans were hiding cargo secrets from them. The missionaries protested their innocence and the vine was removed, the natives once more pledging their allegiance to Christianity. Nevertheless, the Sacraments were withheld from those congregations which seemed to be the worst affected, until their members showed signs of spiritual improvement.

The second conference was held in the following year at Sangpat, between Suit and Galek, on the Rai Coast. On this occasion, the native

[1] Hannemann, *Village Life*, op. cit., pp. 38–9.
[2] A free translation from the Pidgin English in Hannemann, 'Le Culte de Cargo', op. cit., pp. 945–6. Where Pidgin English words are quoted, I have altered the spelling slightly to suit my own orthography. *Kanaka* is a Pidgin English term of contempt for the unsophisticated native.

delegates deliberately segregated themselves from the Europeans by stretching a length of wire through the church and sitting exclusively on one side of it. There was another discussion, in which similar accusations were made. Again the missionaries, supported by loyal evangelists and teachers, protested and withdrew the Sacraments. But by this time such measures were useless. A large proportion of both the Lutheran and Catholic congregations had become thoroughly convinced of the missionaries' duplicity. No amount of argument, even from sincere native Christians, could restore confidence.[1]

The secret which the missionaries were supposed to be hiding was capable of various interpretations. Some believed that those parts of the Bible translated into native vernaculars and Pidgin English omitted the relevant information, and that if they had been taught proper English they would have discovered it for themselves by reading the Scriptures in full.[2] The Garia, who were being prepared for baptism during the middle 1930's, thought that the missionaries had not taught the true *osa*, some form of special prayer or the esoteric name of God, the repetition of which would force him to send cargo.[3] But here again there were at least two interpretations. A few assumed that this was largely the fault of the native helpers, who had not listened carefully to the missionaries. Because they were so stupid, the missionaries had decided to evangelize the whole of New Guinea, including the recently opened Central Highlands, in the hope of finding people of sufficient intelligence to be entrusted with such important knowledge. The majority, however, were satisfied that the missionaries were using this as an excuse to prevent God from sending the cargo lest the natives became their equals and challenged their privileged position.

During this period of speculation,[4] the most constructive ideas came from the peoples of the Madang area. They were now relatively sophisticated and had behind them a long tradition of cargo thinking. In this area, as already mentioned, the Second Cargo Belief had been forgotten

[1] Details from Inselmann, *Letub*, op. cit., pp. 107–10. The use of the vine by Europeans was probably fortuitous, but that of the wire by natives may well have symbolized cargo. This kind of symbolism, like *tok bokis* itself, was common in the Cargo Movement.

[2] It was not until after 1956 that the whole of the New Testament was translated into Graged (Yam). The volumes of Bible Stories hitherto produced for the people were necessarily very small.

[3] The Garia said that the Lutherans had taught only *Anut sisiebu*, a form of audible address to God, without using his secret name (the essence of *osa*, true ritual). *Anut sisiebu* was of course useless by itself. For some time the Garia thought that the secret might lie in the Blessing of the Communion Wine and showed considerable interest in this rite.

[4] Speculation seems to have been rife also on Karkar, and around Finschhafen. See Worsley, *The Trumpet Shall Sound*, op. cit., pp. 213–14.

by all but a few of the more conservative for nearly twenty years. Those who preserved it continued to discuss it among themselves. In Yabob, for instance, there were attempts to integrate it with Christian theology: because of their bitter quarrel, Manup and Kilibob were tentatively identified as Cain and Abel respectively, Manup having been the originator of sorcery and warfare. But the younger men, who had attended mission schools, dismissed such suggestions as dangerous heathen nonsense (the temptation of the 'satans'). They laughed the old men to scorn and clung to the doctrine of the Third Cargo Belief.

Yet as the years went by and it became evident that the adoption of Christianity had proved abortive, the old men began to get a more respectful hearing. This was especially true when certain events occurred which seemed to prove the validity of the Kilibob-Manup myth. It will be remembered that in Yabob there was the tradition that the two brothers would eventually return to Madang to inaugurate a period of peace and plenty after an earthquake and general war. Manup's return would be heralded by the arrival of a native canoe from the north, and Kilibob's by the discovery of a Siasi wooden plate at sea to the south.

It is still believed that this prophecy was partially fulfilled. First, about 1935–6 a native canoe with the name *Gipsy* painted on her hull put in at Yabob from the north. She was manned by a single half-caste or European. He had her carried into the Yabob church, while he himself slept on the floor of a native house, using only a single blanket as bedding. He accepted only vegetable food, and refused all offers of fowls and other delicacies. He said very little to the people, and gave them neither a message nor his name.[1] He stayed in Yabob only one or two days, and then journeyed on to the south. Second, quite soon after this event, a rubber dinghy or raft was discovered at sea south of Yabob. The *Gipsy* was easily identified as the canoe which was to herald Manup's return—a view reinforced by the mysterious behaviour of her owner. The rubber dinghy or raft was equated with the Siasi plate which was to announce Kilibob, doubtless because of its association with the dinghies believed to have been refused by the natives in the Second Cargo Belief. Moreover, at about this time the natives may well have picked up scraps of loose talk about the possibility of a new war in Europe, which would have given these events even greater significance.

[1] Dr A. L. Epstein suggests that he may have been the Czech canoeist who visited Rabaul and caused speculation among the Tolai about the same time.

These coincidences and the mounting unpopularity of the missionaries reawakened widespread interest in the Second Cargo Belief. It was discussed among Lutherans and Catholics all along the coast from Sek to Bogati, and probably also on Karkar, where there appears to have been a similar tradition. But this did not mean the complete abandonment of Christianity. Twenty years of mission teaching could not have been eradicated on the spur of the moment without leaving a tremendous cultural hiatus. A compromise had to be achieved. Thus the Fourth Cargo Belief was essentially an amalgam between the Second Cargo Belief and specially selected themes from Christianity. In the three major cults involved, the reversal of the roles of Kilibob and Manup in the earlier forms of the myth was retained. The Letub Cult, which began several years before the Japanese War, was based on the second version of the myth. The Tagarab Cult, which began just before the Japanese Occupation, and the Bagasin Rebellion, which occurred in 1944 (a few months after the recapture of Madang by Allied forces), were based on the first version.

### The Letub Doctrine and Cult[1]

Letub doctrine was thought out probably in the Catholic village of Sek.[2] The cargo cult with which it was associated first came to the attention of Europeans after the beginning of 1937. It was most active just before and during the Japanese Occupation.

The vital content of the original Letub doctrine seems to have been that the cargo secret hidden by the missionaries was the true identities of God and Jesus Christ. God was, in reality, Dodo (Anut),[3] and Jesus Christ was Manup. This could be easily demonstrated. God and Dodo were the first deities mentioned in Christian Scripture and Sek mythology and, allowing for a few minor points of difference, could be regarded as having performed roughly the same creative functions. Again, as has been seen, missionaries habitually referred to God by the native name Dodo (Anut). Hence it was obvious that God and Dodo were one person, and that their two important sons, Jesus Christ and Manup, were also one person.

[1] My research into Letub is by no means definitive. I discovered and recorded the mythology myself, but otherwise rely on Inselmann, *Letub*, op. cit., the only contemporary account there is.

[2] I never discovered the true originator of Letub but it is important to note that the doctrine was well known to the native inmates of Alexishafen Mission Station by 1942, when one of my informants, now a Catholic catechist, heard it openly preached by other native mission helpers.

[3] As the doctrine came from Sek, I use the Sek name Dodo rather than the more general Anut.

This was explained by a syncretic myth: In the beginning, God-Dodo brought two deity sons into being at Sek[1]—Kilibob and Manup. They quarrelled, as already related, and God-Dodo ordered them to leave. Kilibob made a native canoe and sailed to the north. But God-Dodo showed Manup how to build a proper ship with engines and a steel hull, and to make the rest of the cargo as well. In the meantime, as a separate act of creation, he had brought Adam and Eve into being in or near Sydney, Australia, but had not produced ships or cargo for them, or enabled them to make these things for themselves. They lived in the same way as the natives of New Guinea—that is, without any European material comforts at all. Thus Manup, with the power given him by his father, became the cargo deity and culture hero of the Madang people, while Adam and Eve were the culture heroes of the white men.

Manup took his ship from Sek to Madang and then down the Rai Coast, offering each native he put ashore the choice between a rifle and a bow and arrow, and between a dinghy and a canoe. As already recorded, in every case the native chose the bow and arrow, and the canoe. The people of Sek also adopted the dance which Manup had invented, the Letub. Thus the New Guinea natives forfeited the cargo, which was now carried away to Australia. When Manup reached Sydney Harbour, he found the white *kanakas*, to whom he gave his ship and everything left in her. He also made them other ships, built them the city of Sydney, the Harbour Bridge, and all the wharf and dockyard installations, and constructed stores and warehouses, which he filled with all the goods they desired.[2]

When he had finished, Manup surveyed his work and thought once more of his true followers, the people of New Guinea. He wished that he had been able to do for them what he had done for the Europeans, and decided to return to Madang to make amends. Thus he transformed himself into the Holy Ghost, entered the womb of the Virgin Mary, and was reborn as Jesus Christ.[3] He intended to go back with the missionaries, but the Jews conspired against him, as they did not want the New Guinea natives to share the wealth they now enjoyed. They

[1] The people of Sek claimed their area as the birthplace of Kilibob and Manup.

[2] By this time a few natives had visited Sydney and could describe it to their people at home. Others had probably seen photographs.

[3] Worsley, *The Trumpet Shall Sound*, op. cit., p. 212, is quite wrong in claiming that in the Letub Kilibob and Manup were identified as the sons of Noah. Informants, with whom I checked the point most carefully in 1958 (after the publication of Worsley's book), denied ever having heard of such an identification. Nor have I found any support for it in the literature.

crucified Jesus-Manup and held him captive in Heaven (in or above Sydney). They prevailed on the missionaries to keep this secret from the natives, and the missionaries, who also did not want to let any of the new wealth out of their hands, agreed.

The cult ritual associated with the doctrine was designed to free Jesus-Manup from his bondage. Its aim was to see that God-Dodo brought him back to New Guinea with ships and cargo—especially the rifles he had taken away—and that the spirits of the dead got it from him on arrival and delivered it to the people. This would neutralize the trickery of the Europeans, who were stealing the natives' property while it was at sea. Like the doctrine itself, the new ritual was at the outset essentially syncretic, the main features of Christian worship being retained but combined with pagan ceremonies which had been officially discarded for at least twenty years.

The Christian features of the cult were, of course, derived from the Catholic Mission. Although little is known about the actual rubric of the services, churches were still kept up as centres of religious exercise. Prayers of some type were offered for the return of Jesus-Manup, and ordinary Christian hymns were still sung and sermons preached.

There were two main pagan elements. First, sacrifices were made to the spirits of the dead. In the village cemeteries,[1] small tables or platforms were erected, covered with lengths of cotton cloth, decorated with flowers in bottles, and heaped with gifts of food and tobacco.[2] Invocations were made to the spirits to get cargo from Jesus-Manup as soon as he appeared with his ships. In some villages, although the evidence does not suggest that the practice was frequent, gardens, pigs, and other forms of property were destroyed or thrown away to impress on the cargo deity and the ancestors the natives' poverty and need of immediate relief. They would be shamed into honouring their obligations to the living.

Second, the Letub dance,[3] Manup's special gift to the people of Sek, was revived. Although I have never seen it performed, from informants' descriptions it appears to have been very little distinguished from other dances of the Madang District. It probably took the form of a ballet divided into a series of episodes, portraying scenes from native life. Traditional dress was worn: feather headdresses, face

[1] Which had, of course, replaced traditional methods of exposing corpses, by Administration law.

[2] The Pidgin English term for this rite is *bilasim tewol*, 'to decorate a table'. I have never heard a vernacular equivalent.

[3] It was from this dance that the Letub Cult took its name. The term Letub by itself always refers to the cult rather than the dance.

paint, ornaments of bone and shell, flowers and croton leaves, and bark girdles. But it had one special feature—the general shaking and uncontrolled antics of some of the dancers.

The Letub dance had a dual significance. It was sacred to Jesus-Manup and was performed in his name; and, like most dances in the southern Madang District, it was intended to honour the spirits of the dead. The dancers thought of their ancestors, and believed that the display and general excitement of the occasion would please them. Thus the dance was always staged at the time of a funeral, a long procession of dancers in full regalia accompanying the corpse from the church, where it had been laid out in state, to the grave.

The shaking fits and uncontrolled antics were adopted not only as features of the Letub dance but also as a general physiological condition for cult members even on non-festal occasions, when no dance was being held. Devotees swayed and shook their bodies without ceasing. Outbreaks were most virulent and intense after visits to the cemeteries. In view of this, although Inselmann, who made his observations under extremely difficult conditions, is not explicit on the point, it seems quite clear that the meaning given by the people themselves to this form of behaviour was that those afflicted were somehow in communication with the spirits of the dead or even Jesus-Manup. While in this condition, they were better able to receive special messages about future events such as the arrival of the cargo.[1]

From Sek, Letub doctrine and ritual spread through the coastal villages (such as Bilbil) which possessed the second version of the Kilibob-Manup myth, although they did not at this time gain a foothold among the Sengam, Gira, and Som on the Rai Coast. These peoples were too far away to be proselytized immediately. Later the cult was taken into the hinterland of Alexishafen: the Catholic villages of Halopa, Hapurpi, and Muguru seem to have been very active in disseminating it. From there it travelled south to the Lutheran area: villages such as Kurog, Kauris, Kamba, and eventually Nobanob, where the Lutherans had built their first inland station. It gained a following also in the Madang (Yam) Congregation.[2] But it never crossed the Gogol to enter the Bagasin Area. (See Map VI.)

[1] This is in keeping with what is known about traditional religions in the whole area and was the explanation given Yali, who witnessed a version of Letub ritual in 1947. For a fuller account of the swaying, see Inselmann, *Letub*, op. cit., pp. 113–14.

[2] *Sic* Inselmann, *Letub*, op. cit., pp. 117–18. It is puzzling that Letub should have spread to the Yam, for whom Kilibob rather than Manup was the traditional hero. But from Inselmann's account, it is possible that the Yam interpreted it only as the Second Coming of Jesus Christ (as such) and ignored the syncretic myth at this stage.

The diffusion of the cult was influenced, to a large extent, by cultural factors. The inland villages had no rights to the Kilibob-Manup myth. As in the case of traditional ritual, a definite copyright was involved: any group making use of ritual to which it had no inherited or purchased rights was regarded as having committed theft. In the same way, rights to the Letub Cult had to be bought by groups in the hinterland. As a result, doctrine and ritual ceased to have a rigid uniformity.[1] Many variations were probably closer to the Third Cargo Belief and quasi-Christian worship than to the Sek original. It is likely that hinterland groups bothered to master only Letub ritual (the food offerings and dance) but disregarded the syncretic myth explaining its origin. They may well have even continued to address their prayers to God and Jesus as such (that is, in the forms they had learnt from the missions) without being aware of the new identifications of God as Dodo (Anut) and Jesus as Manup, which had been adopted by the coastal natives. This again had its parallel in the process of cultural diffusion in the past, when inland leaders learnt only the ritual formulae for the dances they bought but ignored the validating myths, being satisfied that the people in the places of origin knew them.

Nevertheless, the Letub can be considered as a single phenomenon: a quasi-Christian revisionist cult. The people themselves understood it in this way. They were outwardly friendly towards the Administration and stressed their hostility to the missionaries—although they doubtless harboured thoughts of a war against all Europeans, for which Jesus-Manup would provide the arms. They continued to regard themselves as Christians but seceded from their missions. Although they offered no physical violence, they refused to associate with European missionaries and loyal mission helpers,[2] or to attend mission sponsored services. They claimed that the cult was ordained and commanded in the Bible: it was the true way to worship God and the cargo secret previously hidden from them.[3] These attitudes were implicit also in the periodic statements made by the new leaders who began to emerge, some of them Administration headmen and others mission helpers.

In 1941, a native 'conference' was held at Barahim village. It was attended by both followers of Letub and natives still loyal to the missions. At this gathering it was clearly stated: 'What the missions have given us is good. We like the Word of God. But they have given us

---

[1] Inselmann, *Letub,* op. cit., p. 103.
[2] Although loyal mission helpers attended the Barahim 'Conference'.
[3] Inselmann, *Letub,* op. cit., pp. 114 and 129.

only one part—merely the shell. The kernel they keep for themselves.'
When, in 1940, the cult spread to the Madang Lutheran Congregation,
one of its local leaders (who seems to have been a former mission
helper) prayed for two hours with two men, one standing on his left
and the other on his right. They were to inform the people, who were
dressed in their best clothes, of the arrival of the Lord. Suddenly the
leader shouted: 'The King is coming!'; and the message was relayed
to the assembled natives. Another leader, Kaut, the *Tultul* of the
Lutheran village of Kauris, claimed to be the Apostle St Paul and to
have a wireless set like those of the Europeans, through which he
received messages about the future from Heaven.[1]

Between 1940 and 1942, the Letub Cult gathered a tremendous
following in the Madang area. The two missions could do little to
combat it because its adherents included not only a large proportion
of their parishioners but also many of their native helpers. Yet at this
time it never achieved a widespread centralized organization. Only one
man, Kaut of Kauris, made any attempt to claim supreme authority
over the whole affected area. His ambition was to become King of
Madang but until the end of 1942 he met with only a limited response.

The time was hardly ripe for the emergence of a single powerful
native leader. The people had had as yet no experience of this sort of
organization and felt no need of it. Above all, the Administration still
had their respect. Although the maximum penalty it could impose on
natives responsible for cargo activities was six months' imprisonment
for 'spreading false reports', this was a sufficient deterrent to block
any such move. Hitherto the District Office had avoided intervening
in mission affairs, partly because of its declared policy of religious
neutrality and partly because of its ignorance of the undercurrents in
native Christianity. But, in 1940, after receiving complaints from the
Lutheran Mission, it began to take counter-measures against the Letub.
The *Luluai* of Kurog and other leaders from both the Lutheran and
Catholic areas were put in gaol for a month. The Paramount *Luluai* of
Kauris was demoted to the rank of ordinary *luluai*, and Kaut (*Tultul* of
Kauris) lost his office entirely. The Madang leader who had announced
the Coming of the Lord was arrested but released after a night in gaol,
when it was ascertained that he had not been referring to the Germans.[2]

These punitive measures were hardly severe and, far from causing
any real hardship, only convinced the people of the truth of their new

[1] For details in this paragraph see Inselmann, ibid., pp. 115, 117–18, and 124.
[2] Inselmann, ibid., pp. 116–18. The Administration's main concern at this stage of the
war was to discourage native interest in German reoccupation of the Territory.

doctrine. The leaders had been gaoled or demoted because the Europeans were afraid that they had at last discovered the cargo secret. Even so, the Administration's intervention at this point prevented the emergence of a widespread seditious organization under a single native leader or oligarchy. Although the cult was hardly driven underground, the ritual had to be performed with a certain amount of caution under purely local leaders.

In 1941, towards the end of the Mandate, the Administration tried to take constructive action by providing a school at Mis (Sagalau) and enrolling a hundred and fifty pupils from neighbouring villages.[1] As English was one of the subjects taught, the school aroused considerable interest and enthusiasm. Many people—both those who followed the Letub and those outside it—believed that at last they would be able to read the Europeans' Bible *in toto* and discover the cargo secret for themselves. Accordingly, many natives bought English hymnals and translations of parts of the Bible in anticipation. The new school, however, had little effect on the Letub and native unrest generally. It was forced to close down early in 1942 when the Civil Administration was withdrawn after the first Japanese air raid. Thereafter the Letub passed into a new phase. Hatred of all Europeans was now quite unmasked, and the cargo expected was military equipment with which to drive them out. This is described in a later context.

### Tagarab's Doctrine and Cult

In 1942, five years after the beginning of the Letub and during the period in which A.N.G.A.U. was theoretically in control of the southern Madang District, a new quasi-Christian revisionist cult broke out in the Lutheran hinterland of Yabob village. It was profoundly influenced by the important events of the day: the rapid succession of Allied military reverses and the apparent imminence of the Japanese occupation of the area. Unlike the Letub, with which it has often been confused, the new cult had a single leader, Tagarab of Milguk, and a rudimentary hierarchical organization—men who were recognized as second, third, and fourth in command, and to whom Tagarab explained his doctrine and ritual with special care.

Tagarab had had a long association with Europeans. In 1929, he was employed as either a labourer or policeman in Rabaul and was involved in the General Strike, for which he served a term of imprisonment. After his release, he worked for a time at Wau and then joined or rejoined the Police Force. When the Japanese War broke out, he

[1] See p. 48 above. For a fuller account see Inselmann, *Letub*, op. cit., pp. 120–1.

was on duty at Madang. Late in 1941 or very early in 1942, he was sent in a police party to Karkar Island to arrest those held responsible for the Kukuaik Cargo Cult, which had recently got out of hand. The Second Coming of Jesus followed by the arrival of the spirits of the dead with cargo, volcanic eruptions, an eclipse of the sun, and various other phenomena had been prophesied.[1] The prisoners had been taken to Madang Gaol. Among them was a well-respected Lutheran native helper, who was in an obviously disturbed state of mind. Although he never foretold the arrival of cargo, he claimed to the native police that he had learnt in a dream from the spirit of a deceased native teacher that soon Jesus would return and the Japanese bomb the town. When the second event did, in fact, occur very soon afterwards (21 January 1942) and the Civil Administration was immediately withdrawn, Tagarab was visibly impressed. Like many other native policemen in Madang and other main centres, he mutinied and deserted to his own village. The N.G.V.R. and A.N.G.A.U. units now responsible for civil order made no attempt to arrest or force him to return to duty.

Soon afterwards Tagarab began his cult. He had a considerable fund of cargo knowledge at his disposal. He had heard all the talk associated with the Rabaul Strike in 1929: that the Europeans were stealing the natives' share of the goods sent via the ancestors. He had heard more of this sort of grumbling in the Police Force during the 1930's. He had heard lengthy accounts of the prophecies from Karkar and had either witnessed or learnt about events which seemed to prove them true: the bombing of Madang, and the fall of Rabaul and (later) Lae. The meaning of these prophecies must have been accentuated for him by the censorship Europeans had tried to impose on war news until now. He could not have been unaware of the Third Cargo Belief and the Letub. What was more important, as an inhabitant of Milguk he had rights to the first version of the Kilibob-Manup myth. This enabled him to draw on the recent theological speculations of the Yabob people, with whom his own group had close ties. The Yabob natives' interest in the Second Cargo Belief about 1935–6 had been intensified by the outbreak of the Letub a year or two later. But their participation in the new cult was inhibited because, according to their own version of the basic myth, Manup could not be the cargo deity.

[1] See Hannemann, 'Le Culte de Cargo', op. cit., pp. 948–9, and Worsley, *The Trumpet Shall Sound*, op. cit., p. 214. The cult was stimulated by a sermon preached in 1940 about the Return of Christ. Although I have no final proof, it is possible that this was interpreted as the return of Kilibob or was in some way connected with it. See Chapter VI, p. 165 (note 1).

Thus they tried to work out a parallel identification of Kilibob, their culture hero, as God or Jesus Christ.

The salient theme in Tagarab's doctrine, therefore, was the first version of the Kilibob-Manup myth. The secret hidden by Europeans was that Kilibob was the true cargo deity. But, apart from the reversal of the roles of the two brothers, the new doctrine differed from that of the Letub in two ways. First, Kilibob was identified as God rather than Jesus Christ because, in Milguk, Anus (the local name for Anut) was of no importance. Kilibob had always been the primary operative deity and thus had to be treated as God, the primary deity of the Europeans. Second, Manup was identified as Satan because of his 'badness'.[1]

Tagarab taught the people as follows:[2] Recently, while he had been on guard duty in the Police Force in Madang, he had seen a great light and fainted. Kilibob had revealed himself in a vision and given him certain information. In the beginning, there was the earth. Then, in the bush near Milguk, there came into being a man called Wain.[3] He was the father of Ankor, who was the father of Anus. Anus married a woman called Kikori and they had two sons, Kilibob and Manup. They too lived in Milguk. Wain, Ankor, and Anus were only ordinary men with no superhuman powers. But Kilibob and Manup were *tibud*, the first great deities.

Manup was 'bad'. He used love magic to commit adultery, and he killed people by means of sorcery and physical violence. He was, therefore, Satan, who had invented and taught the black arts. But Kilibob was 'good'. He invented wood-carving, canoe-building, agriculture, pottery, and all the useful arts. He delegated power to various human beings to preside over these crafts as demigods. But (as already recounted) he tattooed the pudenda of Manup's wife and a bitter quarrel ensued.[4] Manup tried several times to murder Kilibob, and the two brothers had a running fight in the bush. At last they came to Sek, where they both decided to leave the Madang area.

Manup made a native canoe. Kilibob built a steel ship with engines, which he called the *Mengga* (although Europeans called her the *MacDhui*[5]). He filled her with native men, artefacts, and food plants,

---

[1] I discovered no parallel identification of Kilibob as Satan in Letub doctrine.

[2] Tagarab died before I began field work. I learnt his doctrine from his two sons and several of his followers.

[3] The Milguk people claimed their area as the birthplace of Kilibob and Manup.

[4] Paradoxically, Tagarab (like the people of Bilbil) followed the Yam rather than the Yabob account of the original myth in this respect (see pp. 22–3) in spite of the close ties between Milguk and Yabob.

[5] A ship on the New Guinea run, sunk by the Japanese during the Second World War.

and the cargo, all of which he had created. Then the two brothers put to sea. The wind and waves were very strong, and Manup's canoe was driven towards the Sepik. But Kilibob started the engines of the *Mengga* and rode out the storm. As he left Sek, he fired a big gun and so carved out Madang Harbour, the Yam Islands, and Dallman Passage. He took the *Mengga* to Manus and Karkar, and then down the Rai Coast, where he put a native ashore in each of the coastal villages. In every case, of course, the native stupidly preferred traditional artefacts to the cargo, which he therefore forfeited.

Thereafter Kilibob sailed the *Mengga* to Sydney, where he left her by the beach. He went to Jerusalem (which appears to have been part of Sydney) and hid there. In the meanwhile, the white men, who had lived until now without cargo like New Guinea natives, found the *Mengga*. They were anxious to possess her and other ships like her, and all the goods in her holds. For a hundred years or more they looked for Kilibob everywhere.

Kilibob now decided to become the God of the Europeans. (They called him God but the natives were to call him Kilibob.) God-Kilibob's first act was to appear to Moses in or as the Burning Bush and give him the Ten Commandments. The people were not to be arrogant in their personal dealings, abuse others, steal, fight, or commit adultery. They were to live soberly and amicably together. Moses relayed these instructions to the Europeans, who obeyed them and were accordingly rewarded with gifts of cargo.

In Tagarab's doctrine, Jesus Christ played a relatively unimportant part. He was the son of God-Kilibob, who sent the Holy Ghost into the womb of the Virgin Mary to cause his conception and birth. As the son of God-Kilibob, Jesus had an established place in Heaven, where he was the guardian of the spirits of the dead. But he was not closely associated with the cargo, which was made by God-Kilibob alone and carried by the ancestors to the ships in Sydney Harbour.[1]

A vital part of Tagarab's teaching was that Satan-Manup held the New Guinea natives in bondage. They had displeased God-Kilibob by refusing the cargo he had created before he left Madang and accepting not only his own inferior products (the indigenous material culture) but also the black arts of love magic and sorcery invented by Satan-Manup. As a result, adultery and feuding were integral features

---

[1] It is implicit in the account that the relationship between Heaven and Sydney was thought to be the same as in the Third Cargo Belief. Heaven was either part of Sydney or above it in the sky but connected to it by a ladder. It is not clear, however, whether Jerusalem was equated with Heaven or regarded as a separate place.

of native life, whereas the Europeans, who had accepted the Ten Commandments, lived in peace with each other. For a long time God-Kilibob had been so angry with the natives because of their stupidity that he had had no desire to return to Madang. It had been very easy for the Europeans to keep him in their own country and monopolize the benefits he could confer.

Now God-Kilibob's attitude was changing. For some time he had relented towards the natives and sent the missionaries to New Guinea to alter their way of life so that they too could get the cargo. But the missionaries had failed to tell the people the truth: that God and Kilibob were one person, the true cargo deity. Instead, they had taught them to pray to Anut (Anus in Milguk),[1] who was only an ordinary human being with no special powers. Thus the natives' prayers had been craftily deflected from the true cargo deity to a fraud, who had no ability to help them even if he were disposed to do so.

Because of this duplicity, God-Kilibob was now going to punish the Europeans by taking away the blessings they had enjoyed and heaping them on the natives instead. He would leave Australia and return to Madang with his ships full of cargo: not only ordinary trade goods but also rifles, ammunition, and other military equipment. These he would hand over to the spirits of the dead, who would appear in the guise of Japanese servicemen. They would bring the goods to the natives by aeroplane and help them drive out the Europeans, missionaries included. At the same time, God-Kilibob would change the colour of the natives' skins from black to white. These events would be heralded by the occurrence of storms and earthquakes of unprecedented severity and number.

Before the cargo could arrive, however, the natives had to fulfil certain obligations to God-Kilibob and the spirits of the dead.[2] Tagarab had a dais built in the bush near Milguk, where he used to summon his followers to hear his teachings. He ordered them to carry on with the outward form of their religious life as they had been instructed by the Lutheran missionaries. Especially were they to obey the Ten Commandments, which were the laws originally given by God-Kilibob to Moses and the basis of the Europeans' material prosperity. Like the

---

[1] That is, of course, the term used by the missionaries for God.

[2] The information about ritual in the cult was given me by Tagarab's sons and followers. Other details are taken from Penglase, 'Report June–September 1942', H.Q. Ramu District, 30 September 1942', A.N.G.A.U. War Diary, Vol. I, No. 8, Appendix 45. But this document is wrong in suggesting that the cult ritual was purely pagan. The investigating officers did not have time to go into details. Penglase's comments were denied by informants.

Europeans, they were to please God-Kilibob by living in peace with one another. They were to eliminate sorcery feuds and brawling by giving up love magic and adultery (the customs invented by Satan-Manup). Furthermore, they were to conduct their church services—singing hymns, praying with their hands clasped, and listening to sermons—in the Lutheran manner. The only difference was that now they should perform these rites in honour of God-Kilibob rather than God-Anut (Anus) and accept Tagarab's version of the Scriptures.

The people were to watch for a star in their dreams, which would mean that God-Kilibob was about to return with his ships. Tagarab would have advance warning of the event through another medium: God-Kilibob had given him a symbol of his arm, a length of iron rod which would transmit messages about the future. In anticipation of the arrival of the cargo, the natives had to build storehouses, which in the future were to be used for keeping it in good condition but were now filled with taro, yams, and other local produce. This food, together with pork and fowls, was set out in the cemeteries as offerings to the ancestors in order to ensure that they appeared as soon as possible. The people awaited the event with mixed feelings, for the prophecy of storms and earthquakes caused a certain amount of fear. But Tagarab told them not to be afraid: those who were loyal to him would not be harmed and would be rewarded with cargo; whereas those who were disloyal to him would have their houses wrecked and would be killed. There were various other features of the cult: all European tools, trade goods, and money in the natives' possession were entrusted to Tagarab's care; and the days of the week were renamed, Tuesday becoming Sunday, Wednesday becoming Monday, and so forth.

The new doctrine won immediate acceptance in the area around Milguk. The natives waited for the promised star in their dreams, and spoke of Tagarab and his supposed association with God-Kilibob with bated breath. In view of the imminence of the cargo's arrival—and also because the A.N.G.A.U. Administration was too preoccupied to patrol the region—gardens, roads, and villages were neglected.[1] Finally, about August 1942, after much praying, preaching, offering of food in the cemeteries, and other religious activities, Tagarab summoned the people to the dais and prophesied that the cargo would arrive in aircraft piloted by the Japanese (who would be the spirits of the dead) in a very few days. There was renewed excitement: more

[1] There is no suggestion in Penglase's or my informants' statements that gardens and pigs were wantonly destroyed. Gardens were neglected as they were no longer necessary; and pigs were killed as food offerings to the ancestors.

food offerings were set out so that the ancestors should not go hungry at this special time; and church services were intensified. But nothing came of it and some natives began to lose faith.

The cult was temporarily broken up about September 1942, when the A.N.G.A.U. Administration at last got wind of it and found time to take serious action. Tagarab, however, received advance intelligence of the coming of the raiding party and escaped. His lieutenants and many of his other followers were arrested and gaoled. Tagarab was, in fact, never caught by the A.N.G.A.U. Administration. He kept hidden until the arrival of the Japanese when, as will be seen, he was able to regroup his followers and become again an important power in the new political situation.

The Administration's intervention was too late to have any lasting effect. Tagarab's cult was already firmly established in most of the villages near Milguk—O'u, Molsihu, Efu, Ulugun, and Barahim—and down towards the Gogol Valley. It had aroused interest in the Bagasin Area, mainly among the Kein and northern Girawa, although they were not directly involved at this stage. Also in Madang and the area bordering Letub country,[1] it had drawn off those who had previously experimented with Letub but did not feel at home with Letub doctrine, which contradicted their own belief that Kilibob rather than Manup was the cargo deity of the pre-Christian era. (See Map VI.) Indeed, there was some rivalry between the adherents of the two cults. The Letubists regarded Tagarab as a false prophet because he claimed that Kilibob, whom they regarded as a nonentity, was the cargo source. He was delaying the return of Jesus-Manup. Tagarab and his supporters made counter-accusations against the Letubists: that they were following Manup, who was Satan, and keeping New Guinea in servitude to him by observing his customs. Tagarab cited the body-swaying of Letub men, which he associated with adultery.[2] This promoted sorcery feuds and brawling, which were the most serious offences forbidden in the Ten Commandments and did more than anything else to prevent the return of God-Kilibob.

The overall development of the Cargo Movement in the southern Madang District on the eve of the Japanese Occupation can be summed up in these terms: Virtually the whole native population was familiar with at least one of the cargo beliefs propounded and the idea that Europeans were hiding the cargo secret. The peoples of the outlying

[1] As at Barahim village, for instance, where in 1941 there had been a Letub 'conference'.
[2] I cannot say if this assertion was true, although, as noted, sexual licence was a feature associated with some traditional dances in the Madang area.

areas (in most of the Bagasin Area, in the Ramu Valley, and on the Rai Coast), apart from their own initial and probably fleeting identification of Europeans with deities or spirits of the dead, had heard of the Third Cargo Belief and the general opinion that the missionaries were cheating them. Around Madang itself, where the natives had passed through the consecutive stages of the First, Second, and Third Cargo Beliefs, there were now the two revisionist doctrines of the Fourth Cargo Belief, which professed to have discovered the hidden secret: that of the Letub mainly in the area north of Madang—in the villages bordered by Sek, Halopa, and Ramba—but also in Bilbil to the south; and Tagarab's doctrine in the area to the south-west, in the villages inland from Yabob. (See Map VI.) Differences in doctrine—especially between the Third and Fourth Cargo Beliefs, and the two versions of the Fourth Cargo Belief itself—although they had some local significance, were not of overriding importance in the total situation. The recurrent theme of Christian teaching in both the Third and Fourth Cargo Beliefs gave the majority of the natives a sufficiently uniform system of ideas for the events that now occurred to be interpreted in a relatively consistent way.

### Native Reactions to the Japanese Occupation

When Japanese troops landed in Madang on 18 December 1942, the natives were hardly taken by surprise. During the previous eleven months, the war had surged all around the area and the Australian forces remaining were obviously too small to resist any serious attack. There were continual prophecies and rumours that the new occupation was about to begin. The inland natives, who had not been involved in the cargo activities near Madang, believed that God had brought the war to New Guinea to punish the Europeans for their dishonesty. Tagarab and the Letubists were more specific: they claimed that the Japanese were the spirits of the dead, or special human beings, sent by God-Kilibob or Jesus-Manup with military equipment to liberate the people from European rule, and help establish a more prosperous way of life. The people were not to be afraid of them but welcome them with gifts of food and offers of any services they required.[1]

According to one eye-witness account,[2] at the very beginning the

---

[1] Europeans who left the area at this time have told me of the huge amounts of food prepared for the Japanese by the natives. It did not seem as if the natives were merely being polite to their new rulers. They expected them, and regarded them as something rather more than ordinary human beings.

[2] Mr Franz Moeder, who lived in Madang for about three months under the Japanese before escaping to the Allied lines.

Japanese did not behave in the friendly manner expected of them. They regarded the natives as cheap labour and treated them accordingly. But soon their attitude changed and they adopted a policy of fraternization. Although they could not fulfil native hopes of huge presents of trade goods, having brought none themselves and finding the stores in Madang already looted, they made promises which appeared to corroborate those of Tagarab and the Letub leaders. The Germans and Australians, they said, had treated the natives badly, robbing them of their land and doing nothing to help them materially. The Japanese had come to give them a better way of life and a higher standard of living. On the Rai Coast, they went as far as stating that after the war there would be a policy of intermarriage between themselves and the natives. On Karkar Island, they established a school, where native children were taught Japanese and Japanese servicemen were taught Pidgin English. The school was used as a centre for disseminating propaganda for the Greater East Asia Co-Prosperity Sphere. Natives from all over the Madang District were encouraged to attend.

Native reactions to the Japanese varied considerably. There were those who showed the greatest loyalty to the Australian Administration and the missions. Some escaped to join their old employers or the Allied forces. Others remained behind but behaved with tremendous dignity and courage. When the missionaries were interned, some natives protested openly against the humiliation they were made to suffer. When the Japanese forced the people of Nobanob village to bring them the cattle at the Lutheran Mission Station at Amron and offered them a heifer as payment for the work, the *Luluai* refused it, declaring that the beasts did not belong to the natives and, as Christians, they did not wish to steal.[1] There was the Nobanob teacher who had struggled incessantly to keep his congregation from joining the Letub and collaborating with the enemy. Dissident members of the congregation captured him and, when he steadfastly refused to recant, handed him over to the Japanese as a traitor. He was slowly roasted to death over a fire. Again, there were loyal supporters of the missions who tried to remain practising Christians. They were arrested because it was alleged that their prayer meetings were the occasions for subversive discussions. They defended themselves on the grounds that they were praying only that their country might be spared further horrors of war, and were eventually acquitted.

Others maintained a strictly neutral position, which was summed up

[1] Inselmann. *Letub*, op. cit., p. 134.

by one informant who told Japanese officers: 'We natives are like women. First came the Germans and we were married to them. Then came the Australians and we were married to them. Now you Japanese have chased out the Australians—and we are married to you. Do not ask us to do things of which we should be ashamed.' Such men did what they could to protect themselves and their fellows without actively collaborating. They obeyed the Japanese without volunteering to help them. They taught the soldiers Pidgin English, which was essential if there were to be any sort of administration. They allowed themselves to become headmen and acted as buffers for their people. Some of them at least tried to ameliorate the lot of Allied prisoners by dissuading other natives from molesting them or attending their executions, as they were encouraged to do by the Japanese.

There were, however, very many natives who wholeheartedly collaborated with the enemy. Some did so because of bad personal experiences with Europeans in the past but the majority because, as avid participants in the recent cargo cults, they were convinced that the Japanese had come as liberators. They plundered European houses and stores. They willingly offered their services as spies and scouts in the new Native Police Force. Most prominent, of course, were Tagarab, Kaut, and their various henchmen, who were given high ranks in the Police Force, their sense of importance being enhanced by the Japanese swords they wore as symbols of office. Kaut claimed to have realized his original ambition. He assembled Letub followers and told them that the Japanese had recognized him as King of Madang and assigned him one of the European boats captured in the harbour.[1]

As the collaborators literally believed that their hope of a better future lay with their new masters, they did everything they could to please them. They told their followers that if the Japanese were to 'open the road of the cargo', which the Europeans had persistently 'closed', they must help them conquer all New Guinea. They must help kill or drive out every white man or woman, regardless of nationality or status: Australian, German, American, serviceman, or civilian. As a result, many ugly incidents occurred. Allied airmen and other prisoners (including natives) captured in the bush were bound hand and foot, slung on poles, and carried in to the Japanese. It is said that while they were ceremonially beheaded, the natives held dances in honour of the event.

[1] Inselmann, ibid., p. 132. As Inselmann comments, Kaut probably elaborated Japanese statements to his own advantage. In any case, at the beginning of the Occupation the Japanese spoke no Pidgin English and communication was limited.

On the Rai Coast, there were several acts of native collaboration which had serious repercussions after the war. With the fall of Madang, the small A.N.G.A.U. detachment at Saidor, with the Lutheran and Catholic missionaries from Biliau and Gumbi, withdrew across the Finisterres. The only Europeans left in the area were the coastwatchers, one party at Maibang and the other on the upper reaches of the east bank of the Nankina. After the Japanese had taken over the Rai Coast seaboard, the natives east of the Nankina remained loyal to the Administration, mainly because of close personal ties with one of the coastwatchers. West of the Nankina, the Ngaing (except the Sibogs for reasons explained below) remained neutral. With the Nurton incident still in their memories, they were not prepared to antagonize Europeans again. As they were rarely visited by the Japanese, it was not hard for them to maintain this position. But along the coast, although some of the Som supported the Allies, the Sengam and Gira sided openly with the Japanese.

There were two reasons for Sengam and Gira disloyalty. First, as their villages were occupied, their very existence depended on some measure of collaboration. The Japanese made the usual propaganda for good relations but also left it quite clear that they would not tolerate disobedience. Second, although the Sengam and Gira had never actively participated in the Letub Cult, they were aware of its doctrine and objectives. Thus they were quickly won over to the policy of collaboration in Madang. Early in 1943, they were visited by trade friends from Biliã and other Madang villages, who urged them to help the Japanese. (But there was still no attempt to establish the Letub Cult on the Rai Coast at this stage.) At least one Sengam native left home for Madang to seek his fortune under the new regime. He became an important contact man for the Japanese.

As a result, during 1943, the Sengam and Gira were responsible for three acts of hostility against the Allies. A party of Sengam natives led a Japanese patrol to Maibang, the coastwatchers escaping only by a hair's breadth. A Gira native led the Japanese in an abortive raid on the coastwatchers on the inland east bank of the Nankina. Finally and most important, a Sengam native—a Lutheran mission helper who had assumed leadership under the Japanese—persuaded the Sibog natives to kill three coastwatchers in the interior.

This man had summoned a meeting of Galek natives and their inland trade friends, the inhabitants of Sor, Paramus, and Sibog. Brandishing a Japanese sword, he relayed the propaganda that had recently come from Madang: that the Japanese had to be received as friends who would bring the cargo withheld by the Europeans; and that the people should help them by killing all the white men they could find. He then directed their attention to the coastwatchers known to be operating in the upper Nankina region.

The people of Sor and Paramus refused to take any action. They had decided on a policy of neutrality and their relations with the people of Galek, in spite of the old trade tie, had become strained since their adoption of Catholicism after 1933.[1] But the Sibog people, who were at the time relatively unsophisticated and, like the Sengam, had become Lutherans, were easily persuaded. They returned home and made plans to kill Lieut. Bell and his party, who were encamped near their village. Bell apparently heard about the conspiracy and shot one of the natives involved, but thereafter he and the others were murdered. The Sibog people were severely punished after the war.

Apart from giving practical assistance to the enemy, the Madang collaborators carried on with their cargo cult activities. Still believing that the new occupation was the fulfilment of their prophecies, Tagarab, Kaut, and the other leaders kept up their various rituals in the hope that even more Japanese soldiers and larger supplies of military equipment would arrive to ensure the final defeat of the Allies and the establishment of the more prosperous future. Their following was increased. For instance, after the death of the Nobanob teacher mentioned above, many members of his congregation, who had previously been loyal to the Lutheran Mission and Administration largely because of his efforts, went over to the Letub. Even Nobanob, the centre of the congregation, succumbed.

As far as is known, there were few changes in the rubric of cargo rituals during this period. Contrary to what might have been expected, contact with the Japanese had very little effect for, although they taught their language, they seem to have done little to disseminate their religion. The humiliation and deportation of the missionaries in 1943 probably led to modifications in the Letub in the immediate vicinity of Sek where, according to some informants, the Christian elements of the cult were eliminated and Manup was honoured as a purely pagan god by means of traditional or quasi-traditional ritual (especially the Letub dance). Food offerings to the spirits of the dead were, of course, continued. But among the inland groups which had had to purchase rights to the Letub, the ritual seems to have remained

---

[1] The details are explained in Chapter V. Sengam evangelists were said to have been angry because they failed to convert the Ngaing and other inland natives, who were their trade friends.

syncretic. These people knew too little about the underlying pagan mythology to make innovations on their own. Tagarab's ritual was never altered. His followers claim that elements of Christianity (especially the Ten Commandments) were so crucial to his doctrine that they could not have been easily eradicated.

Relations between natives and Japanese continued to be friendly until the tide of war turned. But when, in 1944, Saidor fell to the Americans and the Australians moved up to Shaggy Ridge, they became strained. The Japanese were hard pressed and, in areas where their troops were engaged in military operations, demanded an ever-increasing supply of labour, for which they no longer bothered to pay. Failure to co-operate was swiftly and severely punished. As the Allied armies advanced, the position became worse. Completely disorganized and without food or other necessities, the retreating Japanese became desperate. They robbed gardens, coconut groves, and banana and sugar-cane plantations. They stole pigs, dogs, and fowls. Finally, they shot and ate natives themselves.[1]

During these days, those natives who could ran away to the bush. Their leaders were powerless to protect them. Tagarab is said to have protested to the Japanese about their behaviour. He told them that he was responsible for their coming and had helped them because he had believed that they were his people's friends. But now he would support them no longer. He would work, through his ritual, for the arrival of the Americans and Australians. The Japanese curtly replied that they too had finished with his services, and had him shot at once to discourage any further native disturbance. Very soon afterwards Allied troops reoccupied Madang.

### The Bagasin Rebellion

It was remarked earlier that the recapture of Madang in April 1944 was regarded by the natives as a mixed blessing. Although the loyalists were pleased—especially to see their kinsmen return from war service —the majority were at best cynical. They were not unduly perturbed by the arrest and imprisonment of Kaut and the other collaborators. Little else could be expected and, especially around the town where the people had suffered most, the view was widespread that these men had been failures. The Japanese, from whom they had been promised so much, had behaved worse than their previous masters. They too

---

[1] Japanese cannibalism is well attested by natives not only throughout the southern Madang District but also in other parts of New Guinea. Even Japanese war dead were not spared.

had to run away and, what was more, far from bringing cargo had pillaged and murdered as they left. Many natives had lost much of whatever property they already possessed.

Yet the Madang natives' change of attitude towards the collaborators and the Japanese did not reflect any greater enthusiasm for Europeans as a whole. The American and Australian soldiers were, of course, popular for their friendliness, but it was realized that they would depart as soon as the campaign was over, and behind them was the A.N.G.A.U. Administration which left no doubt that eventually prewar conditions were to be re-established. There was a grave shortage of trade goods, which even the liberality of the troops could not offset. Moreover, in a few outlying areas, such as the Rai Coast seaboard and the northern Bagasin Area, which had had no unpleasant experiences during the enemy's retreat, the people were still openly pro-Japanese and anti-European. This was especially true of the Sengam and Gira, and Girawa and Kein natives.[1]

It was not long, therefore, before there was further unrest, which again took the form of cargo activity. Whatever opinions they held about their earlier leaders and the Japanese, the mass of the people had not given up their cargo beliefs. But, for obvious reasons, natives in the areas previously most affected by the Cargo Movement could not participate in it now as blatantly as they had done in the past. The Madang people, although they conducted Letub and Tagarabist ceremonies as often as possible, were inhibited by the presence of large numbers of garrison troops at the beck and call of the Administration. Along the Rai Coast, the Sengam and Gira, who as yet had no experience of cult ritual, could do no more than sulk and grumble for fear of the A.N.G.A.U. detachment near Saidor, which had already rounded up and imprisoned their main collaborators.

In fact, the only place left where these conditions did not apply and a serious disturbance could break out unimpeded, was the Bagasin Area. As noted, the people there were still pro-Japanese. Apart from A.N.G.A.U. recruiting patrols, they were entirely ignored by Allied troops. Last and most important, the Japanese had left behind in this region considerable supplies of war material, especially hand grenades.

The new leader who seized the opportunity to exploit this situation

---

[1] The Japanese did not harm the Sengam and Gira when they fled into the Finisterres. It was among the inland Ngaing, M'na, and N'dau that they were forced to adopt ruthless methods to get food. Again, the light forces in the Bagasin Area had withdrawn quickly without leaving havoc in their wake.

was a Kein native, Kaum[1] of Kalinam hamlet (near Sekwari village). Before the war he had been in the Native Police. He claims to have been at Rabaul, the capital of the Mandated Territory, in 1937 during the volcanic eruption which damaged the town, when he had certain visionary experiences. He left the service before 1941 to become *Luluai* of Sekwari. While he was in the Police, he had got to know Tagarab and, although not involved in his cult in 1942, had been one of his very keen followers during the Japanese Occupation. He was the leading collaborator in the Bagasin Area.

After the Japanese evacuation,[2] Kaum took possession of the military equipment left behind. He then assembled a large number of natives from the Bagasin Area (from as far away as E'unime and Kolu in Garialand) and the Gogol Valley, and set up a large camp near Sekwari, which contained between 1,500 and 2,000 people. (See Map VI.) The camp had 109 houses, some of them large enough to hold fifty persons, and was surrounded by a high palisade. Sentries armed with Japanese hand grenades were posted at the main gates and also along the roads leading to them. They were given orders to report the arrival of Europeans to Kaum at once and to capture or, if they put up any resistance, kill Allied native soldiers and policemen. Other natives were provided with wooden imitation rifles. Kaum, helped by his second-in-command Sisumaibu, drilled them as a small army unit.

The new disturbance was, therefore, both a cargo cult and a military uprising. Kaum's intention was to acquire cargo, above all more weapons with which to drive out the Europeans from the District. In theory, his cargo doctrine was that of Tagarab, which he had learnt during the war and then, to the extreme annoyance of the people of Milguk, stolen. The Bagasin Area peoples had no traditional rights to the Kilibob-Manup myth but Kaum tried to justify his theft on the grounds that one of his ancestresses came from Milguk[3] and that God-Kilibob had appeared to him in visions only just after he had done so to Tagarab.[4] Now that Tagarab was dead, he had inherited his position.

---

[1] His real name is Kaumaibu but he is invariably known by the shortened form. He also appears in some literature wrongly as Gomaip.

[2] The following account is based partly on my own field notes, partly on Blood, 'Report of Patrol to Bagasin Area, Madang District', *A.N.G.A.U. War Diary*, Vol. IV, No. 2, H.Q. A22, Appendix E, 21 December 1944, and partly on personal communications from Captain Blood himself and Mr D. Parrish (Department of Native Affairs).

[3] This was almost certainly untrue. The Kein were too far away from Milguk for inter-marriage in the past.

[4] In later years Kaum claimed that his visions occurred in Rabaul in 1937, thereby preceding those of Tagarab.

In practice, however, Kaum's knowledge of Tagarab's doctrine was far from perfect. He was never able to recite the syncretic myth of God-Kilibob's journey to Sydney either correctly or in detail.[1] Furthermore, he never seriously attempted to explain to the mass of his followers the identification of God as Kilibob. This was something he discussed mainly with his lieutenants. Indeed, when preaching to the people as a whole, he normally referred to the cargo deity simply as God[2] and emphasized Christian elements in his ritual. (From now on, therefore, although I refer to his cargo deity as God-Kilibob, it must be remembered that this represented his private belief, which was not fully understood by the majority of his supporters.)

Kaum validated his leadership by asserting that God-Kilibob had already sent him the equipment with which he had armed his soldiers, and that more would come if the people performed his ritual and observed his rules of conduct. Prayers to God-Kilibob and the ancestors had to be recited, and food offerings set out on tables, covered with cotton cloths and decorated with flowers in bottles, in the cemeteries. Gardens were destroyed and pigs wantonly slaughtered to impress the deity and spirits of the dead with the people's poverty, and so ensure that they fulfilled their obligations.[3] The people had to sing hymns from the Lutheran song books. Together with Dabus, a local Lutheran teacher who had become prominent in the cult, Kaum gave them a great deal of religious teaching, most of which repeated Tagarab's instructions about the Ten Commandments. The natives had to live soberly and in peace with each other, especially avoiding sorcery and quarrels over women, which were the main causes of social disruption.[4] To demonstrate their acceptance of the new rules they had to own up to every former transgression. For this purpose, Kaum and Dabus held separate confessional services every Monday.[5] They told the people that when they had satisfied God-Kilibob of their future good intentions, he would turn their skins white to symbolize his covenant with

[1] As is shown by the version he dictated to me in 1950. See my 'Cargo Cult', op. cit., p. 17.

[2] Garia informants who had heard Kaum preach described the doctrine as if it were purely quasi-Christian. Although some of them suspected that a local deity was involved at this stage, they never heard Kilibob's name mentioned. This accounts for and corrects my wrong interpretation of Kaum's first two cults in my 'Cargo Cult', op. cit., and 'The Madang District Cargo Cult', op. cit.

[3] Cf. the Letub belief, p. 94.

[4] Especially in the Bagasin Area, where there is a very strong sorcery complex. See my 'Sorcery among the Garia', op. cit.

[5] The Lutheran Mission had made use of confession in its work in the Bagasin Area before the war.

them. Kaum also hoped to establish schools to take care of the education of the young.

Provided that the above ritual and rules were carried out, God-Kilibob would send the cargo through the spirits of the dead, who would bring it by aircraft rather than by ship so that the predatory Europeans could not steal it *en route*.[1] To help the spirits, therefore, an airstrip and storehouses were built in the bush. First would arrive rifles and ammunition to replace the dummy weapons with which some of the troops were now armed. Then would arrive European foodstuffs and other luxuries. Finally, God-Kilibob would send back an army of Japanese. To reinforce this claim, Kaum could point to two Japanese already in his camp. They were stragglers from Finschhafen and remained at Sekwari for several months.

With the Japanese as allies, Kaum planned to attack Madang. But the natives had to be ready for the war. Thus a great deal of time and energy was spent in drilling the troops. Military exercises took up every morning. After midday the soldiers rested. The late afternoons and evenings were devoted to prayers and religious instruction, which very often lasted till the small hours of the morning. As the months passed, Kaum's talk became more undisciplined and incoherent. He prophesied the destruction of Sek by fire and, as his self-confidence became inflated, styled himself first as Captain, then as King, and finally as Jesus Christ.

The Bagasin Rebellion came to a sudden end on 4 November 1944, when Captain N. B. N. Blood led a party of native police and European troops to Kaum's stronghold. The operation was a long one: it began on 20 October, and involved careful planning and strategy, including the sending in of native spies, who passed themselves off as supporters of the cult and brought back information about the disposition of sentries and general state of preparedness in the camp. Eventually the Administration troops moved in during the early hours of the morning, while Kaum was haranguing his followers. The two Japanese had already departed but Kaum and his lieutenants were arrested. Kaum, who was absolutely fearless in the presence of his captors,[2] was imprisoned for nine months, for spreading false reports and being in illegal possession of firearms.

[1] Cf. the Letub belief, p. 94.
[2] Mr D. Parrish, one of the officers who arrested Kaum, has told me that during the subsequent interrogation Kaum refused to be pinioned by native policemen, but stood erect and proud before Captain Blood and gave his statement without holding anything back. This is supported not only by my personal knowledge of Kaum but also by his statement recorded in Blood's report.

The defeat of the Bagasin Rebellion saw the end of the first phase of the Cargo Movement in the southern Madang District. As has been shown, virtually the whole native population was united in anti-European sentiment and had, in the Third and Fourth Cargo Beliefs, a roughly uniform ideology. So far, despite the dissemination of doctrine, actual cargo activity had been carried out on a limited regional basis under the direction of purely local leaders, who had their own idiosyncrasies of doctrine and were at times divided by petty rivalries. But with the death of Tagarab, and the imprisonment and discrediting of Kaut and Kaum, the Movement was left without leaders of any standing. Thereafter it moved into a second phase, in which it crystallized around a new leader from an area hitherto regarded as a backwater: a man who was so far removed from the cabals of Madang that, although it was quite outside his original intention, he automatically appealed to the people as a whole and so transcended sectional differences. How this came about as the result of a series of accidents is described in the following chapters.

# CHAPTER V

# THE NEW PHASE

WHEN the Civil Administration took office in January 1946, it realized that it had to face considerable problems but, certainly in the southern Madang District, it did not fully understand their nature and complexity. Apart from the work of material reconstruction, which was largely a matter of efficient utilization of money, technical skill, and time, it was appreciated that the recurrent labour troubles (such as the strike in Madang which coincided with the demobilization of A.N.G.A.U.), the periodic expression of pro-Japanese feeling, and the outbreaks of cargo cult such as the Bagasin Rebellion demanded special administrative attention. But there was no real comprehension of what lay behind these disturbances. None of the officers knew about the existence, let alone the history, of the different cargo beliefs described, and none of them had ever had the time or curiosity to examine the epistemological bases of the cargo ritual which had come within their experience. They regarded cargo cult as mere *kanaka* absurdity, a farrago of greed and superstition, and attributed all forms of unrest, both secular and religious, to the cunning of unscrupulous demagogues and prophets, who exploited the gullibility of the rank and file to line their own pockets and satisfy their own lust for power. That both leaders and led might be acting in terms of, and might be sustained by, an elaborate and consistent intellectual system had never been given the slightest consideration.

Thus, although the Administration cannot be accused of complacency, many of its officers were prone to assume that their difficulties could be overcome by what they regarded as sound, well-tried, routine procedures more easily than was, in fact, possible. Moreover, they believed that when the new liberal policy that was now being inaugurated was fully understood, with education and political progress, and increased economic advantages from War Damage Compensation and cash crops, native antagonism would disappear and confidence in the Australian Government be restored. The immediate problem was to disseminate propaganda to neutralize the irresponsible demagogues and cargo prophets, and eradicate pro-Japanese sentiment.

PLATE 4

(a) *left:* Native Lutheran church near Madang (1952)

(b) *right:* Yali at Yabalol (1956)

A certain amount could be done by the officers themselves but it was recognized very soon that for propaganda of this type to be really effective it must come from accredited native leaders. What was needed was natives who understood and supported the Administration's new aims, who had the respect of their own people, and who could go among them, patiently explaining what was being done and what was being planned for their future. The most likely recruits for such positions were the native soldiers, who had demonstrated exemplary loyalty during the war. Their experience and good relations with Europeans, their discipline and sense of service—these surely were the qualifications needed for the years of reconstruction ahead.

As it happened, a man of exactly this type had emerged in the southern Madang District. Not only the natives but also many Europeans were quick to appreciate his potentialities, and already by the time the Civil Administration had been installed he was an acknowledged power in the new political situation. Eventually he became perhaps the most controversial native leader in post-war New Guinea. As the development of the Cargo Movement was from now on inseparable from his career, we must consider his life story, and his character and personal outlook, in some detail.

### Yali's Early Career, c. 1912–45 [1]

The new leader, Yali of the Rai Coast, was born in the Ngaing bush area of Sor, a member of Walaliang patriclan and Tabinung (Jatko)[2] matriclan, about 1912.[3] His father was respected in the community as a leader for his mastery of traditional sacred knowledge, and prowess in warfare and other major activities. Yali, however, by his own account, never achieved status along traditional lines. As a boy, he was fully initiated into the Kabu Ceremony but was never properly trained in garden ritual, sorcery, or other similar skills. As he left home at a relatively early age to work for Europeans and spent much of his life until 1945 in close association with them, he never bothered to fill this gap in his education.

Yali's later childhood and adolescence saw the extension of Administration authority and mission influence on the Rai Coast. At about the

---

[1] Unless otherwise acknowledged, all information about Yali was given me by himself when I was living in his village in 1956. The most important supplementary source was official records.

[2] A red and black parrot.

[3] The date is conjectural. There was no Sor Village Book when Yali was born. His birth was therefore unrecorded.

time of his birth, only the seaboard was under full control, but during the 1920's the neighbouring bush groups of Amun, Sor, and Paramus were brought within the administrative organization, being concentrated in three villages (bearing the same names) and placed under official headmen. Sengam natives, and possibly a few Ngaing, had entered European employment under German rule, but it was only during and after the First World War that the bulk of the Ngaing began to be seriously recruited.

As already described, two Lutheran Mission groups were active on the Rai Coast after 1922–3. The party of Yam evangelists led by the Samoan Congregationalist worker was successful in converting the coastal natives. The Ulap native mission helpers established themselves in the inland Nankina area around Sibog. But neither group was warmly received by the Ngaing as a whole or other sub-coastal peoples. This was partly because there were too few evangelists to cover the area effectively and partly because the sub-coastal natives were unwilling to give up their Kabu Ceremony and dance (*ola*), which, as had been decided at the Nobanob Native Elders' Conference in 1923, was essential for full conversion to Lutheranism. The evangelists put what pressure they could on the Ngaing, promising rewards in Heaven and on earth and prophesying damnation in Hell, but failed to make any headway.

About 1928, or perhaps a little earlier, Yali went to Wau as an indentured labourer. He served as bar boy or waiter in the hotel. He enjoyed the work, especially the alcohol with which he and his fellow native employees appear to have been clandestinely supplied. His only complaint was about the amorous advances of some of the male Europeans in the hotel to himself and other natives of his own age.[1] Even so, he was not particularly upset and seems to have shrugged the matter off as a puzzling, if annoying, hazard of service with white men. It certainly did not warp or embitter his subsequent relations with them.

During his period at Wau, Yali for the first time heard cargo talk and expressions of antagonism to Australian rule. Several natives, who had recently been in prison for participating in the Rabaul Strike of 1929, came to work on the goldfields. One of them was Tagarab of Milguk, who for a while cultivated Yali's acquaintance on the grounds that they were both from the same general area and virtually trade

---

[1] Neither male nor female homosexuality is a feature of southern Madang District cultures. It is restricted to ex-labourers who have learnt the practice in the compounds.

friends.[1] Tagarab had a great deal to say about the Rabaul Strike. Although he did not emphasize its religious background, he described the general feeling among the policemen and labourers that their European employers were both underpaying them and holding back the cargo sent them by their ancestors. Yali claims to have taken very little interest in the affair. He was young and not personally involved. He was primarily concerned with seeing the world, drawing his pay, and enjoying life. Furthermore, when he left home the Ngaing, although familiar with cargo doctrines, had not been unsettled by them, and so the full significance of Tagarab's remarks was lost on him.

Yali returned to the Rai Coast about 1931 and became *Tultul* of Sor village. He was now personally involved in the wider concerns of the Administration and missions. As a *tultul*, he had access to the Patrol Officers in the area and enjoyed extremely cordial relations with them. The Administration was by now beginning to push its authority into the hinterland and Yali accompanied many of the patrols. He was with Patrol Officer Nurton on two important occasions: first, about 1932, when Nurton dispersed the religious gathering at Sibog at which the Second Coming of the Lord and the arrival of cargo appear to have been prophesied; and second, in 1936, when Nurton led his ill-fated expedition to Aiyawang village.

With the establishment of Gumbi Station by the Roman Catholics in 1933, the mission situation on the Rai Coast became more complex. There were strong objections to this move from the Lutherans, who claimed that religious rivalry would disrupt their evangelistic work. But the natives of the sub-coast—including the Ngaing and inland Gira—were quick to recognize that there were advantages to be gained. Although they would be under considerably greater pressure to be converted, with two missions to beg their favours, they would be able to bargain for more favourable terms.

Yali claims to have been partly instrumental in bringing the Catholics to the sub-coast. While he had been at Wau, he had met natives from the Rabaul area who had asked him if the Rai Coast had yet been brought under mission influence. He replied with some bitterness that the Lutherans were trying to convert his people, and were always urging them to give up their Kabu Ceremony and dance. The Rabaul natives expressed surprise and told him that they had the

[1] In effect, they had no true partnership, their villages being only indirectly linked in this way. But in the labour compounds, it is usual for natives to make use of such tenuous ties to build up a network of personal relationships in the new situation.

Catholic Mission, whose priests were quite lenient towards native religious ceremonies. Above all, they did not prohibit native dancing. Thus, when a Catholic priest arrived on the Rai Coast, Yali, the *Luluai* of Masi (a village west of Maibang), and other returned labourers who had heard similar reports about the tolerant attitude of his mission, contacted him and invited him to work on the sub-coast. They informed him they would be interested in becoming Catholics as long as they were allowed to keep their Kabu Ceremony and dance.

Accordingly, the Ngaing and inland Gira now adopted Catholicism. The new priest, left in no doubt about their motives, behaved with extreme caution. He placed catechists in all the important centres[1] but gave them the strictest orders not to force the pace of conversion. During the nine years of his incumbency (1933–42), he made no attempt to baptize any of the natives. He was most circumspect in all matters concerning the traditional religion, adopting the policy of not trying to change or eliminate any of its beliefs and rituals until he had learnt as much about them as he could.[2] The whole issue of the Kabu Ceremony he very prudently kept at arm's length, suggesting at most that the people should give up only those parts of it which were held secret from the women but not, apparently, being unduly disturbed if they failed to do so.

As has been seen, however, these precautions did not halt the spread of the Third Cargo Belief.[3] The Ngaing now heard it not only at second hand from Lutheran sources on the beach and in the Sibog region but also directly from their own catechists. As a result, they voluntarily gave up their old totemic beliefs and allegiances in favour of the Christian Story of the Creation, which they interpreted in terms of traditional concepts: Adam and Eve were regarded as universal totems (*sapud* or *supud*) for all mankind.[4] Also they paid particular attention to the care of their cemeteries and used to visit them after church services in the hope that gifts had been left there by the spirits of the dead.

Yali himself showed little interest in the Catholic Mission after it

[1] In the Ngaing-Neko area: one catechist for Sereng, Gabumi, and Aiyawang; one for Maibang, Goriong, and Damoing; and one for Sor, Paramus, and Amun.

[2] Fr A. Aufinger, the priest concerned, made extensive ethnographic studies around Amun. His material was lost during the war, and our knowledge of the Rai Coast is thereby the poorer.

[3] The priest was unaware that it was being spread.

[4] In 1953, when I first visited the Rai Coast, many younger Ngaing had difficulty in re-calling their matriclan totems.

had started work in his area and, certainly at this stage, ignored cargo talk. Moreover, at about the end of 1936 or the beginning of 1937, his wife died. He had been very much attached to her and was considerably upset. He decided to leave home again, resigned his office as *Tultul* of Sor, and joined the Police Force. As a recruit, he went to the Police Training School at Rabaul and saw the earthquake. After his training, he was drafted to Lae. He served at Wau, in the Markham Valley, and in the Huon Gulf area generally, during the next three years. He was in Lae at the outbreak of war in Europe in 1939 and, like many other natives, soon knew about it, in spite of the Administration's efforts to keep it secret, by picking up bits of careless European gossip.

During these years in the Police Force, Yali had two kinds of experience which later greatly influenced his career. First, on his own admission, he witnessed and was allowed—even encouraged—to indulge in brutalities for which native police have always had a bad reputation: the beating up of male prisoners and the rape, or forcible seduction, of female prisoners. According to his own account, the native policemen kept watch while the officers went to the female prisoners; and then the officers would do the same for the policemen.[1]

Second, in the Police Force he again heard cargo talk and expressions of dislike of Europeans. There was still much grumbling about rates of pay. Yali's comrades were all sure that the cargo secret, which was rightfully theirs, was being withheld. It was believed to be hidden somewhere in Christianity and the missionaries were accused of not having revealed it. As the news of the European War became more widespread, many policemen were talking openly among themselves about the need to rid New Guinea of the Australians and replace them with other masters who would be more likely to 'open the road of the

[1] As he states in his Foreword, Mr J. K. McCarthy has reservations about Yali's statement. He says that, although the practice described may have been more common in the early years of the Mandate, certainly after 1930 discipline was very strict. I accept Mr McCarthy's statement as a general view—certainly in the case of the officers (many of whom, as I have already remarked, were men of the highest integrity) but with more hesitation in the case of native police when they were not under direct European supervision. The actions of Nurton's police at Saing in 1936 should not be forgotten. Moreover, although incidents of the kind mentioned may have been infrequent in 1937, when Yali joined the Force, I do not regard his claim as necessarily invalid. As Mr McCarthy says, we cannot deny that such incidents *ever* happened. It needed only one such experience under a European officer for Yali or any other native policeman to regard it as fully sanctioned behaviour. It is possible, too, that Yali was quoting older policemen's experience as if it were his own. But Mr McCarthy's caution should be borne in mind in other contexts where I refer to Yali's statement.

cargo'. One of the ringleaders of this talk was said to be Mayeng, son of Bumbu, Paramount *Luluai* of Busama, near Lae.[1]

Later, during 1940–1, reports began to reach Lae of increasing Letub activity near Madang. The people of Bilbil[2] had expected ships to arrive with cargo, and had destroyed their pigs and gardens, and cut down their betel nut and coconut palms, to hasten the event. Yali, now older and more reflective, began to take an interest in these affairs and the talk associated with them, and relate them to what he had heard from Tagarab ten years earlier and the mission helpers on the Rai Coast before he had joined the Police. His curiosity was stimulated by the war rumours he had heard in Lae. About August or September 1941, he went on his first three months' leave. He travelled by ship to Madang and then walked down to Saidor by the coastal road. Although he knew nothing about the underlying Letub mythology, he wanted to go through Bilbil and see for himself the way in which the people had destroyed their property. He slept a night in the village, looked cursorily at the stumps of the palm trees and, without asking the local people about what they had done, went home to enjoy an otherwise uneventful leave.

In the following November or December, Yali returned to duty and was stationed in Madang. It will be recollected that another member of the Police detachment in Madang at this time was Tagarab, with whom he had had a fleeting acquaintance at Wau ten years earlier. Together with Tagarab, Yali accompanied the party to Karkar to arrest the natives accused of instigating the Kukuaik Cargo Cult. Like Tagarab, he heard the prophecies in Madang Gaol that the town would soon be bombed, but he did not remain there long enough to witness the event. A day or two before the air raid he was transferred to Lae, but when he heard the news of the attack on Madang and saw the fall of Lae, he had tremendous respect for the visionary capacity of the native mission worker he had helped arrest.

As it was, however, from now on Yali was caught up in the war and had little time to speculate about clairvoyance. When Lae was occupied by the Japanese at the end of February 1942, there was chaos on the mainland: native police were openly deserting; labourers were trying to scurry home; and European civilians were being evacuated

[1] For an account of the characters of these two men, see Hogbin, *Transformation Scene*, op. cit., pp. 150–63. It is interesting that the quasi-Christian cargo belief, or something very like it, was current in a heterogeneous group such as the Native Police Force. The Third Cargo Belief in the southern Madang District had its counterparts elsewhere.

[2] Who had the second version of the Kilibob-Manup myth, on which Letub doctrine was based.

as speedily as possible. In the midst of all this, Yali maintained exemplary discipline. He helped Madang and Rai Coast labourers on their journey through the Markham Valley to their own area, and he remained steadfastly loyal to his officers.

After the fall of Lae, Yali made his way with Captain G. C. ('Blue') Harris and other native police by launch to Finschhafen. From there they were sent to ·New Britain to help evacuate refugees. After that they spent a period at Madang and on the Rai Coast during May and June 1942, before proceeding to Talasea (New Britain) for coast-watching duties. Here, in November 1942, they were attacked by the Japanese, who killed one native and two European members of the party. They were withdrawn a month later. Harris and Yali, who were by this time firm friends, reported to Port Moresby, where Yali was promoted to the rank of Sergeant of Police, and were then sent to Queensland for six months' special training in jungle warfare. As could only be expected, this first visit to Australia made a very deep impression on Yali. From our present point of view, his important experiences were: his reactions to the country and its way of life; and the circumstances under which he resigned from the Police and joined the Australian Army.

In Brisbane and Cairns, Yali saw things which he had never before even imagined: the wide streets lined with great buildings, and crawling with motor vehicles and pedestrians; huge bridges built of steel; endless miles of motor road; and whole stretches of country carrying innumerable livestock or planted with sugar cane and other crops. He was taken on visits to a sugar mill, where he saw the cane processed, and a brewery. He listened to the descriptions of other natives who saw factories where meat and fish were tinned. Again, he suddenly became more aware of those facets of European culture he had already experienced in New Guinea: the emphasis on cleanliness and hygiene; the houses in well-kept gardens neatly ordered along the streets; and the care with which the houses were furnished, and decorated with pictures on the walls and vases of flowers on the tables. In comparison, his own native culture—his rudimentary village with its drab, dirty, and disordered houses, the mean paths in the bush, the few pigs that made a man feel rich and important, and the diminutive patches of taro and yam—seemed ridiculous and contemptible. He was ashamed. But one thing he realized: whatever the ultimate secret of all this wealth—and this he understood in very much the same way as other natives—the Europeans had to work and organize their labour supply to obtain it. Again he compared this with native work habits and organization. He felt humiliated by what he considered the deficiencies of his own society.

The system of enlisting natives in the Australian Army in 1943 was not, if we are to accept Yali's information, very carefully controlled. When Yali left the Police and joined the Allied Intelligence Bureau (A.I.B.), the special unit within which the Coast Watching Service was incorporated, he and other recruits were given a propaganda address by a European officer in the following terms: 'In the past, you natives have been kept backward. But now, if you help us win the war and get rid of the Japanese from New Guinea, we Europeans will help you. We will help you get houses with galvanized iron roofs, plank walls and floors, electric light, and motor vehicles, boats, good clothes, and good food. Life will be very different for you after the war.'[1] Like the other recruits, Yali was very much excited by what he had heard. He literally believed that the Administration would remodel New Guinea along Australian lines. He and the others joined up with this thought firmly in their minds.

About June 1943, Harris and Yali returned to New Guinea. They were sent first to Buna, and then somewhere inland from Bongu to watch Japanese troop movements between Madang and Lae. In September, they were in the party which landed at Finschhafen about a week before its recapture by Australian troops. They were then re-drafted to Queensland, first to Townsville and then to Brisbane. There Yali helped train recruits for the A.I.B. at Tabragalba Camp. He was promoted to the rank of Sergeant-Major, higher than which no native could rise in the Australian Armed Forces.

During this period, Allied forces were converging on Madang. Their hold on Papua and southern New Guinea was virtually complete. The High Command now worked out plans to by-pass the Japanese on the north-east coast of the mainland by creating beachheads at Hollandia and Aitape in preparation for the drive for the northern Pacific. It was decided to send in a coastwatching party to Hollandia before the principal landing. Harris was placed in command and Yali was his senior native N.C.O. There were six other Europeans, three other natives from Australian New Guinea, and an Indonesian interpreter—twelve in all.

[1] The address was delivered in Pidgin English. The above text, given me by Yali, may be an exaggeration of the original but there can be no doubt that an address with substantially the same message was made. Yali definitely still believes that this was what he heard. Other natives in the southern Madang District have told me that army recruiting officers made similarly grandiose promises of material rewards for service against the Japanese.

After about five months at Tabragalba Camp, Harris and Yali reported at Finschhafen. The party embarked in the U.S. submarine *Dace* on 18 March 1944 and reached its destination four days later.[1] The landing was dogged by ill luck from the beginning. Much of the equipment was damaged or lost while getting ashore, and local natives almost immediately reported the party's arrival to the Japanese. Eventually there was an ambush, in which Harris was captured and killed, and four others died. Seven of the party managed to escape: three Europeans, the Indonesian interpreter, and three of the native soldiers, one of whom was Yali.

We are not concerned with the individual escape stories of the other members of the party, but that of Yali and Sgt Buka, a Manus native, is of considerable importance. When it was obvious that further resistance was useless, Yali and Buka got away from the battle into the jungle. They had neither food nor matches. Buka was unarmed, but Yali had a carbine and about fifty rounds of ammunition, a bayonet, and a compass, in the use of which he claims to have been proficient. Both had wristwatches and could tell the time. With these slender resources, Yali managed to return from Hollandia to Vanimo and then Aitape by an inland route, arriving after the landing of the main American forces. Buka failed to reach Allied lines. He became very ill, under circumstances to be described later, and although Yali supported him to the end, he was lost somewhere in the hinterland of Vanimo. Yali's escape was, and still is, regarded as one of the native epics of the war in New Guinea. It won him great respect among European troops at the time[2] and, as will be seen later, had an even more significant effect on the natives of the southern Madang District. The distance of the journey was about a hundred and twenty miles, and the time spent in the bush about three months. Yali and Buka existed on the hearts of black palms, bush fruits, any vegetables they could find in gardens, and the few animals they were able to shoot. At one stage, they came upon a Japanese outpost under bombardment by Allied aircraft. They made use of the temporary absence of the Japanese in their slit trenches to rob a house of matches, taro, and other necessities.

Yali appears to have reached Aitape about June or July 1944. After reporting to A.N.G.A.U., he was sent at once to Finschhafen, where he dictated an account of his adventure[3] and spent about two months

[1] For a full account of the operation see Feldt, *The Coast Watchers*, op. cit., pp. 364–374.
[2] Cf. Feldt, ibid., p. 373, who originally organized the Coast Watching Service, and wrote of Yali's courage and resource in the highest terms.
[3] See Feldt, ibid., p. 372.

in hospital. In August or September, he was drafted once more to Brisbane, where he underwent a further six months' training.

On this visit, Yali saw various other aspects of Australian life. With a party of native soldiers he was shown over the Brisbane Zoo and the Queensland Museum. It was at this time also that he heard from a Manus native, Paganau, who was also under training in Brisbane, of the system of 'licensed' brothels in Queensland. Paganau had not been inside one of these houses but had been told about them by some Australians with whom he was on friendly terms.

In February 1945, Yali was sent to Sydney. Here he was shown over the Harbour Bridge, an aircraft repair shop, and the Burns Philp stores and warehouses. He returned to Lae and was posted to New Britain. Between May and July 1945, he was granted leave for at least a month, which he spent at home at Sor on the Rai Coast. He then reported to his unit in Madang. He was sent to Lae and was there when the Japanese War came to an end in August. He spent three months at Nadzab, inland from Lae, and was demobilized in November 1945.

### Yali's Character and Outlook

One of the most significant results of Yali's experiences—especially his wartime experiences—was that they gave the unprejudiced Europeans who liked and supported him a one-sided appreciation of his character and outlook. When he first came to their serious attention during and after 1945, he impressed them at once as an exceptional native. He was of fine physique and much taller than the average native of the southern Madang District, well spoken and dignified without ever being impertinent. He was always scrupulously clean and well turned out, bathing regularly, and wearing a spotlessly white singlet or shirt and immaculately ironed shorts.

These externals set aside, Yali had even greater qualities. In the first place, he had a deep sense of responsibility. At the beginning of the Japanese invasion, when many policemen on the mainland were openly deserting, Yali remained loyal. As he put it himself, he had made his contract to serve in the Police, had always had good relations with Europeans, and saw no reason why he should show bad faith. In action he behaved with consistent gallantry and, as already mentioned, his escape from Hollandia won him the deepest respect. Nor were his loyalties reserved for Europeans. There is no reason to doubt his own word that on the journey from Hollandia to Vanimo and Aitape he gave Sgt Buka every possible support to the end. While he was with Harris on the Rai Coast in May or June 1942, he and a fellow-policeman,

Mas, seduced two women of Sigi (inland from Mindiri). Yali wanted to marry Sunggum, the girl with whom he slept, but Harris persuaded him to wait until after the war. As soon as he was demobilized in November 1945, he went to Sigi and claimed Sunggum as his wife. He learnt also that the girl seduced by Mas had borne an illegitimate son. As Mas had died after the Hollandia raid, Yali adopted the boy.

In the second place, Yali gave the impression of almost complete Western rationality. He genuinely liked Europeans, took pleasure in their company, and wanted nothing more than to count them among his friends. His close personal associations with them as *Tultul* of Sor, policeman, and soldier, and his reputation as a war hero, gave him ease of manner in their presence. He could talk about service and administrative affairs, and his experiences in Australia with a degree of seeming sophistication. Thus generous Europeans regarded him as a native who had really seen into their world: who had grasped some of the essential concepts at the basis of their own culture—hygiene, organization, and hard work.

Yet this was only a surface image below which such Europeans did not probe with sufficient care. They never had long and searching discussions with Yali, and those they did have were of such an elementary nature that it was very easy to put a purely Western construction on everything he said.[1] Yali's was the tragedy of all men who want to assimilate an alien culture, but can see only its externals and hence never leave their own behind. Inevitably, in the testing time, they are forced to turn to their own culture, which alone can provide them with a coherent system of values and concepts. Yali's understanding of Western life was very shallow. He was completely illiterate, and had not attended even a mission school or been baptized.[2] He had been away from home so long that he spoke Pidgin English in preference to Ngaing, but he had no knowledge of English itself. In Australia he was quite unable to discuss what he saw with ordinary

[1] I fully confess that this is wisdom after the event. Indeed, as late as 1956, when I was studying Yali's career in retrospect and was closely associated with him, I still found it difficult to see into his mind. My first impressions were much the same as those of many Europeans in the early post-war period, and it was only after several weeks of continual conversation with him that I realized the truth. Even then my wife had once or twice to prevent me from accepting some of Yali's statements at their face value (i.e. European value). My analysis is *not* intended to bring Yali into public hatred, ridicule, or contempt. On the contrary, he is one of the most remarkable men I have known. Only the strong pressures to which he was continually subjected brought him into conflict with European values.

[2] Worsley, *The Trumpet Shall Sound*, op. cit., p. 218, states that Yali could read and write. This is quite incorrect. At most, Yali had been taught by some of his followers after 1945 to print his name in block letters so that he could sign documents.

K

people and, by all accounts, none of his officers took the trouble to give him careful explanations. During his visits to Queensland, he lived in camp or barracks with other native soldiers. He and they invariably interpreted their experiences in terms of New Guinea cultural idiom.

In the last analysis, Yali's social and intellectual outlook was still that of a southern Madang District native. Although he was certainly a man of deep loyalties, he expressed them solely at a personal level. His sense of obligation was directed towards the individuals with whom he was or had been involved: kinsmen and trade partners, officers under whom he had served, fellow policemen and soldiers, the woman and child for whom he felt directly or indirectly responsible. But although this range of values was considerably wider than its traditional counterpart, it was still primarily egocentric. Yali had no abstract social principles: no true concept of a wider society in which everyone had equal importance and rights irrespective of specific personal relationships with himself.

Although Yali showed only a spasmodic interest in the actual doctrines of the Cargo Movement he heard before the war, it must not be forgotten that they were based on intellectual assumptions which he shared with his own people, which by 1942 were part of his own culture, and which therefore governed his thinking. Although he did not elaborate it precisely, his conception of the cosmic order was the same as that of other natives: a purely physical world inhabited by human beings, spirits of the dead, and two classes of gods (those of European and those of native origin), whose functions were clearly defined.

On the one hand, knowing virtually nothing of the two versions of the Fourth Cargo Belief, he assumed that white men had God and Jesus Christ, who were ultimately responsible for their material culture. This did not conflict with what he saw or otherwise learnt of industrial Australia: the sugar mill, brewery, tinned meat and fish factories, and the aircraft repair shop. He was aware that Europeans could make their own goods, but he nevertheless believed that their God had taught them the requisite secular techniques, just as Rai Coast deities had taught his own people secular techniques for planting and other important activities. Moreover, the Europeans' God could, if properly invoked, supplement human production by sending cargo ready made and direct in times of shortage and adversity. This explained the vast fleets of ships and aircraft which suddenly came to New Guinea during the war. As Yali had good reason to know, in 1942 the Allies had practically no armaments in the area. Yet in a few months they were able to challenge the might of the Japanese. Even allowing for European methods of work and organization, human beings alone could not have turned out so much equipment so quickly. The only explanation was divine intervention.[1]

This sheds considerable light on Yali's personal reactions to the promises he believed were made by the recruiting officer in Brisbane in 1943. Although convinced that the Administration would offer a substantial material reward, he did not imagine that it would reveal the formula for obtaining cargo direct from God, for that was a secret belonging to Europeans. But he did assume that, in return for loyalty and help, some of the goods which were so abundant and could be augmented by special ritual techniques would be made available to his people. The natives would continue to be dependent on Europeans but this was to be the strong bond between the two races. Because of his faith in the integrity of the white men he knew, he was quite content that the goods had been promised and did not worry who had the final control of their source. His confidence had been strengthened by the friendly behaviour of American and Australian troops, and by Army radio broadcasts in Pidgin English, offering the people a better future if only they would assist in driving out the Japanese. On one occasion, it is true, Harris found Yali drinking in one of these propaganda broadcasts and told him not to rely on it. But any doubts Yali had as a result of this were subsequently dispelled when he was invited himself to record a radio talk in Brisbane and was allowed to encourage his people in similar terms. Again, after the Japanese surrender, there was much discussion between Australian and native troops about the Labour Government's plans for reconstruction. Finally, before he was demobilized at Nadzab, Yali attended some form of Army Education lectures for native troops, in which it was intimated that the peoples of New Guinea were to enjoy a higher standard of living now that the war was over. They were to start businesses of their own and, if they needed help, they would get it from the Administration.

[1] As we have seen, Yali was deeply impressed by the fulfilment of the Karkar mission helper's forecast of the imminent bombing of Madang in January 1942, but he did not bother to relate it to any part of his belief system. It merely reinforced his already existing assumptions about the validity of prophecy based on revelation by deities or the ancestors. He also believed that Europeans had special ritual for protection in battle. During a camouflage exercise in Queensland, he and other native troops were taken into a paddock, in which (Yali claims) there were few rocks, undulations in the ground, or trees. The instructor hid himself so successfully that the troops were unable to find him. Although Yali's account is probably exaggerated, he is still convinced that the man became invisible through ritual techniques which he did not reveal.

On the other hand, although he implicitly accepted the tenets of the Third Cargo Belief, Yali had never been so much influenced by them that he had lost his trust in his own religion. When the native soldiers returned home, they naturally talked about their wartime adventures: the actions in which they had fought the Japanese and, above all, how they had escaped death because of their bushcraft and ability to hide. An aspect of the fighting that had impressed some of them deeply was that their casualties had been very light especially in comparison with those of European troops.

The explanation was once more sought in religion. There were, of course, some who believed that native soldiers had been saved by the cunning of God, who had deflected the bullets and bayonets of the Japanese. Yet many of the native soldiers themselves in the last analysis preferred to rely for protection on the well-tried war ritual of the past. They attributed their safe return to their knowledge of the traditional deities, who had given them strength to survive and made them invisible at times of danger. Accordingly, although Christianity in one form or another was still a main basis of cargo doctrine—God, God-Kilibob, or Jesus-Manup being acknowledged as cargo deity—there was now a growing attitude that the 'satans' (the old gods) had performed great services for the people.

Yali himself fully endorsed this view. Before he left the Rai Coast in 1942, he took the precaution of learning the elements of war ritual from some of the old men of Sor and subsequently, according to his own account, made frequent use of it. There were at least two occasions when he believed that his faith in the old religion was wholly justified.

The first incident occurred during his and Buka's escape from Hollandia. On the journey they slept each night under a shelter of boughs. As noted, their only food was what they could find in the bush, until one day they came upon an opened tin of fish by the road. Yali's first reaction was that it was a Japanese booby trap and that the fish had been poisoned. But, as there were no footprints nearby, he decided to try it. Buka, who was a practising Catholic, tried to dissuade him, saying that Satan[1] had put the tin there to deceive them. But Yali risked drinking the fluid from the top of the tin and, as he found it palatable and suffered no ill effects, they both shared the fish. Two

[1] As Buka was a Manus and not a Madang native, Yali could not be sure whether he referred to the Devil of orthodox Christianity or to one of the local deities. Manus religions appear to be very different from those described in this work. See Fortune, *Manus Religion.*

days later, as both of them were still quite well, Buka decided that God had put the tin there to help them.

Some time afterwards they saw a man. Thinking he was a Japanese they ran off but the man did not follow. Yali claims that he vanished and that all they could see was a dog. That night Buka said he saw a man who appeared to turn into a cassowary. He had the same experience the following night also. At first they were mystified but later interpreted what they had seen as the spirit of one of their companions killed at Hollandia, who had followed them to see how they were faring on their journey.

Then occurred the most important episode of the whole adventure. Yali and Buka found a crocodile. Buka at once wanted to shoot it for food. Yali, however, remarked that it was odd that there should be a crocodile in the bush with no river nearby. It was probably, he said, a local deity and they had better respect it as such. Buka replied: 'Let us think only of God. This is meat. You and I must not think about local deities.' Yali gave in. Buka shot the beast in the head and then Yali shot it through the heart. They had cut up the animal and were making a fire to cook the meat when, Yali claims, it became quite dark. They could no longer see each other. Then wild pig, wallabies, cassowaries, possums, and other animals surrounded them, and bared their teeth as if to attack and kill them.

When at last the sun rose, they packed up the crocodile meat—although neither of them had dared eat any—and went on, walking all day. But at sundown they came back to the same shelter in which they had spent the last terrifying night. They did the same thing next day, and now Yali was convinced that the crocodile had been in reality a local deity. They threw the meat away. Yali reproved Buka for thinking only of God and having no respect for the local deities, and Buka became very frightened. Thereafter things went from bad to worse. Buka, now positive that the local deities would kill him for his responsibility for shooting the crocodile, became so ill that Yali had to carry him. They staggered on for several days and by this time were in the hinterland of Vanimo. They heard the sound of shooting nearby and Yali, in the hope that Allied forces might be in the area, left Buka under a tree and went off to get help, marking the trees so that he would know the way to return. He met some retreating Japanese and immediately ran away. But he avoided going back at once to the place where he had left Buka because he did not want the Japanese to follow and capture him. Later, when he judged it safe, he went back to look for Buka but he had disappeared. He searched everywhere but could not find him and at last was forced to give up. He then made his way to Vanimo and finally Aitape. Subsequently he concluded that the local deities had devoured or carried off his companion as punishment for having insisted on the shooting of the crocodile, one of their number. He himself had been saved not by his wits or physical endurance but because, although he was not entirely blameless, he had shown some respect for the old religion.

The second incident occurred in 1944-5, during Yali's third visit to Australia, when he and other native soldiers were shown over the Queensland Museum. The Western exhibits—the old cars, aeroplanes, and pieces of machinery—did not impress or surprise them at all. These were things they expected to see in any case, for they normally associated them with Europeans.[1] But what did shock them was the natural history and ethnographic section of the Museum, where there were showcases containing skeletons of prehistoric animals, and specimens from Papua and New Guinea: face masks from the Sepik, a smoked mummy from the Kukukukus, bows and arrows, and statues of the old gods. Yali and the others stared at these exhibits in silence. At last Cpl Son of Kurog (one of the Letub villages near Madang) found his voice: 'Why', he asked the European officer conducting them, 'do the missionaries urge us to root out the "satans" (Pidgin English, *rausim Satan*), and then other white men come and collect all these things invented by the "satans" (Pidgin English, *ologeta despela samting bilong Satan*) and put them in this Museum?' The officer seems to have made a vague reply by way of explanation, but the soldiers paid little attention to him. It was the question rather than the answer that was important.

Although Yali did not at this stage attempt to give it any specific interpretation, this incident, like Buka's disappearance in the hinterland of Vanimo, helped consolidate his respect for his own religion. It left him with the impression that, whatever the missionaries and native helpers with their superior religious knowledge might have said and done in the past, the general run of Europeans could not hold the pagan gods in utter contempt if they were sufficiently interested to collect and preserve paraphernalia used in traditional religious ceremonies. Thus he adopted a flexible attitude towards Christianity and paganism: each had a legitimate place in the scheme of things he saw. This and his trust in the Brisbane promises of 1943 accounted for many of his actions after his return to civilian life.

[1] They did not, apparently, even recognize that these exhibits were old and out of date. They were merely aeroplanes, cars, and pieces of machinery, as far as they were concerned.

## Yali becomes the New Leader

When he revisited the Rai Coast in the last year of the war, Yali little imagined that within twelve months he would have emerged as the most influential native leader the southern Madang District had ever known. Certainly this had not been his ambition. Yet his rise was meteoric: he swiftly, if fortuitously, won the acclamation of the coastal peoples between Saidor and Sarang; he was given strong support by the Administration; and, although they were less ready to accept him at first, he was eventually recognized by the missions.

Yali was flung into the maelstrom of cargo politics when he went on leave to Sor between May and July 1945. When he reached Finsch-hafen from Aitape, after his escape from Hollandia the year before, he was told by one of the coastwatchers who had worked in the inland Nankina region that the whole native population of his section of the Rai Coast (including the Ngaing) had been disloyal. They had helped the Japanese raid the coastwatchers in Maibang and east of the Nankina, and they had murdered Lieut. Bell, Lieut. Laws, and their half-caste companion near Sibog. As he was particularly concerned that his own people should have a good reputation after the war in view of the reward promised in Brisbane, Yali decided to look into the matter as soon as he got home.

Accordingly, the first question Yali asked his fellow-villagers was why they had turned pro-Japanese. They replied that the majority of the Ngaing had remained neutral. Only the Sengam, Gira, and people of Sibog had openly collaborated. They told him how Sengam and Gira natives had led the Japanese against the coastwatchers, and how the Galek mission helper had persuaded the Sibogs to murder Bell and his party, on the grounds that the Europeans had 'closed the road of the cargo' and the Japanese had come to 'open' it. They also told him that the seaboard peoples were still perpetuating the belief that white men were determined to keep them in a state of poverty and that one day the Japanese would return to liberate them.

Thereafter Yali paid careful attention to the attitude of the coastal natives. They were continually sullen, and their behaviour generally supported what his kinsmen in Sor had told him. He therefore ap-proached the A.N.G.A.U. officer in charge of the Rai Coast and told him how distressed he was that the natives of his own area should conduct themselves so badly. He had been in Australia, where he had been told what the Administration meant to do for the natives in the future, and he knew that the idea that Europeans wanted to keep goods from them was nonsense. The officer replied that it was quite true that the Administration had in mind plans for better conditions for the natives after the war. Although he was circumspect and did not specify the exact nature of these plans, Yali understood his remarks as tacit confirmation of the Brisbane promises. The officer added that he too was extremely worried about the prevailing atmosphere of hostility and suspicion among the coastal people. As Yali had been in Australia, he encouraged him to impress on as many natives as he could the honest intentions of Europeans and the stupidity of believing that they were withholding cargo secrets.

This conversation was overheard by a native of Yaimas village (Gira), who had been hiding under the officer's house. He at once gave an extravagant account of it to his own people: that Yali had discovered that the natives were to get large supplies of cargo after the war. They at once came to Yali and asked him to address them on matters of Administration policy and their own future. As the officer approved the request without any hesitation, a day was fixed for an assembly. Yali had imagined that he would speak informally to a small group of his Nankina-Mot people. He did not realize that word had been sent out for miles around and that a huge crowd of natives from all over the Rai Coast would come to listen to him.

Yali began his speech[1] by describing all he had been through and seen during the war: his actions against the Japanese, his miraculous escape from Hollandia, and his impressions of Australia. Then he went on to reprove the coastal natives for collaborating with the enemy. Why had they done it? The Europeans were not keeping cargo from them. Anyway, had the Japanese given them any cargo? At this point, several Sengam and Gira spokesmen challenged him by stating that the Japanese had treated them well and wanted to 'open the road of the cargo'. Yali cut them short, telling them that the Japanese had never meant to give them anything at all. As he had been saying, the Europeans were not stealing or holding back their cargo and, if the people would only help the Australians drive out the Japanese for good and all,[2] the Administration would reward them when the war was over. He then outlined the Brisbane promises of 1943: the Administration had plans for the natives to have decent housing, electricity, motor vehicles, boats, good clothes, and machinery for tinning their

---

[1] All Yali's speeches paraphrased or referred to in this book were delivered in Pidgin English.

[2] The war was still in progress in northern New Guinea. Also small parties of Japanese were thought to be in hiding in the higher mountains of the Finisterres.

own pigs, game, and fish.[1] These promises, it was true, had been made originally to the soldiers, but, he added, if the civilians would only demonstrate their loyalty, they too would get a share of the benefits in store. They must stop sulking and grumbling, and hoping that the Japanese would return. The Japanese were gone for ever. The people must help get the District in working order again and provide all the labour necessary to support the troops in action. Once more he impressed on the Sibogs their folly in killing Bell and his companions. By this time they and the coastal natives were thoroughly ashamed. Only one Sengam spokesman tried to exonerate his people by explaining how their Madang trade friends had visited them and bribed them to collaborate with promises of huge material gifts in the future.

As was only to be expected, the address made a great sensation. The Rai Coast seaboard peoples swiftly became pro-European. Messengers from Biliau village (Sengam), which had been notoriously pro-Japanese, immediately carried the news to their trade friends in Madang. Very soon they returned with a deputation from Yabob, Bilbil, and Siar, which formally invited Yali to visit Madang and repeat the speech he had recently made. Yali agreed provided that he should first have the permission of the Officer Commanding his unit. He said that he would address them when he reported in Madang at the end of his leave.

About the end of June 1945, Yali went back to Madang. He walked along the coast road and on the last night of his journey slept at Bogati. The people there had already heard the news from the Rai Coast and were keen to talk to him. They revealed to him a great deal about the Third Cargo Belief, and their convictions of the dishonesty of Europeans in general and missionaries in particular.[2] They told him about their pre-war Lutheran missionary Rev. R. Hanselmann, whose memory they still revered. They believed that Hanselmann had been on the brink of disclosing the cargo secret to them, when the other missionaries transferred him to prevent his doing so.

The discussion was charged with bitterness. Yali by now was becoming fully aware of the gulf between Europeans and natives over the cargo issue. Although he did not argue with the Bogatis, the night's experience strengthened his determination to act as the white men's ambassador and try to persuade the people to adopt a more reasonable attitude towards them. Thus when he was given permission

[1] Yali's reference to this machinery was an exaggeration of the promise of better food originally made in Brisbane in 1943.
[2] The Bogati people had the first version of the Kilibob-Manup myth but did not, on this occasion, expound either Tagarabist or Letubist doctrines to Yali.

to speak to the Madang natives at Mis (Sagalau), he included new arguments in his address. After describing his war experiences, upbraiding those who had collaborated with the enemy, and outlining the Brisbane promises, he added bits of information he had heard discussed during the last year or two and attempted to give a more precise explanation of what he had seen in Australia. First, he told the people that in the future Europeans and natives would play sports such as tennis, cricket, and football together.[1] Second, recalling his visits to the sugar mill and brewery, and trying to impress on his audience the present goodwill of the Europeans, he said: 'I have seen the way in which food (*kaikai*) is produced in Australia. The white men will not keep anything secret from us any longer.'[2]

The last remark, which Yali had intended in all innocence, set the seal on his popularity but undermined his whole position from the very beginning. The people were quick to seize on its cargo undertones.[3] After he had departed for Lae towards the end of the war, his address was repeatedly discussed and corrupted in Madang. His claim that he had seen *fesin bilong wokim kaikai* (methods of food production) was soon twisted to mean that he had seen *fesin bilong wokim kako* (methods of cargo production). This, of course, could not be understood in purely secular terms and had to be rephrased in religious idiom. It was openly stated that Yali had discovered the cargo deity: that while he was in Australia he had seen God, God-Kilibob, or Jesus-Manup, according to whether people held the Third or either version of the Fourth Cargo Belief.

Yali, being away from Madang, could do nothing to put an end to this talk, which between July and November became progressively wilder. He became the new Messiah through whom the cargo would come. The most extravagant interpretations were placed on his war career, especially the escape from Hollandia. It was said that he had been killed in this action by the Japanese and had come back as a spirit of the dead. In this capacity he had gone to Australia, where he had seen the King. He had then gone to Heaven, where he had seen God (or God-Kilibob or Jesus-Manup), who had promised him cargo for his people after the war. God[4] would send it to the King,

---

[1] This has to some extent actually happened in Madang, certainly since 1950.

[2] The Pidgin English text of this sentence was: '*Mi lukim fesin bilong wokim kaikai long Australia. Wetman noken haitim samting moa.*'

[3] These undertones were due to careless phraseology, which Yali fully admits, and the fact that cargo talk (Pidgin English, *tok kako*) has its own idiom, which is often capable of several interpretations.

Or, alternatively, God-Kilibob or Jesus-Manup.

who would see personally that it was loaded in the ships and sent direct to New Guinea from Sydney. Yali would then distribute it among the natives. Furthermore, those who had assumed leadership of the Letub and Tagarab's cult were quick to claim association with Yali. They carried on with their rituals as before but now performed them in his honour, regarding him as their intercessor with the cargo deity. In at least one region, popular enthusiasm got out of hand. In August 1945, the people of Halopa (a strong Letub centre in the hinterland of Sek) openly refused to co-operate with the Catholic Mission, whose representatives had by now returned to Alexishafen. They proclaimed that they were followers of Yali, 'the Black King'.

The Administration's support of Yali was less spontaneous, but in the long run it was just as real. While he was at Nadzab, he toyed with a suggestion that he rejoin the Police but gave it up in order to continue the propaganda work he had already begun. He conceived the idea of starting what amounted to a limited rehabilitation scheme on the Rai Coast. Because of the encouragement from European officers while he had been on leave, because nobody had contradicted the speeches he had already made, and because of the generally propitious tone of the lectures he attended before he was demobilized, he now had no doubts about the validity of what he had heard in Brisbane in 1943. His policy would be to urge his people to co-operate with the Administration, rebuild their villages and roads, and try to adopt the living standards he had seen in Australia.

In the meanwhile, the Madang District Office had been somewhat disturbed by reports from the Catholic Mission connecting Yali's name with events at Halopa. For a time it was decided that he should make no more speeches in public. Yet soon the evidence was quite clear that he was in no way personally responsible for the Halopa affair, which in any case did not express antagonism to the Administration. Moreover, the fact remained that the District Officer wanted a native leader to counteract pro-Japanese sentiment and Yali had had a marked effect on native morale. There was still a certain amount of grumbling, and labour troubles were by no means at an end but, especially along the Rai Coast, the people were on the whole much less sullen and were co-operating with the Administration with a far better grace. Thus when Yali returned to the Saidor area about November or December and continued to make his propaganda, the District Officer was by no means displeased. In January 1946, he sent a Patrol Officer to examine the situation and, on receiving a favourable report, allowed Yali to carry on with his scheme.[1] But, at the same time, he cautioned him not to depart from a purely secular programme and, above all, not to get involved in cargo cult. He was to speak out against it and try to put down the ritual wherever he found it. He was to act in a purely private capacity and receive no salary for his work. Yali was quite content with these terms.

Yali's acceptance by the missions was slower and more grudging because of the Halopa incident. The Catholic Mission, whose followers were involved, was at first particularly hostile. With its pre-war experience of the Letub, it distrusted Yali's addiction to making speeches and, most unfairly, was all too prepared to attribute the new disturbance to his desire to stir up trouble, without waiting for a full investigation to be made. Later, however, when Yali had been exonerated and shown to be both pro-European and well disposed towards the missions, and when it became obvious that he was a new power to be reckoned with, the Catholics did everything they could to win his friendship and use him to their advantage. In the same way, the Lutherans, who at this time appear to have been much more open-minded about him, hoped that he would help to spread Christianity and tried to maintain good relations with him.

### The Bases of Yali's Leadership

By early 1946, in the midst of the material and social chaos left by the war, as a result of an almost unique combination of circumstances rather than by his own design, Yali had become the key figure in the southern Madang District. Yet his position was essentially ambiguous. There were at least three distinct interpretations of his leadership.

The natives understood his aims exclusively in terms of the Cargo Movement. He was a superhuman being who had discovered the cargo source: who would see that the cargo deity ushered in the millennium for which they had worked and waited so long. The fact that there was some disagreement about the identity of the cargo deity was irrelevant. Yali, having announced no specific doctrine but merely having made general statements which could be construed in terms of all the different versions of cargo belief current at that time, automatically and unconsciously rose above sectional ideologies and gained a following far larger than his own people of the Rai Coast. In addition, after

---

[1] Apart from the Halopa incident, the District Office was unaware that Yali's propaganda had already been widely reinterpreted as cargo doctrine and that he was regarded as a Messiah. At this stage, natives avoided discussing his affairs with Europeans.

the arrest of the principal collaborators around Madang, the people there had no outstanding leaders. There were no rivals in his way.

The Administration and, to some extent, the missions, being largely unaware of the true nature of the Cargo Movement, and assuming that Yali's apparent willingness to speak out against it meant that he was uninfluenced by its teachings, looked on him as a secular propagandist who would recreate native goodwill and thereby help the work of reconstruction. He would get the people to settle down again and pave the way for the return of routine administration, the new economic, educational, and political reforms being worked out in Canberra and Port Moresby, and the parallel re-establishment of Christian influence. He would prepare the people for the long, slow road to material, social, and spiritual advancement by indoctrinating them with the gospel of hard work.

Yali's point of view was different again. As we have seen, he implicitly accepted the basic assumptions of the Cargo Movement but did not expect the Europeans to reveal their ritual secrets to the natives. He believed that the search for the cargo secret was now no longer necessary because of the Administration's Brisbane promises. There would be a bulk hand-out of goods which, although deriving ultimately from a divine source, would be a secular transaction—at least as far as he and the other natives were concerned. In other words, he was prepared to combat cargo cult not because he was convinced of its false logic but because he assumed that it angered Europeans as intended theft of their property, and that he had found a satisfactory and practical alternative.

Here, then, was a new attempt at *rapprochement*—just as after the German Occupation. But again it foundered on the misunderstanding between the parties concerned. Not only were the fundamental differences irreconcilable but also the situation was further complicated because everybody automatically supposed that everybody else's aims were identical with his own.

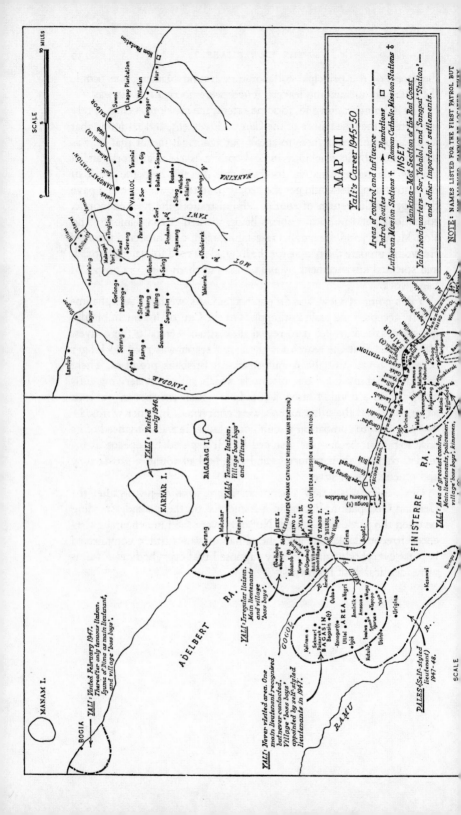

# CHAPTER VI

# THE RAI COAST REHABILITATION SCHEME

## 1945–7

A CASUAL visitor listening to discussions among Europeans in the Madang Club and Hotel during the 1950's could hardly have been blamed if he came to the conclusion that Yali's Rehabilitation Scheme (or 'the Yali Movement', as it was loosely called) suddenly came into being as a single masterstroke of organization. Yali is generally credited with having built, on his own initiative and by the end of 1945, a complete administrative system, by means of which he was able to extend and consolidate his hold over the natives of the entire District. It was said to be staffed with his own personally selected henchmen, 'policemen', couriers, and secretaries, through whom he could send out written orders from the Rai Coast to the Morobe District, Bogia, and even the Sepik region, and with his own appointed 'boss boys', whom he had placed in all the outlying villages to translate into action his carefully planned policies. The only point of disagreement discernible would have concerned the aims of the organization. Some Europeans were fully convinced that the Rehabilitation Scheme had been devoted to seditious ends from the beginning: that Yali had returned to civilian life with the cold-blooded intention of fermenting a native insurrection based on a particularly sinister form of cargo cult. Others were convinced that he and his closest native supporters had been pro-European and anti-cargo cult to the end but had been misrepresented by irresponsible followers.

None of these statements bears more than a partial resemblance to the truth. In the first place, although an organization of this kind did eventually come into being, it was certainly not in existence by the end of 1945 or even 1947. When it did take final shape in 1948, it was not the product of Yali's individual genius and it never functioned with the smooth efficiency attributed to it. It grew up in the same fortuitous way as Yali had emerged as popular leader; and, although it gave him a measure of direct control on the Rai Coast, it enabled him to maintain only an irregular liaison with Madang, and the most tenuous links with places such as Bogia, Finschhafen, and the Bagasin Area. In the second place, Yali's programme was neither carefully planned nor consistent. Although at the beginning he based it on a few straightforward principles, it was very soon dictated by the situation as it developed and reflected the changing pressures to which he was subjected. Thus at the outset he was strongly pro-European and, although not entirely blameless in this respect, did not regard cargo cult as in any way essential to his work. Yet when this approach failed to produce the results he had anticipated, he was quite capable of pursuing an entirely contradictory policy.

### Yali inaugurates the Rehabilitation Scheme[1]

When Yali returned to Sor village in November or December 1945, like many other ex-servicemen he had to begin civilian life all over again. He had been away, except for brief intervals, for almost nine years, during which his old house had fallen in ruins and much of his property had been lost or destroyed. For the next few months he had to set about re-equipping himself. The people built him a new house at Sor and, as he was now a person of considerable importance, made it far bigger than the traditional type in the area. He had to acquire cooking pots, plates, and other necessary household gear; and he had to get ready to plant gardens in the coming year to feed himself, his new wife, and his adopted son. There was little time for political activities. By the end of the year he had done no more than summon a meeting of the Rai Coast peoples at Yamai, a coastal Sengam village.[2] The bulk of the Nankina-Mot population, as well as natives from adjacent regions, and visitors from Madang and Finschhafen, attended. His address repeated much of what he had said six months earlier, but now he included more positive instructions for the future.

Yali's primary objective was to evade the issue of cargo cult by impressing on the people that their hope of a higher standard of living depended on friendship with the Australians. He emphasized that had it not been for his and the other native troops' loyalty, the Allies would not have been careful to preserve the people's lives when they recaptured Saidor. They certainly would have shot many of the beach natives who had collaborated.[3] From now on, therefore, the natives had to do everything possible to win back their good name if they

[1] For the main events of Yali's career in the Madang District after 1945, see Map VII.
[2] The village of the senior (but not paramount) *luluai* of the Rai Coast.
[3] This was, of course, an exaggeration. Collaborators were only imprisoned. But it is interesting that Yali's claim was confused with an important circumstance in the reoccupation of Saidor. Leaflets in Pidgin English were circulated among the people, warning them to keep out of the way of the fighting. It was now said that Yali had been personally responsible for these leaflets: he had gone to the American Commanding Officer and asked him not to kill his people. This enhanced his already considerable reputation.

wanted the Administration to honour the Brisbane promises. They were to cease living in small hamlets in the bush and must regroup themselves in large villages, as the Administration had always wanted.[1] The houses were to be built in straight lines with streets between them, as he had seen in Queensland. They were to be well made and looked after; and the streets were to be kept clean of weeds and refuse, and decorated with shrubs and flowers in the European manner. Pigs were to be kept in proper sties outside the villages. Roads should be cut again and kept open, not just for the occasion of an Administration patrol, as had been the practice in the past, but all the time. They were the people's roads, to be used to maintain communications between the different settlements.

The natives were to pay particular attention to health and personal cleanliness. They must try to live like Europeans. Not only should they keep their houses tidy and in good repair but also they should dig proper latrines in the bush near their villages. They should wash their bodies at least once a day and their hands always before meals. They should clean their teeth and fingernails, launder their clothes regularly, and scrub out their pots and plates after using them.

The women, Yali went on, had special responsibilities. In Australia he had seen people as numerous as leaves on the trees. In New Guinea it was as if the trees had been stripped almost bare. There were far too few people. The old practices of abortion and infanticide must be eradicated. Women were to be encouraged to have as many babies as possible and to take good care of them. Again, the enmities of the past had to be forgotten. People had to live in harmony together. Whenever it could be arranged, girls should marry outside the traditional limits so that affinal and kinship ties would link Saidor to such distant places as Bogati and Madang.[2] Above all, it was essential to put an end to quarrels over adultery. Infidelity was no reason to start fighting. They never saw Europeans do this. The husband was to be compensated with a few shillings and the offence forgotten.[3] No one was to resort to sorcery, which was from now on outlawed.

Yali wound up his address by returning to his opening theme: the need for good relations with Europeans. The people had seen the

[1] The Administration's policy of concentrating the people in large villages had never been entirely successful. Cf. my *Land Tenure among the Garia*, op. cit., pp. 40–1. During the war many of these artificial concentrations had broken up.

[2] Several marriages of this kind have taken place since 1945.

[3] Yali was merely endorsing the Rai Coast custom permitting extramarital liaisons between cross cousins. The custom had been discouraged by the missions so that, whenever it occurred, it led to recrimination, especially in coastal villages.

friendly attitude of American and Australian troops: this was a promise
for the future. But Administration officers, planters, and other white
men would fraternize with them only when they made a real effort to
live decent, clean, and orderly lives. They must co-operate with
Australians in every way: by providing labour for the plantations; by
giving European visitors food and hospitality; and by helping Patrol
Officers carry out their duties as quickly and efficiently as possible. In
matters of religion, the natives were free to choose for themselves,
although Yali advised those who had already become Christians not to
give up their faith. But, in any case, the missionaries were to be shown
every courtesy. All the old talk about their dishonesty over the cargo
was to be forgotten. It was from the missionaries that the people
would get the education which would enable them to meet Europeans
on equal terms—certainly until the Administration had established its
own schools, as it had promised. Thus the children had to attend
mission schools.

Like those preceding it, the address had an immediate effect. Yali's
instructions were quickly obeyed. Village routines were completely
reorganized. According to one European eye-witness account,[1] in
Biliau (Sengam), the natives modelled their lives on what they had seen
in Japanese and Allied army camps. They literally lived by the whistle:
one blast to get up in the morning; another for bathing in the sea;
another for breakfast; and so forth. In other villages the natives were
lined every morning and given instructions for the day's tasks by the
headmen.[2]

These activities soon aroused the interest of the Catholic Mission
and the Administration. The new priest, who had arrived at Gumbi
in January 1946,[3] quickly made Yali's acquaintance and began to
exchange regular visits with him. They appear to have had long
conversations, mainly about religious matters. On one occasion, the
priest, who was staying as Yali's guest in Sor, sprinkled his new house
with holy water and blessed it, and prayed for the success of his work.
Again, as already mentioned, the Administration sent a Patrol Officer
to investigate the Rehabilitation Scheme. The District Officer was
apparently so satisfied with the report that he invited Yali to pay a
short visit to Karkar, where the natives were still pro-Japanese. Yali
went over to the island and gave an address to the local head-

[1] Rev. P. Freyberg of the Lutheran Mission.

[2] In imitation of the Administration practice of lining the people whenever a patrol
visited a village.

[3] The Lutheran missionary did not reoccupy his station at Biliau until 22 May 1946. He
became friendly with Yali thereafter.

men similar to those he had already given on the Rai Coast and at Madang.

## The Perversion of the Rehabilitation Scheme

So far the Rehabilitation Scheme had fulfilled all the requirements of the District Office: its programme seemed entirely secular. But it was not long before it attracted attention from another quarter—the cargo enthusiasts on the Rai Coast and at Madang. After Yali's return from Karkar, his house began to be thronged by a large number of natives clamouring to enter his service. Among them were many Lutheran and Catholic mission helpers who, as Yali was illiterate, styled themselves as his secretaries, dealing with his correspondence, compiling lists of workers, and writing down his instructions.[1]

The new hangers-on were men of two kinds. The first group included a few loyal Christians untainted by the cargo belief. They had good reasons for supporting Yali. His advocacy of co-operation with the missions did much to restore the prestige they had lost during the Letub and Tagarabist period, and the Japanese invasion. Moreover, Yali was offering what they, in common with most other natives in the District and all considerations of the Cargo Movement set aside, in their hearts desired: a higher standard of living and a reasonable *modus vivendi* with Europeans. They saw Yali as the saviour who would lead them to a Promised Land. One Lutheran evangelist from Gal (east of Saidor) compared him to Moses when he led the Israelites out of captivity in Egypt.[2]

The second and larger group was a motley of renegade mission helpers and laymen who, like the mass of the people, were deeply imbued with cargo doctrine. Their main concern was to bring the Rehabilitation Scheme into line with the general Cargo Movement. These were men of far stronger personality than the loyal Christians, whom they speedily ousted from positions of influence at Sor. Eventually one of them, Kasan—a congregational elder of Biliau (Sengam) and a reputed collaborator, who accompanied the Japanese when they raided the coastwatchers at Maibang—became Yali's chief secretary.

[1] I have seen some of these documents. They deal exclusively with Rai Coast affairs. There were no despatches to outlying areas at this time. The documents show no appreciation of the meaning of letter-writing and the material they contain could have been better handled verbally. They served more than anything else to enhance the writers' importance.

[2] Yali was now openly called *Mesa*. There is some doubt whether this was derived from the word *Messiah* or corrupted from the title *Sergeant-Major*, Yali's army rank. Possibly it had a dual connotation: for mission helpers, that of Messiah; and for ex-soldiers, that of Sergeant-Major.

Kasan and a select band of four or five Rai Coast and Madang mission helpers now began to indoctrinate Yali with the quasi-Christian cargo belief. They pointed out that their aims were identical with his, and that were he to forbid polygyny and himself be baptized, God would automatically speed up the arrival of the Administration's promised reward. They cited as proof his escape from Hollandia: God was obviously interested in him for he had saved him from the Japanese and watched over him throughout his perilous journey. They urged him to get rid of his pagan wife Sunggum and marry a Christian. Finally, they put continual pressure on him to order the abandonment of all forms of the traditional religion still practised on the sub-coast, especially the Kabu Ceremony, which the Ngaing kept on celebrating openly and which, they declared, displeased God and so 'closed the road of the cargo'.

Yali resisted this proselytism as best he could. He was prepared to see the introduction of monogamy because he believed that the natives should follow the European example. But he stoutly refused to be baptized and maintained that it was not God but the New Guinea deities who had saved him after the Hollandia debacle. Had he trusted in God and shown immediate disrespect to the crocodile, which was the incarnation of a local deity, he would have been destroyed in the same way as Buka. He would not entertain the idea of divorcing Sunggum for whom he felt personally responsible. He dismissed any suggestion to ban the Kabu Ceremony and other pagan ritual, which he knew from past experience would cause bitter resentment among his own people. When, at one assembly at Yamai, Lutheran elders wanted to display a gourd trumpet and a bullroarer to the women and children to symbolize the Rai Coast's total rejection of paganism, he ordered their immediate removal. But at the same time, he omitted to make it quite clear to the people in general, and Kasan and his associates in particular, that the Rehabilitation Scheme and the Cargo Movement had nothing in common. This was partly because intellectually he was no match for Kasan[1] and partly because of his equivocal attitude towards cargo doctrine generally. As his only counter-argument was his trust in the Brisbane promises, he tried to remain non-committal.

What was more important, Yali did nothing to prevent Kasan and other Sengam (Lutheran) mission helpers from making quasi-Christian cargo propaganda along the Rai Coast littoral. Before their own

---

[1] I knew Kasan well before he died in 1957. He was extremely intelligent, with great clarity of mind and ability to present an argument.

missionary had returned to Biliau in May 1946, and while the new Catholic priest at Gumbi was too inexperienced to appreciate the true significance of their activities, they held a 'conference' in Galek and sent out instructions for a mass return to Christianity. The people were to reform their congregations under the guidance of local evangelists, teachers, and elders. Kasan and his associates did not hesitate to use Yali's name and pervert his ideas. The people were not only to pray to God to send cargo but also to follow Yali's ideas and live at peace with each other in large villages, especially avoiding quarrels over adultery. This was the same as obeying the Ten Commandments, as had previously been advocated by Tagarab and Kaum in the Madang and Bagasin areas. It would augment the goodwill God already felt towards the people because of the loyalty of the native soldiers. This led to much fervent religious activity all along the seaboard. In Wab (near Saidor), the people attended prayer meetings, which were led by their congregational elder and lasted into the late hours of the night or early hours of the morning.[1]

The consequences were fatal. From now on the Rehabilitation Scheme got seriously out of hand. A deputation arrived in Sor from the Letub village of Kurog (near Madang). Its leaders, Son and Bul'me, claimed immediate access to Yali on two counts: they were indirectly trade partners of the Rai Coast people; and Son had served in the A.I.B. and known Yali in Australia, visiting the Queensland Museum with him in 1944-5. They brought with them two rolls of money (£5 each in shillings) and two red laplaps, which were decorated with designs of ships, aircraft, and various types of European goods, and which they called 'flags'.[2] They presented these gifts to Yali and told him that the people of Kurog claimed that God had sent them through the spirits of the dead to the local cemetery in his name. They asked him for his opinion on the matter.

Yali's position was extremely embarrassing. On the one hand, not only did he believe that the Kurog assertion might well be true but also he was beginning to realize that his present popularity depended on the people's belief in his superhuman qualities. If he denied what the Kurog natives were reported to have said, he might forfeit his prominent position, which he was beginning to enjoy, and the Rehabilitation Scheme, which he sincerely thought would help implement the

[1] The Wab people freely admitted that these prayer meetings were intended to bring the cargo. They were witnessed (at a distance) also by Fr J. Wald (S.V.D.), although he did not recognize their full significance.

[2] In some accounts, they brought also a *salip* (sickle for cutting grass) decorated with flowers. This Yali denies.

Brisbane promises, would collapse. On the other hand, he did not want to jeopardize his reputation with the Administration any more than he had already done by turning a blind eye on the recent activities of Kasan and the other Sengam mission helpers along the seaboard. Thus he tried to evade the issue by being delphic and making a public statement which would preserve his good name with both sides.[1]

There was another assembly at Yamai, again attended by people from all over the Rai Coast. The two rolls of money and 'flags' were displayed, and the natives invited by the Madang delegates to comment on their meaning. The local people were bewildered and had nothing to say. Hence the discussion was opened by Son, Bul'me, and the Sengam mission helpers, who proclaimed that God had sent the goods to Yali as an earnest of his future intentions. At the end, Yali spoke. He said: 'These things—I did not get them from Europeans during the war. I was given army documents, rank, and number—but not these things. They are something belonging to you people [of Madang].'[2] He well realized that the last sentence was capable of two interpretations. If it came to the ears of the Administration,[3] he could translate it in these terms: 'I know nothing of these things. We never had flags during the war and this money I have never seen before. They are the concern of you Madang people and nothing to do with me.' But the mass of the people would understand the remark in a completely different way: 'These things do not come from the Europeans but belong to you people of Madang. They come from the source and in the way you have already suggested.'[4]

When the news of the assembly reached Madang, Yali was widely confirmed in native circles as the figurehead of the Cargo Movement. He was now openly referred to as King. In addition, however, the Sengam were encouraged to import ritual based on, or leavened with, the Fourth Cargo Belief that had already begun to creep down the coast from Madang.

During 1945–6, Uririba, a native of the Girawa (Bagasin Area) village of Ulilai, who had served in the N.G.I.B., settled at Erima (near Bogati). He seems to have known something of Tagarab's and Kaum's

[1] I discussed this very carefully with Yali. He fully admitted that this was his intention.

[2] The Pidgin English text of the speech was given me by Yali: '*Despela samting mi no kisim long wetman long woa. Mi kisim pas wantaim namba bilong pait—tasol despela samting nogat. Despela samting i samting bilong yupela.*'

[3] Which it did not. Only the Lutheran missionary at Biliau seems to have learnt about the affair, and then only in 1948.

[4] The phrase '*samting bilong yupela*' is capable of many interpretations according to context.

doctrines, and to have begun a minor cult in the hope of getting cargo from God-Kilibob. Although the doctrine was perfectly intelligible to the Erima people (who had the first version of the Kilibob-Manup myth), little notice was taken of the ritual, which was probably swallowed up in the general excitement and rumour-mongering of the time.

Again, in the early months of 1946, there was another minor cult at Komisangel (further eastwards along the Rai Coast). Its leader, or one of its most ardent supporters, was Pales, who had been a Lutheran mission helper before the war and later had seen service with the Allied forces in various capacities. Although the cult's doctrine was probably based on the Third Cargo Belief, the ritual included food offerings to the ancestors as well as prayers and hymn-singing, and thus seems to have been strongly influenced by the Fourth Cargo Belief.

Yali knew nothing of Uririba's cult at Erima but was fully aware of what was going on at Komisangel. Although he himself had not seen the ritual when he had passed through the village *en route* to Madang, he had been told about it by his brother-in-law, the *Luluai* of Paramus, who had been a day or two ahead of him on the same journey and had watched one of the seances. Once more Yali ignored the affair. He sent no instructions to the Komisangel people to abandon the cult, on the excuse that they did not come within his sphere of influence.

Emboldened by his seeming attitude of connivance, Kasan and his associates obtained Yali's agreement to experiment with cargo ritual of their own. Although they planned to introduce Letub practices from Madang, they told him only that they would pray to God (rather than Jesus-Manup) and place food offerings in the Galek cemetery for the spirits of the dead. Nor did they attempt to introduce the Letub dance. Yali took great care to prevent the Administration from hearing about these seances but very foolishly attended them as a spectator. He could not himself take a leading role because he lacked the necessary religious knowledge. Probably he was mainly curious: to discover how the much talked of ritual was performed and whether it would produce the results claimed for it.

Thereafter nothing of importance occurred before the end of 1946. The situation may be summed up as follows: Yali, living at Sor on the Rai Coast, had made several propaganda speeches to the local natives, which had established his reputation as far away as Madang but not as yet in the Bagasin Area and Ramu Valley. His most practical achievement had been the re-establishment of many coastal villages along pre-war lines. Otherwise, he had only helped to make matters far worse than they had been. His secular ideas had been widely misinterpreted: along the whole Madang–Saidor coast, the true basis of the natives' allegiance to him, and of their readiness to co-operate with the Administration, was their belief that he was in contact with the cargo deity. What was worse, he had attracted around himself a small band of renegade mission helpers who, under pretence of acting as his secretaries, were spreading cargo doctrine in his name and had persuaded him to become involved secretly in the ritual. In other words, at this stage, far from having the efficient centralized organization attributed to it, the Rehabilitation Scheme was being manipulated by the cargo enthusiasts and was virtually out of control.

## Yali visits Bogia

In spite of all this, at the beginning of 1947 the District Officer was still satisfied with Yali's work. He knew nothing of the intrigues beneath the surface and appreciated only the Rehabilitation Scheme's obvious successes, especially its contribution to the improvement of race relations.[1] Although still far from perfect, the situation in the southern Madang District contrasted favourably with that in the north around Bogia, where the people were still openly hostile to the Administration and Europeans in general, and—according to Yali's own account—were expressing the hope that the Japanese would return to New Guinea. The District Officer, therefore, invited Yali to make a propaganda tour of the area.

Yali, with a group of his closest followers, went first to Madang, where he was briefed at the District Office and issued with rations for the journey. He was asked to make the same propaganda at Bogia as on the Rai Coast, especially impressing on the people that the Japanese had gone for ever and that the Australian Government was now finally in control of the country. He should also try to reinforce the authority of the official headmen by looking for native ex-servicemen like himself, whose war records proved their loyalty and whom he could establish in the villages as 'boss boys'.[2] They were to act as third in command to the *luluais* and *tultuls*, help supervise the work of reconstruction, and generally guide the people towards co-operation with European officials.

---

[1] In this context, a Patrol Officer's comment in the Sor Village Book for 2 June 1946 is of interest. It said that it seemed clear that Yali was discrediting the cargo cult.

[2] 'Boss boy' (Pidgin English, *bosboi*) is a term used for a native supervisor on a plantation. He is in charge of the work line and receives higher wages. The term was taken over for a general village supervisor or superintendent.

With these limited ends in view, Yali left Madang about 30 January 1947, but in the course of his journey his stock of propaganda was supplemented by the Catholic Mission. He was travelling by the coastal road, which ran through Sek and skirted Alexishafen Station. As the party went by, Yali was invited to the station and was interviewed by one of the high dignitaries, who asked why he was going to Bogia. As this man listened to Yali's reply, he realized that the situation could be turned to the mission's advantage. He urged Yali to persuade the natives to show a greater interest in Christianity and particularly to give up polygyny. They should divorce their second wives and contract only monogamous unions in future. The priest is said to have indicated that should Yali adopt this policy, he would receive the blessing and support of the Catholic Mission for his work. Otherwise, the mission would not only withdraw its support but also openly oppose him.

At this time Yali was happy to accede to the priest's wishes. For the reason already given, he was himself in favour of the natives adopting monogamy. Again, the missionary at Gumbi had revealed, in the course of their discussions on religious matters, his hope that eventually polygyny would be eradicated, and Kasan had continually repeated to him the slogan that two wives angered God and 'closed the road of the cargo'. He was finally prevailed upon at Bogia, where he was interviewed by a local priest who endorsed the arguments he had heard at Alexishafen.

Thus for the few weeks he was in the Bogia area, Yali sedulously carried out the instructions of both the Administration and the Catholic Mission. He made more speeches, promising the people Administration help if they would give up their pro-Japanese attitude. He appointed Iguma of Dima (ex-Sergeant, A.I.B.) as his main lieutenant in the region and other native ex-soldiers as village 'boss boys'. He also spoke out strongly against polygyny and sent the 'boss boys' through the area, forcibly divorcing all second wives.[1]

Yali left Bogia for Madang, again by the coastal road, on 28 February 1947. He believed that he had carried out his work carefully and adequately. In fact, however, he had left behind a very grave situation. Many of the 'boss boys'—together with a renegade catechist—like his

[1] The account of Yali's journey to, and activities in, Bogia is based on his own description. For an additional account see Burridge, *Mambu*, op. cit., pp. 137-8 and 196-202. Worsley, *The Trumpet Shall Sound*, op. cit., p. 217, quotes me ('Cargo Cult', op. cit., p. 5) as saying that it was believed that Yali had been sent to Bogia to arrange for the delivery of the cargo. This is again a mis-statement: I neither said nor suggested it. The passage quoted refers to events elsewhere later in 1947.

secretaries on the Rai Coast, deliberately translated his instructions into cargo propaganda and claimed him as their authority for doing so. Even worse, the enforcement of monogamy had caused great misery. There were several cases of suicide, and one woman died as the result of the physical injuries she suffered when her husband evicted her. The new District Officer, who had arrived in Madang during February, at once sent Yali back to Bogia to revoke the ban on polygyny and ordered him, on his return a short time later, to give evidence at a judicial inquiry. Yali was finally exonerated by the Court when it emerged that the true responsibility lay with the Catholic Mission.[1] But he was severely reprimanded by the District Officer, who told him that, as he had agreed to work for the Administration, he was to leave the missions to run their own affairs in future. The Administration was neutral in matters of native marital and religious custom, and he was to follow its example.

### Yali tries to Assert Himself

This discomfiture did little to impair Yali's reputation among the Madang and Rai Coast natives. The very fact that the Administration had sent him to Bogia to settle the affairs of the Sub-District showed its growing dependence on him and heightened his prestige. While he was in Madang for the legal inquiry, he was lionized everywhere. The people sang a form of the National Anthem (Pidgin English, *Singsing long King*) in his honour, and he was persistently courted by Lutheran, Catholic, and Seventh Day Adventist native leaders. They asked him to leave the Rai Coast and settle in Madang. They again tried to persuade him to be baptized, divorce his pagan wife, and marry a Christian. They said to him: 'You have seen the Hand of God. We have seen the Light of God on your body, but if you remain married to Sunggum, soon that Light will be extinguished.'[2] He was attributed special powers from God: any sorcerer or other evildoer who touched or shook hands with him would be struck dead in his tracks. Some natives were so afraid of this that they fainted when he approached.

But Yali was in no mood for flattery. In view of the Brisbane promises, he dreaded an open breach with the Administration and was bitterly ashamed of his rebuke from the District Office. He blamed his

---

[1] There was no inquiry into the Bogia cargo activities in this Court. Yali was not held personally responsible, even by the Assistant District Officer at Bogia, who was less enthusiastic about him than his superiors at Madang.

[2] The Pidgin English statement ran: '*Yu lukim Han bilong God pinis. Mipela lukim Lait bilong God long sikin bilong yu. Tasol yu stap marit long Sunggum, orait liklik taim Lait ikan pinis.*'

humiliation on the officiousness of the Catholic priests and native Christians, who had given him false advice. He decided at last to take a strong stand. He would follow the District Officer's advice and keep aloof from all Christian activities: those of the European missionaries and the cargo ritual of the Sengam mission helpers, both of which he regarded as part of the same religious complex.[1] From now on he would devote his energies to purely secular affairs.

Back in the Saidor area in an extremely truculent mood, Yali told the Catholic priest and Lutheran missionary that his close association with them was at an end. He informed Kasan that he would no longer attend the cargo seances in the Galek cemetery.[2] Finally, he made it even clearer to the people than he had done before that they were absolutely free to choose for themselves in matters of religion. He refrained from making a direct attack on Christianity or those who still adhered to the missions, and he continued to encourage the people to send their children to the mission schools. But he let it be known that he himself was on the side of the pagan religion: he gave up attending church services and openly supported the Kabu Ceremony. When asked by the Catholic priest, who was beginning to prepare the people of the sub-coast for baptism and wanted to eradicate the more obvious features of paganism, if he would ever urge the abandonment of the Kabu, he made the deliberately evasive reply that it was a matter for the Administration to decide.[3]

At the same time, Yali flouted the missions over the issue of sexual morality and polygny. After his return from Bogia, luluais and other leaders both in Madang and on the Rai Coast, believing that he possessed special power from the cargo deity, offered him girls to sleep with. They not only wanted to win his favour but also assumed that any offspring resulting from these temporary unions would turn out to be as exceptional as their father. He did not hesitate to accept these offers[4] and also began negotiations to marry a second wife, Rebecca of Matokar (on the coast north of Sek).[5]

[1] Like most natives, he did not distinguish between official Christianity and the Third Cargo Belief, and as yet he knew nothing of the doctrines of the Second and Fourth Cargo Beliefs.

[2] Although the seances are said to have continued well into 1948 (and even 1949), without Yali's presence. See p. 199.

[3] Knowing by now, of course, that the Administration was pledged to neutrality in religious matters.

[4] Apart from his wanting to flout the missions, he was unsqueamish about infidelity. The Ngaing had a relatively lax moral code. Yali's police experience may have been a contributory factor.

[5] The marriage did not take place until 1948.

Paradoxically enough, these sexual activities soon brought fresh advances from Kasan and other cargo enthusiasts. This was due to a new and devious interpretation of Tagarab's doctrine, with which Yali's secular propaganda had already been associated. It will be remembered that Tagarab had ordered his disciples to obey the Ten Commandments, avoiding especially quarrels over adultery. Yet his emphasis differed from that of orthodox Christianity. He attached no importance to the moral evil of sexual laxity as such but stressed heavily the dangers of the sorcery feuds it provoked. It was because they had eradicated all forms of hostility among themselves that Europeans had acquired cargo from God-Kilibob. After the war, as the result of casual conversations with American and Australian soldiers about their premarital experiences, and the discovery of the 'licensed' brothel system in Queensland, it began to be supposed that Europeans avoided feuding over women by means less exacting than self-control. It was imagined that they solved the problem by making women free to all men and, as everybody could indulge in uninhibited libertinism, eliminating all causes of resentment and friction. Yali, therefore, was now thought to be setting a practical example of harmonious living in the true European manner.

This view was bound to find acceptance on the Rai Coast, where extramarital licence between cross cousins had been a feature of traditional society before it had been discouraged by the missions. Indeed, Kasan and other Sengam congregational elders had already probed the idea of pleasing the cargo deity in this way. In the middle of 1946, the Lutheran missionary had suggested to them that they should institute sporting activities for the young people of both sexes. After a slight hesitation the elders told him that they would like to organize moonlight swimming parties for unmarried men and girls, who would afterwards lie on the beach and indulge in either petting or sexual intercourse. The missionary is said to have given a cautious reply.

Kasan now had even more grandiose ideas. With a Catholic catechist from Madang, he asked Yali to agree to the opening of a brothel (Pidgin English, *haus pamuk*) on the Rai Coast, claiming (probably because of the Lutheran missionary's cautious reply) that the missions approved the scheme. All unmarried girls were to be put into it and all unmarried men—even married men, if they so desired—should have access to it.[1] Yali advised Kasan to summon an assembly at Biliau.

[1] The Ngaing assumed that sexual relations only between cross cousins would be permitted, although I doubt whether this was ever discussed.

Natives from distant villages attended, including Pales, who had been prominent in the small cult at Komisangel.

The discussion was led by Kasan, the Madang catechist, and the Sengam mission helpers who had participated in the cargo ritual in the Galek cemetery. They put forward two arguments: First, Yali had urged women to have more babies so as to increase the population. What better way was there to achieve this than the plan suggested? Second, they referred to the belief already outlined, that 'free love' would please the cargo deity by eliminating feuding and help usher in the millennium. Many people were openly in favour of the scheme, not least, according to Ngaing informants present at the meeting, the women themselves. But eventually it was squashed. The parents of some of the girls were old-fashioned: they did not relish the thought of their daughters being saddled with children without husbands to provide for them. Furthermore, Yali made use of the occasion to indicate his dissociation from cargo activities, although he did so on not intellectual or moral but severely practical grounds. The Queensland brothels, he said, were regularly inspected by qualified doctors. On the Rai Coast there was no native capable of doing this. He could not, therefore, agree to the proposal. But, even though the project of the brothel was abandoned, it is certain that in Biliau the tradition of cross cousin licence was revived, with Kasan as the ringleader. Also, as will be seen, the idea of the brothel was reintroduced to the Cargo Movement in another area later in 1947.

Having demonstrated, as he thought, his aloofness from religious affairs—apart from the pagan rituals of his own village —Yali turned his attention to secular politics and economics. This he was quite content to do. Christianity and cargo doctrine were not important for his immediate objectives. His main concern was to preserve good relations with the Administration so that the Brisbane promises, on which he still pinned his hopes, would be honoured.

Although it had been necessary to reprimand Yali for his stupidity at Bogia, Native Affairs officers continued to take an interest in his Rehabilitation Scheme, thinking that it could be used as a preparation for the Government's political and economic reforms. They described to him the Village (now Native Local Government) Councils, which were eventually to replace the system of village headmen. But they did not do so with sufficient care. They left Yali with the impression that the 'boss boys' he had appointed in the Bogia area were the equivalent of councillors under the new scheme and automatically superseded existing officials.[1] Thus he began to install 'boss boys' in the villages around Madang and on the Rai Coast, and to indicate that they took precedence over *luluais* and *tultuls*. Otherwise, their duties were the same as at Bogia although, especially on the Rai Coast, they were expected to make occasional reports to Yali about the progress of reconstruction in their villages.[2]

The appointment of 'boss boys' gave the Rehabilitation Scheme at last a semblance of organization. Unlike many of the official headmen, the 'boss boys' were young and energetic, some of them ex-servicemen, and all of them owing allegiance solely to Yali. As he himself had installed them, he did not have to share their loyalty with the Administration. This gave him a measure of personal control over the Nankina-Mot sub-coast[3] and, as already suggested, a means of liaison with Madang and Bogia. But the system was still extremely inefficient. Even within his own immediate area, Yali could not as yet guarantee that his orders were promptly and properly carried out, and there was little he could do if they were misunderstood or disobeyed. In outlying areas such as Madang and Bogia, where the 'boss boys' were given few if any instructions after their first briefing and were left to carry on by themselves, he had no direct control. As had already happened at Bogia and was soon to happen inland from Madang, the most extravagant propaganda could be spread and attributed to him without his being able to repudiate it, even if he was aware of what was being said.

Yali's economic experiments had equally little success. He had already tried to revive the old Madang–Rai Coast trading system, which had become very irregular during and after the 1930's. He arranged for the Rai Coast natives to send a large consignment of wooden plates and bark cloths to Madang. The plan failed. The situation in the southern Madang District became so confused during the next few years that a return consignment of clay pots was never sent.[4] Now, however, acting on the advice of the District Office, Yali attempted to promote Western business enterprise. He encouraged the Rai Coast people to plant cash crops, the most prosperous venture being a vegetable garden at Sibog. He collected and banked several hundred pounds for buying a motor

---

[1] 'Boss boys' were often addressed as *konsel* (councillors). Cf. my 'Cargo Cult', op. cit., p. 6.

[2] I doubt if these reports were either frequent or detailed.

[3] But not over the Rai Coast beach villages which were under the influence of the mission helpers. The only exceptions were Yaimas and Wab, near Saidor.

[4] The debt was still outstanding in 1958, and I have not heard that it has been paid since. The exchange at Yamai on the Rai Coast (p. 27, note 3) in 1953 did not apparently settle it.

launch to stimulate local trade.[1] He also became a recruiter of native labour.

With the backing of several planters, Yali was given a contract by the Administration to provide native workers for Cape Rigney, Lagap, Nom, and Melamu[2] plantations. He received £1 a month for each worker, from which he had to pay a wage of 15s. He also had to supply food to the labour lines. He organized this by borrowing land near Cape Rigney and Galek, on which he planted special gardens. He employed other natives to supervise them.

The project ran through 1947–8 but ended dismally. There was no proper supervision by the Administration. The monthly profit of 5s. a head, from which food had to be provided, was far too small. Yali himself had no comprehension of European economic principles, and his secretaries, despite their basic literacy, understood little more. Such accounts as they kept were in a hopeless muddle.[3] Moreover, after the beginning of 1948, under circumstances to be described, Yali began to be financially embarrassed. There is evidence that a number of his labourers were not paid full wages. Towards the end of 1948, his licence had to be revoked by the District Officer, who paid a special visit to Saidor to announce the decision.

### Yali summoned to Port Moresby: Events during his Absence

By the middle of 1947, Yali was being talked about by higher Administration officers, who were worried by the reports from Bogia and thought that he needed special guidance. It was agreed that he and nine other outstanding natives from the Madang District and Finschhafen region should visit Port Moresby for a period of indoctrination: to learn something of the long-range plans for native development. They left Madang about the middle of August 1947 and returned about the middle of the following December. Their experiences are described in Chapter VII. Here we are concerned with Yali's personal reactions, and those of the people at large, to the announcement of the visit.

Yali expected to achieve three things in Port Moresby. First, he saw the visit as the culmination of his Rehabilitation Scheme. The Administration would now honour the Brisbane promises and make arrangements for him to take delivery of his reward: building materials,

---

[1] The launch was never bought, and the money was handed back to the contributors after 1950.

[2] Also called Konstantinhafen by the Germans. After 1921, the German name was given up.

[3] I have seen these documents, which are now in the hands of the Administration. They are quite incomprehensible.

tools, an electric light plant, machinery for tinning meat, and trucks to solve transport problems. These goods would be sent to him by instalments for distribution to the people.

Second, he had ambitions of a more personal nature. Native Affairs officers and planters had occasionally remarked to him that his work was equivalent to that of a Patrol Officer. During the five days he spent in Madang before leaving for Papua, it was mentioned to him that soon he would be given an official and salaried position within the Administration. It was quite unjustifiable that he should be expected to continue his work without any recognized status or remuneration. In view of the earlier remarks, he took this to mean that he would, in fact, be made a Patrol Officer or at least receive similar status.[1] He welcomed the idea. Over the last two years he had developed a taste for power and his greatest wish had always been to be treated by Europeans as an equal.

Third, if he was to have official status within the Administration, he wanted his relationship with the missions clearly defined, especially after his humiliation at Bogia. What authority did they have over him and the other natives? Was the society he was helping to build to be dominated by them and have entirely European-Christian laws? Or, apart from its new material culture and the laws imposed by the Administration, could it incorporate the traditional way of life and, above all, religion? In this context, the crucial problem was the Kabu Ceremony. Was it to be eradicated or perpetuated?

These were issues about which Yali was both angry and confused. He had been told to be neutral in religious matters. Yet religion was the source of all his worries. He had been under continual pressures from the missions and ordinary village natives, who represented opposed points of view. The Catholic priest at Gumbi, and the Catholic and Lutheran native mission helpers were urging him to forbid the Kabu and work for full conversion to Christianity. Yet this could only incur the antagonism of the people of the Nankina-Mot sub-coast, for whom the Kabu, largely because of the circumstances of their adherence to Catholicism, had come to symbolize their cultural and social identity. Again, native mission helpers had persuaded the peoples in some areas to give up traditional hunting and fishing rights which, as has been shown, were vested in small clans or similar groups, and adopt a system of communal ownership, on the grounds that, under

---

[1] It was reasonable for Yali to suppose this. There were no special administrative positions for natives above those of village headmen, and he had been told that he was regarded as their superior.

God, all land, sea, and reefs were free to all men. As a result, coastal natives were perpetually seeking his advice about how to settle the vexatious disputes that arose from the new communalism advocated by the mission helpers. He anticipated that in Port Moresby these difficulties would be resolved once and for all.

Yali discussed these affairs with his close associates in Madang and, as was only to be expected, information quickly leaked out. Soon after his departure there was a flood of speculation on the basis of the cargo ideas which had already crystallized around his name: he was at last going to collect the goods promised him by God during the war; and he would return from Port Moresby as a District Officer with a special charter for native society. This speculation was followed by a great wave of cargo cult activity in the Bagasin Area, in the Ramu Valley, and near Madang and Saidor. It was believed that it would guarantee the success of Yali's mission to Papua.

Until now Yali had been no more than a name to the people of the Bagasin Area. He had never visited them or sent them any messages, and they had not been involved in his Rehabilitation Scheme. But henceforth he was to be well known to them. Between August and October 1947, certain irresponsible individuals, who had never had close contact with him and cannot be regarded as having acted on his orders, styled themselves as his lieutenants and journeyed through the villages south of the Gogol. They included three native ex-soldiers (two of them from Girawaland) and one or two known cargo enthusiasts from Sopu country. They spread new cargo prophecies—a mixture of the popular elaborations of Yali's own secular propaganda, and of Tagarab's and Kaum's doctrines. The following account, given by informants in the Somau-Iwaiwa region of Garialand, seems to have been typical of their activities.[1]

The people were assembled to hear a series of addresses. The first to speak were the ex-soldiers, who were on the whole comparatively restrained. They rehashed Yali's official propaganda, augmenting it with what he was known to have said at Bogia and relatively straightforward versions of the new rumours at Madang. They described how God had saved Yali during the war, both at Hollandia and in other actions against the Japanese, and had enabled him to go to Australia, where he had seen the King. The King had told him that, although in the past Europeans had not shown proper friendship towards the natives, they were now going to make amends because of the loyalty of the New Guinea soldiers to the Allies. Yali was to get the country

[1] See also my 'Cargo Cult', op. cit., pp. 4–5, which this account supersedes.

into order again after the ravages of war. Then ships would be filled
with goods for the natives and sent to him for distribution. As his
work was completed in the coastal regions, he had gone to Port
Moresby to collect this cargo. He would return as an Administration
officer, and give it first to the returned soldiers and then to civilians.
But the people of the Bagasin Area were not yet ready or worthy to
receive their share. They had not heard Yali's official propaganda,
which had been approved by the King and the Madang District Office.
If they wanted cargo, they would have to listen to it now and do as the
coastal people had already done.

The ex-soldiers then issued the following orders: The people were
to give up living in hamlets and come together in large 'camps',[1]
which were to have their houses built along streets, and be beautified
with flowers and shrubs. Each 'camp' was to have a new Rest House,
which was no longer to be called a *haus kiap* but a *haus Yali*. It was
to be used by Yali when he visited the people in his capacity as an
Administration officer. Each 'camp' had to have proper latrines, and
new roads had to be cut throughout the area.

As this was a programme demanding energy and organization, said
the ex-soldiers, the old headmen were inadequate and would have to be
superseded by 'boss boys'.[2] They were to supervise the work of reconstruction and also see that Yali's orders were carried out. The population had to be increased: all women were to be forced to have many
children; and abortion and infanticide were to be wiped out. Polygyny
would no longer be tolerated and monogamy would be enjoined. All
second wives were to be divorced and remarried to bachelors.[3] If Yali
visited them[4] and discovered that they had ignored these rules, they
would get nothing from him and remain bush *kanakas* for ever.

This was followed by a second address by the cargo enthusiasts.
These men put a religious slant on everything the ex-soldiers had said,
reciting the even wilder rumours about Yali that had been fermenting
for the last two years. It was not to be thought that Yali was a mere
human being: he was a spirit of the dead. He had been killed at Hollandia and had gone from there, in spirit form, to Australia, where he

---

[1] In Pidgin English, *kem*. The term came into use during the war. It is now used for
any large collection of dwellings.

[2] They were meant to take full command of the villages but by 1949, when I first
visited the area, had become only assistants of the *luluais* and *tultuls*.

[3] This must have been based on Yali's Bogia propaganda, which had already been
countermanded. It strongly suggests that the ex-soldiers and cargo enthusiasts were not
acting on Yali's orders. Enkol of Paisarek, his main lieutenant for the Bagasin Area (see
Diagram I), was never mentioned to me in connexion with these activities.

[4] Which he never did.

had seen not only the King but also God himself in Heaven. God had told him that he had been wanting to 'open the road of the cargo' for the natives for a long time and would do so now if they would re-organize their way of life along European lines. He ordered Yali to return to New Guinea and urge the natives to build large 'camps', see that the population increased, and eradicate abortion, infanticide, and polygyny. This had been done on the Rai Coast, and at Madang and Bogia, and thus God had instructed the King to send ships with cargo to Port Moresby, where Yali would now take delivery of it. As the ex-soldiers had said, only the Bagasin Area was lagging in the task of reorganization. Unless the people there did something about it, they would get nothing, for both God and Yali would be angry with them. Moreover, they would be in great danger. The goods Yali was to bring back from Port Moresby would include military equipment: especially big guns, aircraft, and tanks. He was preparing a new war against the Europeans, and if the Bagasin Area people had no arms and ammuni-tion, they would be unable to save themselves from destruction.

Speeches like these were made throughout the whole Bagasin Area. The people were quick to react. 'Boss boys' were installed, 'camps'[1] built, and second wives divorced and remarried, in some cases to boys in their teens.[2] As at Bogia, the enforcement of monogamy caused a great deal of unhappiness and at least two suicides occurred.[3] But this did not deter the people from carrying out the programme. In addition, they were given indirect encouragement by some of the local Lutheran mission helpers, who had so far kept aloof from cargo activity. These men were interested in what was going on for two reasons. On the one hand, they approved the abandonment of polygyny and the increase in church attendance—even though both were due to the belief that cargo would at last arrive from God. On the other, they were deeply im-pressed by the prophecy of a new war, and were easily persuaded by less reliable elders and evangelists to hold mass baptisms.[4] Several thousand Girawa, Garia, and Sopu converts were made in this way. The mission helpers explained their conduct on the grounds that, as many people were likely to be killed in the course of hostilities, their only hope of salvation lay in quickly joining the Church.

These activities also provoked another minor cult in Garialand

[1] Some of them, the remains of which I saw in 1949, must have housed over 500 people.

[2] This angered older Garia, who had been brought up under rigid sex taboos. As noted, adolescent boys were allowed no close contact with women.

[3] They were not reported to the District Office.

[4] As noted, the Lutheran Mission had begun official baptism in Garialand only in 1937, and the process had not gone very far.

about November or December 1947.[1] Its leader was Polelesi, a young woman of Igurue, who had recently married a local evangelist. She herself had attended only village school.

Polelesi claimed that an angel had warned her in a dream of the imminence of a Second Flood to destroy the 'wicked' and usher in the arrival of cargo for the 'Elect'. She had a house built on tall stilts, where she was believed to receive messages from God. She organized a programme for the rooting out of Satan: those who still practised agricultural ritual, love magic, and sorcery were to recite their secret formulae to her and promise to give them up entirely. If they did this, God would save them from the Flood by turning Igurue Mountain into an island, whereas the rest of the area would be covered by water. She advised other Garia to leave their settlements (the 'camps' they were in the process of building) and join her at Igurue. Those who did not would be drowned or eaten by crocodiles. In a clairvoyant moment, she proclaimed that she had seen God, Jesus Christ, angels, and the spirits of the dead in the clouds above the mountains. She had seen a storehouse as well. Soon, when the Flood came, God would send the ancestors with ships and pinnaces full of cargo for the survivors at Igurue.

The cult gained a following in Igurue and Tapopo, and also around Somau-Iwaiwa. Some people destroyed their property and slaughtered their pigs before leaving home, again to shame God and the ancestors with their poverty. Apart from making her disciples reveal ritual formulae, Polelesi ordained special prayers to God and the spirits, and later, when it began to rain, announced that this was a divine sign that the Flood was about to begin. She ordered everyone to sit outside and be washed by the rain as if it were a form of baptism. But after a few weeks people grew tired of her unfulfilled prophecies and the cult disbanded, the immigrants going back somewhat sheepishly to their homes.

Some time between August and November 1947,[2] cargo activity spread to another region which, as far as is known, had been hitherto unaffected. Pales, who had been prominent in the Komisangel cult in 1946 and had attended the recent discussions at Biliau about the possibility of a Rai Coast brothel, went inland to Dumpu in the Ramu Valley. He claimed to have been sent there by Yali and the Lutheran Mission, to baptize the people and lead them to the true way of God. His doctrine was a mixture of the Third Cargo Belief and the revision-

[1] This account corrects my 'Cargo Cult', op. cit., p. 4, in which the cult is dated as before mid-1947, This was the only cult I recorded led by a woman. For a comparable instance see Belshaw, 'Recent History of Mekeo Society', pp. 5-8.

[2] In my 'The Madang District Cargo Cult', op. cit., I wrongly dated this cult as 1945-6. This is now corrected.

ist theories current during and since the war. God had turned his face from the natives because of the stupidity of their ancestor Ham. But now, if they obeyed the Ten Commandments, gave up sorcery feuds over women, lived in peace with each other, and generally followed Pales' teachings, the situation would be changed. Special prayers were instituted in a church which Pales described as 'just the same as the white men's Jerusalem', and the bones of the dead which had been buried at random in the bush were exhumed and reinterred, with solemn rites, in new and carefully prepared cemeteries. Finally, Pales instituted what was either a brothel or an extensive system of wife exchange which, for the reasons already given, would ensure harmonious living and hence the arrival of the cargo. The cult lasted into 1948 and spread all along the Ramu Valley to the west as far as the Sopu village of Kutulu[1] on the Pike River, on the western Garia border.[2]

Madang also became a hotbed of cargo ritual during Yali's absence. Letub seances were revived, and Kaum of Kalinam began a new cult on the outskirts of the town itself. After he had served nine months in gaol for the Bagasin Rebellion, Kaum entered European employment for about a year. He returned to his village at the end of 1946 and at once began new ritual, again based on Tagarab's doctrine, for which he was imprisoned for a further six months in March 1947. On his release in September, he once more entered European employment in Madang.

At this time Kaum was living in the Madang Labour Compound.[3] He collected around himself a number of workboys, largely but not exclusively from the Bagasin Area, and told them that while he had been in prison he had died as result of severe treatment by the native police.[4] He had then gone to Heaven and seen God-Kilibob, who had given him a new skin—it would turn white in due course—a new name, Konsel (Councillor), and instructions to perform new ritual, which would bring ships and aircraft with cargo to Madang. This was to be a parallel supply to that which Yali would bring back from Port Moresby. In fact, the ritual would ensure the success of Yali's own enterprise. When the cargo arrived, God-Kilibob would cause an earthquake and tidal wave to destroy the Europeans. Thereafter, while

[1] Called Obsau by the Administration.
[2] The Garia refused to join Pales' cult. Because of their rigid sex taboos, they were horrified by the idea of a brothel or any system of permitted promiscuity.
[3] The following corrects my 'Cargo Cult', op. cit., pp. 5–6.
[4] In imitation of the belief that Yali had been killed at Hollandia and had gone to Heaven. Kaum's claim was, to some extent, justified: he was severely maltreated by native police in gaol, as is evidenced by his broken ear lobes from which his ear-rings have been torn out at some time.

Yali ruled Madang and the Rai Coast, Kaum would become District Officer or King of the Gogol and Bagasin areas. In anticipation, he dressed for the part, wearing a white shirt and necktie. He appointed his close associates second and third in command, and had other work boys cook for him.

While he had been in Heaven, Kaum claimed, he had seen God-Kilibob and the spirits of the dead making cargo. God-Kilibob had also given him a symbol of his arm—it appears to have been a small gunshell[1]—which could go direct to Heaven and bring back messages about the future. This symbol was most important in the ritual.

The seances were held at night in the Labour Compound. Kaum would set up a small table, cover it with a cotton cloth, decorate it with flowers in bottles, and set out offerings of food and tobacco for the ancestors. In the middle, standing on its base, was 'the arm' of God-Kilibob. As soon as he had eaten the meal prepared by his attendants, the people would assemble and, folding their hands in the Lutheran manner, pray to Kaum thus: 'O Father Konsel, you are sorry for us. You can help us. We have nothing—no aircraft, no ships, no jeeps, nothing at all. The Europeans steal our cargo. You will be sorry for us and see that we get something.' Thereafter Kaum, acting as intermediary, would relay this prayer to God-Kilibob. He would then dismiss the company and, together with his second in command, sleep near the table. He would claim that during the night he dreamt of God-Kilibob, the ancestors, and the coming of the cargo, and that the gunshell had been to Heaven to bring back information. According to some informants, he used to hold it as if it were a telephone and pretend to have conversations with God-Kilibob.

The ritual seems to have been carried on undisturbed for about two months, during which the people accorded Kaum great honour. They gave him a woman from the Ramu area as a mistress. She was renamed Maria.[2] But although the cult was never discovered by the Administration, it came to an end some time in November, when Kaum was transferred to a work team at Saidor.

On the Rai Coast, Kaum lost no time in impressing the local natives with his own importance. He told them that he had been deported because his earlier ritual had caused lightning to strike the Madang Electric Power Station[3] and the Administration was afraid of him. He

[1] In imitation of Tagarab's 'arm' of God-Kilibob, a length of iron rod.
[2] I could never discover the significance of this.
[3] Lightning did actually strike the Madang Electric Power Station some time between April and August 1947. Kaum was then in gaol and not, as far as is known, performing

joined forces with a native called Angge, who had once been a Lutheran mission helper on Karkar Island and claimed to have been involved in the Kukuaik cult before the Japanese invasion.[1] Together they began new seances in Wab, Yaimas, and Wilwilan villages, which were within easy reach of the Administration Station. The doctrine and ritual were much the same as those used in the Madang Labour Compound. Kaum and Angge prophesied the arrival of ships, submarines, and aircraft with war material and other cargo. They aroused a great deal of interest among the Nankina-Mot people.

Those who showed the greatest interest were the Sengam mission helpers who had been dabbling in cargo ritual since 1946. They now intensified their efforts in the belief that they would help Yali achieve his ends in Port Moresby. He was expected to return soon with a fleet of ships and sail along the Rai Coast to Madang. Special look-out houses were built, and the horizon scanned day and night for his arrival.

Moreover, it was now widely accepted that Yali would return as a District Officer and, at the very least, assume control of the Rai Coast. A proper 'station' had to be built for him. The people of Galek, as the coastal trade partners of the people of Sor, voted him a strip of land at Sangpat (between their own village and Suit) for this purpose. By the beginning of 1948, they had erected a new and very large house for himself, together with smaller dwellings for visitors and hangers-on, on the site.[2] The buildings were laid out along the lines of the Administration Station at Saidor.

The situation was now at crisis point. Yali had unwittingly unleashed forces which, during his four months' absence, gathered tremendous momentum and plunged most of the southern Madang District into a ferment of cargo activity. The question now was whether, when he returned to Madang, he would be able or willing to control them. On this depended the future of both his Rehabilitation Scheme and the Cargo Movement as a whole. His reaction to the problem was decided not by any previously held convictions or principles but by his experiences in Port Moresby.

---

any cargo ritual. But the Rai Coast natives were not to know that. (Personal communication from Mr Brian Stonebridge of Madang.)

[1] Cf. Chapter IV, p. 99 (note 1). Karkar has the first version of the Kilibob-Manup myth. The fact that Angge could co-operate with Kaum so easily suggests that the Kukuaik cult may well have incorporated the myth in some way. Angge also claimed that he had preached the same doctrine as Kaum's on Karkar. I could never check this with him because he was killed in a motor accident before I knew of his existence.

[2] Yali claims to have paid the people of Galek £60 for the work.

# CHAPTER VII

# YALI IN PORT MORESBY

THE party which went to Papua consisted of the following: Yali of Sor, Rai Coast (ex-Sergeant-Major, A.I.B.); Iguma of Dima, Bogia Sub-District (ex-Sergeant, A.I.B., and Yali's main lieutenant in the northern Madang District); Wagara of Wilwilan, Rai Coast (ex-Corporal, A.I.B.); the *Luluais* of Biliã and Silibob, Madang; the *Luluai* of Sio, north-west of Finschhafen, Morobe District; Kore of Yabob, Madang; Bate of Furan, near Madang; Don of Matokar, north of Madang; and Kasan of Biliau, Rai Coast (Yali's chief secretary). Kasan kept a diary from the beginning to the end of the journey. I have used it to date many of the events described.[1]

## Departure and Arrival

In view of the importance attached to it by the Administration, Yali himself, and the natives, the journey to Port Moresby was humiliating. The group had assembled in Madang by 12 August, Yali having left Saidor by Administration ship on the 10th and Kasan having followed him from Biliau by the Lutheran mission vessel a day later. Thereafter they had to suffer every conceivable kind of delay and irritation. Originally it was intended that they should all travel together by sea, but their ship broke down in Madang Harbour and alternative arrangements had to be made for them to go by air. They were routed in several groups via Lae, where they were to reassemble and wait for other aircraft to take them to Port Moresby. Yali left for Lae on 16 August and Kasan and the others joined him there by the 23rd.

This was hardly an auspicious beginning but worse was to come. The party was held up in Lae for well over a month until the end of September, when at last bookings could be made for the second stage of their journey. Kasan's diary during this period records several acts of bad temper on Yali's part. Although his anger was directed overtly against his companions and several local policemen, who roistered about and disturbed his sleep, there was probably a deeper, sub-conscious reason—the indignity to which he was being subjected. He, who was being sent on a special embassy to Port Moresby, who was

[1] The diary is now in the possession of the Administration.

treated with awe by the natives, and respect by the Europeans, of his
District, and who was to become a paid official of the Administration,
had to cool his heels and wait, like any ordinary native, until space not
wanted for urgent freight could be found for him in an aeroplane.[1]

The feeling of depression subsequently deepened as a result of a
small but important incident. A letter arrived for Yali from one of his
keenest supporters in Madang, a catechist. This man described how,
some time after the party had left Madang, he had dreamt that the
spirit of his dead father had brought him bad news. The spirit had said:
'The Administration intends to put an end to (Pidgin English, *katim*)
Yali's work.' This was understood to mean that the Administration intended to prevent Yali from getting the cargo that had been promised.

Because of the widely held belief in the validity of information revealed in dreams, Yali and his companions automatically assumed that
the news from Madang could very well be true. But they reacted in
different ways. Yali, who had staked everything on the Brisbane
promises and had cold-shouldered the missions in order to ensure that
the Administration honoured them, was naturally bewildered and
crestfallen. He did not know what attitude he should now adopt. But
the others, notably Kasan and the *Luluais* of Biliã and Silibob, were
quick to cast around for alternative courses of action. They were still
convinced that the missions, in spite of their past duplicity, possessed
the cargo secret and that any further estrangement from them might
cut the natives off irrevocably from this source of supply. They decided,
therefore, that they should try again to get Yali to modify his views
about Christianity.

The matter was discussed under the following circumstances. Yali
had renewed his acquaintance with Mayeng of Busama, with whom he
had served in the Police Force between 1937 and 1941, and who now
wanted to entertain him and his friends. The party met at the Lae
Police Barracks. A Tami Islander and a Bukawa native were also
present.[2] Yali explained to Mayeng the reasons for his visit to Port
Moresby, and in the course of general conversation the contents of the
letter from Madang were recounted. Kasan and the *Luluai* of Biliã then
suggested to him that, as it was now quite possible that the Administration would not make cargo available, he would be well advised not
to complain about the activities of the missions to higher officials in
Papua. He had better make his peace with the Catholic priest at Gumbi

[1] At this time, natives travelling in aircraft customarily occupied either inferior seats or
space not otherwise being used for freight.
[2] They both belonged to the area of the Neuendettelsau Mission.

and the Lutheran pastor at Biliau, for the missions would be the natives' last hope of getting the cargo they wanted. The suggestion was strongly supported not only by the other members of his own group but also by Mayeng, the Tami Islander, and the Bukawa native.[1] But as far as Yali was concerned, this was only cold comfort. He remained a very worried man.

At last the party began to move off to Port Moresby. Yali, Kasan, and one or two others left Lae on 28 September, and the rest followed on 1 October. On arrival, each group was met at the aerodrome by Advent Tarosi, a Sio (Finschhafen area) native, who was at that time an Administration teacher trainee. He had been selected as mentor and guide to the party for several reasons: he had known Yali on war service in 1942; he could claim a close personal tie with the *Luluai* of Sio; he was interested in the Rehabilitation Scheme; and he could speak, read, and write English as well as Pidgin, and had learnt to use a typewriter. He took the visitors to the officer responsible for their welfare while in the capital.

### The Failure of Yali's Mission[2]

It is impossible to trace the important events of the next two and a half months in detail for the written record is too meagre. Kasan's diary gives only brief mention of everyday occurrences, and other documents do not present them in chronological order. Even so, an overall picture of the party's experiences can be outlined. In the diary, we catch glimpses of Yali and his comrades in the offices of various Administration Departments, discussing problems relating to his work: especially those of Village (Native Local Government) Councils, in which he seems to have been given considerable instruction by both European officers and leading Hanuabada natives.[3] Again, we see them being taught about the new programme for Native Education and visiting the Education Training Centre at Sogeri. There were other important visits: to the Agricultural Station, a workshop, a native sawmill, a Medical School, an electric power station, and the engine room of M.V. *Malaita*.[4] Beyond the official sightseeing, there are glimpses of the

[1] Quasi-Christian cargo doctrine was not discussed on this occasion but it is significant that ideas from Madang were readily understood and endorsed by natives from the Huon Gulf region.

[2] The description of events in the following section is based on Yali's and Kasan's personal accounts, supplemented by the diary and other documents, to which reference is made in context.

[3] Hanuabada was one of the first villages in which a Council was established.

[4] A Burns Philp vessel at that time on the New Guinea run.

more personal side of the party's experiences: letters from home; watching films in Hanuabada; aimlessly wandering around town with nothing better to do than pass disparaging remarks about the local natives and their habits; and being photographed.[1] At various times, Yali and Kasan were ill, and there are again several references to Yali's bad temper.

As in Lae, these outbursts of anger were doubtless caused by Yali's sense of frustration and failure. His visit to Port Moresby had been a complete farce. Although he got some satisfaction in the matters of his future status and the rules for the native society he was helping to build, the Brisbane promises—the primary object of his coming—were, as was inevitable, repudiated. According to Kasan, very soon after his arrival Yali approached the officer in charge of the party and asked him when the reward pledged to the native soldiers four years earlier would be handed over. When would he and his people receive the building materials and machinery he had been told they were to have? The officer is alleged to have replied that the Administration was, of course, grateful for the services of native troops against the Japanese and was, in fact, going to give the people a substantial reward. The Australian Government was pouring vast sums of money into economic, educational, and political development, War Damage Compensation, and schemes to improve medical services, hygiene, and health. It would be a slow process, of course, but eventually the people would appreciate the results of the Administration's efforts. But a reward of the nature Yali had imagined—a free hand-out of cargo in bulk—was quite out of the question. The officer was sorry, but this was just wartime propaganda made by irresponsible European officers on the spur of the moment.

Nine years after the event,[2] Yali had devised arguments to soften the blow he must have felt on this occasion. He told me that he had been apprehensive enough after receiving the letter from the Madang catechist in Lae. Furthermore, quite early in his stay in Port Moresby he attended a meeting of the Hanuabada Council, at which the Papuans asked the European officer present when the village would get electric power.[3] The answer was that the people could have it as soon as they

[1] In these photographs, members of the party are dressed in short or long trousers, shirts, and ties. Several wear shoes and socks. This contrasts with the clothing worn by the general run of natives in 1947: a laplap and possibly a shirt or singlet.

[2] When I discussed it with him in 1956.

[3] For an account of modern Hanuabada, see Belshaw, *The Great Village.* During the war the people of Hanuabada had to evacuate their village for military reasons. After 1945 it was rebuilt by the Administration with European materials. The natives, according to Yali, assumed that they would automatically get the same amenities as Europeans. In the diary account, Yali could have visited Hanuabada Council on 1 October 1947.

could pay for it but not before. This caused much grumbling among the Hanuabadans, who had understood that electricity was a service free of charge. Yali claims that he realized even then that the Brisbane promises would not be honoured.

Nevertheless, by whatever means Yali discovered the truth, his bitterness was very great. His whole war service and loyalty to Europeans had been a mockery. When put to the test, they cold-bloodedly forgot their fine words and let him down. As he put it to me, 'I realized now that the talk of the officers in Brisbane was bullshit—that was done with now—we just wouldn't get anything—the white men had lied to us and didn't want to help us. We just wouldn't get anything to give us a better life.'[1]

There were, however, far more serious implications. As Yali well realized, the bottom had dropped out of his Rehabilitation Scheme. Everything he had said to win friends for the Europeans—on the Rai Coast, at Madang, on Karkar, and at Bogia—had been based on the assumption that soon the Administration would demonstrate its goodwill by guaranteeing a rapid improvement in native living standards. His followers at home were daily expecting an announcement of this kind and now, with nothing but his shame, he had to return and face them. How was he to explain that there was to be no immediate and tangible reward but only general promises of new schools, hospitals, and opportunities to engage in business enterprise in the future? These were things which they neither clearly understood nor appreciated. It was hardly to be wondered that he had little stomach for the remainder of his official programme.

Yali was by no means fully satisfied also in his second hope, that he would become a Patrol Officer. It was justifiably believed that no one should hold such a position who could not speak, read, and write English. Even so, this did not mean that Yali was not to be given a formal rank in the Administration. What appears to have been an entirely special post of Administration Foreman or Overseer[2] within the Department of Native Affairs was created for him. It carried a salary of £4 a month (£48 a year) and rations (including tinned meat, rice, tobacco, and kerosene) for himself and his wife. His duties were to carry on with the propaganda and work of reconstruction he had already begun. Especially, he was to combat cargo cult. Later the posi-

[1] The Pidgin text runs: '*Mi save tok bilong ol kiap long Brisbane em bulsit—em pinis nau—mipela no inap kisim samting—ol wetman igiamanim mipela, oli nolaik halivim mipela. Mipela no inap kisim samting bilong litimapim mipela.*'
[2] Both titles appear in Administration records.

tion was given added importance: a salary of 15s. a month (£9 a year) and rations—again to be paid by the Department of Native Affairs—was approved for his secretary.

The title of Foreman or Overseer gave Yali a status far higher than any native in the southern Madang District had ever enjoyed before under the German or Australian Administrations. The very fact of his receiving a salary at all clearly distinguished him from most ordinary village headmen who, with the exception of Paramount *Luluais*, were unpaid. In addition, what he had already been told in Madang was now restated in unequivocal terms: he was to be treated as their superior.

The other members of the party were greatly impressed by Yali's honour. A document typed in Port Moresby by Tarosi refers to him as a 'new Governor' (Pidgin English, *niupela Govner*)[1] and speaks of him as if he had received his authority in the southern Madang District from the Governor-General of Australia himself. But Yali was luke-warm about the appointment. Although he could tell ignorant bush natives that he was an Administration official and 'just the same as a Patrol Officer', he was himself too sophisticated not to know that it was a poor second best. He realized that Tarosi's and his other companions' enthusiasm was only wishful thinking. He had been rated as a native, even if a very superior one, and would never be treated as a European.

It was only in his third expectation—that his relationship with the missions would be clearly defined and that he would be allowed to draw up a blueprint for the native social order—that Yali received full satisfaction. During the first month of his stay in Port Moresby, he had many conversations with officers in the Department of Native Affairs. He asked about the Administration's attitude towards native culture and religion in general, and the worship of the spirits of the dead (Kabu Ceremony) in particular. He was told that the whole outlook of the Administration had changed. The old system of strong rule was to go. The intention now was to have the best possible relations with natives and gradually pave the way to eventual self-determination. It was hoped to build up a strong New Guinea people with a strong culture based on the best features of the European and native ways of life.[2] Thus the Administration, which had always adopted a neutral attitude in the past, was now actively in favour of the people retaining all those

[1] It would be wrong to read anything sinister into the phrase, but the choice of words shows the people's respect for Yali.

[2] There is no truth in the common European belief that Native Affairs officers sup-ported these statements by referring to the Independence of India and Pakistan. Yali *was* told about this event, but by an officer of the Department of Agriculture on 5 November 1947. (*Sic* Kasan's diary.) Yali himself took singularly little interest in the information.

customs which it had not already banned as impediments to their economic and social development. In religion—except only in the matter of cargo cult—complete freedom of conscience was guaranteed to all. If Yali and his people wished to remain pagans, there was no law to stop them. The missions had no right to interfere. But, he was advised, if he really wanted to revive old customs, he should be careful to see that he did so correctly. As a relatively young man, there was probably much that he had not been taught.[1] He should fill in the gaps in his knowledge by consulting the old men. Yali accepted this as evidence that the Administration wished him to perpetuate the Kabu Ceremony. This view was strengthened later when one of the officers allowed him to keep three naval megaphones, which he found in his garage. Yali wanted them as substitutes for gourd trumpets, of which there were very few left in the Ngaing area, most of them having been destroyed during the war.

At the same time, Yali was encouraged to draw up a set of 'laws', combining the best features of the two cultures, for native society. Helped by Tarosi, Kasan, and other literate members of his party as typists and consultants, he spent a great deal of time drafting several documents in Pidgin English.[2] One document listed influential supporters of Yali in Madang and its hinterland, and on the Rai Coast. Another dealt with the procedures for ordering goods from the stores. Others dealt with various facets of the new society, setting out new and old 'laws', and defining the relations between them. Thus one document covers the following subjects: organization of work in the villages; house-building; marriage rules; sanitation rules; pig husbandry; road-work; water rights; reef rights; land rights; funeral ceremonies; polygyny; pregnancy; betrothal; proper conduct when away from home; the use of sorcery and love magic; penile incision; cargo cult prophecies; ritual honour to the spirits of the dead (the Kabu Ceremony); and work on European plantations. Another deals with various offences punishable by law: playing *laki*;[3] drinking alcohol; fighting and generally disturbing the peace. A final document deals with such subjects as: the rights of the natives under the Court of Appeal; rules for pagans and Christians respectively concerning polygyny; mission work; schools and education; the rights of the individual versus the

[1] This was quite true. Even today, contrary to popular native opinion, Yali is extremely ignorant of the finer points of his traditional culture—and freely admits it.

[2] For reasons of space these documents, hereafter called the Yali Papers, cannot be included as an Appendix. I intend to publish them in a later work.

[3] A card game probably invented by native indentured labourers themselves. As it generally involves gambling, it is forbidden by Administration law.

Administration; Native Village (Local Government) Councils; communal village work; and the duties of native policemen and the limitation of their authority. It was stated categorically that police and mission helpers were not to beat or in any way maltreat prisoners or children in their charge.

The Yali 'Laws' were never, as far as I know, tested by the Crown Law Office for their strict legality. This was probably quite unnecessary, for they do not appear to have contravened the Administration's legal codes in any way. But, although they had been approved by officers in the Department of Native Affairs, it was nevertheless thought proper that they should be submitted to the Administrator for inspection. The 'Laws' were, therefore, formally presented to him on 3 November, when he met the party officially. According to the typewritten account in the Yali Papers, the Administrator received the documents without special comment. But, according to Yali, the Administrator told him personally on this occasion that he fully approved of the 'Laws' and then asked him how much of the old culture he knew. When Yali admitted that he had been so long away from home that he had forgotten a great deal about it, His Honour smilingly repeated the advice already given him by the other officers, that he consult the old men on matters about which he was uncertain—especially in the field of religious ceremonies—so as to be sure of his ground.

After these remarks, Yali believed that his victory over the missions was complete: he need brook no further interference from them, not only in religion but also in all other aspects of native life. Nevertheless, the occasion must have been particularly galling for him. According to the Yali Papers, in order to impress on the party the Administration's new outlook and the extent of its efforts for native welfare, His Honour explained that, whereas before the war the money available for development had been limited to taxes on copra and gold, now the Australian Government was providing large financial subsidies (for economic, political, educational, and medical advancement), for which it expected no return. Yet, apparently, none of this was going to be used to provide the bulk cargo which Yali needed beyond anything else to solve the problems waiting for him in Madang.

### Yali conceives the Pagan Revival

The codification of the 'Laws' was significant in itself as the first written statement of the aims of the Rehabilitation Scheme. But it had even more important results: it led Yali to certain very startling discoveries about European ideas concerning human origins, which in turn caused him to revise his programme when he returned to Madang. One aspect of his conversations with Native Affairs officers had puzzled him—their apparent indifference to Christianity, which after all was officially their own religion, and to the work of the missions. He mentioned the problem to Tarosi and his companions. Tarosi, in the course of his studies, had learnt about the concept of Evolution and had read books on the subject. He answered Yali's question by showing him and the others diagrams which illustrated the gradual emergence of animals, the Great Apes and, finally, Man.[1]

Tarosi no doubt had some appreciation of the meaning of Evolution but it created a sensation among his hearers. It undermined a whole generation or more of Christian education. On Yali the effect was even greater. It will be remembered that among the Ngaing human origins were traditionally explained in terms of totemism, which was one of the fundamental assumptions of the old religion. Moreover, one of the early results of Christianity among the Ngaing had been that, especially within the younger generation, the Creation Story in the Book of Genesis had replaced the matriclan totemic myths and assumed their position of unquestioned authority. Thus, although Yali had never formally adopted Christianity, the information had for him implications which a casual European observer would not have readily appreciated: it struck at the heart of all missionary teaching. He said to Tarosi: 'But I thought that white men believed that both they and we were descended from Adam and Eve! What are all these animals and particularly this *monki*?'[2] Tarosi replied that he had studied in Lutheran mission schools as well as those of the Administration, and had read the Bible. He understood Yali's difficulties. The answer to his question was that it was true that some Europeans believed that they were descended from Adam and Eve, as the Scriptures stated, but others believed that they were descended from the *monki*.[3] There was no full agreement on the subject.

This explanation was completely misunderstood. Natives of the southern Madang District always possessed, as we have seen, an essentially homogeneous intellectual system. They could not appreciate that Europeans were able to live together yet disagree about fundamental issues of religious belief: that some could be orthodox Christians

---

[1] The incident is briefly recorded in Kasan's diary for 19 October 1947.

[2] The Pidgin English term used to describe the Great Apes.

[3] I am paraphrasing Yali's description of the conversation to me. It suggests that Tarosi did not fully understand that evolutionary theory stated that human beings and the apes (*monki*) had a common ancestor rather than that human beings were descended from the apes.

accepting the Bible as incontrovertible truth, whereas others could be atheist or agnostic and adhere to Darwinian theory; and that these differences could be determined by individual conscience rather than *a priori* membership in fixed social groups.[1] Hence Yali interpreted what Tarosi had to say in terms of the beliefs of his own society: one specific group of Europeans claimed descent from the joint totem Adam-and-Eve, while another entirely discrete group claimed descent from the totem *monki*.

Later this interpretation was expanded. Yali thought back to his visit to the Brisbane Zoo, where the animals were properly housed, cared for, and fed at regular intervals. He reflected on the bones of the prehistoric animals he had seen in the Queensland Museum and the European habit of keeping seemingly useless pets, on which they lavished a degree of care and affection unknown in New Guinea villages. Finally, just over a fortnight[2] after his discussion with Tarosi, he visited the Agricultural Station near Sogeri. He had a long conversation with one of the station officers about animal husbandry. He was shown how European animals were housed, and how experiments were conducted to improve conditions for them and help them adapt to the tropics. The officer suggested to Yali that he urge his people to take better care of their own animals, both domesticated and wild. They should feed them properly and, above all, give up the practice of burning off grassland and slaughtering them wholesale.

Suddenly, Yali claims, the truth dawned on him. The animals at the Zoo and the Agricultural Station, the pets in the houses, and the bones in the museum—these were all additional European totems or relics of totems. The Christianity taught the people by the missionaries was false in one vital respect. White men did not have just one or two but multiple totemic origins as did his own people. Apart from the two groups descended from Adam-and-Eve and the *monki*, there were yet others claiming the horse, cow, dog, cat, lioness, tigress, zebra, and other animals as their ancestresses.[3] Furthermore, the attention lavished on these animals and the respect accorded them when dead were of the same order as Ngaing taboos preventing totems from being harmed in any way.

[1] It could be argued that natives had seen a similar conflict between pagans and Christians in their own society. But, as seen, God and Jesus had been absorbed into their own pantheon, in a part, if not the whole, of which everyone believed. It was not a cleavage between faith and atheism.

[2] On 5 November 1947 (*sic* Kasan's diary).

[3] As a Ngaing, Yali thought in terms of matrilineal totems, although a joint totem such as Adam-and-Eve was perfectly legitimate, Eve being the principal totem, of course.

N

Until now Yali's attitude towards the missions had been ambivalent. On the one hand, he had demanded complete religious freedom and, since his discomfiture after his visit to Bogia, he had personally dissociated himself from all Christian activities. On the other, he had always wanted to retain the missions for the education they provided, if for nothing else. Yet now, especially because he believed that they were powerless to touch him, he used them as a scapegoat for all his pent-up bitterness over his failure to get cargo from the Administration. He regarded all Europeans as liars and cheats, but the main force of his fury was turned on the missionaries. They had deliberately deceived the people. They had hidden from them the truth about human origins; and if they were prepared to be dishonest about so simple and basic a matter, it was hardly likely that they would ever reveal the really important secret they possessed—the ultimate source of the cargo. His companions could forget the advice they had given him in Lae. As far as he was concerned, it was an utter waste of time. He was finished with Europeans of every kind.

Yet self-pity was not going to solve Yali's problems. He had some idea from the letters he had received of what was going on around Madang and Saidor during his absence, although he did not fully realize the extent to which the new cargo prophecies had swept throughout the whole southern Madang District. He knew well that he was expected back with ships full of goods. A Rai Coast catechist had written to him suggestively that he had seen the Light of God shining from his house at Sor[1] and that £10 had mysteriously appeared in one of his wooden chests, which had been removed to the new mansion now completed or nearing completion at Sangpat. Yali obviously needed a new policy to neutralize the people's disappointment when he returned empty-handed, and save himself from the disgrace and obscurity which were the fate of all cargo leaders who failed to live up to their promises.

Yali weighed up the position as follows: Both 'roads to the cargo' were 'closed'. The missionaries were determined to keep the people in ignorance of their secret and, at the same time, by discouraging ritual to the pagan gods and ceremonies in honour of the spirits of the dead, were depriving them of benefits from the old religion. The natives were in limbo, as it were, denied advantages from both sources. Again, the Administration had broken its wartime pledge. Nevertheless, it had allowed Yali a large measure of responsibility for the future of his

---

[1] Yali discovered on his return that it was the hurricane lamp which his wife Sunggum kept burning at night while she slept—a very common native practice.

society by encouraging him to frame the 'Laws', to be derived from both European and native culture. Those derived from European culture he had selected because they would promote clean and orderly living, values which, in spite of his present bitterness against all white men, he had personally internalized during his service in the Police Force and army. But those derived from native culture were ultimately of far greater importance to him: as he saw it, they represented an unconditional guarantee of religious freedom not only from the Department of Native Affairs but also from the Administrator himself.

Because of this guarantee, Yali decided that it would be quite within his charter and in the interests of his people to organize a widespread revival of paganism. He would urge them to abandon Christianity and quasi-Christian cargo ritual—between which, like most natives, he made little or no distinction—on the grounds that they could never produce the results expected, and to return to the religious beliefs and practices of the past.[1] They should do this in anticipation of getting *not* cargo but the traditional advantages their old religion had conferred: the bigger crops, the greater abundance of game in the bush, and the larger numbers of pigs in the villages, which were essential for their way of life. They would give up all aspirations to a fully European culture and be satisfied with their lot as natives. But they would be once more men with their own self-respect, for they would be relieved of the burden of frustration and anxiety thrust on them by the defective Christianity taught them by the missions: the hopes that were constantly unfulfilled, and the fear of punishment by the Administration for performing illegal ritual.

One point should be emphasized here. Yali's decision to start a pagan revival was basically a clarification of his rather imprecise ideas before he visited Port Moresby. The main difference was that now, instead of encouraging religious toleration and symbiosis, he was wholeheartedly advocating religious segregation. Although convinced of the duplicity of the missionaries, he did not believe that the Christianity practised by white men had no basis of truth.[2] He assumed that there were two separate religions in New Guinea, each constituted in roughly the same way and each powerful in its own sphere. First, there was Christianity, with its two deities (God and Jesus Christ), spirits of the dead, and multiple totems. God and Jesus Christ were

[1] The abandonment of cargo ritual would also be strictly in accordance with the wishes of the Administration.

[2] As was assumed by many Europeans after the inauguration of the pagan revival. I made the same false assumption in 1949–50. See my 'Cargo Cult', op. cit., p. 16. It is echoed also by Burridge, *Mambu*, op. cit., pp. 199–200.

responsible for the material and social culture of the Europeans: in fact, for everything he had seen in Australia. This was the Europeans' secret. They would never reveal more than its externals to outsiders and would resent any attempt to purloin it—as, for example, by means of cargo ritual. It had never been revealed or sold to the natives, and hence they had no rights to it whatever. Second, there was the native religion, which had its own deities, spirits, and totems.[1] These deities were responsible for the New Guinea material and social culture, to which he would now encourage his people to return. Beyond the European modifications written into the new 'Laws' he had drawn up, there was to be no further compromise between the two ways of life.

This religious policy was worked out by Yali in a vacuum: it was a product partly of his disappointment and fury, and partly of his pressing need to save face. He had not really taken into account the growing strength of the Cargo Movement in the whole southern Madang District while he had been away. It was, therefore, questionable how long his new propaganda would be able to keep it suppressed. Furthermore, the policy was based on the assumption that cargo doctrine was simpler and more clear-cut than in fact it was, and that it was possible to eradicate it merely by replacing Christianity with paganism. There were still factors in the situation which it would have been very difficult to foresee.

---

[1] Yali was unaware that other societies in the southern Madang District had no totemism. When I told him that this was true of the Garia, he assured me that they had been lying.

# CHAPTER VIII

# THE FIFTH CARGO BELIEF

## 1948–50

### *The Return to Madang and the Biliā Assembly*

THE party left Port Moresby in M.V. *Montoro*[1] on 10 December 1947 and, after calling at Samarai and Lae, reached Madang on the 17th.[2] Again they had to travel as natives, living in the forecastle and sleeping on deck. Yali's new status in the Administration did not get him and the others special treatment. With the threat of embarrassment ominously near, this increased his bitterness. According to Kasan,[3] one day when he was sitting on the hatch covers, he burst into a tirade about his treatment in Port Moresby. Four months had been wasted looking at schools, workshops, Councils, and other activities he could have seen just as well in his own area. He might as well have never gone to Papua for all the good he had got out of it.

As it turned out, however, Yali's anxiety about his reception in Madang was unnecessary. As soon as he landed he went to Biliā, where he had trade friends with whom he generally stayed.[4] Next day local natives came into the village. They were all very pleased to see him again and, instead of asking him about his experiences in Port Moresby, told him about the arrangements made by the Administration for an assembly in Biliā on 4 January 1948, at which he was to give another public address. As this was the first he had heard of the matter, he went at once to the District Office to learn more about it and report back officially.

The Administration had good reason to call an assembly. The District Officer had heard about the wave of cargo activity which had swept through the Bagasin Area and Ramu Valley, and Madang and Saidor, since August. Although he did not know the full details, he was aware of the rumours that Yali was a spirit of the dead and would return with ships full of cargo to take over command of the District. He was naturally worried about the information, although he quite

[1] A Burns Philp ship at that time on the New Guinea run.
[2] Dates in this section are again taken from Kasan's diary.
[3] The incident is not recorded in the diary but was recounted to me personally.
[4] They were really trade friends of his Galek trade friends. But in the contact situation such distinctions became meaningless as a result of personal association.

correctly refused to believe that Yali was directly responsible. More-over, as Yali had become a minor official in his own Department, he sincerely wished to clear his name of any suspicion. He believed that the surest way to do this was to hold an open meeting, and enable Yali publicly to deny what was being said about him and repudiate once and for all the illicit activities being carried on in his name. Yali accepted the invitation. It would serve as a useful prelude to his pagan revival which, although it did not by any means reject the assumptions under-lying the cargo belief, was as near as he could get to complete personal dissociation from them.

Nevertheless, before the end of the year, Yali had to maintain even this equivocal position in the face of very strong inducements to the contrary. The two and a half weeks before the Biliā Assembly were too short for him to visit Sor. As he had learnt something of Kaum's and Angge's ritual in the villages near Saidor, he sent Wagara (one of his party) to the Rai Coast to make inquiries and bring back information. He himself asked the Assistant District Officer's permission to investi-gate similar activities said to be going on at Kurog, the village of Son and Bul'me, the two natives who had brought him the money and 'flags' in 1946.

The suggestion was readily endorsed. Yali returned to Biliā and next day, 19 December, was visited once more by local natives, who brought him presents.[1] That night there was a dance in his honour, two teams participating—one from Sek and Riwo, and the other from Biliā. On 20 December, Yali, accompanied by Kasan and a few others, set out for Kurog. Kasan's diary account (the last entry) is very bald and seemingly innocuous: 'Yali went to Kurog to inspect Son's "camp". At night they held a dance until dawn. Yali stayed another night in Kurog. At three o'clock in the morning they danced again till dawn. Yali lined the head-men of Kurog and gave them instructions. Then we returned to Biliā.' In fact, these proceedings at Kurog were far from innocent and, al-though Yali managed to dismiss them at the time, later made a lasting impression on him. We must consider here, first, the nature of the 'dances' performed and, second, the content of the instructions given the headmen.

The 'dances' were literally cargo seances, which were based on some form of Letub doctrine and divided into two parts. At the beginning there was a 'church service', for which the people appeared in their best European clothes: laplaps or shorts and shirts for the men, and blouses

---

[1] The nature of the presents is not specified in the diary but most probably they con-sisted in part, if not wholly, of cash payments.

and fibre skirts for the women. They sat outside on the ground singing hymns and reciting prayers to God[1] in Pidgin English. After his discoveries in Port Moresby, Yali was in no mood to listen to Christian talk and began to show his impatience. He asked sarcastically when the cargo was to appear. Son and Bul'me counselled him to wait, and then directed his attention to a woman in the congregation and told him to watch her very carefully. She began to twitch and tremble all over, and to roll her head and eyes. They then invited him to inspect her body and satisfy himself that she was concealing nothing. He looked in her hands and blouse, and ran his fingers under the waistband of her skirt. There was nothing there. Then she left her place in the congregation and began to wander around the village, shaking, taking drunken steps, and mouthing inanities. Son and Bul'me said to Yali: 'God has entered her body.'[2] A man followed her with a cup of water. Yali was invited to walk beside the pair and observe them closely. Every now and then, as the woman took a few steps, she held out her hand clasped tightly. Then she opened it, with a single shilling in the palm. This she dropped into the cup of water. She then closed her hand again, opened it, and once more dropped a shilling into the cup. She repeated the sequence of actions until there were 10s. altogether. Thereafter she gradually became normal again. When Yali asked her where the money came from, she replied: 'An angel got it from God and gave it to me.'

When this part of the seance was over, the congregation dispersed and removed their European clothes. Later they reassembled wearing traditional dance dress: bark girdles or fibre skirts, bone and shell ornaments, floral decorations, and so forth. They lined up as a team and performed what was presumably a version of the Letub dance.[3] For a while nothing spectacular happened. Then a man began to dance with his hands above his head. Again Yali was invited to inspect his body and found nothing. The dancer then staggered about and produced ten single shillings in exactly the same way as the woman had done. This money also was said to have come from God. At the end of the seance Yali, remembering his experiences in the Galek cemetery in 1946, asked Son and Bul'me if they did not lay out food offerings for the ancestors. They replied that they had given up the practice but had used it in the past with marked success. They showed him a bag of money and some

[1] God was the only deity mentioned. Yali never heard the name of Manup (or Kilibob) mentioned, as one would have expected in Letub country. It is possible that Kurog had learnt the ritual without the underlying mythology (cf. p. 96). The situation in the area needs further research.

[2] The Pidgin English text ran: '*God ikam pinis long sikin bilong meri.*'

[3] Yali, who knew nothing of the local culture, described it as *Laloi*, a Sengam dance.

cartridges, which they claimed had been sent them during the war, by way of proof. When he asked them how they had discovered the ritual, they told him that they had learnt it from the mission.[1] But he did not make any inquiries about the relevant doctrine, automatically supposing that it was derived from ordinary Christianity.

Yali had come to Kurog fully convinced that natives would never solve the riddle of the white man's wealth. Although he still accepted the underlying assumptions of quasi-Christian cargo doctrine, he had no faith in the efficacy of the ritual techniques hitherto employed. But now he was satisfied that he had actually seen shillings sent by God appear before his eyes. He did not recognize that the seance had been rigged. He believed that his examination of the woman's and man's bodies ruled out the possibility of sleight of hand. He made no attempt to contradict the statements made by Son and Bul'me, and allowed them to think that he believed that they were telling the truth.

In spite of this, Yali was not now prepared to become involved in this or any other cargo cult he knew to exist. He was still furious about his failure in Port Moresby, and the pagan revival had become an obsession. In addition, as an Administration official, he did not yet dare risk trouble with the District Office. Thus, when on the morning he left Kurog[2] he lined the headmen, he told them that, although he would not urge the Administration to take action against their cult, it was entirely their affair and they must not look for co-operation from him. On his return to Madang, he felt that his position was fully justified. When he reported what he had seen, the Assistant District Officer shrugged and commented in a resigned tone that he was tired of the whole business. The courts kept on imprisoning natives for cargo ritual but it did not do the slightest good. Yali completely misunderstood the remark: he thought that it proved his point, that what really angered Europeans was the attempted theft of their property.

At this stage, it is essential to reconsider Yali's religious standpoint. So far it had been relatively uncomplicated. As has been stressed, he saw only a simple dichotomy: between Christianity, which was the sole repository of the cargo secret, and paganism, which was not. He had never heard of the Second Cargo Belief[3] and, in spite of his experiences in the Galek cemetery in 1946 and more recently at Kurog, of its syncretic modifications in the Fourth Cargo Belief. These were the hidden

---

[1] Presumably the Lutheran Mission, to which they nominally belonged.

[2] Presumably 22 December, although no dates are given in the diary after the 20th. Yali described the seance as if it was conducted during one night only, although it may well have been repeated the second night, as is suggested by the diary account.

[3] Of which there was no counterpart among the Ngaing.

factors with which he had not previously reckoned and which he had now to learn: the links which had already been forged between Christianity and paganism by the Letubists and Tagarab in the Madang area.

After his return from Kurog Yali had still two weeks to fill in before the Biliā Assembly. He began to put into practice the advice given him in Papua, that he should discuss traditional customs with the old men before trying to reintroduce them. Accordingly, he asked the Biliā people what they could remember of their mythology. They replied that they had been brought up under the Lutheran Mission and were too young to know anything about it. But there was one man in Sek village, the *Luluai* Sagwi, who could tell him all he wanted to know. Sagwi, therefore, was invited to Biliā.

Sagwi was very proud to show off his knowledge, especially to such a distinguished visitor. He claimed to be the sole repository of all Madang traditional mythology.[1] He recounted the second version of the Second Cargo Belief, in which Manup as cargo deity had gone to Australia. His exposition included many details lacking in the version worked out during German rule and borrowed from Letub doctrine: although he did not mention that Manup was believed to be Jesus Christ,[2] he included such features as the building of Sydney and the dockyard installations. He made it quite clear that the cargo secret had been originally a purely native possession, which the white men had acquired by accident.

For the next few days there was a great deal of discussion. Some of the Madang and Rai Coast natives supplied the details which Sagwi had omitted: how Manup had been reborn as Jesus Christ from the Virgin Mary and prevented by the crucifixion from returning with the missionaries to New Guinea. Others expounded Tagarab's doctrine. All of them left Yali with no doubt that it needed only a word from him for the two cults to be co-ordinated on a grand scale under his direct leadership. But again, although he was quite prepared to believe that what he had been told was true, he refused to become involved. The Kilibob-Manup myth was not part of Ngaing culture and for him to make use of it would be illicit appropriation of Madang property. He did not want trouble on that account in the future. He told the

---

[1] This, of course, was not true. There were other old men, as in Yabob and Milguk, who still knew something about pagan mythology.

[2] For reasons I never could discover. It is probable that Sagwi followed the trend apparent during the Japanese Occupation, when the Sek people were said to have eliminated Christian elements from the Letub. In 1956, Sagwi told me the same version of the myth.

people, therefore, that he and the Ngaing had other deities, and would be content to use them for traditional ends.

Thus Yali considered that he could face the assembly sponsored by the Administration on 4 January 1948 with a clean record and a clear conscience. It was a notable function, elaborately staged and well attended. Natives came to Biliā from the Madang hinterland, Bagasin Area, and Rai Coast, and European representatives from the Administration, missions, and commercial community were also present. Refreshments were served by the Biliā people to visitors of both races.

Yali spoke from a specially erected dais, decorated with an Australian flag, as a symbol of his new status in the Administration, and native ornamentation. He was briefly introduced by the District Officer and then spoke himself for a considerable period.[1] His speech, according to his own and other accounts, followed the lines already suggested to him: that he denounce the rumours circulating about himself and dissociate himself from cargo cult in all its forms. He spread himself on both points. First, he denied categorically that he was a spirit of the dead. He was a living man like everybody else, and to think otherwise was nonsense. Second, he stated roundly that he would have nothing to do with cargo ritual. The people would never see him praying to God[2] or the ancestors for ships and aeroplanes to arrive. If they wanted cargo in the future, they must buy it with money earned from business enterprise. Finally, they must obey the Administration and the 'Laws' he had codified in Port Moresby. When he finished his speech, the Administration officers and some of the other Europeans were confident, at least for the time being, that he had clarified his position entirely to their satisfaction. They did not appreciate that he had repudiated cargo cult not on the grounds of rational disbelief but for the reasons he had formulated in Port Moresby and during the last few days in Madang: his fear of being accused of stealing other people's religious secrets.

### The Return to the Rai Coast and the Pagan Revival

As soon as the assembly was over, Yali began to prepare the ground for the pagan revival, his last serious attempt to divorce his Rehabilitation Scheme from the Cargo Movement. He told the natives that he had still a great deal to say about the 'Laws', which would have to wait until he got home. He was referring, of course, to his intention to attack

---

[1] All speeches were delivered in Pidgin English.

[2] This implicitly included Jesus-Manup and God-Kilibob, about whom he had learnt after he had returned from Kurog.

Christianity.[1] He then set out by road for the Rai Coast, followed by a large retinue which, by the time of his arrival, had been considerably augmented by natives from the Erima and Bogati area. Later he was joined by Son and Bul'me of Kurog. When he reached Saidor, he was given first-hand accounts by the Officer-in-Charge at the Administration Station about events during his absence: the building of his own 'station' at Sangpat and the cargo rumours current in the Sub-District.

Sangpat 'Station' does not concern us here. It was formally presented to Yali at a ceremony at which he 'opened the door'[2] of his new house and a dance was held in honour of the event. He now had two houses, the other being in Sor village. He commuted between the two as he had occasion: to Sangpat for 'official' purposes; and to Sor for his ordinary private affairs.

The cargo rumours and ritual, however, were a real problem. Even before he talked with the O.C. Saidor, Yali knew a good deal about them. From the letters he had been sent in Port Moresby, his recent discussions in Madang, and Wagara's scouting expedition, he had learnt that the whole Nankina-Mot seaboard was involved in cargo activities of some kind, that the ritual performed in the Galek cemetery since 1946 was based on the Letub belief that Manup was Jesus Christ, and that Kaum and Angge were using Tagarab's doctrine. But as the ritual still had strong associations with Christianity, he was as keen as the O.C. Saidor himself to suppress it. He could ignore what was going on around Madang, but he did not want his own area involved. He agreed to summon those concerned to the Administration Station and call them to account for what they had been doing. He addressed them in roughly the same terms, and based his arguments implicitly on the same private reasons, as in his speech at Biliã on 4 January. In view of his recent discoveries about the nature of the ritual performed, he added the strong hint that he did not wish to see 'Madang property' stolen to the Rai Coast.[3]

The speech at Saidor was only a prelude to what was to come. Yali had still to announce to the people at large the results of his visit to

[1] This became known to Europeans as 'Yali's secret talk', in which he was supposed to have announced new cargo doctrine. This was wrong. The new cargo doctrine grew up in different circumstances to be described later.

[2] Modelled on the Lutheran ceremony, at which a new building is inaugurated by having a missionary or other dignitary first open the door and then formally go inside.

[3] That is, ritual based on the Kilibob-Manup myth, which he chose to designate as exclusively 'Madang property', even though he now realized that the Sengam and their neighbours on the seaboard had rights to the second version of the traditional myth and knew something about Letub doctrine. He wanted to keep cargo cult as far away from the Rai Coast as possible.

Papua. Towards the end of January, another assembly was held at Sangpat. It was attended by natives from as far away as Cape Rigney and Gal, on both sides of the Nankina, as well as the retinue of Madang and Bogati people which had accompanied Yali on his return. The local Europeans were also present: the O.C. Saidor and his second-in-command, the Lutheran pastor from Biliau, and the Catholic priest from Gumbi. Again Yali appeared on a specially prepared dais, and two Australian flags were flown: one for the Saidor officers and the other in recognition of Yali's new position in the Administration.

Yali did not speak at length. He briefly introduced Kasan, his secretary, who then expounded the 'Laws' prepared in Port Moresby. Kasan went through each document in turn, giving every point equal emphasis, and occasionally asking his hearers to signify that they had understood what they had been told.[1] At the end of the meeting, however, Yali spoke again and introduced what the two missionaries could only regard as an ominous note. He singled out for special attention the section of the 'Laws' relating to the Kabu Ceremony. He stressed that the Administrator himself had told him that the people were free to perform it if they wished. Missionaries and other Europeans had no authority to interfere, and would do so at their own risk. The Kabu Ceremony could unleash terrible power. This had been proved at Aiyawang village in 1936, when Patrol Officer Nurton had been attacked and severely wounded because of the sacrilegious behaviour of his native police, who had purloined gourd trumpets and shown them to some of the local women. This had infuriated the deity Yabuling, who had invented the Kabu Ceremony, and the spirits of the dead, in whose honour it was held. They had jointly brought about Nurton's downfall. The point had added weight because Yali could claim to speak from personal knowledge: he had accompanied Nurton on this patrol.

After the meeting at Sangpat, Yali had to get back to the humdrum affairs of daily life. The official speech-making, flag-wagging, and excitement were temporarily over, and more practical issues had to be taken into consideration. Of these, the most pressing was to forestall the question which, amid all the popular acclaim, it had been possible so far to avoid: Where was the cargo the people had been promised?

Back in Sor, Yali told the people what had really happened in Port Moresby: how the Administration had brazenly dishonoured its wartime pledges; how he had been fobbed off with a dull conducted tour

---

[1] Kasan did not actually read out the documents but used them as notes. Yali, being illiterate, could not have done this, and he had not memorized the 'Laws' well enough to recite them at length.

of exhibits which were of no interest to him or them—things they already knew about; and how Tarosi had shown him that the missionaries had withheld basic secrets about human origins. All that he had achieved was official permission to revive and carry on with the old religious ceremonies. In fact, the Europeans only wanted them to remain *kanakas* and had no real interest in their material welfare. Dramatically he threw away his much-prized European clothing and appeared in a bark girdle. 'If that is all the white men want,' he cried, 'then we shall be *kanakas* in earnest!'

From now on Yali began his campaign against Christianity. He completed the negotiations to marry Rebecca of Matokar as a second wife.[1] He attacked the missionaries in public on every possible occasion. They had robbed the people of the strength their forbears used to derive from the traditional religion by forbidding ritual to the deities and spirits of the dead, and by trying to drive out the deities by sprinkling holy water over their sanctuaries.[2] By way of return, they had tricked the people into accepting the externals of Christianity but had consistently refused to reveal the vital secret which was the key to the Europeans' material wealth. In this way, the natives had been easily held in political subjection. Now they should assert themselves. They should throw out the missions and give up all hope of getting cargo, and they should revert to paganism and their own way of life.

This invective was reinforced by action. Yali allowed no one to conduct Christian worship in his presence. He terrified the local catechists into abandoning church services and school lessons, and their congregations into unprotesting acquiescence. The old men were encouraged to recite traditional mythology, most of which the younger men had never heard. Yali instructed them to make sure that every adult male knew the background of the Kabu Ceremony, which had been performed during the last three years at least without the younger participants knowing the Yabuling myth. By the end of February 1948, to the extent that the old religion could be revived, Sor and Paramus were once again fully pagan villages.

The pagan revival was restricted to a relatively small area. The inland Ngaing and the Rai Coast peoples outside the Nankina-Mot region were too far away to be affected immediately. Even within the Nankina-Mot region, the position of certain villages remained in the balance.

---

[1] A little later he took a third wife, Sasamai, also from the Matokar region, but she left him after a short period because of his alleged cruelty to her.

[2] This was unjustified for the Ngaing area, where the Catholic Mission had been relatively lenient. It had ignored much of the pagan religion—certainly until very recently —and had sprinkled holy water on very few deity sanctuaries.

Wab and Yaimas were still under the influence of Kaum and Angge, who allowed a short interval to elapse after the meetings at Saidor and Sangpat before starting their ritual again. The coastal Sengam villages from Biliau to Suit refused to repudiate Christianity and remained technically loyal to the Lutheran Mission for reasons to be discussed later on. But the sub-coastal villages near Sor and Paramus—Amun, Batak, Sereng, and Maibang among the Ngaing, and Yori and Malangai among the Sengam—were quick to follow Yali's lead. This was due to three factors. First, these villages had never had strong ties with the missions, which could have counteracted the magic of Yali's personality and propaganda, and his new status within the Administration. Second, the natives in these villages were heartily tired of performing dull Christian rituals for no appreciable return. For instance, the people of Malangai, when challenged about their anti-mission attitude, replied that they would no longer pray for the Second Coming of Jesus Christ with the ancestors and cargo. The whole thing was futile and 'their backsides ached'. Third, the pagan revival was an excellent palliative or short-term substitute for Yali's promised reward. The general excitement of the final change-over from one religion to the other, the rediscovery of self-respect, and the endless discussion and local speech-making to which they gave rise, took the people's minds off the disappointment they must have felt. In these villages, therefore, churches and schools were deserted, and mission helpers who had the temerity to object were silenced with threats of physical violence. They either joined the pagan revival or left their posts to return to Gumbi or Biliau. The two missionaries, if ever they tried to intervene, were politely kept at arm's length or rudely asked to leave the village.

### The Birth of the Fifth Cargo Belief

During February–March 1948, the pagan revival ran more or less according to plan. The villages which adopted it prepared to celebrate the Harvest Festival about April. Apart from browbeating the mission helpers,[1] Yali had done nothing to exceed his charter from Port Moresby or to give the Administration cause to interfere. Above all else, he flatly dismissed any new overtures from cargo cult leaders or other enthusiasts. Pales came from Dumpu, bringing a very large amount of money, which he had made by charging the Ramu natives either for enjoyment of sexual promiscuity or for being baptized. He boasted to Yali about what he had been doing. Yali was furious. He

---

[1] Which was no worse than the behaviour of many mission helpers towards their own followers.

ordered Pales to leave Sor, take the money back to Dumpu at once, and tell the people there that he himself was not responsible for anything that had been done in their area.[1]

About the same time, Kaum, who had already proclaimed himself Yali's equal, visited Sor with the aim of bringing the pagan revival into line with his own cult. He was quick to recognize the significance of the new policy. He dropped the name of God entirely from his doctrine and used only that of Kilibob as an indigenous New Guinea cargo deity. He claimed that he was about to produce cargo by means of pagan ritual almost identical with Yali's: Kilibob would soon send ships and military equipment for the war against the Europeans he had been planning since 1944. To prove his point, he brought Yali five old rifles and two machine guns he had found near Wab. He urged Yali to order the people to join in the seances at Wab and to clean up the village cemeteries as a mark of respect for the spirits of the dead.

On this occasion, Yali received Kaum politely but refused his invitation. Although he believed that the Kilibob doctrine might well be valid, he still regarded it as Madang rather than Ngaing property and, for that reason, refused to meddle with it. Again, as the rifles and machine guns were rusty and unusable, and he had no difficulty in recognizing that they had been left behind by the Japanese,[2] he was not convinced that Kaum was as likely to succeed with his cult as he boasted. Finally, he knew about Kaum's record with the Administration and realized that any association with him would be dangerous.

These good intentions, however, were short-lived. About April 1948, Yali was approached by an entirely new cargo prophet, who quickly gained ascendancy over him. In fact, he offered virtually no resistance whatever. The man in question had all the advantages both Pales and Kaum lacked. He did not advocate cargo ritual based on Christianity or New Guinea deities to whom Yali and the other Ngaing had no inherited rights. He was completely unknown to the Administration for cargo cult or any other illicit activities, and could not be an immediate embarrassment on this score.

The new prophet was Gurek, a native of Hapurpi village, inland from Sek. He had been trained as a Catholic catechist at Alexishafen. He had served his mission in this capacity on the Rai Coast until the

[1] Thereafter Pales died in obscurity during 1948-9. I was unable to meet him. According to a European informant, whom Pales visited *en route*, the sum of money he brought to Yali must have been about £400.

[2] As elsewhere, the Japanese had left a great number of weapons behind them in their retreat from the Rai Coast. Not all of them were collected by Allied forces. One of their rifles was found in use as far inland as Yakierak as late as 1953.

Japanese invasion in 1942, when he returned to his own village, and again after the reopening of Gumbi Station in January 1946. During both periods of duty he had worked in Sisagel village, a few hours' walking distance from Sor.

Until 1948, there had been nothing remarkable about Gurek's career. He was unassuming and his work had always satisfied the missionaries under whom he had served. Yet during his period of training and the years of the Japanese Occupation he had been involved in the Letub situation. At school at Alexishafen he had heard the doctrine that Manup was Jesus Christ, and throughout the war he had witnessed Letub seances at Sek and Hapurpi, when pagan elements were beginning to replace those derived from Christianity.

Gurek, therefore, had a considerable working knowledge of existing cargo doctrine. He now developed a latent talent for elaborating new theories. As far as can be ascertained, while Yali had been away in Papua, he had attended Kaum's and Angge's seances at Wab. They doubtless reminded him of Letub ritual. Later he heard Yali's anti-mission propaganda. He now began to surprise the people of Sisagel and Amun by claiming to have visions in which he saw 'lines of deity-soldiers' (Pidgin English,[1] *lain masalai soldia*) drilling and on exercise in the bush. They were Rai Coast deities and eventually they would bring rifles and other Western goods to the people. But the people could not see them because they had anger in their hearts and were perpetually quarrelling with each other.[2] They must follow his example and live at peace together. He then publicly renounced his work as a catechist, and openly supported the pagan revival on the grounds that it was the people's true 'road to the cargo'.

News of these visions and prophecies soon spread. Yali was puzzled when he heard about them, for no one had ever suggested before that his own Ngaing deities were the cargo source. Thus when Gurek came to see him in the hope of winning him over to the programme he had in mind, he was sufficiently intrigued to listen. Gurek told him that he also was disillusioned with the missions. For years he had worked as a catechist without getting any insight into the white men's secret. But now, surreptitiously from a priest at Alexishafen, he had learnt the truth. Yali asked him to explain.

Gurek's doctrine was complex. He modified Letub ideas so as to

---

[1] Which, as a Madang native, he habitually spoke on the Rai Coast.
[2] This seems to have become a catch cry in the Cargo Movement at the time. It hardly applied to the Ngaing who, in my experience, are extremely even-tempered and rarely quarrel among themselves.

bring them into line with the pagan revival, but also incorporated additional pieces of information, which hitherto had been discussed but not satisfactorily interpreted. He began by saying that, as everyone knew, Jesus-Manup, the indigenous New Guinea cargo deity, was held captive in Heaven (above Sydney) as result of the crucifixion. As he could not himself return to his own country, he had to devise alternative means of sending goods to his people. He had discovered that other New Guinea deities were in Australia and had taught them the art of making cargo.

To understand Gurek's claim, it is necessary to reconsider one of Yali's wartime experiences, his visit to the Queensland Museum in 1944–5. It will be remembered that Son of Kurog, a member of the party, asked why missionaries urged natives to 'root out Satan', whereas other Europeans assembled native artefacts (the things invented by the 'satans' or local deities) in the museum. When the troops came home, the incident was frequently debated around Madang and on the Rai Coast. Yali himself had described the artefacts in these terms: 'Our myths are there also' (Ngaing, *parambiknining iretigang*; Pidgin English, *sitori bilong yumi istap*). The word 'myth' (*parambik, sitori*) in this context broadly connoted 'New Guinea culture'. As myths about artefacts were invariably associated with gods or goddesses, it was natural for Gurek to reason that Yali and the others had discovered the New Guinea deities in the museum. Furthermore, although it cannot be proved, Gurek very probably connected Yali's experience with an event that must have caused comment, if not misgiving, among natives around Sek during the interwar years. The Catholics had built up at Alexishafen an ethnographic museum containing dance-masks, hand-drums, decorated skulls, and wooden statues (*telum*) of gods and ancestors. In 1925 and 1932, many of the specimens were sent to the Lateran Museum in Rome.[1]

Almost certainly because of this, Gurek told Yali that the museum he had visited in Brisbane was in fact 'Rome'[2] and what he had seen in the showcases had been the New Guinea deities, whom the missionaries had stolen and sent away. Some had presumably been carried out of the

[1] See *The New Guinea Handbook*, op. cit., p. 464. I am also indebted to Rev. Fr M. Schulien (Director of the Lateran Museum, Rome), Very Reverend Fr J. Schütte (Superior General of the Society of the Divine Word, Rome), and Bishop A. Noser of Alexishafen for personal communications. Unfortunately, while I was in the field, I did not know about the collection and its being sent to the Lateran Museum. Hence I never made the relevant inquiries.

[2] It is worth noting that there is a Roma Street Station in Brisbane, which was the railway terminus for troops travelling down from the north and stationed at Tabragalba Camp. This may have strengthened the idea discussed.

villages and included in the collection from Alexishafen.[1] Others had been conjured away by the Catholics when they sprinkled holy water on their sanctuaries, and by the Lutherans when they made their male converts display their secret religious paraphernalia to the women and children. The deities had made no attempt to stay in New Guinea as soon as the people had ceased to perform ritual to them and turned to useless Christian worship, such as Mass.

'Rome', however, was not only the official residence of the local deities in Australia. It was also directly beneath Heaven, to which, like Sydney, it was connected by a ladder.[2] God-Dodo (Anut), Jesus-Manup, and the ancestors normally lived in Heaven but could journey up and down the ladder as they felt inclined. Thus it was in 'Rome' that Jesus-Manup had at last come face to face with beings from his own country—his fellow New Guinea gods and goddesses. To them he had at once passed on the special knowledge which would save his people from perpetual subjection to Europeans. The 'satans' had become the people's true cargo source. Christianity and the missions were no longer important and could be by-passed. The natives had only to follow Yali's instructions: they should return to their pagan religious cere-monies so that the old gods and goddesses could be lured back to New Guinea to usher in a new period of prosperity.

Yali gave Gurek his support and allowed him to outline his pro-gramme at a public meeting at Sor. He did so for two reasons. In the first place, not only did he firmly believe what he had been told but also it overcame many of his personal objections to becoming involved again in the Cargo Movement. Gurek's doctrine was intellectually satis-fying to him. After his disappointment in Port Moresby and what he was convinced he had recently seen occur in Kurog, he was psycho-logically ready to accept it. Gurek had given his statements the stamp of mission authenticity. This was bound to impress Yali who, despite his bitterness, still admired Europeans. The doctrine clarified a problem which had worried him for years: although he had found an explanation for the bones of the prehistoric animals in the Queensland Museum (as relics of European totems), the significance of the New Guinea artefacts had completely defeated him.[3] At the same time, the new doctrine

[1] I am presuming that Gurek was referring to the statues sent to the Lateran Museum.

[2] The geographical confusion is typical of native vagueness about Australia and the vast distances involved. By 1950, even the best educated natives had only a smattering of world geography. Cf. the world map given by a Manam native in Burridge, *Mambu*, op. cit., p. 10.

[3] He was still puzzled in 1956. When I began to discuss cargo cult with him, his im-mediate question was about the meaning of these exhibits in the museum. Both my wife

necessitated only a slight modification of his previous view that Christianity and the pagan religion were entirely separate but essentially similar systems, each of which had its own specific power and was reserved for a different group (Europeans and natives respectively). Although in the past he had assumed that cargo was an exclusively European secret, Gurek had now shown him that, because of the link between Christianity and paganism discovered by the Letubists, his own religion also shared it by right. There had been a delegation of knowledge from the original cargo deity—a god whom he could associate with the Europeans or the people of Madang as he felt inclined —to all the pagan gods of New Guinea. As long as he did not examine their identities too critically, he could still be satisfied that the Europeans' and natives' gods, although loosely integrated into a single pantheon, functioned independently for all practical purposes.

What was most important from the immediate point of view, however, was that Yali could adopt Gurek's doctrine without feeling that he had stolen anything from either the Europeans or the Madang natives. The cargo secret was the joint possession of himself and every other native in the southern Madang District. They all had rights to it through their own gods, and could combine in one gigantic and concerted cult without the authority of any one particular group being overridden. Although he did everything he could to cover his tracks, Yali no longer had any scruples about ignoring his official undertaking to help eradicate cargo cult. His adoption of Gurek's doctrine was a just return for the Administration's dishonesty over the Brisbane promises and the missionaries' continual lies to the people.

In the second place, it was extremely difficult to prevent Gurek from outlining his programme in public. He had already done so at Sisagel and Amun, and when he had visited Yali other natives had been present at the conversation. Both he and they would obviously spread the doctrine in the future. Yali also realized instinctively that it was only a matter of time before the excitement of the pagan revival died down. The Rai Coast natives, like those of Madang twenty or thirty years earlier, now depended on European goods as necessities rather than luxuries. It was impossible to turn the clock back to the past without taking this into account. The cargo issue would inevitably be raised again, and when that happened Yali would have a serious rival for popular leadership. The wisest plan was to join forces with Gurek at once.

---

and I tried to explain but with very little success. He could not understand that native artefacts could be displayed merely for the instruction of the public. There had to be a deeper religious meaning.

Thus almost overnight the pagan revival became the Fifth Cargo Belief. Although he had described his doctrine in full to Yali and his close associates, Gurek gave only the barest outline to the people at the assembly at Sor, telling them simply that it was now known that the New Guinea deities as a whole were their true cargo source. Yali's new policy was fully justified: the natives must abandon Christianity and go back to their own religion so that the goods they wanted would come. Gurek gave them the following instructions: Traditional rituals for agriculture, important artefacts, pig husbandry, and hunting, and the old taboos associated with them, were to be reintroduced; the Kabu Ceremony was to be performed in full, especially the secret parts of it reserved for adult males; and the Letub *table ritual* was to be instituted. Small tables were to be set up in private houses and near deity sanctuaries. They were to be covered with cotton cloth and decorated with bottles of flowers. Offerings of food and tobacco were to be placed on them for both the deities and the spirits of the dead, who were to be invoked to send cargo.[1] The invocations and offerings would ensure that the deities handed over presents to the ancestors who, pleased by the ritual (especially the Kabu Ceremony), would deliver them to their descendants. At such times, the natives would be told by the spirits during dreams where the goods had been left—in deity sanctuaries or other parts of the bush. The cargo would include rifles, ammunition, and other military equipment.[2]

Gurek made other claims on this occasion. Apart from cargo in its usual sense, the deities would send also European domesticated animals, especially horses[3] and cows. Additional 'laws' were laid down: Yali was henceforth to be addressed as King; and the days of the week were to be renamed. Gurek said that as Yali had been born on a Thursday,[4] it was to be renamed Sunday and observed as the official day of rest from now on.[5] At the end of the meeting, Yali spoke a few words: The

[1] The *table ritual* has often been called the 'Flower Cult' in the southern Madang District, and its origin attributed wrongly and solely to Yali. As we have seen, it began in the Letub, and was used also by Tagarab and Kaum. Gurek merely carried on a tradition.

[2] Gurek did not advocate the destruction of any form of property. Nor was property destroyed at this time on the Rai Coast or in the Bagasin Area. I cannot speak with certainty for elsewhere.

[3] The horse was used as a pack animal by the missions and was much appreciated by the natives because it saved them from having to act as carriers.

[4] A complete fabrication of course. Nobody could have known this, because, as noted, not even the year of Yali's birth was recorded in the Sor Village Book.

[5] Tagarab also renamed the days of the week, but it is impossible to state the reason he gave for doing so.

people had heard what Gurek had to say. He himself believed that it was the truth. The ritual should be put to the test.

For the next few months, Yali and Gurek were inseparable. As Yali was no theologian, he became Gurek's pupil; and as he was virtually illiterate, Gurek acted as his theological secretary. Gurek's main aim was to prepare a full list of all the deities on the Rai Coast. Armed with pencil and notebook, he took Yali on a journey through Ngaing and Sengam territory. He not only recorded all the known deity sanctuaries but also, in moments of inspiration, began to discover other deities, whose existence the indigenes had not hitherto suspected. He found them in ordinary trees, river pools, and the mouths of creeks, which previously had been treated as entirely profane and subject to no taboos. On one occasion, when he and Yali were resting in Malangai, a bird flew overhead. One of the local natives said he would go after it with a bow and arrow, but Gurek reprimanded him, saying that it was no mere bird but a god who appeared in Yali's honour. It was one of the many deities whom the new cargo ritual had persuaded to return to New Guinea.

Once Gurek had laid the foundation of the doctrine of the Fifth Cargo Belief and the cult associated with it, Yali made a few minor additions of his own by attempting to draw parallels between the new ritual and what he had seen of European life. Gurek had said that Mass was a hoax, and that the Kabu Ceremony and *table ritual* were the true 'road of the cargo'. Yali corroborated this by saying that while he had been in Australia he had never once seen Mass celebrated, but he had often observed Europeans dancing and setting out vases of flowers in their houses, restaurants, and other buildings. The dancing was obviously the equivalent of the *ola* of the Kabu Ceremony, in which men and women participated together outside the cult house. Again, floral decorations were the European version of the *table ritual* and, like the Kabu Ceremony itself, were means of honouring the ancestors. Although these ideas added little to the new cult, they were important in that they confirmed Yali's previous conclusions that the European and native religious systems were roughly similar in structure and function.

## Yali's Zenith

During the twelve months after the inauguration of the Fifth Cargo Belief, Yali reached the summit of his power and fame. Although he had been acknowledged as leader of the Cargo Movement since 1945 in spite of his equivocal attitude towards it, he now accepted the role without further vacillation. The new doctrine and ritual, modified only to suit local cultural idiosyncrasies, spread through most of the southern Madang District so as to incorporate the cults already in existence, although in the inland they made only a temporary impact.[1] Along the coast between Matokar and Saidor, the political organization which had begun to come into being in 1947 now took its final shape. It necessitated complicated financial arrangements and, even if it was still far less efficient than has been supposed in retrospect, enabled Yali to challenge and even usurp the authority of the European officers in the Saidor Sub-District.

## The Spread of the Fifth Cargo Belief

In early April 1948, the new cargo cult was restricted to the villages near Sor which had adopted the pagan revival. Thereafter it was quickly established virtually throughout the whole Rai Coast, and was then taken to Bogati, Madang, and the Ramu and Bagasin areas.

On the Rai Coast, Wab and Yaimas were the first villages to be incorporated. Kaum visited Sor again and was received with greater enthusiasm. He now borrowed liberally and shamelessly from Gurek's doctrine, claiming that Kilibob, who had originally gone to Australia, had discovered the other gods in 'Rome' and taught them to make cargo.[2] He would work with Gurek and Yali to bring them back to New Guinea. Thereafter Yali raised no objections when he told his followers that he was conducting his seances in co-operation with him. But Kaum and Angge did not now remain long at Saidor. A few weeks later they were sent back to Madang.[3] Wab and Yaimas then gave up their ritual and joined the new cult on the same basis as the other villages.

The next groups to be brought in were the Catholic villages of the Gira hinterland—Yauniai, Gig, and Kru—and after that the inland Ngaing villages of Waibol, Sibog, Sindama, Aiyawang, Gabumi, and Kilang. In June, the cult spread westwards to Masi, where the people had been baptized as Catholics,[4] with some show of enthusiasm, just before Easter. About the same time (during June and July), for reasons to be described later, Yali made an official patrol through the Finisterres.

[1] I do not deal with the reputed spread of the cult outside the southern Madang District. It was probably taken eastwards towards Finschhafen and the Huon Gulf region, but I have no exact information. It is said to have been taken northwards through Bogia as far as Wewak, but again I have no precise knowledge.

[2] Kaum's emphasis on Kilibob as against Gurek's emphasis on Manup did not worry Yali. They were both 'Madang gods' and, like other natives, he believed that the Madang people could explain the problem if he ever cared to inquire.

[3] Where Angge was killed soon afterwards. See Chapter VI, p. 165 (note 1).

[4] They were the first baptized Catholics on the Rai Coast.

This served to spread the cult inland on both sides of the Nankina and west of Maibang, towards Madang. Thereafter other villages, which had only heard of the cult by rumour, began to adopt it of their own accord.

In the majority of these villages, Gurek's doctrine was never fully expounded. It was accepted on his and Yali's authority that the local deities were the cargo source, and that they had acquired their new power from the Madang god Manup. But of Manup's identification as Jesus Christ and adventures in Australia the ordinary natives knew nothing. Indeed, they appear to have shown little interest. As in the traditional and Letub situations, outlying people were satisfied that there was a validating myth known to other groups nearer its place of origin. Moreover, there was no attempt to designate any particular set of gods and goddesses as the cargo source. All were equally involved: deities of war, taro, yam, the Kabu Ceremony, tutelaries of the spirit pools, and any other deity regarded as the exclusive property of a particular group.

The ritual was generally of the same pattern as outlined by Gurek. Tables were decorated, food offerings prepared, and invocations made to gods and spirits in the way already described. Yali himself is said to have placed the skull of his mother's brother in the middle of the table he set up in his own house. In outlying areas he was invoked to intercede with the gods on the people's behalf. In Aiyawang,[1] the *table ritual* was co-ordinated with the traditional rites to the goddess who was believed to make dogs' teeth and Siasi beads. It was assumed locally that she had a special interest in European valuables, although goods were expected from the other deities as well. In theory, the *table ritual* was performed at any time but, in practice, it was generally combined with the Kabu Ceremony, which was now revived with unprecedented energy. Whereas in the past the Kabu was supposed to last about three months at the longest, in 1948 it appears to have been performed incessantly for the greater part of the year. It was only after May 1949 that it was curtailed as result of Administration interference.

The widespread exuberance of the cult—especially the over-indulgence in the Kabu Ceremony—can be attributed to some extent to the feeling of escape from the boredom of Christianity[2] and the need to show a common front against Europeans.[3] But, apart from this, there was reason for the people to believe that their ritual was proving effective.

[1] Although probably not in Sindama and Sibog, because no one was left who knew the ritual.

[2] Boredom, that is, after it was realized that Christianity was not economically profitable.

[3] Cf. Worsley, *The Trumpet Shall Sound*, op. cit., p. 250.

During the Kabu Ceremony, shillings were easily 'produced' by the simple deception of hiding them in the mouth and allowing them to roll down inside the gourd trumpets in the cult houses. In Aiyawang, the expert in ritual for dogs' teeth and Siasi beads won considerable fame by 'obtaining' sums of European money together with native valuables. Again, apart from those already 'conjured up' by Kaum at Wab, other firearms were found in the bush. They were believed to have come from the deities and spirits, and were interpreted as the fulfilment of the prophecy, derived from the Kilibob-Manup myth, and resuscitated by Kaum's and Gurek's teachings, that soon there would be a war against the white men, in which Yali would play the part of a native general. The idea was quickly taken up around Madang and in the Gogol Valley, where it had always been dormant, and spread inland to the Bagasin and Ramu areas. It led to occasional minor acts of hostility against Europeans, especially the missionaries. On the Rai Coast, the priest from Gumbi was ordered out of Maibang village and threatened with physical violence when he tried to remain.

There was, however, one group on the Rai Coast which refused to join the new cult: the coastal Sengam villages of Biliau, Teterei, Yamai, Galek, and Suit which, as has been noted, had already held aloof from the pagan revival and adhered formally to the Lutheran Mission.[1] There appear to have been three reasons for their decision.

First, the coastal Sengam had been under strong Christian influence since 1922-3. By 1948, they had given up their old religion. They knew something of their traditional mythology but the associated ritual, if not entirely forgotten, could not have been revived without considerable disruption of the cultural pattern to which they had become accustomed. They had been prepared to believe that their missionaries had hidden secrets and to accept the syncretic Letub doctrine that Manup was Jesus Christ but, because of their mission education, they were far too sophisticated to revert to what was little more than frustrated paganism.

Second, coupled with their greater intellectual sophistication, the coastal Sengam had enjoyed a privileged position on the Rai Coast. They had had tremendous influence with the Administration. As the first to be incorporated within the European political organization, the *luluais* of the beach villages assumed responsibility for the groups on their inland trade routes. They acted as interpreters with the Administration before the inland peoples could speak fluent Pidgin English and very often were left to relay the orders of the Administration as well.

---

[1] The inland Sengam villages (Malangai and Yori) had already joined the pagan revival and, therefore, found it easy to adopt the new cargo cult.

THE FIFTH CARGO BELIEF

This meant that their originally mild sense of self-importance as middle-men in the Madang–Rai Coast trade system had been considerably inflated. But, since 1922–3, the Ngaing had always challenged their position. They had elected to become nominal Catholics rather than Lutherans and had remained neutral during the war, thereby gaining a temporary advantage over the Sengam, who had been punished for collaboration with the Japanese. The Sengam had later, to some extent, restored their fortunes by establishing their influence over Yali after 1945, by supplying him with secretaries and other advisers, by per-suading him to connive at their own quasi-Christian cargo activities, and by building the 'station' at Sangpat so that their territory would become the centre of his organization. Thus they were not prepared to join a pagan cargo cult which would have necessitated their having to relearn religious ceremonies from the Ngaing, who had never given up traditional ritual to the same extent.[1] They would have become satellites of people they had come to regard as inferior.

Third, there was probably a deeper reason rather harder to prove. Yali and his supporters always claimed to me that during 1948–9, while the pagan cult was current in the inland, the coastal Sengam carried on with the quasi-Christian cargo ritual they had started in the Galek cemetery in 1946. Moreover, they had opposed the inland cult not on altruistic grounds but because they believed that complete reversion to paganism angered God—or God-Anut (Dodo) and Jesus-Manup—and thus made it even more unlikely that he (or they) would send goods. Although this assertion is consistent with events on the Rai Coast immediately after the war and with the conversation in the Lae Police Barracks in 1947, and was fully admitted by at least one coastal Sengam informant, it cannot be regarded as finally substantiated. But whatever the truth of the matter, the coastal Sengam were shrewd enough to dissociate themselves entirely from Gurek's and Yali's new cult. They guessed that it would eventually get out of hand and bring strong repercussions from the Administration and missions. If they kept clear of this trouble when it came, the good name they had lost because of their collaboration with the Japanese, and their influence with the officers at Saidor, would be restored.[2]

---

[1] It is interesting that both Wab and Yaimas, which had been under Lutheran in-fluence almost as long as the Sengam, literally had to be retaught pagan ritual by the people of Sor. Never having been as influential with the mission and Administration, they did not feel that their pride was at stake.

[2] Their view was justified by 1953, when they were restored to the favour of the Administration, whereas there was always the suspicion that the Ngaing were dangerous troublemakers.

After April 1948, therefore, the inhabitants of these villages had a very ambiguous attitude towards Yali. They were bound to acknowledge his authority as an Administration official and, by continuing to recognize 'boss boys', remained formally within his secular organization. The people of Galek avoided an open breach with him because they were trade friends of the Sors and because Sangpat 'Station' was on their land. Thus when Kasan, who disapproved of a totally anti-Christian policy, left his service as secretary and went back to Biliau soon after the beginning of the pagan revival, Yali replaced him with Kuro of Galek.[1] Even in other coastal Sengam villages there were several individuals who approved of the new cargo cult. But the vast majority rejected it and went on attending Christian services. They withdrew from the councils at Sor and Sangpat, and gave up trying to influence Yali and his associates. He himself accepted their secession with as good a grace as possible. He avoided prolonged contact with them, spending most of his time in Sor and using Sangpat only when necessary.

Other places were quick to adopt the pagan cargo cult from the Saidor area. Around Bogati it was particularly active. The natives, who had long been convinced of the duplicity of the Lutheran Mission, threw off Christianity with a will. They subjected the resident missionary to every possible indignity, shunning him in public and refusing him co-operation of any kind. They performed the *table ritual* and revived, as far as they could, their traditional ceremonies in honour of the spirits of the dead. Both these activities were carried out in Yali's name. Along the coast, where the people had the first version of the Kilibob-Manup myth, it was believed that Kilibob[2] would return from Australia with ships full of cargo, which he would hand over to the deities of warfare, reefs, agriculture, and so forth, and to the spirits of the dead, for distribution. In the inland, where the Kilibob-Manup myth was unknown, the people believed that the mountain gods would send cargo via the ancestors. The cargo expected was largely military equipment.

Similarly, in the hinterland of Madang, the Letub cult was kept going

---

[1] Kuro was not Yali's personal trade partner. He became official secretary at a salary of 15s. a month. Gurek never held the position. He was only theological secretary and received no salary. It is worth noting in this context that relations between the Sors and Galeks had been strained before and during the war but had never been seriously disrupted.

[2] Who was no longer identified as God. He had merely taken the cargo to the land of the white men (now identified as Australia), as in the first version of the Second Cargo Belief.

with renewed vigour, although it is unclear whether Christian elements were perpetuated or suppressed. Again, there is no record that Taga-rab's supporters were active in the Milguk area, but Kaum (who had returned from Saidor) revived his ritual in the Madang Labour Com-pound. He conducted his seances much as before but, following his accommodations to the new pagan cargo belief, treated Kilibob as a purely non-Christian god. He claimed full partnership with Yali and repeated his boast of 1947 that the sovereignty of the southern Madang District would eventually be shared between them. The ritual was per-formed in secret for a long time: it was not reported to the District Office until March 1949, when Kaum was arrested again and imprisoned for six months. He served his sentence at Angoram in the Sepik District.

For the Ramu area, the information is very sketchy. After his rebuff by Yali for his quasi-Christian cargo activities, Pales returned to Komis-angel. Thereafter he or his associates[1] took the pagan cult to Dumpu, where it was combined with the system of wife-exchange inaugurated in 1947.[2]

The pagan cult was introduced to the Bagasin Area in the later months of 1948. Kaum sent envoys from the Madang Labour Com-pound. The Dumpu people sent messages along the Ramu to Igurue. The Bogatis contacted the people of Tapopo via the old Naru trade route. All three sources gave similar instructions: that the natives should perform the *table ritual* and revive all traditional religious cere-monies and dances, especially those honouring the ancestors. But the people were given only the vaguest notion of the doctrine behind the cult: no more than that the local deities would send cargo if the specified rites were carried out. Dances were to be staged in Yali's name. The people should 'think on' him so that he could act as an intermediary with the deities and the spirits of the dead.

Although the people shared the general disillusionment with Chris-tianity, the new cargo cult never took deep root in the Bagasin Area. Propaganda from Madang was strongly discouraged by Gulu, the Paramount *Luluai* of Amele, a very influential and loyal supporter of the Administration, who had consistently prevented his people from meddling with any form of cargo activity in the years before and im-mediately after the war.[3] Furthermore, the natives of the Bagasin Area now had little respect for Kaum, who had failed in his promises on at

[1] If it was Pales, his influence was short-lived for he died soon afterwards.

[2] Wife-exchange was still practised in the area as late as 1953.

[3] Amele is a strategic village on the main road between Madang and the Bagasin Area. Gulu became the leader of the Amele Rice Scheme and first President of the Ambenob Native Local Government Council.

least three occasions and had involved some of them in serious trouble in 1944. Their contempt deepened when his envoys proved to be young men of no consequence, several of whom were known troublemakers in their villages and had been required to leave home for European employment on that account.[1]

The messages from Dumpu were blocked by the people of Igurue. For a while they toyed with the cult but quickly gave it up because they had been ridiculed for their sponsorship of Polelesi's prophecies during Yali's absence in Port Moresby and were bitterly ashamed. Also the association of the pagan ritual with sexual promiscuity along the Ramu Valley outraged their extremely puritan sense of morality.[2] It was only the propaganda from Bogati that made any headway at all. The strongest converts were the people of Tapopo, Nugu, Amasua, Anminik, and Negri, but even their enthusiasm waned after several months.

The ritual of the pagan cargo cult was never elaborately staged in the Bagasin Area and the main evidence of its presence appears to have been the inordinate interest in pig exchanges and dancing. By April 1949, when I first visited the people, there was nothing to suggest that they had ever been involved apart from their hardly veiled antagonism to the Lutheran Mission. They were too far away from the nerve centre of the cult to maintain their interest in it. They had never heard a full exposition of Gurek's doctrine and thus had no concrete authority for believing that their deities made cargo. Also, after the initial messages, they were not visited again by envoys from Madang,[3] Dumpu, or Bogati. Hence it was not deeply impressed on them that people in other areas had mythological justification of the belief even though they themselves lacked it. During 1949-50, they adopted a non-cargo pagan revival on their own account. Although the majority of the people continued to assume that the 'road of the cargo' lay somewhere in Christianity, they no longer trusted the missionaries to lead them to it and preferred to return to their old religion for its traditional benefits.

After the beginning of 1949, therefore, the Garia and their neighbours ceased to be active participants in the Cargo Movement. In the middle of the year, as already recounted, certain rumours, phrased in terms of quasi-Christian doctrine, were spread about myself but were eventually forgotten. Occasionally, labourers returning from Madang brought back reports of an impending war against Europeans but were

---

[1] One had served the Japanese as a policeman and was unpopular for having reported a kinsman for helping the Allies.

[2] As noted, the Garia had no system of extramarital licence.

[3] Until Kaum's return in 1949, as described below.

not taken very seriously. At the end of 1949 Kaum, who had now finished his third gaol sentence, went home to Kalinam. He immediately visited Iwaiwa village, where I was living, in the hope of getting the Garia and myself to support a new cult based on the doctrine he had used in the Madang Labour Compound on his return from Saidor. Christian elements had entirely disappeared from his teaching. Kilibob had invented ships and cargo in New Guinea, but then had sailed away to Australia and given them to the white men. Later he had taught the other New Guinea deities, who had been stolen away to Australia by the missionaries, to make these things. If the people would revive traditional ritual, Kilibob, the other local gods, and the ancestors would send them cargo through the village cemeteries. Kaum still claimed equal status with Yali but even this made little impression. The Garia refused to be enticed and eventually his own Kein people threatened to report him to the District Office if he persisted in his activities. Thereafter, although he continued his seances with a few close associates, he drifted into obscurity.

## Yali's Political Organization[1]

There can be no doubt that the Fifth Cargo Belief and the ritual associated with it spread as far and fast as they did primarily because they suited the people's mood at the time. They were the culmination of a long period of bitter frustration with Christianity. But, to some extent at least, the process was facilitated by the political organization which Yali had at his disposal between 1948–50 and which is set out in Diagram I. We must consider, first and very briefly, the area over which he can be said to have had control and, second and in greater detail, the means by which he established it.

In theory, the organization covered the whole southern Madang District and the Bogia region: in practically every village there was a 'boss boy' who claimed allegiance to, and authority from, Yali. In practice, however, it was very much less extensive. The position in the inland and around Bogia had not changed since 1947. Yali himself never visited the Bagasin and Ramu peoples, nor did he have accredited lieutenants in the Ramu area. His main lieutenant in the Bagasin Area (Enkol of Paisarek) appears to have done little to foster the pagan cargo cult which, as has been seen, the local natives soon abandoned. Similarly, Yali never went again to Bogia to supervise the 'boss boys' he had appointed in 1947. He left them under the nominal command of his

[1] I deal here only with the formal aspects of the organization. Its detailed relationship to Ngaing social structure will be discussed in a separate monograph.

main lieutenant, Iguma.[1] These places, therefore, are ignored in the present account. It was only along the coast between Saidor and Matokar that the organization became more elaborate than it had been before Yali went to Port Moresby. Yet even within this area, he still had only the Rai Coast from Saidor to Mindiri under direct control. Towards Madang and Matokar, although his position was probably stronger than in the past, he never did more than exert influence without any guarantee that his instructions would be correctly interpreted and carried out. The form of the organization is described in relation to these varying degrees of effectiveness.

On the Rai Coast from Saidor to Mindiri, Yali brought into being[2] a rudimentary pyramidal system of which he was the apex. Below him were his secretaries, his 'policemen' or strong-arm men, his lieutenants, and his 'boss boys'. These power relationships were reinforced by kinship and affinal ties in well-defined areas.

Yali's personal position was determined partly by his formal status in the Administration and partly by his role as leader of the Cargo Movement. Both fields gave his now great desire for power considerable scope. In the first capacity, he was formally under the command of the officers at Saidor. Although his charter was to continue the work of reconstruction he had begun in 1945 and stabilize native life on the basis of the 'Laws' drafted in Port Moresby, for a very large part of 1948 practically nothing was done to define the geographical sphere of his authority or supervise his activities. Thus he was able to interpret his position as Foreman-Overseer to suit his own convenience. He set himself up as a virtually independent autocrat: he impressed on the people in general, and on the village headmen in particular, that he had been put in charge of the Rai Coast by the highest officers in the Administration. He was, in fact, *the* Administration, as far as they were concerned. He also made it quite clear that the missions and Administration were entirely separate organizations, and that those who supported the former were the opponents of the latter—that is, of himself. Those who disobeyed him would be punished in the name of the Administration.

These claims were reinforced by a style of living modelled on, and in native eyes almost as luxurious as, that of the officers at Saidor. Yali

[1] The Bogia and Manam people had only occasional contacts with Yali during 1948–50. They are mentioned in context.

[2] It should be emphasized that Yali did not plan his organization as a whole from the outset. He merely appointed people to certain positions in imitation of what he had seen in the Administration in order to enhance his own prestige. Gradually they achieved a rough integration.

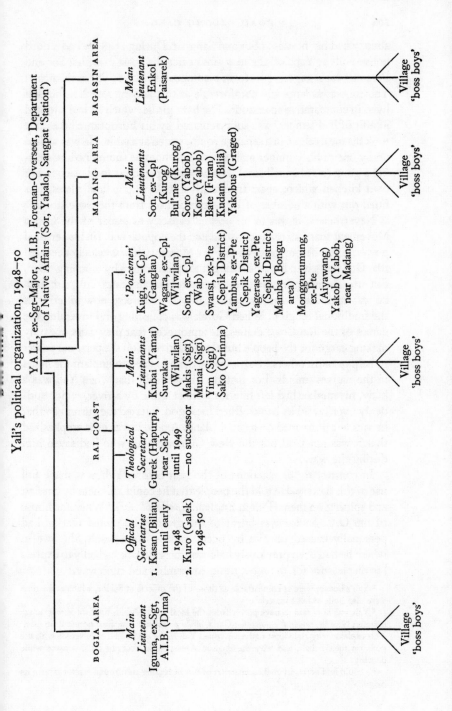

Yali's political organization, 1948–50

YALI, ex-Sgt-Major, A.I.B, Foreman-Overseer, Department of Native Affairs (Sor, Yabalol, Sangpat 'Station')

**BOGIA AREA**

*Main Lieutenant*
Iguma, ex-Sgt, A.I.B. (Dima)

Village 'boss boys'

**RAI COAST**

*Official Secretaries*
1. Kasan (Biliau) until early 1948
2. Kuro (Galek) 1948–50

*Theological Secretary*
Gurek (Hapurpi, near Sek) until 1949 —no successor

*Main Lieutenants*
Kubai (Yamai)
Suwaka (Wilwilan)
Makis (Sigi)
Munai (Sigi)
Yim (Sigi)
Sako (Orinma)

Village 'boss boys'

*'Policemen'*
Kugi, ex-Cpl (Ganglau)
Wagara, ex-Cpl (Wilwilan)
Som, ex-Cpl (Wab)
Swansi, ex-Pte (Sepik District)
Yambus, ex-Pte (Sepik District)
Yageraso, ex-Pte (Sepik District)
Mamba (Bongu area)
Monggurumung, ex-Pte (Aiyawang)
Yakob (Yabob, near Madang)

**MADANG AREA**

*Main Lieutenants*
Son, ex-Cpl (Kurog)
Bul'me (Kurog)
Soro (Yabob)
Kore (Yabob)
Bate (Furan)
Kudam (Bilia)
Yakobus (Graged)

Village 'boss boys'

**BAGASIN AREA**

*Main Lieutenant*
Enkol (Paisarek)

Village 'boss boys'

already had big houses at Sor and Sangpat. During 1948, he had a third house built at Yabalol, the new site nearer the coast at which Sor and Paramus came together to form a composite village. The residence at Yabalol was as large and comfortable as that at Sangpat.[1] Yali himself lived in comparative splendour. The bark girdle, which he had adopted in a fit of bad temper, was soon replaced by his European clothes. He took his meals alone in a separate room, seated at a table. He was waited on by one of his younger male relatives, whom he summoned by beating a gong (an old shell case). His wives prepared his food, each in her own kitchen which, apart from native cooking pots and plates, was fitted out with a number of European utensils from the trade stores.

Nevertheless, it was in his second capacity as leader of the Cargo Movement that Yali really consolidated the popular belief in his personal power. Even before he went to Port Moresby, it was widely accepted that God had given him the strength to kill sorcerers by touching them. But after the inauguration of the pagan revival and cargo cult, although he was attributed a similar quality, it was interpreted now in terms of the traditional religion. When Gurek was collecting and inventing the names of the Rai Coast deities, he announced that they were not only making cargo for the people but also had given Yali the personal power to help or harm others.[2] Stories were disseminated to implant the belief in the natives' minds. For instance, it was said that when Yali was a baby, his mother had left him for a short while by a river, which suddenly overflowed its banks. But a local god diverted the current so that he was left unharmed on a small island. Again, it was now emphasized that it was not God but the New Guinea deities who had saved him during the war.

In contrast to his reactions of the year before, Yali now made full use of this flattery. He told the people that he could kill them by cursing and spitting on them (Pidgin English, *sipetim ol idai*).[3] When the house of the O.C. Saidor was burnt to the ground, he hinted that he had personally caused the fire by occult means. As a result, the awe in which he had been previously held was increased: he had only to express his displeasure for the most timid to tremble and run away.

[1] Yali's houses were as comfortable as those of the officers at Saidor, which at the time were also built of bush materials.

[2] Yali was now said to have power from the local gods (Pidgin English, *sitrong bilong masalai*; Ngaing, *tutyerak amangang*; Garia, *oite'u po soksok*) as against power from God. This explains why Rai Coast natives invoked Yali in the *table ritual* to intercede with the gods on their behalf, and why the Bagasin Area people 'thought on' his name while dancing.

[3] I could find no traditional counterpart of this in Ngaing culture and cannot explain its origin.

Apart from his new title, style of living, and the special powers ascribed to him, there was another visible symbol of Yali's personal authority on the Rai Coast: the 'officials' in his organization already mentioned. As we have seen, Gurek, as unpaid theological secretary, had the important duty of formulating the beliefs of the pagan cargo cult. The duties of the ordinary secretary (Kasan of Biliau until early 1948 and thereafter Kuro of Galek), who now received 15s. a month, were much the same as before: to deal with correspondence and transcribe orders; and to help entertain important visitors. By all accounts, although the Department of Native Affairs saw fit to pay his salary, his position was a sinecure, for he appears to have been consistently under-employed.

The 'Police Force' consisted of some nine[1] native ex-soldiers and other hangers-on (three from the Sepik District, and the rest from the Rai Coast and Madang), who had attached themselves to the Rehabilitation Scheme after 1945. (Their names can be seen in Diagram I.) Yali now gave them 'formal' status to enhance his own prestige. Although it did nothing to disband them until 1950, they were never recognized by the Administration, but in dress and bearing they did everything to imitate, if not outdo, their official counterparts. They wore slouch digger hats, military belts,[2] shirts and shorts or very short laplaps, and they carried swagger canes. But, in spite of their surface spit and polish, they were hardly a well-disciplined body and their attendance to duty was often extremely irregular. They spent some of their time at Sangpat, Sor, or Yabalol, so that Yali could always count on having a small personal bodyguard wherever he happened to be living. Technically, they were supposed to have his permission to take 'leave' but this was often ignored. Several of them at least used to come and go as they pleased. Even when most of them were with Yali, they were not subjected to rigorous discipline. Parades and exercises were very infrequent, and their primary purpose seems to have been to impress the locals. Although greatly exaggerated reports[3] were spread about these 'policemen' among Europeans—as if they were a large private army being prepared for a *coup d'état*—for the most part they were an idle crew which, not being kept under proper control, was only too willing to indulge in any ruffianism that was suggested.

[1] Although the largest number I could account for was nine, it is possible that the total was slightly larger.

[2] There were large supplies of old military clothing in New Guinea at the time. They were sold to natives in the trade stores.

[3] This does not deny that the natives believed that a war against Europeans would eventually break out but, apart from waiting for military equipment, few preparations were actually made.

P

The six main lieutenants never had a clearly defined role. They were said generally to supervise in Yali's name the localities in which they lived. Below them were the 'boss boys', whose duties have already been described and were not changed. Yali used them as contact men. Wherever possible, however, he still relied, for purposes of liaison, on the network of his kinship, totemic, trade, and affinal relationships. This gave him a strong grip, of course, on the Nankina-Mot sub-coast, but it applied also to Sigi (inland from Mindiri), which was the village of his first wife Sunggum. By extending the system of classificatory relationships, he could now treat many people in that region as his affines. They often visited him socially and also to discuss affairs of local importance.

Around Madang and to the north, the organization was by no means so elaborate. In five villages near Madang itself, Yali had his main lieutenants. In most of the other villages there were 'boss boys'. These were his principal agents for transmitting and implementing any instructions he sent. Apart from them, in the Matokar area he had his affines (the relatives of his second wife Rebecca), through whom he was able, as at Sigi, to exercise a considerable degree of influence. Nevertheless, as in the past, the liaison between Yali and his agents in the Madang–Matokar region was still extremely casual: in spite of his great prestige, in the main they continued to make, and act on, their own decisions with little interference from him. From now on, no direct reference is made to their activities.

## Yali's Finances

Yali's political organization on the Rai Coast was expensive to run. His own salary and rations were hardly adequate for even his private establishment. Although his secretary, like himself, was paid by the Department of Native Affairs, and the lieutenants and 'boss boys', like the ordinary village headmen, gave their services free, wages had to be found for the 'policemen' and plantation labourers. The retinue of hangers-on and visitors from Madang and elsewhere had to be fed. Occasionally, important visitors received cash presents of up to £10. There were the almost continual exchanges at Sor and Yabalol, which Yali had to stage in conjunction with the Kabu Ceremony to maintain his popularity. Pigs had to be bought elsewhere, and the accepted price of a fully grown animal was between £5 and £10.

In 1956, when I was first in a position to investigate the problem, it was impossible to recover accurate details. Moreover, the information in Kasan's diary and Kuro's accounts is most imprecise. But the figures mentioned in these documents indicate that the organization's financial transactions were, at the time for natives, on a very big scale.[1] On 3 February 1948, thirty-three people were paid sums varying from £5 to £1. Another entry gives 'Police Constable' Wagara's salary as £4 10s. for three months (£1 10s. a month). For June 1948, there is a list of a hundred and forty-five payments from £10 15s. to £5 5s., totalling about £800.

Yali raised money in various ways, at least two of which were strictly illegal or against the explicit instructions of the District Office. First, he received unsolicited gifts which, as a salaried official of the Administration, he should have refused.[2] It was alleged that he was given large sums by the Bogia natives in February 1947, although the assertion was never investigated because the Europeans who made it would not put it in writing. On his return from Port Moresby in December 1947, the Madang natives brought him presents at Biliā. On what appears to have been 3 February 1948,[3] sums of £400 and £800 were given him at Sangpat. There was also a steady stream of small sums, such as £15 from the *Luluai* of Bogati. Second, although the official head tax had been abolished in 1945, Yali levied his own taxes: as in some villages visited on his first patrol in 1948 and at Tapen-Boana on his third patrol in 1949.

In spite of these very considerable revenues, Yali was often short of money. As a result, he seems to have been tempted to default on payments which he considered unimportant. He floated a scheme whereby the people of Mindiri, who had the only clay deposits on the Rai Coast, should supply pots for him to market on their behalf. For one consignment of about a hundred and thirty pots, worth between £50 and £65, they received £10, three wooden plates, three string bags, and five bark cloths. Again, as already reported, the plantation scheme got out of hand: Yali paid some of the labourers he had recruited less than the requisite wage of 15s. a month, although the Europeans for whom he was acting were fulfilling their part of the bargain. Even so, it would be unfair to lay the blame for this financial chaos entirely on Yali's

---

[1] At a first glance, the sums involved appear to be out of all proportion to native earning capacity. But it is important to remember the hoarding of cash that has been going on in New Guinea villages for many years. Huge sums in silver currency are said to be hidden away. Although individual holdings are probably very small (perhaps only a few shillings a head), *in toto* they represent a considerable economic potential.

[2] At the beginning of 1948, Yali was ordered by the District Officer not to accept presents. He disregarded the order and told me in 1956 that he had been allowed to receive gifts from the people because he was working on their behalf.

[3] According to Kasan's diary, the payments could have been made in February 1947. But at that time Yali was at Bogia. Also the payments were made at Sangpat 'Station', which had not been built by February 1947. Thus the year must have been 1948.

shoulders. It has already been pointed out that his legitimate profits from recruiting were too small and that the secretaries who were supposed to manage his accounts were incapable of dealing with the sums entrusted to them.

## Yali's Political Activities

With the pagan cargo cult and the new political organization behind him, Yali's future actions were a foregone conclusion. Although he was doubtless goaded by his bitterness against Europeans and his own ambition, his position was essentially that of any leader of a popular movement: Was he himself in control of events or had they taken control of him? If he wanted to retain power, he had now no alternative but to promote the pagan cargo ritual and, at the same time, try to keep it secret from the Administration. To do this it was necessary to usurp the authority of the officers at Saidor so that he would be the only link between them and the people, and they could be kept in ignorance of what was going on. He achieved his end by virtually assuming the functions of the Sub-District Court for Native Affairs, by convening his own meetings at Sangpat, Sor, and Yabalol, and by spreading his own propaganda on patrol.

It was surprisingly easy to take over the legal duties of the O.C. Saidor. Yali let it be known that in Port Moresby he had been told to judge the natives of the Rai Coast according to the 'Laws' he had prepared. In future, the Administration was not to be worried with petty disputes, which were to be settled in the villages by the headmen and 'boss boys'. Those that could not be settled in this way were to be brought to him at Sangpat, and only the most serious, such as homicide, were to be referred to Saidor. The people obeyed these instructions and, according to official records, Yali became the *de facto* judicial power in his own area. Only one homicide (the details of which are given below) occurred and was reported to Saidor. Otherwise, apart from those settled on the spot, Yali appears to have dealt with all cases himself, imposing 'fines' or varying periods of 'imprisonment', which consisted in having to cut grass at Sangpat or help with various projects at Yabalol. At least twelve people were 'imprisoned', but no 'gaol' was ever built to house them, as was thought by some Europeans at that time.[1]

[1] It should be remarked that, although these activities were quite outside the law, it is questionable whether Yali's sentences were less just than those sometimes imposed by Administration Courts. In my experience in the southern Madang District, well over 75 per cent of disputes are settled in the villages because traditional means of negotiation are more satisfactory than European decisions. This was hardly affected by Yali's regime. (In the Bagasin Area, where the people are extremely litigious, this was the only part of

The meetings convened at Sangpat, Sor, and Yabalol every week or fortnight were officially sanctioned by the Administration. Yali was allowed to call in the village headmen and 'boss boys' in order to instruct them in his rehabilitation policies: improvement of village hygiene, encouragement of cash crops, and other work. In fact, however, apart from expounding the general content of the new 'Laws', he used these occasions to disseminate cargo cult propaganda. He would address his audience seated in a chair, with several of his 'policemen' drawn up at attention behind him, in imitation of a Patrol Officer. He delivered bitter tirades against Christianity and claimed that he had been ordered in Port Moresby to revive the Kabu Ceremony in all its old glory. This, coupled with the *table ritual*, he told them, would bring the goods they desired.

It was in these talks that Yali appears to have made his most important contribution to the pagan cargo cult itself: the political cover behind which the ritual could be safely performed. He warned the people that they must be careful of the local missionaries and the officers at Saidor, who were in league to 'close the road of the cargo' by stamping out pagan ritual. It was only important members of the Administration— the highest officials in Papua and the District Officer in Madang—who really had their interests at heart. They knew of the cult and supported it. The natives had to be very circumspect in what they said to local Europeans. They were never to repeat their myths to them, for they would steal the gods back to Australia and so impoverish New Guinea once more. Above all, they must never admit that they were performing cargo ritual. If they were asked about the *table ritual*, they were to say that it was to beautify their houses in the European manner. If they were asked about the revival of agricultural ritual and the Kabu Ceremony, they were to maintain that they were no more than traditional religious practices for legitimate ends. In the past, their forbears, using stone axes, could clear only very small areas of land but, with the aid of the old ritual, were able to raise bumper crops. At the present time, although with the steel tools now at their disposal they could clear larger gardens, the crops they grew were negligible in comparison because the missionaries had forced them to give up their old religion without

---

Yali's propaganda to make any permanent impression. The natives continued to conduct their own 'court' cases rather than go to the Administration and justified their actions by referring to what they had heard of Yali's policy.) Many of Yali's sentences were no heavier than those of the proper courts. Moreover, such brutalities as occurred—and they are described in context—had their counterparts under the official Administration organization.

providing them with an effective substitute. They were now reverting to the old ritual in order to improve their dwindling food supply.

This system of double-talk was almost impenetrable. On the surface, it was well within Yali's charter from Port Moresby and for years it was extremely difficult to prove whether he was personally responsible for making cargo propaganda or not.[1] Again, the new cargo ritual was so close to traditional pagan ritual that anyone ignorant of Gurek's doctrine could hardly tell the difference. Political cover of this kind was essential to Yali in his dealings with the District Office in Madang, where he was able to present a case for his activities, which could not easily be broken. If he were challenged about cargo cult, he could always claim that people in outlying villages were misrepresenting his teachings, and point to the rumours which had been circulated the previous year and which he had denounced on his return from Port Moresby.[2] The District Officer was bitterly criticized, especially by the missions, for accepting these protestations of innocence at their face value and refusing a full investigation. Yet he can hardly be blamed. It is extremely doubtful whether any investigation of the overt situation by an Administration officer would have disclosed the truth, unless the missionaries themselves had made available information about their followers' perversion of their own teachings, so that a full history of the Cargo Movement could have been compiled and Yali's part in it seen in proper perspective. But they never did this. They told the District Officer about the pagan cargo cult but not about its quasi-Christian forerunners.

Along the coast and sub-coast between Saidor and Mindiri, Yali was able to spread his propaganda by sending his 'policemen' with messages to his 'boss boys' and, more especially, by manipulating his kinship, affinal, and trade relationships. He accomplished a great deal also through the meetings at Sangpat, Sor, and Yabalol, which were attended by natives from many outlying Rai Coast villages, and occasionally from Bogia and Manam. In April 1949, Manam natives dictated to his secretary a cargo myth, which had points of correspondence with the Kilibob-Manup myth and the Primal Myth recorded by Burridge,[3] an-

[1] In 1953, when I first began to work among the Ngaing after eighteen months' experience in the Bagasin Area, it took much probing to get inside the system. At this time the situation was quiet and Yali had been in gaol for three years. It was not until 1956 that I got conclusive information.

[2] In point of fact, Yali really liked the District Officer. He deceived him merely to save his own skin.

[3] See Burridge, *Mambu*, op. cit., pp. 155–65. The heroes of the Manam cargo myth were two brothers and their mother. Its theme was the invention of ships and the discovery of white men, who had previously lived like bush natives and now were given cargo.

other traditional myth, names of local deities, and rudimentary genealogies of their forbears. Yet, particularly in 1948, there were still many people in the Rai Coast hinterland and elsewhere who had not attended these meetings. Yali obtained permission to make patrols in the hinterland and along the seaboard towards Madang in order to give his work greater publicity and encourage the natives to bring their problems to him. This gave him additional means of circulating cargo doctrine.

Only three patrols were made. The first began during June 1948 and lasted about eight weeks. Accompanied by a large retinue, including several of his 'policemen', Yali took the following route: From Sangpat to Gal (on the coast east of Saidor), and then inland to Boana, Tapen, Windaruk, Kembong, Bambu, Warawang, Kambaiong, Tarignang, Yogayoga, Sabilonge, Ohokierak, Aiyawang, Gabumi, Maibang, Kilang, Usuang, Seremore, Matoko, Funiende, Simuniende, Kuhuparam, Kuhuk, Mebu, Orinma, Sigi, Ganglau, Awaraing, and then back to Sangpat. At each village, he gave an address of roughly the same kind as already described, urging the people to abandon Christianity and revive the old religion with the aim of getting cargo.

The second patrol was carried out during September–October 1948. Yali visited Cape Rigney and Bongu, and was back at Sangpat by 26 October. At Bongu, apart from his usual propaganda, he told the people to stop killing and eating totem animals.[1] The visit considerably inflamed the local situation.

The third patrol took place as result of somewhat different circumstances. It was organized by the O.C. Saidor. At the end of 1948, a Native Medical Orderly from the Saidor Hospital had been sent to Tapen-Boana to examine the people for venereal disease. The people refused to line and ran away. The O.C. Saidor had to take disciplinary action but, instead of leading a patrol himself as would have been correct, sent Yali to deputize for him. The party included, besides Yali, his secretary Kuro and some of his own 'policemen', two Native Medical Orderlies, and two Administration policemen. The two constables from Saidor were included to make it quite clear to the Tapen-Boana natives that Yali was the official representative of the Administration. Yali set out in January 1949. He went straight to Tapen-Boana and returned with the ringleaders of the trouble, together with other men and women

[1] These instructions probably derived from Yali's conversation with the officer at the Agricultural Station near Port Moresby in 1947. It is interesting that this particular propaganda spread into the Bagasin Area in 1949 during my first visit there. As the people had no totem animals of any kind, they were extremely puzzled. They observed taboos on hunting for a short time and then forgot about the matter.

involved. The patrol greatly enhanced his reputation: it substantiated the belief that he was in charge of the Rai Coast.

Apart from anything else, these patrols had one unintended result: they gave Yali and his 'policemen' scope for strong-arm tactics. It has already been mentioned that, during his service with the Police Force before the war, Yali had witnessed and participated in brutalities either instigated or condoned by European officers: rape, intimidation, and beating up. As he now considered himself a Patrol Officer in all but name, he considered that he and his 'policemen' were justified in taking the same liberties. During two of his patrols some extremely ugly incidents occurred.

Before the first patrol there were already signs of opposition to Yali's new policy. It came mainly, as was only to be expected, from loyal native mission helpers (especially the Lutherans), whose position he was openly attacking. At two of the Sangpat meetings, the *Luluais* of Uyerak and Kuhuparam reported that the Lutheran evangelists in their areas were inciting the people to disobey him: he was a 'man of Satan' (Pidgin English, *man bilong Satan*) because he wanted to reintroduce the ritual to the local deities ('satans') and the spirits of the dead.

Yali was furious and determined to teach the evangelists a lesson. When, on his first patrol, he reached the areas concerned, he had them brought before him. He satisfied himself of the truth of the allegations and then ordered his 'policemen' to slap their faces. No real physical injury was done but, as the punishment was inflicted before the assembled villagers, among whom the evangelists had been accepted previously as important men, they were very deeply disgraced and their influence destroyed. Also at the end of the patrol, at Awaring, although he did not have them slapped or beaten, Yali publicly abused and ridiculed the natives who remained loyal to the missions.

On the third patrol to Tapen-Boana, there were scenes of real brutality. Yali had learnt that the underlying reason for the natives' refusal to line for the Medical Orderly in 1948 was that the Lutheran evangelist in the area had told them to disobey the Administration because it was the tool of Satan. Yali realized that this was an insult directed at himself: it was based on the assumption that the Administration's policy was identical with his own pagan propaganda. Again he had the Administration police and his own 'police' slap the man's face in public. Moreover, as the patrol returned to Saidor, several of the women who had been forced to accompany it were raped by various members of the party, including the Administration constables. There is no reason to suppose that this occurred with Yali's connivance, for he was exonerated at a later inquiry. But the question of his failure to provide adequate protection for the women on this occasion was unexplored.

The worst incident, however, did not occur on a patrol. In 1948, there had been a murder in the Suri (Ngaing) area. A man who wanted to marry the wife of the *Tultul* of Isangang bribed a N'dau native[1] to kill him. When the body was discovered, Yali had the widow, her lover, the paid assassin, and several other women suspected of complicity, brought to Sor. Later that evening, it is said, some of the women were raped. Next day, the widow and her lover were stripped naked in public, slapped by the 'police', and then made to run the gauntlet so that their nakedness could be mocked. Thereafter, together with the paid assassin (who appears to have escaped public humiliation), they were handed over to the O.C. Saidor. The woman was not punished but the two men were sentenced to gaol for ten years each.

### Yali's Downfall

During 1948–50, many Europeans in the southern Madang District believed that the local situation was chaotic and that the Administration had completely lost control. Even the planters[2] and missionaries, often at daggers drawn in the past, found common cause in their demands for the suppression of what they regarded as an insurrection, and for the re-establishment of 'British law and justice' by naked force. Yet it is worth pausing to consider the exact nature and extent of the chaos for which Yali alone was widely held responsible.

Yali had, through entirely legal means, inaugurated a pagan revival, which had led to a general eclipse of Christianity. Beyond that, he had listened to Gurek, who had turned his programme into a cargo cult, and quite illegally propagated the new doctrine and ritual. This had fostered the popular belief in a war against the Europeans, and caused minor acts of insolence and threats of hostility. Yali had also usurped the authority of the Court of Native Affairs at Saidor, imposing unlawful 'fines' and 'prison sentences', and had illegally instigated the physical maltreatment of several natives, both male and female, on the Rai Coast in a manner he believed to be in keeping with his status as an Administration official.

In comparison with what has happened in other colonial or ex-colonial territories since 1948—Malaya, Cyprus, and various parts of

[1] I never discovered the exact relationship involved. It was possibly a trade relationship. The N'dau assassin was persuaded because of his lack of sophistication.
[2] Although, as indicated, there was some division of opinion in the commercial community.

Africa—this situation was extremely mild.[1] Very few, if any, Europeans were actually molested, and the planters, in spite of recurring labour problems resulting from cargo propaganda, managed to run their properties at a handsome profit. The missionaries, although justly objecting to the molestation of their native helpers and the raping of women, had no cause to complain if the natives wished to exercise the right of freedom of worship guaranteed by the same law that permitted the unrestricted entry of accredited Christian organizations into the country. In short, what it all amounted to was mainly European uneasiness and resentment at the decay of the pre-war colonial social order. The natives were showing their teeth. Settlers could no longer count on automatic obedience to their slightest commands, and the missions were forced to compete with other ideologies.

As long as he could, the District Officer showed the greatest sympathy for and tolerance of the people's aspirations. Yet even he was eventually forced by continual pressures from the missions to clip Yali's wings. On 26 October 1948, he visited Saidor and summoned Yali, who had just returned from his second patrol to Cape Rigney and Bongu, to the station. He convened a general assembly, at which he announced that henceforth Yali had no authority to recruit labour or hold court. He also denounced the cargo cult, ridiculed the people for performing the Kabu Ceremony in the hope of obtaining European wealth, and strongly advised them to send their children back to the mission schools to get some basic education.

The occasion was a definite setback for Yali. Although the District Officer had not ordered a full investigation of the situation and had been careful not to implicate him in his caustic remarks about cargo cult, he did not invite him to address the meeting and treated him very much as a junior official. Moreover, the withdrawal of the licence to recruit represented a loss of revenue. But worse was to come. After the inquiry into the Tapen-Boana patrol of January 1949, it was decided that, although he could not be proved personally responsible for the brutalities which occurred, Yali was not to be entrusted again with the command of Administration personnel. A new Patrol Officer was sent as O.C. Saidor in May 1949. He saw that all the above instructions were carried out and instituted a few reforms of his own. He gave orders that the duration of the Kabu Ceremony should be curtailed and

---

[1] In 1949–50, I never felt that I was in any way threatened while living in the Bagasin Area. (The Garia even promised to protect me in the event of a general war against Europeans.) Admittedly, the people had withdrawn from the Cargo Movement but even in the vicinity of Madang, where I spent some of my time, there was little evidence of serious unrest.

made it quite clear that the Administration headmen rather than the 'boss boys' were in charge of the villages. He also told the people that the meetings at Sangpat, Sor, and Yabalol were not compulsory. The headmen's only obligation of this kind was to report births, deaths, and marriages every three months at Saidor, unless official patrols went through their areas.

Nevertheless, Yali was as yet by no means in disgrace. In August 1949, he was formally presented to the Governor-General of Australia, Mr (now Sir) William McKell, who was on a tour of inspection of Papua and New Guinea. Native visitors (still often with presents) continued to appear, and he was still as popular as ever with the people. Late in 1949, Japanese stragglers found living with inland Rai Coast natives were taken to him at Sangpat rather than to the O.C. Saidor. But at the same time he realized that he would have to be more careful. He allowed mission schools to reopen in the villages, although he tried to insist that they gave only secular instruction, and he saw that the dance-exchanges and general junketings were carried on with less vigour.

From this time on the pagan cargo ritual began to wane. Gurek, its main advocate, had by now left the Rai Coast for his own village, and many of the people were beginning to lose faith in it. At the end of 1949, Yali cancelled the Kabu Ceremony at Yabalol because of his misunderstanding of the Lutheran Mission's announcement that Advent heralded the Coming of Jesus Christ. He appears to have assumed that the mission was claiming that the Second Coming was imminent, and decided to wait and see if it would really happen, and ridicule the mission if it did not. Finally, by the early months of 1950, he was himself beginning to be disillusioned by the failure of the Kabu Ceremony to produce the results promised by Gurek. He retired with a few followers to the bush, where he performed the ritual associated with the whirling of the bullroarer and decorated a table in honour of its creator deity, in the hope that the latter might send cargo.[1] When this failed, the pagan cargo cult was allowed to lapse.

In the meantime, however, forces were building up against Yali, which eventually led to his downfall. The missionaries were naturally incensed by his anti-Christian propaganda and activities. The Lutherans especially had become his implacable enemies. After the middle of 1948, they began their own investigation of events on the Rai Coast. Their principal informants, apart from the evangelists who had been

[1] Yali took advantage of the lull in the Kabu Ceremony to carry out the bullroarer ritual. As noted, the two had to be kept entirely separate.

humiliated, were the natives of the coastal Sengam villages, who had kept aloof from the pagan revival and cargo cult. The main exceptions were the inhabitants of Galek, only one of whom was prepared to denounce Yali. The others respected their trade ties with the people of Sor.

The investigation started under the following circumstances. It will be remembered that, early in 1948, Kasan left Yali's service because he disapproved of the pagan revival. He returned to Biliau, where he continued to indulge in the traditional system of sexual promiscuity he had revived in 1947. About March or April, one of his adulteries infuriated the village *luluai* who, acting on the assumption that Yali was now the proper judicial authority on the Rai Coast for cases of this kind, referred the matter to him. Kasan, his mistress, and two other women (one of them married) accused of acting as go-betweens, were taken to Sangpat. Yali sentenced them all to 'imprisonment' at Yabalol, Kasan for a month and the women for three weeks. That night they were lodged on the 'station' and, it was claimed, Yali tried to seduce Karong, the second female go-between, who was still a virgin. She refused his advances and he was extremely annoyed. Next day the party was taken to Yabalol, where Kasan was appointed store clerk[1] and the women were put to carrying stones to build a new path from the village to the river.

The whole affair demonstrated Yali's lack of true responsibility for and understanding of the judicial system he pretended to represent. Kasan, according to both his own and Yali's account, had no difficulty in carrying on his intrigue with his mistress and also in beginning a new one with the married go-between. Yali is said to have told his 'policemen' that they too could enjoy the women's favours. Karong, however, still refused to comply. This annoyed Yali even more. It was alleged that he instructed Yakob of Yabob (Madang), the 'policeman' detailed to supervise her work by the river, to use stronger means of persuasion. Yakob took advantage of her when she was alone and burdened with a netbag full of stones, and raped her.[2]

At the end of three weeks the women were sent home to Biliau. But Kasan, who was angry with his *luluai* for having put him in 'court', preferred to stay at Yabalol after the completion of his 'sentence'. He was kept on as store clerk at a salary of 15s. a month, which was now paid by Yali himself. He held the position until the end of Yali's first

---

[1] His duties were hardly arduous. He was supposed to clean and oil the rifles brought to Yali by Kaum.

[2] Yali, while admitting that he 'imprisoned' Kasan and the three women, still denies that he gave Yakob any such instructions.

patrol in June and July 1948. He went with the party as far as Yoga-yoga, where he received a letter inviting him as a congregational elder to attend the Lutheran Conference, which was to be held at Biliau. He accepted the invitation and left the patrol, using his lameness (caused by a bomb explosion during the war) as an excuse.

At the Conference, Kasan began to give information to the European missionaries: about his own and the women's recent experiences at Yabalol (omitting, of course, the full details of his own sexual intrigues), the humiliation of the first evangelist from Uyerak on the patrol he had just left, and the pagan revival and cargo cult, which were now gathering strength. (He did not see fit to describe their quasi-Christian fore-runners.) At the end of the Conference, he rejoined the patrol at Maibang and returned with it to Sangpat. He thus witnessed the slapping of the second evangelist (at Kuhuparam) and the shaming of the loyal Christians at Awaraing. Having collected the additional information he wanted, he left Yali's service for good and returned to live at Biliau.

From these beginnings, the Lutheran Mission began to build up its dossier on Yali. Encouraged by Kasan's example, other natives now volunteered statements of their own. Eventually, the President of the Lutheran Mission believed that he had enough evidence for a trial of strength. In June 1949, he published a signed article in English in the mission's local newspaper *Aakesing*, accusing Yali of promoting cargo cult, destroying all mission work and education, and having people pray to himself rather than God.[1] When the article came to the notice of the Administration, the District Officer of Madang at once trans-lated it to Yali, who categorically denied the allegations it contained. The District Officer, therefore, acting on Yali's behalf, sought legal advice from the Crown Law Office in Port Moresby as to the libellous nature of the article. He was told that, if the statements in question could not be substantiated, a libel action would be justified. Yali then filed suit against the Lutheran Mission.

The libel action was extremely ill-advised. The Lutheran Mission was able to furnish the Administration with such facts about Yali's activities that it was soon dropped. Thereafter there were, first, an Administration and, second, a Police investigation, as result of which Yali was arrested and summoned to appear before the Supreme Court at Madang on 3 July 1950. The charges were: first, deprivation of liberty

[1] It should always be remembered that Yali never claimed to be a god. At most, he acknowledged the claim that he had special power from the gods and allowed people to invoke him in the *table ritual* as an intercessor with the gods.

(the illegal 'imprisonments' already described); and second, incitement to rape (of Karong at Yabalol in 1948). No charge of promoting cargo cult was brought. Probably it was thought too difficult under the circumstances to prepare a watertight case and, in view of the damning evidence on the other counts, hardly worth while for an additional gaol sentence of only six months.

The trial took place in an atmosphere of extreme racial bitterness.[1] The proceedings were in English, with a Pidgin English interpreter for the natives involved. They were conducted strictly according to the law, and Yali was given proper legal advice and protection throughout. Yali was convicted on both charges, and was sentenced to six months' imprisonment on the first and six years' imprisonment on the second, both to be served concurrently. The verdict surprised nobody but the severity of the penalty was very gratifying to local Europeans, whose interest in the trial was almost exclusively political. Their morale was to some extent restored, because they felt that a threat to Australian rule was removed, that the Madang District would be freed from a dangerous agitator for a very long time, and that the natives would realize that anti-European activities would never be countenanced in the future. As the full power of the law was brought to bear on him, they saw Yali as utterly disgraced and his charisma as finally destroyed. He stood in the dock dressed as any ordinary native prisoner, and the District Office[2] did nothing to alleviate his terrible humiliation. In European eyes, he was reduced to a figure of contempt.[3]

Yali served his sentence at Lae. By all accounts, he was a model prisoner, and several attempts were made by officers of the Administration and Armed Services who knew him to have him released. Nevertheless, he was granted only a year's remission. He left gaol and returned to Yabalol towards the end of 1955.

During these five years, Yali's political organization ceased to function. Sangpat 'Station' was demolished and the 'Police Force' disbanded, the three members from the Sepik District being ordered back to their own villages. Only the 'boss boys' remained, although they were no longer given even tacit recognition by the Administration. The

[1] I attended the trial myself and the observations in this paragraph are entirely my own.

[2] Some months before the trial there was a routine transfer of District Officers. The new District Officer had no sympathy for Yali, whereas his predecessor would have spared him whatever humiliation he could.

[3] Yali, in fact, behaved with considerable dignity during the trial. Natives generally reacted to the event quite differently from Europeans. Informants told me later that they did not regard his stature as impaired.

people continued to appoint them merely as third in command to the *luluais* and *tultuls*. The Kabu Ceremony on the Rai Coast was banned indefinitely. This marked the end of cargo activity as a widespread co-ordinated movement in the southern Madang District. Between 1950 and 1961, both during Yali's imprisonment and since his release, there have been occasional outbreaks of cargo cult. Although some of them have been connected with his name, they appear in the main to have been inspired by purely local and independent leaders, and to have lacked central direction. They are described, and their importance is discussed, towards the end of Chapter IX.

# THE CARGO MOVEMENT

## MOTIVATION, MEANS, AND EFFECTS[1]

IF THE Cargo Movement is examined on its own as a phenomenon *sui generis*, it may be regarded as, in the long run, a rudimentary form of revolutionary 'nationalism'—the people's first experiment in completely renewing the world order and achieving independence from European rule. Much of the behaviour of its adherents and many of the declared aims of its leaders point to this conclusion. There were examples of what could be construed, *prima facie*, as the symbolic renunciation of the old way of life: Tagarab's sermons on the Ten Commandments; his and Gurek's renaming of the days of the week; and the mission helpers' efforts to enforce monogamy, reorganize the ownership of land and fishing reefs, and eradicate dancing. In its later stages especially, the Movement introduced important changes in the overt socio-political order—such as Kaum's military and Yali's political organization—and presaged even greater ones had its aims ever been realized. At times, the hope was expressed that Europeans would be either killed or driven out of the country. Nevertheless, an analysis exclusively in these terms would blind us to the very strong, and perhaps more important, forces in the Movement that counterbalanced its radical tendencies—forces that prevented its adherents from ever breaking seriously with their past and that delayed the emergence of militant 'nationalism' in a full sense of the word until a relatively late stage of development.

We shall see the Cargo Movement in clearer perspective if we try to answer in turn each of the questions asked at the outset: Why did the natives of the southern Madang District want cargo? Why did they believe that they could get it largely by means of ritual? And what is the political significance of their attempts to do so? We must begin by reconsidering the nature and extent of socio-cultural change in the area between 1871 and 1950. Significantly, in the total area, there were cargo

---

[1] The ideas on which this chapter is based were first presented in two papers I delivered at the Senior Officers' Course on Native Education in Papua and New Guinea, at the Australian School of Pacific Administration, Mosman, N.S.W., in 1958. They have also been paraphrased by Essai. See my *The Educational Conflict in Papua and New Guinea*, and 'The Background to Educational Development in Papua and New Guinea', op. cit.; and also Essai, *Papua and New Guinea*, pp. 176–9.

cults among many different groups subjected to varying degrees and periods of contact—from the coastal peoples, who bore the full weight of occupation after 1884, to those of the sub-coast and hinterland, far removed from the main centres of European settlement and brought under control only after 1921. This suggests at once that total social or cultural disintegration is not a necessary condition for cargo cult, as is borne out by the work of Berndt, Salisbury, and Reay in the Central Highlands. These scholars have all described cults among peoples whose traditional way of life has been so little disrupted that it is still bound to influence their outlook.[1]

What is more important, if we look at the southern Madang District as a whole between 1871 and 1950, we find that its people, even in regions where contact was greatest, were never faced with anything like total social or cultural disintegration. It can be shown that, although there were very great changes in their way of life, these did no more than give a new cast to its outward forms. In a more vital sense, they were purely superficial. In the economic and social field, the loss of some institutions and addition of others did not seriously affect the basic principles of traditional behaviour and relationships, and the values associated with them. In the intellectual field, the epistemological system, although given new content, preserved its original form. From this point of view, therefore, the Cargo Movement was conservative rather than revolutionary. It was attributable to too little rather than too much change. Although the people may have thought at times that they were creating a different way of life, it was old attitudes and concepts that primarily directed their actions. Even the apparently unqualified innovations already mentioned must be interpreted, in part at least, in this way. Ideas could not be too unfamiliar: to be accepted they had to have some roots in tradition.

This is not to deny that the Cargo Movement was caused by the pressures of European occupation. But here we must distinguish between precipitating and enabling conditions, the one being represented by the history of contact and the other by the native culture. It is by analysing the interaction between the two that we get a true insight into the problems of motivation and means. *Motivation*, or the natives' reasons for wanting Western goods, must be seen as their reaction to the main events of contact in terms of their traditional social values.

[1] See Berndt, 'A Cargo Movement in the Eastern Central Highlands of New Guinea', pp. 40–65, 137–58, and 202–34, and 'Reaction to Contact in the Eastern Highlands of New Guinea', op. cit., pp. 190–228 and 255–74; Salisbury, *An Indigenous New Guinea Cult*, and Reay, *The Kuma*, pp. 194–202. I take into account the changes described by Salisbury in his *From Stone to Steel*.

These reasons were never constant. They varied according to whether the people thought that they were suffering privation and indignity or that they had some hope of improvement. *Means*, or the natives' conviction that they could obtain cargo almost exclusively by ritual, must be seen as their attempt to control the new situation by the same sorts of techniques as they had always had good cause to assume were effective in the old, very largely because they could not conceive any alternative. These two general themes are reflected also in the conduct of the leaders of the Cargo Movement.

Finally, it is only by understanding the absence of real change in values and epistemological assumptions that the *effects* of the Cargo Movement—its political significance both in the past and for the future —can be fully appreciated. In the past, although the Movement saw the first stirring of unity and 'nationalism', conservatism prevented it from realizing its full potential. For the future, unless conservatism is quickly and effectively eradicated, it may well impede the more far-reaching economic, political, and intellectual revolution which we are now trying to achieve.

### The Perpetuation of the Traditional Value- and Epistemological Systems

In Chapter I, it was seen that in the past the value- and epistemological systems were closely interrelated. Each reflected a different aspect of a cosmic order which was conceived as finite and anthropocentric, and as possessing few if any supernatural attributes. Within this order, man saw himself as the focal point of two systems of relationships and derived, or believed he derived, benefits from both.

Social values reflected the actual tendency towards stasis in the socioeconomic order, the first system of relationships. Without forces to create continually changing economic drives and hence alignments between individuals and groups, the pattern of human relationships integrated as a generalized and virtually classless structure with multiple functions in the economic, social, political, and religious fields. It was perfectly capable of carrying out these duties as long as events maintained their settled rhythm, but it did not allow, or even encourage, the individual to advance his own interests at the expense of those of his group. It contrasted strongly with the relatively flexible hierarchical structure of Western society, which consisted of several more or less discrete systems each designed for a specialized function.

The homogeneity of social values was little affected by differences in structural form, of which the individual was quite unaware. He reacted in terms of a constellation of interpersonal relationships, of which he was the nucleus and which he regarded as standard for the whole southern Madang District. At the purely superficial level, where careful inquiries were never made, the attitude was justified. People belonging to different social networks could, and did, have perfectly satisfactory dealings with each other as, for instance, in trade.

From this point of view, the content of social relationships and hence the values they expressed were everywhere the same: the bestowal of reciprocal advantages or the exchange of goods and services on the basis of equivalence, guaranteed by the approximate equality of access to economic resources enjoyed by all members of the society. From this it emerged that harmonious or friendly relationships between individuals and groups could exist only where such arrangements were regularly maintained. Even where there was a surplus of wealth, it was normally 'sold' for personal or group prestige by staging elaborate distributions to outsiders which, again according to the principle of equivalence, had to be returned. In short, material culture, apart from its immediate and practical uses, was also the symbol of all important relationships and social status. Ensuring the success of its regular means of production was an essential qualification for leadership. Conversely, where there was no exchange of goods and services between individuals and groups—no reciprocal distribution of wealth, and no informal give and take in everyday affairs—there could be no harmonious relationship. There could be only complete indifference, where neither party impinged on the other, or a state of hostility and periodic warfare.

The epistemological system had as its referent the wider cosmic order, which included the second network of relationships (between man, deities, ancestors, and totems[1]), and which was implicitly conceived as finite and immutable. The content of these putative relationships was expressed in roughly the same way as in the case of the socio-economic system. Each party did things for the other. Material and social culture was accepted as an automatic concomitant of living. Human beings had complete rights to it because their various deities (each of whom belonged exclusively to a roughly definable geographical region) had invented it and perpetuated it for them, while their ancestors, although rarely creators, helped them exploit it. In return, men ensured the continued co-operation of deities and ancestors by the performance of ritual. 'True knowledge', the intellectual basis of leadership, although it included secular-empirical techniques, was considered

---

[1] As totems were important only in one group (the Ngaing), they are ignored in the general analysis, unless special reference is made to them.

to be primarily the ability to maintain these additional relationships within the cosmic order by the repetition of esoteric formulae and symbolic actions, the mastery of which necessitated the observance of stringent food and sex taboos. These taboos had no other rationale: they were not regarded as ethically desirable behaviour in themselves.

The minimal importance attributed the independent human intellect did not imply mysticism, as was clear from an examination of the cosmic order as it was conceived to exist in space and through time. Spatially, because men, deities, and spirits of the dead co-existed in the same geographical environment and had the same corporeal nature, their interaction was as pragmatic as that between human beings themselves. That these superhuman beings should handle material objects presented no conceptual problems. Important 'work' involved both a compound of secular and ritual techniques, and collaboration from deities and ancestors, no distinction being made between different degrees of reality. Again, the method of reckoning time eliminated the possibility of mysticism. There was no historical tradition comparable to that of Western society. Cosmic time—genealogical time or the period of remembered events plus the age of antiquity or the creation of the culture as recorded in myths—had little chronological meaning and was not associated with the concept of change. As ordinary events recurred with more or less regular monotony, relationships between men and superhuman beings were assumed to be unvarying. Thus the body of religious knowledge was thought to be as certain and fixed as the framework within which it operated: it appeared to be based on perpetually verified fact; and it could be augmented only by further invention and revelation by old or new deities.

In the southern Madang District, the traditional value- and episte-mological systems have so far proved extremely durable under European contact partly because of their own integration and logical consistency, and partly because the changes introduced affected only the externals of the natives' way of life without touching the vital principles under-lying it. This can be demonstrated by reviewing the impact of the West in the economic, socio-political, and intellectual fields, described in Chapter II.

The impact of contact on the native economic system must be looked at from two points of view: its effects on the internal economy of the villages; and its effects on the young men who left home for European employment. From the first point of view, the factor of overwhelming significance was the preservation of the native economy on the basis of stationary subsistence. By 1950, five Administrations had failed to change it into something approaching that of Western society. Although it is true that, after 1871, there was a continuous trickle, if not a large flow, of European goods into native society and that these goods, especially steel axes and bushknives, almost completely replaced their traditional counterparts, economic life was in no way revolutionized. Work was speeded up but there was little alteration in the types of jobs to be performed. Even in exchange economics, the new goods (including money) were used for purely traditional ends: they took the place of indigenous artefacts and valuables in marriage, initiatory, and mortuary payments. Little was done to change the goals of the economy to profit and progress in the Western sense. Although, after 1899, the Imperial German Administration tried to build up native copra, rubber, and guttapercha industries, its rule was too short for them to have any noticeable result and they died a natural death after the departure of the Imperial officers at the beginning of the First World War. The two subsequent Administrations (during the Australian Military Occupation and Mandate) made no real attempt to follow up the German programme. It was only after 1945 that a serious start was made, but by 1950 there was so little headway that the overall situation remained virtually unchanged. At the same time, the Lutheran and Catholic Missions contributed little, if anything, in this field. They did not regard it as their proper concern and, in any case, their policies were directed at keeping native secular culture intact as far as possible.

European business enterprise, although disruptive, did not have the far-reaching effects claimed for it in other areas. The establishment of the plantation system deprived some native societies of much of their best land and, as has been seen, created a good deal of ill will. (This is discussed in a later section.) But it did little to change the fundamental nature of the economy in the whole area. Only the seaboard communities between Sarang and Bogati were badly affected. Moreover, even the inhabitants of villages such as Biliā (Yam, Madang), which lost all or most of their land, did not enter entirely new occupations in order to earn their livings. They joined cognates and affines in other groups, and either borrowed or rented their land. They continued to use natural resources in the age-old way and for age-old ends.

Again, the indenture system, which drew off from the villages considerable numbers of the younger able-bodied men for labour, still left the traditional economy intact. Certainly, in cases where over-recruitment occurred, the women, children, and old people were left without adequate food supplies. But there is little to suggest that this evil was widespread in the southern Madang District, except between 1914 and

1918, when recruiters in the inland were not properly controlled by the District Office, and during 1942–5, when the Japanese and A.N.G.A.U. Administrations were impressing workers for their armed services. As long as the rule preventing the signing on of more than 33⅓ per cent of adult males was not too often and too flagrantly abused, the deficit in manpower was fairly adequately offset by the new steel axes and bush-knives, which had speeded up everyday tasks.

From the second point of view, European employment did nothing to change the outlook of the indentured labourers themselves. Their experiences in domestic service, and on the plantations and goldfields, rarely if ever gave them new economic concepts and values to take back to their villages. Indentured labourers remained essentially subsistence wage earners. Very few of them had any understanding of the purposes of the work they performed: the industrial value of the copra, gold, and other commodities they helped produce. Furthermore, they did not appreciate that the Europeans did anything to earn their livings. White men did no physical labour—certainly little to produce the luxury foods, goods, and machinery they enjoyed in such abundance. At most they carried out minor repairs on ships, aircraft, and motor-cars, but machinery needing serious overhaul had to be sent to Australia. Other-wise, they directed the work of native employees, sat in offices and wrote on bits of paper and, when they wanted fresh supplies of goods, sent their servants with chits to the stores. Until 1945 at least, the meaning of these activities was never explained to indentured labourers, who were therefore neither enabled nor encouraged to become petty entrepreneurs and capitalists with small businesses of their own in the European towns.[1] Even since 1945, very few such businesses have been started.

In the social and political field, the overt changes were more striking. Native societies were reorganized by both the Administrations and the missions. In the administrative system, warfare was outlawed and leadership revised. The old big men were replaced by the official head-men. Although due consideration was paid to local custom in the law courts, the Administrations did not formally recognize the existence of the myriad autonomous indigenous societies in the area. They treated the people as a whole—regardless of linguistic or other boundaries—as so many individual units to be fitted into the new structure as the lowest class in the economic, social, and political pyramid. The natives were linked through their headmen to the European officials who

---

[1] In any case, it is doubtful if they could have competed with the Chinese, who had a monopoly in this field after the end of German rule.

occupied the positions towards its apex. In the mission system, traditional societies were grouped into local congregations under the leadership of native helpers, who acted for the people in their dealings with the European hierarchy but who, in the case of the Lutherans, were also intended to take over the top positions in the future.

Even so, these two systems, although representing considerable change in the overall situation, only modified rather than transformed village social life. As emphasized, neither the Administrations nor missions wanted to interfere with customs of which they did not disapprove. The old networks of interpersonal kinship and trade relationships could still operate efficiently within the new wider framework. The official headmen exercised their authority only in the presence of the Administration. When no patrol was in the area, their insignia stored away, they were indistinguishable from ordinary villagers. The mission helpers put greater pressures on the people, especially when they tried to reorganize marriage and land and reef ownership, and root out paganism, but even they did not change the social structure to a radical degree. Because the subsistence economy was left intact, the traditional systems of feast exchanges (admittedly shorn of much of their religious ceremonial in many Christian villages), of agriculture, and of give and take between kinsmen continued to function, involving roughly the same obligations for people in roughly the same relationships to each other as before.

It often happened that old relationships could be used as they stood for new purposes, as when the Yam Lutheran evangelists took Christianity to their Rai Coast trade friends in 1922–3. Yet even when the contact situation demanded new social alignments, traditional principles were always adopted. When severe land loss at Biliā (Madang) weakened the patrilineal structure and forced the people to rely on cognatic and affinal ties, this was a pattern still recognizably in keeping with the past.[1] When the opening up of the country enabled unrestricted travel, natives who had never met before now had face-to-face dealings with each other. But the resultant relationships were always expressed, as far as possible, in terms of distant kinship and indirect trade ties, which were now treated as if they had always been close and intimate. (Hence, even though the spread of European goods crippled the old trading systems as such, the trade partnerships themselves were maintained as

[1] A similar situation exists in Aiyawang village on the Rai Coast. As the result of Nurton's punitive expedition in 1936, and M'na and N'dau immigration, the old patriclans have been weakened. But most relationships in the village are based on kinship, descent, and marriage ties of some kind.

vital means of communication between groups and individuals.) Even in the labour compounds, where natives from many different Districts were often thrown together, a man tended to address and behave towards his fellow-workers (Pidgin English, *wanwok*) as if they were his brothers. In this way, social values, still associated largely with interpersonal face-to-face relationships of some kind, remained the same.

The native epistemological system would appear, at first sight, to have been most disrupted. By 1942, the missions had made considerable inroads into the old religion, which in very many villages they had ostensibly replaced with Christianity. They had large numbers of nominal adherents, who were at least familiar with their doctrines. Many children of both sexes had passed through their primary schools, and a percentage of the older boys had gone on to their secondary, high, and technical schools.

Nevertheless, there was no revolution in the people's basic ways of thinking. There was virtually no success in giving them Western secular education. The Imperial German Administration had made a good start with its school at Namanula and plans for four others by 1917, but the boys it took from the mainland (twenty-three by 1912, according to the *Annual Reports*), even supposing that the majority of them came from the southern Madang District, were so few that they could not have been expected to have disseminated a rational understanding of the new colonial order. Furthermore, they had not yet reached the standard where they could have taken over the jobs of Asian technicians, as was originally intended. As in the economic field, the Imperial regime's educational programme was abandoned in 1914. By 1942, the Australian Mandate Administration had fallen far short of its promises of 1921, and the new policy inaugurated after 1945 had made only limited headway by 1950. Before the Second World War some natives from the whole area visited Australia, and after 1942 a larger number of native soldiers trained in Queensland. But because there had been no extensive teaching in English, they were not equipped to get a true insight into Western culture.[1]

The missions did what they could to improve the situation. Both Lutherans and Catholics taught some secular subjects in their schools. But, with relatively few exceptions, their pupils showed little inclination for this kind of work. The only teaching that made any serious and widespread impression was religious. There were two obvious reasons for this. On the one hand, Western secular education had no real

[1] In spite of their efforts, the Germans were unable to spread their own language. But after 1914 this was obviously not of such importance.

counterpart in the native intellectual tradition: there was nothing to which it could be readily assimilated. Also, because native economic life remained unchanged, it was of no immediate and recognizable use: it could not be eaten, worn, or consumed. Thus what was imparted was soon forgotten. On the other hand, Western religious teaching had its direct counterpart in the native intellectual tradition, to which it could be at once assimilated. In addition, the people believed that they saw its practical relevance to the economic system of the new colonial society as they conceived it.

Broadly speaking, the net result of the first seventy-nine years of contact was that the values and concepts of the indigenous culture were totally vindicated in the people's eyes. They had, of course, to grapple with the problems caused by the impact of occupation, but their solutions could not be other than entirely traditional. The fact that they had been unable to adopt a pattern of individual economic incentives meant that they could not appreciate those that goaded most European activities and that there still were no forces within their social system to make it more flexible. There were no opportunities in native society for the intelligent and energetic to advance their personal interests by new skills and hard work, and those offered in European employment were negligible. Hence, unable to adjust to the external conditions imposed on them through sharing in, and internalizing the values of, Western commercial enterprise, the natives could judge European behaviour towards themselves only by the standards they retained from the past, reciprocity and equivalence. Again, because there had been no change in their economic and social life, they could not learn or develop on their own new, rational, and secular ideas to explain the vicissitudes of the contact situation. Although they had to think out their position for themselves, they could do so only on the basis of old assumptions so that the Cargo Movement had to have a primarily religious form. In their view, it was knowledge revealed by special deities rather than the incessant struggle, experiment, and achievement of the independent human intellect that was responsible for Western material culture and the economic disparity between Europeans and themselves. This conservatism was further reinforced by the opening up of the country during the interwar years. In the absence of real association with Europeans, the natives inevitably forged closer bonds between themselves. Already possessing a basically common culture and now having in Pidgin English a *lingua franca* capable of expressing it, they began to feel that they belonged to a society far wider than that of their forbears: the common native society of the whole area. Apart from its political significance, which is discussed later on, this enabled them to close their minds against ideas from the outside.

These factors gave the Cargo Movement its strongly conservative character. It represented the continuation of the essential features of the people's old way of life under new external conditions. It was the natives' attempt to maintain their dominant position in the cosmic order, so that relationships between human beings, and between human and superhuman beings, would function to their advantage. In this way, the high degree of integration and consistency that characterized the traditional culture was transferred to the Cargo Movement and was responsible for its almost unassailable logic. This is at once apparent if we re-examine the material presented in Chapters III–VIII: how traditional social values and epistemological assumptions fulfilled separate functions in the fields of motivation and means in the Cargo Movement, while still remaining fully interrelated and contained within a single system, and combining to provide a *modus operandi* for its leaders.

### Motivation: Pressures of Contact; Values and Attitudes in the Cargo Movement

The natives developed an obsession for cargo for two reasons. First, it became an economic necessity: it had obvious advantages over their own goods, which it swiftly replaced as the area was brought under control. Second, it became an index of their self-respect. Because their demand for it always exceeded the supply, the problem of its availability caused considerable anxiety. Hence they attributed to it the same kind of social importance as they had done to their traditional material culture: they came to regard it as the symbol of their status in the new colonial society. If they were enabled to acquire adequate quantities of it or the key to its source in return for the land, labour, and services they were obliged to provide, their relationships with Europeans would be satisfactory and friendly. But if cargo or its secret were withheld, they would be relegated to a position of inferiority and contempt. Thus over the whole period of contact native attitudes towards Europeans were not, as was a common theme in many of the cults described in Worsley's survey of the whole of New Guinea, invariably unfavourable.[1] In the southern Madang District, native attitudes alternated between expressions of friendship and hostility according to whether it was believed that white men were likely to uphold or repudiate the

---

[1] But Worsley, *The Trumpet Shall Sound*, op. cit., p. 54, states clearly that 'anti-European feeling was not necessarily present in the earlier stages of many movements though it quickly became added to most of them'.

principles of reciprocity and equivalence. This alternation prescribed the types of goods the people periodically desired and the purposes to which they were to be put. As will appear in another context, it also correlated with the various economic, social, and political aims of the Cargo Movement.

In the First Cargo Belief, attitudes of both friendship and hostility emerged. Once Maclay had overcome the initial awe and wonder caused by his arrival, and had established his *bona fides*, the people treated him with respect and goodwill. They were able to assimilate him to their own pattern of relationships by exchanging goods and services with him on what they regarded as an equitable basis. Hence they came to think of him as an intrinsic part of their own world and saw no reason to invest the cargo he had brought with any special importance beyond its immediate economic utility. They wanted trade goods to make their lives more comfortable: steel axes, adzes, and other tools.

During the later stages of the First Cargo Belief, however, race relations and racial attitudes deteriorated. The Germans ignored the principle of equivalence. They treated the coastal people with the greatest arrogance. They stole their land and demanded their labour, and in return were prepared to offer only the most niggardly compensation from the vast wealth in their possession.

In the people's eyes, this was the denial of a true relationship. Cargo was now regarded as both the reason for, and the symbol of, European military and political supremacy. Inevitably friendship turned to enmity, which eventually culminated in the Madang Revolt of 1904 and the doctrine of the Second Cargo Belief. At this time (the periods of active and passive resistance), the greatest importance was attached to military equipment for a war against Europeans. This was apparent in the attempt, in the course of the Revolt, to seize the police rifles and in the dominant emphasis on rifles in the revised versions of the Kilibob-Manup myth. It was rifles that the cargo deity had taken away, and it was with rifles that he was expected to return to redress the balance.

The twenty years of the Third Cargo Belief saw a complete *volte face*. The final demonstration of German power in 1912 and two years in exile predisposed the Madang natives to a policy of accommodation. They were encouraged in this by what seemed to be strong evidence of a change in European attitudes: the solicitude of the Lutheran missionaries and the Australian Military Administration's ready permission for them to return home. Thus hostility gave way to a concerted effort to create friendly relationships with Europeans, the content of which was to be fair distribution of the new wealth that had come into the country. Again there was a change in the type of goods desired and the purposes for which they were to be used. There was no more talk of military equipment. The natives once again wanted ordinary trade goods, which in many places had become essential to their way of life and would, as they saw it, grant them full social equality with white men.

With the Fourth Cargo Belief, there was a return to enmity. Again the cargo became the symbol of European oppression. As we saw, during the Mandate race relations were very bad. European title to land stolen from the Madang natives was confirmed, and the people of the whole area received little share of European wealth. Socially and politically, they were kept firmly in their place by the white masters. Even the missionaries, from whom so much had been expected, were now treated with suspicion. Moreover, as a larger proportion of the native population was being recruited than before, common experience in employment could serve only to spread and strengthen the spirit of resentment that had been building up around Madang, the main centre of black–white interaction. At first, the people expressed their hostility by withdrawing from the missions and establishing their own 'Church' under the Letub leaders, and by hoping for the return of Jesus-Manup with rifles. Later, with the outbreak of the Japanese War, they became more aggressive: they openly prophesied an invasion by enemy troops and, on their arrival, brazenly collaborated with them against their former rulers.

For two and a half years after the Second World War, largely because of the personality and propaganda of Yali, there was a partial and temporary return to the policy of accommodation. Yali was able to persuade the people that relations with Europeans would very soon improve and that huge supplies of cargo would be made available to them. Until the second half of 1947, prophecies of military equipment were rarely made. Hopes were redirected to ordinary trade goods, building materials, machinery, and social equality with the whites.

In 1948, the final realization that the Europeans would not share their wealth led to new and even more widespread expressions of hostility. The lack of cargo once more symbolized the people's subjection to foreign rule. Hostility was expressed first, in the pagan revival, by attempting to minimize dependence on Europeans and later, in the Fifth Cargo Belief, by the prophecy of the arrival of arms for a renewed struggle against them. The prophecy was thought to be partially fulfilled by the discovery of rifles and machine guns on the Rai Coast.

## Means: The Epistemological System of the Cargo Movement

The natives believed that they could obtain cargo largely by ritual because, for reasons already given, their assumptions about the nature and dynamics of the cosmic order were virtually unchanged. The conceived geographical environment was, of course, gradually expanded. But the total cosmic order was still regarded as finite and anthropocentric—with few if any supernatural attributes—and the relationships between its human and superhuman personnel as specified and predictable. It existed solely for the benefit of man. Its origins could be accounted for only by myth. It could not have come into being except for the activities of a deity or deities, who then surrendered, subject to certain conditions, to human direction.

It was impossible to regard cargo as the product of human endeavour and skill. It had to be the crowning achievement of the creator god or gods. Thus the means devised to solve the technical problems of explaining its source and exploiting it to the natives' advantage were of exactly the same kind as those used in the case of the traditional material culture. By studying, in each of the five cargo beliefs, the conceived spatial dimensions of the new cosmos, we shall see how relationships between human beings, cargo deity, and ancestors were so defined as to establish the natives' inalienable rights to the cargo as a concomitant of living, and thereby reflect and validate their successive attitudes towards Europeans. The new cosmic order, as seen through time, emphasized the immutability of these relationships, rights, and attitudes. The perpetuation of the traditional concepts of knowledge and work gave the people techniques for translating their desire for cargo into the type of action they believed would produce it, and confirmed man's central and paramount position in the cosmic order.

The remarkable uniformity of this epistemological system in the whole area was due, as has been obvious throughout, to the similarity of both the indigenous pagan religions and the intellectual pressures (mainly Christian teaching) to which the people were subjected. This homogeneity was increased when basic concepts from different regions were translated into Pidgin English. The limitations of its vocabulary glossed over petty idiosyncrasies and hence accentuated the essential oneness of meaning.[1]

[1] Thus the Pidgin English word *masalai* embraced all those classes of superhuman beings I have called deities: Ngaing *tut* (god); Sengam, Som, and Madang *tubud* or *tibud* (god), and the demigods (who lacked vernacular collective names); and Garia *oite'u* (god). Again, the Pidgin English phrase *Singsing Tambaran* covered not only the Ngaing Kabu Ceremony but also equivalent, although never completely identical, rituals honouring the ancestors in other places.

There were, of course, occasional differences in the pattern owing
to local variations in both the traditional and contact situations. For
instance, Tarosi's information about Evolution was particularly important to Yali as it could be interpreted as something akin to Ngaing
totemism, which after 1933 had given way to the teachings of the
early chapters of Genesis. This did not interest natives in other parts of
the area to anything like the same extent, because totemism was either
insignificant or entirely unrepresented in their cultures. Again, in the
Letub version of the Fourth Cargo Belief, the identification of Manup as
Jesus Christ and the prominence given the Virgin Birth were obviously
attributable to Catholic influence in the Sek region. In Tagarab's version, the identification of Kilibob as God, the relative unimportance
of Jesus Christ, and the stress on the Ten Commandments reflect
Lutheran (Protestant) influence. But in the broad picture, which alone
concerns us here, these differences meant little and can be disregarded
from now on.

## The Spatial Dimensions of the New Cosmos

Spatially, the conceived cosmos remained unaltered during the First
Cargo Belief. The natives interpreted Europeans as part of the physical environment they had always known: as gods (or possibly spirits)
who had always been either in their midst or in some way associated
with them, and who had now suddenly appeared in visible form. The
reaction of the Astrolabe Bay natives to Maclay was particularly important. His fearlessness and friendly behaviour proved his identity as
a Bongu–Sek coastal deity, perhaps even Kilibob or Manup. This at
once defined in strictly traditional terms the way in which the people
understood their relationship with their European visitor–cargo deity,
established their rights to the goods he had made and brought them,
and reflected their initial friendship for the white men. As Maclay was
one of their own gods, they at once assumed that the wealth he provided was as much theirs by right as the culture given them by other
deities in the past. They obviously reciprocated his goodwill towards
them. The behaviour of the later German settlers was interpreted in the
same way, although now the people's resentment was expressed by the
belief that the new white men were gods from a hostile area. This suggests a temporary abandonment of rights to the cargo on the grounds
that, in the age of antiquity, the deities of some areas had often given
their followers special artefacts and resources (such as clay deposits),
which deities in other areas had denied to theirs.

With the Second Cargo Belief and greater experience of white men,

the cosmos was expanded geographically for the first time, although it
was still understood as a purely physical realm. For the coastal peoples,
it was no longer merely the Sarang–Saidor littoral and Siasi Islands,
but now incorporated a vague land across the sea, inhabited by Europeans. White men were classified as human beings and their presence in
the native world was attributed to Kilibob's or Manup's having taken
them to, or found them in, their country at the end of his journey.
They were, therefore, another island society either linked to the natives
at the time of the creation or entirely separate. The natives' claim to the
cargo and mounting hostility to Europeans were stated clearly by the
belief that the latter had obtained exclusive possession of a valuable
commodity invented by a deity to whom they had only partial rights
or no original rights at all. If Kilibob or Manup created both white
men and natives, then the white men should have given the natives
their quota of cargo. If Kilibob or Manup had only discovered the
white men in their distant home, then the cargo belonged primarily to
the natives. In either case, the ties between the two races were so negligible that the natives were justified in fighting for their rights.

After the introduction of Christianity and the rise of the Third
Cargo Belief, which showed an even greater knowledge of Europeans,
the boundaries of the cosmos were further extended, and the relationships between human beings and the cargo deity revised. Sydney was
accepted as the home of the white men, and Heaven was either a part of
Sydney or a place above Sydney but linked to it by a ladder. The
physical unity of the cosmos was maintained. Moreover, the adoption
of Christianity did not mean strict conversion to monotheism. The
world was believed to be inhabited by a greater number of deities than
before. God (the cargo deity), Jesus Christ, the Virgin Mary, the
Saints, the angels, and the ancestors lived in Heaven. The old deities,
still powerful in their own spheres, continued to occupy their sanctuaries in New Guinea, although they were now designated as 'satans'.
The natives' return to an attitude of friendship towards, and dependence on, Europeans was now expressed by means of a putative
genealogy, which was derived from, and substantiated by, the Scriptures, and had its obvious counterparts in traditional social structure
and mythology. Both natives and Europeans had a common pair of
ancestors, Adam and Eve; and more particularly, they were jointly
descended from Noah. As the heirs of the favoured sons, Shem and
Japheth, the white men were obliged by the rules of kinship to succour
their less fortunate 'brothers', the progeny of Ham. This also vindicated the ultimate rights of all New Guinea natives to the cargo. God

was part of their cosmic order. He and the wealth he had created had originally belonged as much to them as to the Europeans. Now he had ordered that their confiscated inheritance be returned to them.

In the Fourth and Fifth Cargo Beliefs, the spatial dimensions of the cosmos were not enlarged to any extent. The main emphasis was on a redefinition of the relationships between its inhabitants: between human beings and gods, and between human beings themselves. In the Fourth Cargo Belief, its physical boundaries were thought to be the same as during the nominally Christian period. The principal change was that two of the 'satans', Kilibob and Manup, were now identified by different groups as God and Jesus Christ, as cargo deities. This expressed the return to hostility towards Europeans and a reassessment of native rights to the cargo. In the Letub version, natives and Europeans were genealogically separate: natives were associated with Manup, and Europeans with Adam and Eve. There was, therefore, no basis of kinship obligation between them. Manup had been enabled to create cargo only in New Guinea and hence it was the natives' exclusive property. The Europeans had acquired it, first, by accident (when Manup gave it to them because the natives had refused it) and, second, by blatant fraud (when the Jews crucified Jesus-Manup to prevent his return to New Guinea). This amounted to theft and justified the natives' later collaboration with the Japanese. In Tagarab's version, although the point is not explicit, natives and whites appear to have been genealogically discrete. Kilibob took the cargo away from its legitimate owners and gave it to an entirely alien people, the Europeans, whom he found in another land. They had demonstrated their ill will by refusing to teach the natives the true identity of the deity (God-Kilibob rather than the purely human and impotent God-Anus) from whom they could obtain a share of their property. Again, collaboration with the Japanese was justified.

The pagan revival represented a second temporary renunciation of rights to cargo, which was believed to be derived from deities (God and Jesus Christ) under exclusive European control. In the Fifth Cargo Belief, as the result of the wartime experiences of native troops in Australia, Brisbane and 'Rome' (the Queensland Museum) were added to the cosmos. Once more its physical unity was maintained, 'Rome' being said to be connected to Heaven by a ladder. The renewed hostility towards Europeans was implicit in the view that Christianity and paganism were only tenuously linked systems. Each represented a different origin, and provided a different set of deities, for Europeans and natives. Moreover, through Jesus-Manup (prim-

...iea god), the cargo was still the property of the
...he had created it originally only for the peoples of
...'Rome' he had handed on the secret to the deities of
... that every inhabitant of the southern Madang
...itomatic right to it. The Europeans still had cargo
...d trickery. Not only had they accepted it from Jesus-
...etences and then prevented his return to New Guinea,
... tried to strengthen their hold on it by stealing the
...ell and teaching the natives the mere externals of

... interpretations of the triadic relationship between
...is, and the cargo deity corresponds very closely with
...lysis of successive native attitudes towards Euro-
...ans. It demonstrates the interdependence between the value- and
epistemological systems of the Cargo Movement. Good and bad race
relations in the actual situation invariably had their parallels in the
ideology. Where there was native goodwill or hostility at the socio-
political level, current cargo doctrine was automatically adjusted to
reflect an identical attitude. A pattern of supposedly pre-existing inter-
relationship or its opposite was always manufactured to explain why
the natives should regard Europeans alternately as friends or enemies.
At the same time, the natives' rights to the cargo were always vindicated through their original association with the relevant deity.[1] In
other words, ideological relationships were continually reformulated in
the light of practical experience. This is summarized in Table IV.

## The New Cosmic Order as Seen Through Time

Traditional methods of reckoning time were unaffected by contact. No
historical tradition in the Western sense emerged. Events were not seen
as unique and infinitely variable but as having a predestined place in a
fixed cosmic framework. In cargo doctrine as a whole, there was no
chronological system which could depict Western technology as the
end product of innumerable years of gradual progress. Like the native
material culture, it was believed to have been brought into the world in
its final form, ready made and ready to use. This might appear to be
contradicted by the account of the development of the five stages of
cargo belief in Chapters III–VIII, based largely on descriptions by
native informants. Yet it would be wrong to assume that the majority
of the people saw these beliefs in their true chronological perspective.

[1] With the possible exception of the later stages of the First Cargo Belief and definite
exception of the pagan revival, when rights to the cargo were abandoned.

R

TABLE IV

Native–European ideological relationships

| Cargo Belief | Values and Attitudes towards Europeans (Type of Goods Desired) | Religion | Conceived Nature of Europeans | Native Rights to Cargo |
|---|---|---|---|---|
| 1st | Initial friendship; trade goods to be obtained only for their economic value | Pagan | Maclay an indigenous deity | Rights through Maclay (own god) |
|  | Later hostility | Pagan | Germans deities from hostile area | ? Temporary abandonment of rights |
| 2nd | Hostility; rifles desired for driving out whites | Pagan | Europeans humans from separate land; possessed cargo by default | Cargo deity native god. Natives lost cargo because of forbears' mistake |
| 3rd | Friendship; trade goods desired for social equality with whites | Christian | Europeans human, 'brothers' through Adam, Eve, and Noah; would restore natives their share of cargo | God once natives' deity. Natives lost cargo because of stupidity of ancestor, Ham |
| 4th | Hostility; rifles desired for driving out Europeans | Syncretic Pagan-Christian | Europeans human but genealogically alien. Stole natives' cargo secret | Cargo deity originally native god. Natives lost cargo because of forbears' mistake and Europeans' duplicity |
| Pagan Revival | Hostility; renunciation of dependence on Europeans | Pagan | Europeans human; exclusive owners of cargo secret | Temporary abandonment of rights |
| 5th | Hostility; modern military equipment desired for driving out Europeans | Pagan | Europeans human but genealogically alien. Stole natives' cargo secret | All pagan deities cargo deities. Natives lost cargo because of forbears' mistake and Europeans' duplicity |

The most perceptive knew, of course, that within the span of the previous three or four generations there had been five major attempts to explain and get control of the new situation, and that as each attempt failed it was succeeded by another. Beyond this, however, they regarded each attempt at explanation—each cargo belief or myth—as in itself a separate and complete 'history' of the world. It bore no relation to earlier attempts at explanation, which were all in error and had been, as it were, erased.[1]

The first two cargo beliefs need not be discussed from this point of view. They were explanations of the contact situation in terms of the pagan religion, which at this stage had undergone little or no modification. The analysis of time-reckoning presented in Chapter I applies automatically in their case.

It can be demonstrated that the same principles applied also in the three subsequent cargo beliefs. In the Third Cargo Belief, cosmic time was divided into the same rough periods as in the past: the age of antiquity; and the period of remembered events. The age of antiquity was that of the Creation as described in the Bible. It was the time when God made the world, confiscated the cargo from Adam and Eve, gave it back to Noah and his two sons Shem and Japheth, but denied it to the third son Ham, whom he exiled to New Guinea. Simultaneously, God brought the 'satans' into existence, enabled them to invent the local material culture, and gave Ham and his descendants mastery over them. The period of remembered events was that in which Europeans came to settle in New Guinea and when, above all, God had ordered the missionaries to lead Ham's descendants back to Christianity.

The total time depth, the recognized age of the cosmos, was still extremely shallow. The time of the Creation was still only just over the horizon of remembered events. It was remote in that it was not witnessed by living men but it was not separated from them by an immense period of time. Thus, according to one highly sophisticated informant on the Rai Coast, Jesus Christ was crucified only three generations ago—that is, on the borderline between remembered events and the age of antiquity, just beyond, but not too far beyond, the range of living memory. Furthermore, within the total time depth, although events were conceived as having occurred in a definite sequence, there was still no suggestion of slow human advance from a simpler to a more elaborate way of life. Adam and Eve in the Garden of Eden enjoyed, apart from clothing, all the amenities of modern Madang. Noah's

---

[1] Except in one instance: the Fifth Cargo Belief incorporated Letub doctrine without revising it.

Ark was a steel-built ship like the vessels on the Islands run, and Noah himself wore the uniform of the skipper of a modern merchantman.

In the Fourth Cargo Belief, there was again the same chronological dichotomy. In the age of antiquity, according to the Letub version, God-Dodo (Anut) brought Kilibob and Manup, and the native material culture, into being in New Guinea, and then enabled Manup to make cargo. Meanwhile, he had created Adam and Eve and their white descendants in Australia, but had not given them cargo or its secret. Later, Manup went to Australia, where he built the city of Sydney, became Jesus Christ, and was crucified. According to Tagarab's version, Kilibob brought the local material culture and the cargo into being in New Guinea, but took the cargo to Australia, where he became the God of the Europeans.

The period of remembered events in Letub doctrine dovetailed very neatly with antiquity. It began just after Jesus-Manup's crucifixion, when the missionaries arrived in New Guinea and taught the people false doctrine. In Tagarab's version, it covered the deceit of the missionaries and God-Kilibob's consequent anger. The recognized age of the cosmos was as short as before. The separation between the remote and near past was indistinct, and there was no sense of historical development. Manup's Sydney (with its Harbour Bridge, dockyard installations, and warehouses) was the city of the 1930's, and Kilibob's *Mengga* was, apart from her cannon, the M.V. *MacDhui* seen in New Guinea waters until the Second World War.

In the Fifth Cargo Belief, it was assumed that during the age of antiquity God-Dodo (Anut) and Manup created the cultures of the seaboard peoples and cargo, while the other deities of the southern Madang District brought the other local cultures into being. During the period of remembered events, the missionaries came to New Guinea, taught false doctrine, and removed the indigenous deities to 'Rome', where Jesus-Manup found them and taught them to make cargo. The dividing line between the remote and near past was once more extremely faint, and there was no hint of gradual material and social development. This was obvious, of course, in Yali's misunderstanding of Evolution: he could imagine only an immediate transformation from Ape to Man according to the pattern of Ngaing totemic myths.

The significance of the natives' failure to adopt or work out a true historical tradition was that they could not realize that their world was now irrevocably involved in a process of continual change, to which they had to adjust by purely rational, secular-intellectual means. Instead, they could envisage only a cosmic order in which relationships between human beings, cargo deity, and ancestors were so ordained that their own rights to the cargo were guaranteed, and their desire for it would be satisfied, not just for the present and immediate future but for all time. At the moment, the situation was temporarily unfavourable to them but, with the aid of one further act of ritual manipulation, it would be restored to their perpetual advantage. They would instantaneously acquire the entire material culture now enjoyed solely by the Europeans. They would have achieved the millennium, after which there would be no further change. The idealized and realized cosmic order would be as finite and immutable as in the traditional past. Human and superhuman beings would go on fulfilling their predetermined obligations to each other for ever. This applied equally to all the cargo beliefs in turn. Each one reflected a cosmic order that alone was authentic and, as has been mentioned, automatically cancelled those that preceded it.

## The Concepts of Knowledge and Work

Ideas about the dynamics of the new cosmic order reiterated two general themes from the original culture. First, as the human intellect on its own still counted for nothing, the only valid sources of important knowledge were assumed to be myths and revelations by deities during dreams or other singular experiences. Such knowledge again consisted in the possession of correct ritual secrets, which depended for success on the observance of taboos (avoidance of specific types of conduct) or obedience to positive codes of behaviour, instituted by the cargo leaders. These were the recognized means of establishing advantageous relationships with the cargo deity and ancestors in the absence of personal interaction with them. They were still intended to place superhuman beings in a position where they had automatically to 'think' and confer material benefits on men. The main difference was that after the adoption of Christianity the expansion of the cosmos led to more complex relationships between men and deities. The environment was inhabited by a wider assortment of gods than before, and the problem was to discover the true cargo deity or deities and the proper ritual procedures for approaching him or them. As we have seen, the subsequent history of cargo doctrine was a series of theological experiments along these lines.

Second, this experimentation correlated with a continuing emphasis on materialism and anthropocentrism. Deities were 'good' or 'bad' according to the type of wealth they represented. Values such as purity and sin still received little attention. Non-observance of ritual and taboos had no real spiritual significance, but was thought merely to obstruct those processes within the cosmos that would give the natives complete mastery over it. As in the traditional situation, this unswerving belief in the effectiveness of ritual and taboos, especially during the later stages of the Cargo Movement, was not mere irrational mysticism but had its own pragmatic logic. This was implicit in the natives' concept of work.

The information about the first two cargo beliefs is too meagre for an analysis of this kind. Yet a general feature of Maclay's experiences is of considerable importance. Although the coastal natives regarded him as one of their own deities, they behaved towards him as if he were a human being. There is no suggestion that they performed ritual in his name. At first sight, these two attitudes appear contradictory. But it must be remembered that, in native eyes, deities were only superhuman beings, whose visible presence among men, although unnerving at the outset, was perfectly reasonable and had precedents in traditional mythology. Thus the content of the relationship, once it had been created, could be the same as that of ordinary human relationships. As long as the bestowal of services and gifts produced the responses desired, there was no need for ritual activity. This strongly supports the view that the natives always regarded ritual as an alternative to direct interaction with gods and ancestors. It accounts for the importance of the dream or equivalent experience in both the traditional culture and the Cargo Movement: leaders and prophets treated it as a means of establishing exactly this kind of personal relationship with superhuman beings.

The last three cargo beliefs, however, clearly illustrate the two themes outlined. In the Third Cargo Belief, the first theme was expressed as follows: God (the cargo deity) was far removed from native society, in Heaven (Sydney). The Bible (the cargo myth), which came from an unquestionably divine source, had revealed to men (especially the missionaries, on whom the natives depended) the proper means of contacting him: the ritual techniques of church services, prayer meetings, preparation for baptism, and Holy Communion. But these would be effective only if reinforced by the new taboos on extramarital intercourse, polygyny, homicide, sorcery, love magic, and the other pagan religious practices which the missionaries had forbidden.

The Fourth Cargo Belief represented a modification of these ideas. 'Orthodox' Christianity had failed. The identity of the cargo deity and his relationship with the natives, together with the content of cargo ritual, had to be revised. The Christian God was too remote to take notice of the people, and Christian ritual too unpragmatic and impersonal to establish intimate contact with him. A more effective alternative had to be devised. Kilibob and Manup were therefore identified as God and Jesus Christ, and adopted as substitute cargo deities, by different groups because they had close traditional ties with the people and obviously would be more likely to help them. Everything was done to remind the new cargo deities and the ancestors of their personal obligations, and to achieve close association with them. In the Letub, the dance invented by Manup was reintroduced. In the Letub, Tagarab's cult, and the Bagasin Rebellion, food offerings were set out in the cemeteries. In the Letub and Bagasin Rebellion, pigs, gardens, and palm trees were destroyed so as to win immediate sympathy for the people by accentuating their poverty. But even then ritual had to be supported by taboos, such as Tagarab's and Kaum's ban on sexual promiscuity and quarrelling.

All this involved a good deal of speculation, but the human intellect on its own still had no authority. The final doctrines were not accepted as 'true knowledge' until they had been substantiated by accredited claims of divine revelation. This is amply demonstrated by the cases of Tagarab and Kaum, who consistently told their followers that God-Kilibob had given them instructions in the course of visions and (in Kaum's case) a visit to Heaven.

The return to paganism during the Fifth Cargo Belief was the final variation on the general theme. The identity of cargo source was extended to all the pagan gods. 'True knowledge' for the manipulation of these deities was now regarded as traditional ritual, coupled with the *table ritual* imported from Madang and buttressed by the observance of traditional taboos. Yet although Gurek personally invented the new doctrine, he was careful not to admit responsibility for it. He substantiated it to Yali by claiming that the knowledge had been given him by a Catholic priest at Alexishafen and that he had also had visions of 'deity-soldiers' in the bush. Yali himself admitted that this claim was one of the reasons why he believed that Gurek was genuine.

The second theme of materialism and anthropocentrism is equally clear in the last three cargo beliefs. The people still had no sense of obligation to gods who were economically worthless or inferior, and would exchange them for others who offered better prospects with as little compunction as the Garia in the case of their agricultural deities. Thus, in the Third Cargo Belief, the old gods were 'bad' ('satans') merely because they represented the traditional material culture as

against the cargo. But the two 'satans', Kilibob and Manup, who were
identified as the cargo source in the Fourth Cargo Belief, changed their
character immediately. The same applied to all the pagan gods in the
Fifth Cargo Belief.

Again, the taboos and positive codes of behaviour associated with
the different stages of cargo ritual were strictly non-spiritual and non-
ethical. They were not seen as referring to and maintaining a state of
society that was an absolute good in itself, but as a means to an end.
They were 'moral renewal'[1] only in the sense that they represented a
new set of prerequisites for placing the cargo deity and ancestors in a
position where they had to fulfil their obligations to men. The ban on
extramarital intercourse, polygyny, and so forth in the Third Cargo
Belief was 'good' only because it had been ordained by God and its
observance, together with the performance of ritual, would leave him
no option but to send cargo. Exactly the same is true of the codes of
behaviour advocated just before and after the Japanese Occupation.
Tagarab's injunctions to establish complete social cohesion by eradi-
cating love magic, adultery, and sorcery feuds, although doubtless
derived from missionary antagonism and the Administration's penal
sanctions against adulterers, were valid only because they were the
hard core of the Ten Commandments, which were given Moses by
God-Kilibob.[2] That they did not represent internalized values is
strongly suggested by the way in which they were reinterpreted, admittedly by other groups, after 1945. Whereas sexual promiscuity had
been condemned by Tagarab because it produced enmity, of which
God-Kilibob disapproved beyond all else, it was later encouraged on
the Rai Coast and at Dumpu because it was now thought to contribute
to, if not constitute entirely, the social cohesion that was part of the
secret of the Europeans' wealth. Even Yali's secular propaganda between 1945 and 1947—to rebuild villages, recut roads, and remodel life
along Australian lines—was understood in the same light. Although
it represented values to which Yali personally attached a great deal
of importance, it appealed to the people as a whole largely because
they believed that it was a necessary precondition for the arrival of the
soldiers' reward from Heaven. Once hopes had been disappointed, the
propaganda was forgotten, especially in outlying villages. For the
majority, it was cargo rather than the ideal of harmonious and orderly

---

[1] Worsley, *The Trumpet Shall Sound*, op. cit., p. 251.
[2] By the same token, Manup was identified as Satan by Tagarab only because he had
invented the black arts which Kilibob opposed. But Kilibob, in spite of the Ten Commandments, could be prevailed on to tattoo the pudenda of Manup's wife.

community life that was important. The reintroduction of pagan taboos in the Fifth Cargo Belief needs little discussion. As indicated, they bore the same relationship to pagan ritual as they had done in the past. But it is worth noting that in many places the Christian taboos against polygyny and extramarital intercourse (where the latter did not run the risk of detection by the Administration) were automatically abandoned as having now no economic utility.

The conviction that these taboos were the commands of the cargo deity did nothing to remove man from his central and paramount position in the cosmic order. It did not indicate a nascent feeling of complete human dependence on an unpredictable divine will. Provided his instructions were carried out, the cargo deity himself had no further freedom of action. Nor did the non-observance of taboos lead to an embryonic sense of sin or spiritual evil.[1] There is nothing to suggest that the natives were beginning to fear lest they were morally unworthy. With the possible exception of Kaum's confessional services in the Bagasin Rebellion in 1944, they made no attempt to atone to the relevant deity for their past wickedness in having ignored his precepts, whenever they changed from one cargo belief, and hence one set of ritual and taboos, to another. They had been merely stupid, or misled by the 'satans' or ill-disposed human beings. But they were not in any way irreclaimably iniquitous, and it was now enough that they had at last arrived at the (presumably) correct solution to their problem. Even Kaum's confessional services were intended not so much to rid his followers of the burden of moral guilt as to enable them to establish a right relationship with God-Kilibob for purely mundane ends. Ritual and taboos were still no more than parts of the religious 'technology' given man for him to realize his destiny. Even in cargo doctrine there was no hint that the natives' present economic inferiority was due to the sinfulness of their forbears. The ancestors who refused the rifles and dinghies, and Adam and Eve, and Ham, who had the cargo confiscated from them, were portrayed as obtuse rather than evil. They took wrong turnings on the road mapped out for them, and their mistakes were far more in the nature of 'cosmic bad luck'[2] than a permanent fall from grace in an ethical or spiritual sense.

From the analysis so far it can be understood *how*, during the contact period, the natives experimented with the deities within their enlarged pantheon without ever departing from the principles and assumptions derived from their traditional religion. Yet at least one

[1] Cf. Burridge, *Mambu*, op. cit.
[2] Inglis, Review of Burridge, *Mambu*, op. cit., p. 383.

question remains to be answered: *Why* did the people believe that ritual alone was adequate to produce cargo? In the traditional culture, the growing of crops and production of important artefacts involved both secular and ritual techniques. It was fully recognized that mere repetition of esoteric formulae and symbolic actions by men who had scrupulously observed the requisite taboos during their training would be useless unless secular processes were carried out as well. Yet in the Cargo Movement there was no evidence of any secular activity which imitated the production of Western goods. The question is doubly pertinent because individual cargo cults were invariably referred to as 'work'—as, for instance, in Pidgin English, *wok bilong Tagarab, wok bilong Kaum*, and *wok bilong Yali*.[1]

It is not enough to answer the question by stating, with Sundkler and Ballandier,[2] that religion was the only form of expression left the people, especially after the final humiliation of the Madang natives in 1912. This does not explain their unwavering conviction of the logic of their actions. The real solution lies in reconsidering, first, the traditional concept of work, which like other basic ideas had hardly been affected by contact, and second, everyday European behaviour as seen through native eyes.

Important work, it will be remembered, was regarded as a compound of both ritual and secular activities, which ensured co-operation between deities, ancestors, and human beings. But because gods, spirits, and men all lived in the same geographical environment and had the same corporeal nature, the activities of all of them had the same pragmatic validity. Furthermore, both secular and ritual techniques were parts of the same complex: both were derived from the deities, and this was the ultimate guarantee of their efficacy. The gods could do anything without human aid, as was apparent when they created the original culture, but it was up to man to keep them under his direction by means of ritual and taboos.

As already explained, the natives never saw Europeans doing physical labour, nor was there anything in European behaviour to suggest that there was any other kind of work than the one they knew. They could not comprehend the economic system behind office routine and the presentation of chits at the stores, and they had no evidence that white men themselves actually produced their own goods. Again, as

[1] In their message to Rev. R. Hanselmann in 1933, the Madang natives stated, 'We understand all the work of Europeans (Pidgin English, *ologeta wok bilong wetman*).' This referred to Christian rituals and taboos.

[2] Sundkler, *Bantu Prophets in South Africa*, p. 100, and Ballandier, *Sociologie Actuelle de l'Afrique Noire*, pp. 477–9.

they did not work in metals or cloth, they could not imagine, at second-hand, the industrial processes by which these goods were manufactured.

All that natives saw was the arrival of ships and aircraft, which unloaded huge quantities of cargo at the wharves and aerodromes. As the Europeans obviously had not contributed to the total operation the secular labour that might normally have been expected, the only possible conclusion was that it was carried out entirely by a deity who was helped by the ancestors and was under human direction. There was plausible evidence for this view also in the behaviour of Europeans when they received consignments of cargo.[1] Living, as many of them did, on isolated plantations and sub-stations, Europeans were perpetually faced with the problem of eking out short supplies of essential goods. They treated the arrival of a ship or aeroplane as an occasion for mild celebration. They assembled for a few drinks and to renew friendships with the master or pilot. The whole gathering could easily give the impression—especially to those already conditioned to see it in that light—of marking the successful culmination of a ritual undertaking.

Yet once more there was no element of mysticism. The cargo deity was doing no more than other deities had done in the past and, just as annually ripening crops and large catches of fish continually substantiated traditional religious beliefs, so the regular arrival of ships and aircraft authenticated the cargo belief. Because the cargo deity too was conceived to have the same physical nature and to belong to the same realm of existence as human beings, there was still nothing uncanny about his actions or illusory about the processes believed to set them in motion. Moreover, just as no ritual was performed in the First Cargo Belief because the people had satisfactory face-to-face dealings with Maclay (the first cargo deity), so in later beliefs, when such dealings became impossible, secular techniques could give way quite easily to ritual. Because both had equal validity as parts of the same body of knowledge, the natives' tendency to give prominence to one or the other represented only a shift of emphasis within the original concept of work rather than the adoption of an entirely new one.

### The Cargo Leaders: Social Values and Epistemological Assumptions

The conclusions drawn so far apply also to the leaders in the Cargo Movement. Admittedly, they often had qualities which they did not necessarily derive from the original culture. Kaut, Kaum, Yali, and

---

[1] I am indebted to Dr A. L. Epstein, who read this work in manuscript and drew my attention to the points made in the remainder of this paragraph.

Tagarab all had outstanding, even dominant, personalities, although this was not an absolutely essential qualification for leadership. For instance, Polelesi of Igurue, when I met her between 1949 and 1953, seemed little different from other Garia women. Again, individual leaders often showed considerable political intuition and skill. Kaut and Tagarab exploited the Japanese Occupation to their own advantage, and Yali was particularly adroit in his dealings with Europeans.

The political importance of the cargo leaders' careers is considered in a later context. Here we are concerned only with the basic principles that governed their conduct. From this point of view, we may regard them as the catalysts of the Movement, around which its different cults crystallized and grew, precisely because in most of their activities they operated within the limits imposed by traditional values and assumptions, which they accepted as automatically as did their followers. The only possible exception was Yali between 1945 and 1947.

In this field, there were two relevant features of traditional leadership. First, the leaders' most important duties were to initiate and organize annually recurrent undertakings, especially in economic life. The mainspring of these undertakings was the people's recognition of their importance (as, for instance, in agriculture) and desire that they be carried out. The leaders' roles as policy-makers were extremely limited: they rarely, if ever, originated entirely new schemes but only acted in ways that their followers had already intended. Second, the acknowledged intellectual basis of leadership was the mastery of ritual which would guarantee the completion of the enterprises discussed. The leaders were believed to possess the esoteric formulae and other information originally taught human beings by the deities during the age of antiquity in the course of personal association with them or in dreams. Occasionally they could have similar experiences themselves. But although their knowledge was sanctioned by divine origination, the real test was personal success. When a leader failed or was overshadowed, his followers might transfer their allegiance to others.

With the possible exception already mentioned, the cargo leaders who emerged after 1914[1] were the direct successors of these men. Their careers, although normally shorter because of the nature of external conditions, depended on the same sort of considerations. Their roles as policy-makers were still governed by the demands of their followers. They might initiate new doctrines but had to suit them to the people's current aspirations and intellectual assumptions. Although they

---

[1] That is, during and after the Third Cargo Belief. I ignore the first two cargo beliefs in this context as no relevant information is available.

claimed their knowledge from a divine source they had to demonstrate success or fade into obscurity. They may be divided into three groups: the renegade mission helpers; the prophets of the Fourth Cargo Belief and the period after the Second World War; and Yali.

During the Third Cargo Belief, the renegade mission helpers almost entirely replaced the traditional leaders and eclipsed the official headmen. As they exercised *de facto* control over Christian teaching within their congregations, they easily convinced the people that they alone could provide the new wealth for which, with the opening up of the country, there was a growing demand. They were thought to have learnt the cargo secret from the missionaries, who had either inherited it from their predecessors in the period of the Christian Creation or even themselves been taught it in the course of personal meetings with God and Jesus Christ.[1]

After 1933, with the rise of the Fourth Cargo Belief, the mission helpers lost their influence. As they could not satisfy the demands of their followers, they had to give way to a new group of prophets or, as is illustrated by the case of Dabus in the Bagasin Rebellion, attach themselves to new cults as 'technical advisers'. The laity had no compunction about deserting them for other leaders who not only offered better hopes of success but also matched their own growing sense of hostility to the Europeans by promising them weapons for waging war. These new prophets—Kaut, Tagarab, Kaum, and, after the war, Pales and Polelesi—still claimed to derive their authority from the same kind of source as the mission helpers. But, in keeping with the current native mood, they no longer acknowledged dependence on white men. They did not rely on second-hand instruction from the missionaries (from whom they deliberately dissociated themselves on the grounds that they were false teachers) but claimed to have acquired their special knowledge on their own account. They had established the close personal association with the cargo deity and ancestors denied them by Europeans. They had met the cargo deity and spirits in visions; they had died and gone to Heaven; or, like Kaut in the late 1930's, they impersonated important biblical figures and claimed to have contacted the cargo deity by mechanical means.

Yali was far more complex as a person than the other cargo leaders, partly because of his more varied personal experiences and partly because he had continually to satisfy the demands of two distinct groups —Europeans and natives. Yet ultimately even he cannot be excluded

---

[1] The Garia, for instance, believed that Europeans could actually meet and talk with God and Jesus Christ on the streets of Sydney. 'Photographs' in Bibles proved the point.

from the general category. On the one hand, his Rehabilitation Scheme can be described at first sight in almost rational terms. It appeared to be a definite break with both the traditional past and the Cargo Movement: a secular programme based on the expectation of Administration aid in return for the wartime loyalty of native troops, which was designed to satisfy the people's economic aspirations. That the District Office at this time saw it in this light is clear from its consistent support: it sanctioned Yali's appointment of secretaries and 'boss boys', if not 'policemen', and it employed him in the Department of Native Affairs. The ideas he himself expressed at the outset were far in advance of those of his predecessors in the Movement. Although he expected a free hand-out of goods at Port Moresby, it was to include primarily building materials and machinery with which the people were to re-equip themselves. An improved standard of living would not be instantaneous but would be achieved only by some physical effort and village reorganization. Yali had at times considerable social and political intuition. He appreciated early on that the natives needed the missionaries for reasons of education. After his return from Bogia, he worked for the definition of the missions' authority in relation to his own, especially *vis-à-vis* property rights, marriage, and religion. Because the Administrations had so far chosen to remain neutral on this issue, he had no defence against the meddling of native mission helpers. He rectified this in Port Moresby by drawing up his 'Laws' and having them sanctioned by the Administration. He was a born manipulator: his usurpation of the authority of the O.C. Saidor and deluding of the District Office about his activities after 1948 showed the greatest shrewdness.

On the other hand, to judge Yali purely at this level and see him as a primarily secular leader would be to misunderstand him. The task he had undertaken was sufficiently Herculean to daunt even the most skilled and best-trained administrator of the day, but he was barely fitted for it. In spite of his experience of, and fellowship with, Europeans and his adoption of their personal living habits, he had never really rejected the values and assumptions of his own society. Although he had not been fully trained in traditional ritual, he accepted the native interpretation of the nature and dynamics of the cosmic order without question. He never divorced its secular from its religious aspects. He saw the involvement of gods and ancestors in human affairs not as remote and indirect but as immediate and instrumental. He was convinced that he had been saved after the Hollandia debacle by his respect for the local deities. He subscribed to the general principles of the Cargo Movement. He believed the prophecies from Karkar in 1941-2. He was quite satisfied that the money and 'flags' brought to him in 1946 could have been sent by God and the spirits, and he was fully persuaded that he had himself witnessed similar phenomena at Kurog nearly two years later. He never really saw beyond the exterior of Western culture and was not aware that it was based on entirely different principles from those underlying his own. He understood the Brisbane promises, on which his Rehabilitation Scheme ultimately rested, merely as a means of evading the issue of cargo cult, which aroused antagonism among Europeans only because it was an attempt to steal their property. Although actual dealings between natives and Europeans would be secular, the goods to be made available were still derived, directly or indirectly, from a cargo deity, who would remain under exclusive European direction. He saw the future relationship between Europeans and natives as being very like those between groups linked by trade in the past, when finished goods (clay pots and wooden bowls) could move freely from one area to another, although the ritual secrets involved in their production were jealously guarded by their owners. Although he recognized that the people would have to work to raise their standard of living, beyond modernizing their villages with new building materials, he was never very clear about the form such work would take. He certainly did not believe in an instantaneous transformation of native society, but he thought that it would be achieved in relatively few years. He could not see that it would require the re-education of a whole new generation.

Thus Yali did not turn to religion to solve his problems after the collapse of the Brisbane promises solely for reasons of convenience. Admittedly, under the terrible pressures of the moment, he saw it as the best means of saving his reputation, and of revenging himself for the personal humiliation and betrayal he had suffered. But, at the same time, there was nothing in his own mind to inhibit the decision. It is significant that his spontaneous reaction, after Tarosi's disclosures about Evolution, was to try to regain control of the situation through the pagan revival. When Gurek's genius transformed the pagan revival into the Fifth Cargo Belief, he immediately found the new doctrine intellectually acceptable, his one misgiving being fear of administrative reprisal and his own disgrace. Thereafter there was little in his behaviour to distinguish him from the cargo prophets who had preceded him. He impressed on the people that he had special knowledge of, and power from, the new cargo source—the pagan deities. After 1948, he glossed over in public the secular propaganda for hygienic and orderly living he had stressed between 1945 and 1947, although it still remained his personal standard. Of all the 'laws' he brought back from Port Moresby, the only one he consistently expounded was that authorizing the Kabu Ceremony. The strength of his personal commitment to the new cargo doctrine was shown by his disregard of the District Officer's indirect warning at Saidor in October 1948 and participation in the ritual until a few months before his arrest in 1950. Only after two years of persistent trial was he finally disillusioned.

This endorsement of traditional values and intellectual assumptions was vital for the position of the leaders of the cults described. Burridge has written of their counterparts in the northern Madang District as the 'new men' of native society: they would restore dignity to their followers and win them the respect of Europeans. This description fits also the cargo leaders of the southern Madang District. Yet it must not be taken to mean that these southern leaders were idolized as a completely different type of human being, qualitatively apart from ordinary natives, as Burridge[1] seems to imply for the Bogia area. They were 'new men' only in that, *as ordinary natives*, they would achieve the success their followers desired. They would vindicate before the world the values for which ordinary natives had always stood, and the assumptions which ordinary natives had always held. Even the honour accorded Yali—his large houses at Sor and Yabalol, the 'station' at Sangpat, and his *de facto* recognition as 'District Officer of the Rai Coast'—was intended to mean not that he himself belonged to a new social class but that he had at last forced the white masters to accept the people as a whole on their own terms.[2]

From a severely practical point of view, had the cargo leaders of the southern Madang District attempted to expound doctrines based on ideas entirely foreign to their people, they would not have got the automatic following they did. Before they could have inaugurated their schemes they would have had to expend a great deal of time, energy, and patience in explaining them in order to get a hearing at all. In fact, however, as they kept close to the concepts of their culture, they could win rapid acceptance merely by announcing a programme of ritual and taboos that purported to satisfy the people's economic demands and current socio-political aspirations, and by substantiating it by some plausible claim of having been in contact with the cargo

[1] Burridge, *Mambu*, op. cit., p. 259. But see Firth, *Elements of Social Organization*, op. cit., p. 113, who stresses the importance of the affirmation of native values in cargo cults.

[2] Yali, of course, claimed publicly to be superior to ordinary natives. But the masses regarded him implicitly as a more powerful version of the traditional big man—essentially as *primus inter pares*.

deity and spirits of the dead. As long as both doctrine and ritual stayed within these limits, the cult would gather its own momentum and need very little reiteration of the specific beliefs underlying it, especially among the mass of its devotees. We have seen several cases where, just as in the traditional situation, outlying peoples were prepared to adopt a particular form of ritual without inquiring carefully into the teachings associated with it, on the grounds that it was perfectly consistent with their ideas about the workings of the cosmic order and that there were others nearer the source who knew the myth of origin. Thus, whereas the Third Cargo Belief was widespread because of the general mis-interpretation of Christianity, in the Fourth Cargo Belief many inland peoples, who supported the Letub, Tagarab, or Kaum, knew very little about the Kilibob-Manup myth. Inland Letub villages appear to have retained Christian beliefs with slight modification. A few of Tagarab's less attentive followers assumed that the cargo deity was God rather than God-Kilibob. This was even truer of the majority of Kaum's sup-porters, who were never given a crystal-clear account of Tagarab's doctrine. In the Fifth Cargo Belief, although the natives of the inland Rai Coast were all aware that the pagan gods were now claimed to be the cargo source, they knew very little of the theological argument which had linked God and Jesus to Dodo (Anut) and Manup, and Jesus-Manup to the other 'satans' in 'Rome'. In all these cases, Kaut, Tagarab, Kaum, Gurek, and Yali were able to carry all before them by force of personality and demonstration of personal conviction. The rank and file were confident that their leaders were in full possession of all doctrinal details, although they themselves were at best only par-tially informed.

The only occasion when a leader did not address himself to his fol-lowers in this way was the inception of the Rehabilitation Scheme in 1945, when Yali tried to introduce a programme that did not include ritual activity. The project got out of control almost at once. As Yali promised everything the people wanted, he got as quick and favourable a response as had his forerunners. Yet, because he did not take suffi-cient pains in explaining the scheme, was careless in his choice of words when relating his experiences in Australia, and did not clearly dissociate himself from general cargo ideology, the people distorted his propaganda by the end of the year. It had to be made consistent not only with their economic and socio-political aspirations but also with their intellectual assumptions. They could not understand that Yali in-tended to achieve his aims by means which were at least an attempt to evade cargo cult, even though he never denied its validity. They had to

s

interpret him as a conventional cargo prophet before he and his teachings could be intelligible. Like his predecessors, he had to have received the charter for his programme from the cargo deity during some special experience. He had been killed at Hollandia in 1944 and had visited God in Heaven as a spirit of the dead. He had seen the Hand of God, and the Light of God shone on his body.

### Effects: The Political Significance of the Cargo Movement

The past and future effects of the Cargo Movement must be treated separately. The one must be analysed against the background of native society as it emerged during the contact period. The other involves some consideration of the Administration's development policy in the southern Madang District since 1950. The past effects must be understood in terms of the interplay between the Movement's conservative and revolutionary 'nationalist' tendencies. We can say at once that its steadfast conservatism in the fields of motivation and means is no argument for classifying it as dominantly 'nativistic' or 'revivalistic' in Linton's sense. It did not consistently seek to 'revive or perpetuate selected aspects of [the traditional] culture'.[1] The people reacted to European occupation in terms of their old values and assumptions largely because, as has been shown, they knew of no alternative. Beyond this, although there were two occasions when 'nativism' as Linton defined it did appear, the Movement was primarily forwards-looking. Its overall aim was not to turn the clock back to the pre-contact past but to enrich the present and future with European goods. Nevertheless, its revolutionary and 'nationalist'[2] potential was never fully realized. As has been the case with many movements of its kind, although it led to and envisaged certain changes in the traditional socio-

[1] Linton, 'Nativistic Movements', p. 230. See also Worsley's trenchant criticism, with which I agree (The Trumpet Shall Sound, op. cit., pp. 272–6).

[2] I define 'nationalism' or 'embryonic nationalism' below. Otherwise I distinguish between three terms: reform, revolution, and rebellion. For reform and revolution, I follow Hobsbawm, Primitive Rebels, pp. 10–11: 'Reformists accept the general framework of an institution or social arrangement, but consider it capable of improvement or, where abuses have crept in, reform; revolutionaries insist that it must be fundamentally transformed, or replaced.' Cf. also Talmon, The Origins of Totalitarian Democracy, p. 49. For rebellion, I follow Gluckman, Rituals of Rebellion in South-East Africa, pp. 20–3: the socio-political order is to be neither reformed nor replaced; only the relative statuses of individuals within it are to be changed. I may be criticized for using these terms with undue rigidity. I do so purposely so as to emphasize what I regard as the Cargo Movement's most dangerous tendency: conservatism. But I do not deny the existence of the tendencies which the terms defined suggest. (The only exception is the 'Bagasin Rebellion', which does not coincide with Gluckman's definition and would be called more properly a revolt. But as the name has been used in official documents and now has general currency, I have not changed it.)

political order, its conservatism prevented it from seriously modifying the principles on which that order rested, let alone from replacing them with entirely new ones. For the future, the evidence suggests that, although the Cargo Movement in the form described may have come to an end, its ideology will be strong enough either actively to resist or imperceptibly to undermine the Administration's attempts to introduce a substantially new cultural and socio-political order.

## The Past

For the past, the Cargo Movement has had two important effects on the native socio-political order. First, it has helped bridge sectional cleavages between separate linguistic units and thus create a larger regional grouping by giving the people of the southern Madang District as a whole a sense of oneness. Second, it has given rise eventually to a form of 'embryonic nationalism'. Yet, although both were reactions to roughly uniform pressures of contact, neither represented a regular or stereotyped process.

The growth of the natives' sense of solidarity during the first seventy-nine years of contact was too erratic to be regarded as the Cargo Movement's consistent masterplan. It was largely its by-product. It was determined by the content of the five cargo beliefs and the difficulties of overcoming the parochialism inherent in the natives' traditional political outlook. A cargo doctrine could prosper only where it could be automatically accepted without the infringement of acknowledged rights to religious secrets or where its prophet was prepared to spread it. The first consideration depended on the identity of the current cargo deity, and the second on whether the prophet was able or willing to go beyond his own and his local group's desire for cargo and recruit followers elsewhere. In such a case, the leader had to have a personality which could attract the attention of people with whom hitherto he had had no direct relationship. He needed also the political instinct to manipulate the ritual, taboos, and, occasionally, destruction of property he had instituted in such a way that, although they were seen by his supporters only as the means of acquiring Western goods, they had the unconscious function of enforcing discipline and conformity.[1]

By 'embryonic nationalism' here, I mean a political structure of indigenous growth which expresses *militant opposition* to European rule,

---

[1] Cf. Worsley's penetrating analysis (*The Trumpet Shall Sound*, op. cit., pp. 247–51). I should stress, however, that I regard the creation of unity as an effect or unconscious function of ritual and taboo rather than the deliberate purpose of the leader, who probably acted only instinctively.

and is designed to hold together a *permanent* combination of hitherto autonomous political groups or equivalent associations by means of centralized authority and an incipient ranking system. On the basis of this definition, it can be shown that 'embryonic nationalism' has not been an invariable feature of the Cargo Movement. It was clearly recognizable at only a relatively late stage and was preceded by the emergence or expectation of essentially 'non-nationalist' or reformist structures. It did not necessarily correlate, therefore, with the sense of pan-native identity, which could at times express completely different aims. Rather, it was governed by the succession of native attitudes towards Europeans which, as has been shown, alternated between friendship and hostility, and by the historical accidents of contact. Furthermore, none of the new structures—reformist ('non-nationalist') or 'nationalist'—was truly radical. Although the actual or projected social framework might be far larger than in the past, there was no departure from the old concept of relationships. Even the hierarchical institutions of 'embryonic nationalism' were only very rudimentary and inefficient. They never turned to full advantage the people's desire for unity by providing an effective political organization wide enough to embrace all the outlying groups that would have liked to have been recruited. Nor did they attempt to function in complete isolation from the already existing networks of kinship and other ties. There was no sense of what we might call 'civic responsibility' or the personal obligations a hierarchy involved.

About the period before 1914 we can only speculate. But it seems safe to assume that during the First Cargo Belief there was no growth of a sense of unity or attempt to create a new type of socio-political system. Because the coastal natives wanted Maclay's trade goods solely for their economic utility, they did not envisage any further change in the cosmic order they had always conceived. It would continue to function as it always had done, only enriched by a new and superior material culture.

During the Second Cargo Belief, such native unity as had been achieved seems to have been very slight. It was limited to the peoples of the Sek-Bongu seaboard, who alone offered prolonged opposition to the German Administration and showed interest in the new cargo belief. But even their political outlook was still extremely narrow. Neither they nor their leaders could see that wider unity would be to their advantage. They never tried to merge the two new versions of the Kilibob-Manup myth into a single consistent doctrine. They did not invite the coastal natives north of Sek and east of Bongu to make common cause with them, as would have been feasible. These natives had been brought under control by 1910, and had trade ties with Madang and rights to the Kilibob-Manup myth. The peoples of the inland, of course, were as yet unaffected by the Occupation and, in any case, could not have adopted the Second Cargo Belief as they had no rights to the Kilibob-Manup myth.

It would be a mistake to regard the Second Cargo Belief, in spite of its anti-European attitude, itself as a full expression of 'embryonic nationalism', although it was certainly a forerunner. The Madang Revolt in 1904 was more than rebellion in Gluckman's sense: its aim was to drive out the whites and abolish the political structure they had created. Yet it was only a small alliance between local and hitherto mutually hostile groups, which probably would have dissolved as soon as its limited objectives were achieved. Although the Siars and Grageds took the lead, this did not mean the birth of a new hierarchy. The conspirators probably conceived no more than the restoration of their pre-contact social system complete with its traditional cleavages. This is suggested by the defection of several groups before the plot matured and its final betrayal by a Biliā native. If the expulsion of Europeans was to involve also the loss of their goods, the revolt can be understood as an example of 'nativism'. Again, it does not seem likely that during the subsequent period of passive resistance (1904–12) there was a marked change in the political outlook. The Cargo Movement was once more forwards-looking with the hope of Kilibob's or Manup's return with trade goods and, more particularly, weapons for driving out the whites. But there was still no suggestion of centralized leadership and a wider 'national' group, and during the unrest of 1912 the people's loyalties were by no means undivided. Once again the most that seems to have been anticipated was a return to the old system of relationships, with the additional content of European goods.

During the Mandate, the situation both along the coast and in the inland was altered by the establishment of administrative authority and the dissemination of the Gospel. The peoples of the whole area began to acknowledge a sense of oneness with each other. This was fostered not only by the uniform demand for Western goods and common experience of Europeans but also by the universalist nature of Christianity, which offered but the one God for every group, and the homogeneous ideology of the Third Cargo Belief. The process was given added impetus by the active proselytism of the renegade mission helpers. Their wide enforcement of congregational discipline left the people with the feeling that they belonged to a single community.

This new sense of common identity which emerged during the Third Cargo Belief prepared the ground for but did not yet represent militant 'nationalism'. The people's outlook at this time was essentially reformist: they wanted to retain and improve the existing colonial order. They created no hierarchical institutions of their own—apart from those introduced by the Administration and missions—and pursued the policy of accommodation. They implicitly expressed the desire for a 'non-nationalist' composite society, in which the natives as a whole and Europeans should live together harmoniously. But although the structure of the new society was to be considerably larger than in the past and its culture was to incorporate all the new rules of behaviour introduced by the missionaries (especially monogamy), it was still conceived according to the traditional model. Among themselves the natives invented no new types of relationships but only reformulated those already existing or fabricated others in their image. Europeans were to be brought into the system on the same basis. They were regarded as new immigrants who by settling in the country had augmented its economic resources. As they were to be received in friendship, and provided with land and labour, they were supposed to reciprocate, in the same way as wealthy traders in the past, by making available to their hosts some of the advantages they themselves enjoyed. A network of interpersonal and intergroup linkages between the two races would result.

The Fourth Cargo Belief after 1933 failed to exploit the solidarity that had been built up during the previous decade and accentuated when Christianity fell into disrepute. If anything, it weakened that solidarity. It restored the traditional cleavages, on the one hand, between the coastal natives, who had the Kilibob-Manup myth, and those of the inland, who did not, and, on the other, between those coastal groups which followed its different versions. Although the new doctrines spread quickly through the local villages, there was no widespread attempt at conversion. The Letubists did not try seriously to win over the Sengam, Gira, Som, and other Rai Coast peoples, who shared their (the second) version of the Kilibob-Manup myth, until 1943.[1] When Kaum used Tagarab's doctrine for the Bagasin Rebellion, the people of Milguk, far from welcoming or even approving his action, regarded him as a thief. Admittedly, the differences between the Third and Fourth Cargo Beliefs, and between the two versions of the Fourth, did not neutralize the mounting bitterness against Europeans

---

[1] Even then they do not seem to have spread Letub doctrine on the Rai Coast at this stage but merely to have urged the people to help the Japanese.

or prevent any natives from interpreting the Japanese invasion in a way to justify collaboration. Yet the fact that the Letubists and Tagarabists preferred to disparage each others' doctrines without ever trying to reach a compromise does not suggest that the need for widespread social and intellectual conformity at all costs was uppermost in their minds.[1]

It was during this period, however, that militant 'nationalism' began to appear. The two doctrines of the Fourth Cargo Belief were uncompromisingly anti-European, and the new leaders—Kaut, Tagarab, and Kaum—began to create hierarchical organizations by styling themselves as Paramount rulers over groups of villages (which previously had had no political unity) and by appointing other natives as their deputies. Their declared aim was to see the end of Australian rule. Kaum built up a military organization for this purpose. But the experiments were on a very small scale and did not last very long, partly because of doctrinal rivalries and partly because of the contact situation. Before 1942, Kaut was unable to realize his ambition of becoming King of the Madang area because of the Mandate Administration. During the A.N.G.A.U. interregnum in 1942, he had a competitor in Tagarab. After 1942, in spite of his boasts to the people, both he and Tagarab lost any chance of autonomy by becoming officials in the Japanese Native Police Force. Even if the Japanese had remained, it is inconceivable that either of them would have been allowed to operate independently. Kaum was crushed by the A.N.G.A.U. Administration.

After 1945, the principle of common identity was more than reaffirmed when Yali became the figurehead of the Cargo Movement. It was encouraged by active proselytism, as in the Bagasin Area in 1947, and clearly enunciated in the Port Moresby 'Laws', which purported to represent the whole native population. Until the end of 1947, the general change of attitude towards Europeans from hostility to friendship as result of the Brisbane promises saw a comparable swing from 'nationalism' back to reformism—to the pre-war ideal of a composite society. As is again clear in the 'Laws', both races were to live together and contribute to each other's welfare. The 'Laws' were hardly revolutionary: they did not advocate a radically new socio-cultural order but stood for a compromise between the two cultures and societies involved. Far from attempting to give precedence to European-Christian rules of behaviour—even to the same extent as

[1] The only suggestion of a move in this direction was the Barahim 'Conference' in 1941. Yet its influence seems to have been short-lived and it took place a year before the emergence of Tagarab's Cult.

during the Third Cargo Belief—they enjoined toleration. Some aspects of life were to be governed by European-Christian rules, and others by traditional rules. Where there was conflict between the two, the individual was left to make his own decision according to his conscience, without attempting to influence his neighbour.[1]

Between 1948 and 1950 native solidarity, already strengthened since the war, received its greatest declaration in the Fifth Cargo Belief. The only significant ideological cleavage became that between Christianity and paganism. Those between the different pagan religions were bridged by the link between Jesus-Manup and the other 'satans': each religion now provided the true cargo source for its followers. (Even the cleavage between the two versions of the Kilibob-Manup myth ceased to matter. Kaum claimed a parallel link between Kilibob and the other 'satans'.) This time native solidarity correlated closely with militant 'nationalism', which was at last a clear political reality. For a short period the pagan revival had witnessed a return to 'nativism', in which Yali's stated intention was to recreate the old way of life with as little dependence as possible on European goods. But 'regression' of this kind was clearly impossible. It was not long before many natives in the whole southern Madang District were demanding a new war against the Europeans under Yali's leadership, and a European standard of living.

The new hierarchical structure on the Rai Coast with its theoretically graded 'office bearers' was to some extent a response to this demand. It was the Movement's closest approximation to a truly revolutionary experiment. Yet it still had significant limitations. For a start, Yali, although his personal prestige rested heavily on the belief in his power from the local deities, still owed a great deal to the consistent backing of the Administration and his status in the Department of Native Affairs. Both these factors gave him freedom of action for a considerable period. Of his secretaries, 'boss boys', and 'policemen', the first attached themselves to him uninvited, the second were installed initially at the suggestion of the Madang District Office, and only the third appear to have been his own invention. Again, it is questionable to what extent his effective organization represented an expansion of the traditional political horizon. Although the people of a large part of the Madang District acknowledged him as the figurehead of the Cargo Movement, beyond advocating a wider network of marriage ties, he never seriously tried to build up institutions which would exploit

---

[1] Yali's views were, of course, altered when he began his pagan revival. The 'Laws' reflected his earlier aspirations for his people.

their desire for unity to the full.[1] He ignored close liaison with distant supporters whom he did not regard as important for his personal position. Admittedly, poor communications were always a problem, but it is still significant that between 1948 and 1950 his activities were concentrated in the Saidor region. It was there that he humiliated mission helpers, disseminated propaganda, and urged the people to preserve a common front against Europeans by refusing to reveal pagan secrets. Apart from one short patrol to Bongu, he never tried to strengthen his influence in the Madang, Bagasin, Ramu, and Bogia areas. Although visitors from these places were treated with every show of welcome and respect, they normally came of their own accord rather than in response to a direct summons. Yali's main concern seems to have been to establish complete social conformity and his own power among the peoples of the Saidor area of the Rai Coast in order to save face after the collapse of his undertakings to them in 1945 and make himself as secure as possible. He realized that opposition to his policy and careless talk to Europeans near at home would lead to the administrative intervention he feared. He could explain away what was said against him elsewhere as pure misrepresentation by the ignorant. Thus he had no incentive to expand his effective organization beyond the Rai Coast and did not want to do so as an end in itself.

Finally, even in the Saidor area where Yali exercised greatest control, the hierarchical structure never operated independently of the existing social system. Traditional relationships and values continued to channel and sanction most social behaviour. The widespread resurgence of paganism, and especially of the Kabu Ceremony and pig exchange, gave new strength to patriclan and kinship bonds. Even Yali found it more effective to exert pressure through these personal ties than through his 'officials'. On the Nankina-Mot sub-coast, his hold on 'boss boys' who happened to be related to him was far stronger than on those who did not. In the Sigi area, the home of his first wife, three of his four main lieutenants were also his close affines. He could achieve far more by manipulating these relationships than by sending a 'policeman' with instructions to the local 'boss boys'. (The same applied to a far greater extent, of course, to his link with Matokar, north of Madang, the village of his second wife.) The hierarchy itself did not imply an entirely new concept of society associated with a sense of equal obligation to every one of its members. Morality was

[1] In this context, it is interesting to remember that in 1947 Yali refused offers to unite and lead the Letub and Tagarabist cults because he could not claim rights to their doctrines. He thought only in terms of Ngaing rights to cargo doctrine.

still dictated by the old range of personal relationships. Thus, although he was doing no more than imitate the behaviour of the less scrupulous members of the European administrative staff, Yali showed an extreme lack of responsibility towards the persons he took into 'custody'. He disregarded Kasan's continued adulteries while 'serving sentence' at Yabalol, on the grounds that Kasan's personal behaviour was no concern of his. He took no action when some of his female 'prisoners' were severely maltreated, because they were not related to him in any way. It goes without saying, of course, that the other people involved had exactly the same attitude.

## The Future

During the decade following Yali's imprisonment and the end of large-scale co-ordinated cargo activity in 1950, the southern Madang District has seen the beginnings of what could be real change. The Administration, through its economic, political, and educational policies has tried to create the institutions which alone can give the natives the higher standard of living, unity, and liberty they demand. Every effort is being made to turn their minds away from the turbulent and sterile past by providing them a fresh and more realistic focus of interest for the future. A new type of personnel has been trained to help with the programme: European officers in charge of agricultural extension work, Co-operative Societies, political development, and schools and medical training establishments; and their native assistants, clerks, members of the Local Government Council, teachers, and Medical Assistants.

Significant advances have been made: the Amele Rice Scheme and its subsidiary at Yar; the Ambenob Native Local Government Council; Administration Schools at Madang, Saidor, and elsewhere; and a number of Native Medical Aid Posts. But when I was last in the area in January 1958, the officers concerned were not unanimously satisfied with the current rate of development. In several cases, the natives had shown initial curiosity about, even interest in, the opportunities offered but had then drifted into apathy. There are, of course, obvious factors involved: poor planning and instruction, weak propaganda, and administrative blunders. These must be eliminated as soon as possible. Even so, where there has been antagonism or indifference to, or misunderstanding of, the new policy, an additional principal cause has been continuing native interest in cargo ideology, which is still a force to be combated.

We could perhaps take comfort from Worsley's conclusion that cargo cult is destined to give way to some form of secular or orthodox politics: that it 'is typical only of a certain phase in the political and economic development of [the people of Melanesia], and that it is destined to disappear or become a minor form of political expression among backward elements'.[1] Although this is perfectly acceptable as a long-range generalization, which is what it is intended to be, we should nevertheless be extremely cautious about adopting it in any single area as a short-term prediction, which may be all that we are allowed to make.

From an overall point of view, Worsley makes it clear that such a transition will depend on increasing urbanization, which will throw up a population capable of seeing the world through Western eyes. But it is more than questionable whether New Guinea has the resources for urbanization of this kind and whether it has been seriously envisaged for the foreseeable future. The Australian Liberal Government's aim has always been broad development in local communities with only a relatively small native elite being brought into the towns. The impact of such an elite on mass rural opinion can be only very limited. Under these conditions, it could be fatal for us to assume that any cargo movement, especially if it has had a long and unbroken history, will suddenly and automatically wither away in conformity with some theory of evolutionary determinism. If it is allowed that the culture I have described is fairly typical of coastal Melanesia, it would be naive to expect people, for whom the religious and secular are so inextricably interwoven in the same order of existence that it is impossible to classify any important event as exclusively either one or the other, to switch from a non-rationalist to a rationalist outlook in the matter of a few years. By itself such a process would in all certainty take much longer than the limited time at our disposal in New Guinea, and we must be prepared to force its pace. As the country is already groping towards political independence, and as cargo cult is by no means restricted to the small area I have discussed, the risk is that we shall leave in our wake an ideology which will still be politically disruptive in the new nation-state we are trying to build.

From a narrower point of view, we should be careful about using Worsley's conclusion as a short-term prediction in the southern Madang District. The Madang native urban population is negligible and likely to remain so for a long time. Moreover, Worsley's suggestion that the Cargo Movement in the area was an example of an

[1] Worsley, *The Trumpet Shall Sound*, op. cit., p. 255. The generalization is echoed also by Mair, 'Independent Religious Movements in Three Continents', op. cit., p. 134.

incipient trend away from religious millenarian to orthodox politics must be qualified. The Movement's tendencies in that direction before 1950 were very slight and short-lived, and during the last decade its doctrines appear to have been cherished in their original form by a large number of people. Plans for the next, probably crucial, decade must take this into account.

Before 1950, the vast majority of the Movement's followers at no time moved away from a purely religious epistemological system. The most significant possible exception was Yali who, between 1945 and 1947, appeared to be 'moving in the direction of orthodox politics, not millenarism'.[1] This is certainly true of some of his actions, which were rationally directed: for instance, his early attempts at *rapprochement* with the missions and his framing of the 'Laws'. Yet his Rehabilitation Scheme as a whole can be regarded as a secular development only if the wider cosmic order in which he conceived it to operate is ignored. It was not based on assumptions unshared by cargo ideology, from which he was not at any time emancipated. In his view, ordinary cargo processes would continue to function, for he never questioned that the goods to be made available by the Administration would come ultimately from a divine source. He never did more than try to by-pass cargo cult. When this proved impossible, he unhesitatingly adopted cargo ritual as soon as he was satisfied that he was not infringing other people's rights. Thereafter even tenuous secularism disappeared from the Movement.

The cargo cults that have broken out in the southern Madang District since 1950 have been small and lacking in central direction in that they have been pagan and quasi-Christian at random. Yet they have been distributed all along the coast and sub-coast between Saidor and Sarang. In 1951 and 1953, while Yali was in prison, there were two pagan cults at Bogati, the second on the eve of the Coronation. Yali was expected to return to Madang with warships and merchantmen laden with cargo to take over the reins of government. The horizon was scanned for his arrival, and pagan ritual revived to speed it up. About the same time, there was a quasi-Christian cult at Yakierak (N'dau) on the Rai Coast. It was believed that mass baptism would bring cargo from God. In 1956, a year after Yali's release, Ku of Kaliku (near Bongu) claimed to have died and visited Heaven, where he saw God and a man who appears to have been the late King George. He came back as the Black Jesus, who would intercede with God on the natives' behalf as the White Jesus had done for

[1] Worsley, *The Trumpet Shall Sound*, op. cit., p. 219.

Europeans. He enjoined Lutheran prayers, the *table ritual*, and sexual promiscuity on his followers. The cult lasted in secret for about six months but was eventually stopped by the District Office. In the Madang area in 1957, cargo activity formally closed down: the Letub, after a period of some twenty years, was abandoned and its adherents received back into the missions. But at the same time, there was a fresh outbreak of minor cultism (of which I heard the first tentative rumours in 1956) in the Rempi area, north of Madang. These cults seem to have run on intermittently until 1961. The most important was led by Lagit, *Luluai* of Abar and an ex-catechist of the Catholic Mission. He killed a man in front of the assembled villagers by slitting his throat with a bushknife. His reason was that it was necessary for a native to make the same sacrifice as Jesus Christ had made for Europeans before the native standard of living could be raised. The incident was obviously prearranged because the victim, far from offering resistance, went voluntarily to his death.[1]

Taken individually, these small cults may appear of slight importance, as now only the 'minor form of political expression among backward elements' of which Worsley speaks. In comparison with events before 1950, they have caused little social disruption. Nevertheless, collectively they are still cause for considerable anxiety, for the 'backward elements' involved must represent the bulk of the population for a long time to come. They augur two potential problems: First, although they may not lead to a Cargo Movement as militant as before, they may yet contribute to widespread passive resistance to the Administration's policy. Second, even if such a fear is baseless and the new policy is given a fair trial, they give grounds to suppose that the Administration's aims could be seriously distorted.

Should the first problem arise in the near future, the figurehead of any resistance will most likely be Yali. He returned to the Rai Coast in 1955 very embittered by his five years in prison. For the first two years at least, he did everything to impress the District Office, as he had already impressed the prison officers in Lae, with his good behaviour. By the end of 1956, his only move had been to obtain permission to revive the Kabu Ceremony, which he ostentatiously kept free from all overt suggestions of cargo ritual. His motive was to make it plain that he still had influence with the Administration and that the missions, which had been very active in trying to recover lost ground during his absence, could even now be disregarded. He still saw the missions as his main enemies; and this makes it very unlikely that he was in any

[1] Information from *The South Pacific Post*, Port Moresby, 14 July 1961.

way responsible for the petty cargo cults beginning in other areas, for many of them incorporated Christian beliefs.

Nevertheless, it was quite obvious that many people continued to regard Yali as their leader. Visitors from distant coastal villages brought him news and sought his advice about local affairs. It was not long before they came with the first invitation to dabble in native politics again. In 1953 and 1957, there had been volcanic eruptions on Long and Manam Islands, which he was said to have caused by invoking the local deities in order to express his hatred of Europeans. In 1957-8, the natives of Manam and the north coast approached him clandestinely to stop the volcano by interceding with the gods once more, and appear to have offered him a considerable sum of money as payment. Subsequently he has attended several large gatherings between Saidor and Bogati, where it is likely that he has at least been asked to resume the position he enjoyed in the old days and that the Fifth Cargo Belief has been discussed. Born manipulator and embittered as he is, he must find such temptations hard to resist.

It is quite possible, therefore, that, if these meetings reawaken widespread interest in pagan cargo ritual, the adherents of the petty cults north of Madang and elsewhere will renounce their quasi-Christian doctrines and merge with those who have remained Yali's loyal followers. Much would then depend on Yali's attitude towards the Administration. But even if he remained non-committal, refraining from either subverting or supporting the new policy, the situation could still be ominous. The people would see him and themselves as a power rivalling not only the European Administration but also the Native Co-operative Societies, Local Government Councils, schools, and health services it has created. Without positive direction from him but knowing his previous attitude, which is still largely their own, they would automatically obstruct all development sponsored by these bodies. In this context, it is significant that by 1958, although Yali had enrolled his son in the Saidor School, he had obviously not encouraged his fellow-villagers to plant cash crops. Largely at his instigation, they were spending much time producing food for the Kabu Ceremony, and were thus economically far poorer than the inland villages such as Sibog and Aiyawang, which were making substantial profits from the sale of European vegetables. These two villages had by now rejected his leadership and refused to re-introduce more than an attenuated form of the Kabu, on the grounds that it interfered with their business enterprise.

At the same time, it would be extremely shortsighted to attribute every setback to the direct or indirect influence of one man, as some Europeans in the past have been too prone to do. Yali, at the very worst, could only exploit already existing attitudes and assumptions. These attitudes and assumptions, the crux of the second problem, can themselves create perhaps far greater difficulties. On their own they are diffuse, and hence less easy to detect and counteract. It should never be forgotten that, even if it has no accredited prophet, cargo ideology has now become an intrinsic part of the culture of the southern Madang District. It is no longer just grafted on to but virtually represents the natives' whole way of life. It provides, as Burridge[1] has well pointed out, a tremendous feeling of self-respect under European domination. As an intellectual system, it explains European economic superiority with much greater logic in native eyes than any description of Western financial transactions, industrial research, and factory organization with all their complexities and seeming contradictions can ever hope to offer. To reject the cargo belief completely for untried schemes, the logic of which is not at once apparent, would involve renewed dependence on the white man and hence a sacrifice of pride. It would mean also an intellectual challenge that comparatively few are as yet either willing or equipped to accept. Thus it is inevitable that for some time to come cargo ideology, or at least the type of thinking it represents, will promote undesirable reactions to the new economic, political, and educational institutions.

By 1958, large-scale economic development in the southern Madang District, with the notable exception of the projects already mentioned, had not been received with the widespread enthusiasm anticipated. Several natives with whom I discussed the matter admitted freely that they were little concerned. They planted cash crops only because the Administration had told them to do so. They had been quite prepared to 'work' for European goods by means of ritual, which they understood, but now that that had proved ineffective they were unwilling to experiment with new skills, which they could not see as likely to provide abundant wealth as quickly as they desired. They still assumed that they should acquire the whole material culture of the Europeans as an automatic concomitant of living and could not appreciate that they would have to work their way towards it slowly from small beginnings.[2] Some even confessed that they believed that the

[1] Burridge, *Mambu*, op. cit., *passim.*
[2] The same attitude was apparent in reactions to the Native Clubs started at Madang and Saidor in 1956. At first, there were numerous applications for membership, but a year later the numbers dropped. It emerged that the people had assumed that membership

limited financial returns they would get from cash crops might be a hindrance to obtaining real wealth. Should the true 'road of the cargo' ever be discovered, the cargo deity and ancestors, seeing that the people had a little money with which to buy goods, might refuse to bring them bulk supplies.

On the surface, the establishment of Native Local Government Councils appears to have been a success, but there have been incidents that have caused experienced officers some uneasiness. Many natives have been unhappy about the scheme because they have believed that allegiance to a Council would cancel their nominal allegiance to a mission. Although they are not imbued with fresh Christian fervour, they do not want to become the centre of new recriminations. They have had to be reassured that the missions fully supported the Councils: that God had given authority to the Queen, who had vested it in the Australian Government and Administration; and that the Administration was now delegating some of it to the Councils. Cases such as this suggest that the people still have no comprehension of the multiple systems within the wider state structure that is slowly being built up, and are looking for a single generalized system that will govern every facet of their lives as did the system they had in the past. It is also most unfortunate, for reasons that should be by now abundantly clear, that they should have to be reminded of the association between the Divine Will, the Monarchy, and the Administration. The Madang natives in 1953 were reported as saying that the new Queen, as a woman, would be less hard-hearted than a man and would perhaps reveal the cargo secret.[1]

In a climate of opinion such as this, mistakes or failures by a Council could be fatal. As long as a Council can be provided with adequate funds by the taxes it levies, and its discussions be directed towards vigorous and rational plans for development, the danger of misrepresentation can be averted. But, as Maher[2] has stated in the case of the Tommy Kabu Movement in the Purari region of Papua, should such programmes break down for lack of economic support, the voices of cargo prophets could easily be heard once more. One very active

---

would at once grant the right to drink alcohol, the ban on which was always resented. When this was found to be untrue, interest soon waned. (Personal communication from Mr L. Williams, District Commissioner of Madang, and Mr K. Dyer, then Assistant District Officer at Saidor.)

[1] It is interesting to note that after the visit of the Duke of Edinburgh to New Guinea in 1956 there was a widespread rumour that His Royal Highness had said in public that he was ashamed to see so many natives without European clothes.

[2] Maher, *New Men of Papua*, op. cit., p. 122.

member of the Ambenob Council was a cargo prophet in the past and, during its first term of office, another was one of Kaum's personal lieutenants. Kaum made a bid, through him, to use the Council as a front for new cargo activities, but was silenced by its more responsible members. In 1960, Professor Guiart discovered that there was still a live interest in the Letub among members of the new Council on Karkar Island, even though the cult had been officially disbanded on the mainland three years earlier.[1] In 1958, I was myself asked in a village within the Ambenob Council area if my consistent interest in cargo doctrine meant that I was preparing a new cult in Australia to help the natives.

I cannot quote comparable evidence from the new Native Schools in the southern Madang District. But Sinclair's[2] suggestion for the whole of New Guinea is probably fully applicable: that the 'belief in the magical effects of learning to speak English and the belief in its supposed power to confer all the material benefits of our culture may be an important underlying drive towards the acquisition of a European "education" '. The attitude of the pupils' parents may well be typified still by the comment of a Karkar Lutheran congregational elder soon after 1945 when he heard that the Administration and missions were starting an English language programme. 'Now we shall have aeroplanes and ships!' he said.[3] It would probably not be difficult to find around Madang parallels to the example of the lad in the Wewak Administration School, who wrote to an Australian pen friend asking for 'magic for think'—not just 'think about', he stipulated, 'but magic for think'—so that he could get into a higher class.[4]

Whichever of these two problems (passive resistance to or misrepresentation of the new policy) becomes more acute, the most urgent general issue facing the Administration in the southern Madang District is what has been described for other countries as the battle for men's minds. We must somehow accelerate the transition to a secular and rational outlook. To achieve this, we should seriously consider at least three points. First, we must strengthen our liaison with the people. Not only must we improve race relations immediately but

[1] Personal communication from Professor J. Guiart. I presume that the Karkar natives identified the Letub with their own Kukuaik Cult, especially if the latter incorporated the Kilibob-Manup myth.

[2] Sinclair, *Field and Clinical Survey Report of the Mental Health of the Indigenes of the Territory of Papua and New Guinea*, p. 19.

[3] Personal communication from Rev. G. O. Reitz of the American Lutheran Mission.

[4] Information from *The Sydney Morning Herald*, 19 March 1960, and Mrs W. Henley of French's Forest, Sydney, N.S.W.

T

also learn from the shortcomings of Western policy in South-East Asia that it is useless to pour in 'aid' from air-conditioned offices without going outside to discover and take into account the people's own ideology, and their likely reactions to what is being offered them. That there is a danger of this is suggested by the increasing bureaucratization, which has led natives in many areas, and also a number of senior and junior officers, to complain that the Administration is becoming too remote.

Second, in building up closer liaison with the people, we must acknowledge and respect cargo ideology as a carefully integrated intellectual system which, as has been shown by its persistence over eighty years, is extremely durable. Yet cargo ideology does not always come out into the open. It may be only occasionally and fleetingly visible to Europeans unless they are trained to discover it for themselves. Europeans will never understand it until they realize its pervasiveness, and cease viewing it as a loose collection of unrelated beliefs and customs, each of which a relay of experts can isolate, eliminate, and replace: the European Agricultural Officer, the European legal adviser, the European schoolmaster, and the European doctor—all proficient in their own fields yet totally oblivious of the native interpretation of the work they are trying to do. As Stanner[1] has remarked, 'increased "economic opportunities" or "reasonably devised" education' will not be 'simple panaceas'—especially if they are introduced as uncoordinated institutions. If we do no more than present them to the people as such, they can be received (unless they are flatly rejected) only in either of two ways. Either the people will adopt them merely as meaningless customs, which they will do their best to copy but, under pressure from elsewhere, readily abandon for others purporting to offer quicker results. Or, as in the case of Christianity during the interwar years, they will interpret them according to their own values and assumptions, ultimately producing burlesques of the originals, which are doomed to collapse and ridicule. In either case, the Government and Administration, which have accepted sole responsibility for development since 1945, will be in the same position as the missions after 1933. They will be blamed for the failure, but the price they will have to pay will be far higher. The people's goodwill will have been alienated for ever.

Third, as we are dealing not with a farrago of superstition but with a coherent system, we should seek out carefully its weakest point for the spearhead of our attack. Above all, we must not repeat the former

[1] Stanner, *The South Seas in Transition*, p. 71.

error of stopping short at the cultural exterior but push through to the underlying social values and intellectual assumptions, which must be replaced by entirely new ones. We must so co-ordinate and introduce our programmes of development that the mass of the people have no alternative but to accept them as the only logical solution to the problems of modern living.

The weakest point in the total system is neither the socio-political nor the belief structure. They have evolved under certain conditions and cannot be attacked successfully until the conditions themselves are altered. It has been shown in this book that the cardinal factor which determined the nature of native socio-political and intellectual life, both before and after European occupation, was economic. Because the traditional economy was virtually stationary—because it did not promote the search for new resources, new goods, and new methods of production—social alignments varied little and the human secular intellect was completely dominated by a religious epistemological system. During the first seventy-nine years of contact, the fundamental changes in native culture as a whole were negligible. Most serious of all, the subsistence economy was barely affected so that there were still no internal pressures to create new social attitudes and ideas. The resultant situation had to be interpreted according to traditional values and religious beliefs. Therefore, to induce social attitudes and ideas comparable to those of the Western world, our primary objective should be at all costs to overcome native apathy and introduce radical change in the economic field. Once we have achieved this, we can follow up with development in the other two fields more quickly and efficiently. The people will then have to establish among themselves entirely different types of social and political relationships and, in order to meet the needs of the new way of life, be forced to think for themselves—not according to their old assumptions, which will at last have been proved inadequate, but according to the new ones we are trying to introduce. This should promote a rational demand for Western political institutions and education, which will be built into, rather than tacked on to, the emerging culture. Then, perhaps, the people will have discovered the true 'road' for themselves. Their pride and self-confidence assured, they may undertake their journey into the future with greater chance of success.

# POSTSCRIPT

SINCE 1958 many natives in the southern Madang District seem to have accepted development as a potentially satisfactory alternative to cargo cult. In the economic field, the growth of native business, the establishment of Madang's first factory (for making cigarettes), and higher urban wages, won by the Madang Workers' Association, have given the people greater access to European goods. On the Rai Coast there is a nascent coffee industry, already requiring motor roads to help with transport problems. In the Bagasin Area the Garia are moving down to Usino Airstrip in the Ramu Valley to plant cash crops, which will be flown out to market. In politics there are more native public servants (especially clerks and Patrol Officers), there is a Native Local Government Council at Saidor and the first National Elections for the House of Assembly in Port Moresby were held in February 1964. In education, more children attend primary and secondary schools, and young men and women go to Port Moresby and even Australia for advanced training. In rural areas race relations seem better, with good-will towards Europeans, especially since the removal of the ban on native drinking in 1962, together with pride in the native *élite*. In and near Madang, however, there is less improvement. European and native attitudes are often bad. Even the new drinking laws may breed native resentment because of inevitable, if unofficial, racial segregation.

Racial friction set aside, the main problem, in both country and town, is still how far progress is being impeded by the two factors discussed on pp. 267–71: a series of small but active cargo cults possibly coupled with Yali's influence or, as now appears more likely, diffuse cargo thinking. A few insignificant cults have been reported: one from Kesawai and another started by Kaum in 1963. Yali himself is less popular. He has resisted all offers to return to the Cargo Movement, although cash gifts and women are still offered to him. In July 1965 he proclaimed that cargo cult—originally imported from Madang—was dead on the Rai Coast. In the National Elections of 1964 he was soundly beaten in the Rai Coast Electorate, where even many Ngaing villages did not support him, although in the Madang Electorate some 3,000 informal votes were cast in his favour.[1] The failure was offset in 1964 by his winning the Presidency of the Saidor Council. Yet in 1966 he

---

[1] For excellent accounts, see T. G. Harding, 'The Rai Coast Open Electorate', and C. A. Hughes and P. W. van der Veur, 'The Elections: An Overview' (p. 403), in *The Papua–New Guinea Elections, 1964*, edited by D. G. Bettison, C. A. Hughes, and P. W.

failed to retain even this office. Otherwise, he appears to be buttress-
ing his position in two ways: as traditionalist and as entrepreneur. In
the first role, while renouncing cargo cult, he has tried to demonstrate
his authority by urging a return to the Pagan Revival (especially the
full Kabu Ceremony) of 1948. Even among the Ngaing the response
has been lukewarm. In the second role, he again recruits and employs
native labour, with his own copra and coffee interests. Yet he is still no
businessman and is overshadowed by his rival Gegang of Sibog, who
was largely responsible for establishing coffee on the Rai Coast. Without proper supervision, Yali's new concerns could fail in the same way
as those of 1947–8. For a while, as a lucrative sideline, he sold bottled
water believed to be impregnated with his power from the deities and
thus effective against illness and misfortune (cf. p. 206).

The main danger to progress appears to be diffuse cargo thinking!
In the economic field, the collapse of a large co-operative society in
1965 led to strong resurgence of cargo talk. In politics, Local Government Councillors and Members of the House of Assembly are constantly worried by the antagonism between orthodox programmes
and belief in the millennium. Cargo demagogues are quick to seize on
failures in achieving material progress. (Hence it is imperative to save
the Rai Coast coffee industry from stagnation by building motor roads
soon.) Furthermore, there is now the danger that native public servants,
already embittered by reduction of their salaries in 1964, might use
cargo ideology as a form of protest and compensation. This has already
happened in the case of a well-educated mission teacher, who could
speak very good English but had an inferiority complex towards his
European colleagues. He told his pupils that God was sending the
ancestors with ships full of cargo. In the schools, even senior students
have expressed cargo ideas. Cargo thinking is still a rich field to be
exploited by frustrated men. How close it is to the surface is illustrated
by an incident on the Rai Coast in 1965. A Ngaing informant had
made a point of stressing to me that cargo cult was now dead in the
area. I told him how natives around Rabaul believed that a giant egg,
filled with cargo, would descend from Heaven. When a helicopter
landed among them, they assumed that it had arrived. 'And there *was*
cargo inside, was there?', he asked. 'No,' I replied, 'only an Agricultural
Officer.' He then reaffirmed, with even greater emphasis, the Rai
Coast's rejection of the cult.

---

van der Veur (Canberra, Australian National University Press [1965]). But I found no
confirmation of the derivation of '*Haus Lo*' (a Pidgin term for the House of Assembly)
and its suggested cargo significance on p. 403.

# SELECT BIBLIOGRAPHY

*Aakesing*, Lae, American Lutheran Mission, June 1949.

*Annual Reports on New Guinea*, 1900–1 to 1904–5 and 1906–7 to 1912–13, Imperial German Administration (translated by H. A. Thomson). Library of the Australian School of Pacific Administration.

— 1921–2 to 1939–40, Australian Mandate Administration, Canberra, Government Printer.

AUFINGER, A., 'Wetterzauber auf den Yabob-Inseln in Neuguinea', *Anthropos*, xxxiv (1939), pp. 277–91.

— 'Die Mythe vom Brüderpaar *Kilibob* und *Manup* auf den Yabob-Inseln Neuguineas', *Anthropos*, xxxvii–xl (1942–5), pp. 313–15.

*Australian War Memorial, Jungle Warfare*, Canberra (1944).

BALLANDIER, G., *Sociologie Actuelle de l'Afrique Noire*, Paris, Presses Universitaires de France (1955).

BECK, C. VON, *Das überseeische Deutschland: Die deutschen Kolonien in Wort und Bild* (compiled by C. von Beck *et al.*), Stuttgart, Union Deutsche Verlagsgesellschaft (1911).

BELSHAW, C., 'The Significance of Modern Cults in Melanesian Development', *Australian Outlook*, iv (1950), pp. 116–25.

— 'Recent History of Mekeo Society', *Oceania*, xxii (1951), pp. 1–23.

— *The Great Village* (*The Economic and Social Welfare of Hanuabada, an Urban Community in Papua*), London, Routledge & Kegan Paul (1957).

BERNDT, R. M., 'A Cargo Movement in the Eastern Central Highlands of New Guinea', *Oceania*, xxiii (1952–3), pp. 40–65, 137–58, and 202–34.

— 'Reaction to Contact in the Eastern Highlands of New Guinea', *Oceania*, xxiv (1954), pp. 190–228 and 255–74.

— *Excess and Restraint* (*Social Control among a New Guinea Mountain People*), The University of Chicago Press (1962).

BIDNEY, D., 'Meta-anthropology', in *Ideological Differences and World Order* (ed. by F. S. C. Northrop), New Haven, Yale University Press (1949).

BLOOD, N. B. N., 'Report of Patrol to Bagasin Area, Madang District', *A.N.G.A.U. War Diary*: Vol. IV, No. 2, HQ A22, Appendix E, 21 December 1944.

BODROGI, T., 'Colonization and Religious Movements in Melanesia', *Acta Ethnographica*, ii (1951), pp. 159–292.

— 'Some Notes on the Ethnography of New Guinea', *Acta Ethnographica*, iii (1953), pp. 91–184.

— *Art in North-East New Guinea*, Budapest, Publishing House of the Hungarian Academy of Sciences (1961).

BURRIDGE, K. O. L., *Mambu* (*A Melanesian Millennium*), London, Methuen (1960).

*Custodian of Expropriated Property, Catalogue of New Guinea Properties, Second Group* (*Sale of Expropriated Properties in the Territory of New Guinea*), Melbourne, Government Printer (1926).

— *Catalogue of New Guinea Properties, Third Group* (*Sale of Expropriated Properties in the Territory of New Guinea*), Melbourne, Government Printer (1927).

*List of New Guinea Properties Sold by the Custodian of Expropriated Property as at 1st January, 1928*, Melbourne, Government Printer (1928).

DEMPWOLFF, O., 'Sagen und Märchen aus Bilibili', *Baessler-Archiv*, i (1911), pp. 63–102.

ESSAI, B., *Papua and New Guinea (A Contemporary Survey)*, Melbourne, Oxford University Press (1961).

EVANS-PRITCHARD, E. E., *The Nuer*, Oxford, Oxford University Press (1940).

FAIVRE, J.-P., AND SOKOLOFF, V., 'Mikloukho-Maklai (1846–1888): À l'Occasion du Centenaire de sa Naissance', *Journal de la Société des Océanistes*, Paris, Musée de l'Homme, iii (1947), pp. 93–102.

FELDT, E., *The Coast Watchers*, Melbourne, Oxford University Press (1946).

FIRTH, R., *Elements of Social Organization*, London, Watts & Co. (1951).

FISCHER, D., *Unter Südsee-Insulanern (Das Leben des Forschers Mikloucho-Maclay)*, Leipzig, Koehler und Amelang (1956).

FORTUNE, R., *Manus Religion (An Ethnological Study of the Manus Natives of the Admiralty Islands)*, Philadelphia, The American Philosophical Society (1935).

FRAZER, SIR J., *The Golden Bough (A Study in Magic and Religion)*, Vol. I, London, Macmillan (1913).

FREEMAN, J. D., 'The Joe Gimlet or Siovili Cult (An Episode in the Religious History of Early Samoa)', in *Anthropology in the South Seas* (ed. by J. D. Freeman and W. R. Geddes), New Zealand, Thomas Avery & Sons Ltd. (1959).

GLUCKMAN, M., *Rituals of Rebellion in South-East Africa*, Manchester University Press (1954) republished in 1962.

GREENOP, F. S., *Who Travels Alone*, Sydney, K. G. Murray Publishing Co. (1944).

GUIART, J., 'Forerunners of Melanesian Nationalism', *Oceania*, xxii (1951), pp. 81–90.

*Un Siècle et demi de Contacts Culturels à Tama, Nouvelles-Hébrides*, Paris, Musée de l'Homme (1956).

*Handbook, The New Guinea Handbook*, Canberra, Government Printer (1943, reprint).

HANNEMANN, E. F., *Tibud (New Guinea Legends)*, New Guinea Section of the Board of Foreign Missions of the American Lutheran Church (1934).

'Le Culte de Cargo en Nouvelle-Guinée', *Le Monde Non-Chrétien*, viii (1948), pp. 937–62.

*Village Life and Social Change in Madang Society*, mimeographed (n.d.).

*Papuan Dances and Dancing*, mimeographed (n.d.).

HOBSBAWM, E. J., *Primitive Rebels*, Manchester University Press (1959).

HOGBIN, H. I., *Transformation Scene*, London, Routledge & Kegan Paul (1951).

*Holy Bible, The Book of Genesis; The Gospel According to St Matthew*, Authorized Version of 1611.

HORTON, R., 'A Definition of Religion, and Its Uses', *Journal of the Royal Anthropological Institute*, xc (1960), pp. 201–26.

INGLIS, J., 'Cargo Cults: The Problem of Explanation', *Oceania*, xxvii (1957), pp. 249–63.

Review of Burridge, K. O. L.: *Mambu (A Melanesian Millennium)*, in *Journal of the Polynesian Society*, lxx (1961), pp. 381–4.

INSELMANN, R., *Letub, The Cult of the Secret of Wealth*, mimeographed, Kennedy School of Missions, Hartford Seminary Foundation (1944).

JACOBS, M. G., 'Bismarck and the Annexation of New Guinea', *Historical Studies of Australia and New Zealand*, v (1951), pp. 14–26.

'The Colonial Office and New Guinea, 1874–84', *Historical Studies of Australia and New Zealand*, v (1952), pp. 106–18.

*Katekismo Katolik, A Catholic Catechism in New Guinea Pidgin for the Natives of New Guinea*, Sydney, Franklin Press (1945).

KEYSZER, C., 'Mission Work among Primitive Peoples in New Guinea', *International Review of Missions*, xiii (1924), pp. 426–35.

*Eine Papuagemeinde*, Kassel, Bärenreiter-Verlag (1929).

LAWRENCE, P., 'Sorcery among the Garia', *South Pacific*, vi (1952), pp. 340–3.

'Cargo Cult and Religious Beliefs among the Garia', *International Archives of Ethnography*, xlvii (1954), pp. 1–20.

'The Madang District Cargo Cult', *South Pacific*, viii (1955), pp. 6–13.

*Land Tenure among the Garia (The Traditional System of a New Guinea People)*, Canberra, Social Science Monographs No. 4, Australian National University (1955).

'Lutheran Mission Influence on Madang Societies', *Oceania*, xxvii (1956), pp. 73–89.

*The Educational Conflict in Papua and New Guinea*, mimeographed, Library of the Australian School of Pacific Administration (1958).

'The Background to Educational Development in Papua and New Guinea', *South Pacific*, x (1959), pp. 52–60.

'The Political System of the Garia', in a symposium on *Political Systems in Papua and New Guinea* (ed. by K. E. Read, n.d.).

'The Religious System of the Ngaing', in a symposium on *Some Religions of Seaboard Melanesia and the New Guinea Highlands* (ed. by P. Lawrence and M. J. Meggitt, n.d.).

LEESON, I., *Bibliography of Cargo Cults and other Nativistic Movements in the South Pacific*, Sydney, South Pacific Commission Technical Paper No. 30 (1952).

LINTON, R., 'Nativistic Movements', *American Anthropologist*, xlv (1943), pp. 230–40.

LYNG, J., *Our New Possession (Late German New Guinea)*, Melbourne Publishing Co. (1919).

*Island Films*, Sydney, Cornstalk Publishing Co. (1925).

MCAULEY, J. P., 'We are Men—What are You?', *Quadrant*, xv (1960), pp. 73–9.

'My New Guinea', *Quadrant*, xix (1961), pp. 15–27.

MCCARTHY, J. K., 'The Rabaul Strike', *Quadrant*, x (1959), pp. 55–65.

MACKENZIE, S. S., *The Australians at Rabaul (The Capture and Administration of the German Possessions in the Southern Pacific)*, Official History of Australia in the War of 1914–18, Vol. X, Sydney, Angus & Robertson (1934).

MAHER, R. F., *New Men of Papua (A Study in Culture Change)*, Madison, University of Wisconsin Press (1961).

MAIR, L. P., *Australia in New Guinea*, London, Christophers (1948).

'Independent Religious Movements in Three Continents', *Comparative Studies in Society and History*, i (1959), pp. 113–36.

MEAD, M., *New Lives for Old*, New York, William Morrow (1956).

MIKLOUHO-MACLAY, N. N., *Sobranie Sochenenii*, Vol. III, Moscow, Academy of Sciences (1951).

NEUHAUSS, R., *Deutsch Neu-Guinea*, Vol. I, Berlin, Reimer (1911).

PENGLASE, N., 'Report June–September 1942, HQ Ramu District, 30th September 1942', *A.N.G.A.U. War Diary*: Vol. I, No. 8, Appendix 45.

PHILLIPS, J., *Judgement: Delivered at Madang, on Wednesday the 25th day of May, 1932*.

READ, K. E., 'Effects of the Pacific War in the Markham Valley, New Guinea', *Oceania*, xviii (1947), pp. 95–116.

'A "Cargo" Situation in the Markham Valley, New Guinea', *Southwestern Journal of Anthropology*, xiv (1958), pp. 273–94.

REAY, M. O., *The Kuma (Freedom and Conformity in the New Guinea Highlands)*, Melbourne University Press (1959).

REED, S. W., *The Making of Modern New Guinea*, Philadelphia, Memoirs of the American Philosophical Society, Vol. XVIII (1943).

ROMILLY, H. H., *The Western Pacific & New Guinea*, London, John Murray (1886).

ROWLEY, C. D., *The Australians in German New Guinea, 1914–21*, Melbourne University Press (1958).

RUDIN, H. R., *Germans in the Cameroons (A Case Study in Modern Imperialism)*, London, Jonathan Cape (1938).

SALISBURY, R. F., *An Indigenous New Guinea Cult*, mimeographed, Berkeley (California), Kroeber Anthropological Society (1958).

*From Stone to Steel (Economic Consequences of a Technological Change in New Guinea)*, Melbourne University Press (1962).

SCHMITZ, C. A., 'Zum Problem des Balum-Kultes in Nordost-Neuguinea', *Paideuma*, vi (1957), pp. 257–80.

'Zur Ethnologie der Rai-Küste in Neuguinea', *Anthropos*, liv (1959), pp. 27–56.

'Zwei *Telum* Figuren aus der Astrolabe-Bai in Nordost-Neuguinea', Stuttgart, *Tribus* (1959).

*Historische Probleme in Nordost-Neuguinea (Huon-Halbinsel)*, Wiesbaden, Franz Steiner Verlag (1960).

SCHWARTZ, T., 'The Paliau Movement in the Admiralty Islands, 1946–1954', New York, *Anthropological Papers of the American Museum of Natural History*, xlix Part 2 (1962), pp. 211–421.

SINCLAIR, A., *Field and Clinical Survey Report of the Mental Health of the Indigenes of the Territory of Papua and New Guinea*, Port Moresby, Government Printer (1957).

SOKOLOFF, V., AND FAIVRE, J.-P., see under Faivre, J.-P., and Sokoloff, V.

*South Pacific Post, The*, Port Moresby, 14 July 1961.

STANNER, W. E. H., *The South Seas in Transition*, London, Australasian Publishing Co. (1953).

'On the Interpretation of Cargo Cults', *Oceania*, xxix (1958), pp. 1–25.

SUNDKLER, G. M., *Bantu Prophets in South Africa*, London, Missionary Research Series No. 14, Lutterworth Press (1948).

*Sydney Morning Herald, The*, Sydney, 19 March 1960.

TALMON, J. L., *The Origins of Totalitarian Democracy*, London, Mercury (1961).

THOMASSEN, E. S., *Biographical Sketch of Nicholas de Miklouho-Maclay, Member of the Imperial Russian Geographical Society*, Brisbane, Geographical Society (1882).

U

TYLOR, E. B., *Primitive Culture* (*Researches into the Development of Mythology, Philosophy, Religion, Language, Art, and Custom*), Vols. I–II, London, John Murray (1903).

WALLACE, A. F. C., 'Revitalization Movements', *American Anthropologist*, lviii (1956), pp. 264–81.

WORSLEY, P. M., 'N. N. Mikloukho-Maclay, Pioneer of Pacific Anthropology', *Oceania*, xxii (1952), pp. 307–14.

    *The Trumpet Shall Sound* (*A Study of 'Cargo' Cults in Melanesia*), London, MacGibbon & Kee (1957).

WULLENKORD, A., *Duebuk*, Finschhafen, American Lutheran Mission (1946).

# INDEX